Sport, Leisure and Physical Education
Trends and Development
Volume 2

ASSOCIATION INTERNATIONALE DES ECOLES SUPERIEURES D' EDUCATION PHYSIQUE (AIESEP)

Gudrun Doll-Tepper/Wolf-Dietrich Brettschneider (Eds.)

Physical Education and Sport

Changes and Challenges

WORLD CONGRESS
PHYSICAL EDUCATION AND SPORT '94

Meyer & Meyer Verlag

Die Deutsche Bibliothek – CIP-Einheitsaufnahme

Physical education and sport :
changes & challenges / Wolf-Dietrich Brettschneider/Gudrun Doll-Tepper
(Hrsg.).
– Aachen: Meyer und Meyer, 1996
(Sport, Leisure and physical education ; Vol. 2)
ISBN 3-89124-320-0
NE: Brettschneider, Wolf-Dietrich [Hrsg.]; GT

Cover design: Walter J. Neumann, N & N Design-Studio, Aachen
Cover exposure: frw, Reiner Wahlen, Aachen
Printed by Druckerei Hahnengress, Aachen
Printed in Germany
ISBN 3-89124-320-0

Physical Education and Sport: Changes and Challenges

Preface

The last decade has brought enormous social and political changes to our world which affect all aspects of our societies. In 1994, Berlin hosted the AIESEP World Congress which was designed to identify political, economical, social and cultural changes and explore the challenges they pose for practice, preparation of professionals, and research in sport and physical education. Berlin, a city where the breaking down of political barriers and the separating wall is most obvious, was a unique site to experience and discuss the new era of globalization and unified efforts to offer improved quality of life to all individuals. Among the specific changes and challenges that were explored in this congress were the political and social relationships in the world, the rise of health on the modern value scale, the rediscovery of the body, the aging population, individuals with disabilities, the commercialization of sport, the development of multi-cultural societies, the changing roles of schools, and sport organizations in society. There are two major trends that currently affect a great number of our societies and they are well reflected in the world of sport and physical education: the trend towards globalization and the trend towards individualization. Above all, the new communication super highways and increasing migration have contributed to the idea that sport is a homogeneous cultural flow across national and state boundaries. Sport provides a generative frame of unity in which diversity can take place.

On the other hand, modern life is increasingly characterized by a growing particularization of areas of life such as family, leisure time and education. Parallel to this development, secure traditional ties provided by the family and religious value systems are declining in our societies. Unlike the generation of their parents and grandparents, young people today are called upon to be the producers of their own biographies. These changes have allowed for a growing spectrum of options for the individual; at the same time these changes have proven to be a complex challenge.

The purpose of this book is to highlight interdisciplinary approaches and contributions that help to clarify these current developments and trends in our societies and their effects on sport science as a scholarly discipline, on sport with all of its facets, and on physical education as a subject in schools.

The present collection of papers contains a variety of topics including: sport and physical education in the context of political, social and cultural changes; the changes in sport and their impact on sport pedagogy; teacher education and physical education in schools; fair play in sport and in physical education; the changes in sport and their challenges for research; the changes in society and the opportunities for adapted physical education; sport in the lifespan, and the role of competitive sport.

The large number of manuscripts submitted created a great challenge for the editors: a difficult selection problem had to be solved since only a limited number of papers could be included in this volume.

We wish to extend our sincere thanks to everyone who was involved in this international scientific event and thus contributed to the success of the Berlin World Congress. All of us gained a deeper insight into each other, which helps to provide more tolerance towards each other. We hope that this book can make a modest contribution to the dissemination of knowledge and information to all involved in physical education and sport and that it will contribute to a better understanding of our current and future professional challenges worldwide.

We would like to pay special tribute to the tireless efforts of Silke Böttge, Katrin Jenne, Michaela Nickel, Erika Schmidt-Gotz, Sigrun Schulz and Susanne Voß for their commitment and endurance in bringing together these proceedings.

Gudrun Doll-Tepper, Wolf-Dietrich Brettschneider 1995
Freie Universität Berlin

Contents

Teacher Education

School P.E.

Fair Play in Sport - Fair Play in P.E.

3. Changes in Sport: A Challenge for Research

Methodological Reflections

Measurement in Sport

4. Changes in Society - Chances for Adapted P.E.

5. Sport in the Life Span

6. Competitive Sport

List of Contributors

Barrette, Gary T.
Adelphi University, Department of Physical Education,
South Avenue, Garden City NY 11530, USA

Brandl-Bredenbeck, Hans Peter
Freie Universität Berlin, Institut für Sportwissenschaft, Hagenstr. 56,
14193 Berlin, Germany

Buckley, Charles
Trinity and All Saints College, Brownberrie Lane, Leeds LS18 SHD,
England

Capel, Susan
Canterbury Christ Church College, North Holmes Road,
Canterbury CT1 2RW, Kent, England

Crum, Bart
Hélène Swarthlaan 33, 1422 KG Uithoorn, The Netherlands

De Knop, Paul
Vrije Universiteit Brussel, HILOK, Pleinlaan 2, 1050 Brussel,
Belgium

Dowling Naess, Fiona
Norwegian University of Physical Education and Sport,
222 Sognsveien, 40 Kringsjå, 0807 Oslo, Norway

Dresen, Paul
State University, Department of Human Movement Sciences,
Postbus 72, Bloemsingel 10, 9700 AB Groningen, The Netherlands

Gabler, Hartmut
Eberhard-Karls-Universität Tübingen, Institut für Sportwissenschaft, Wilhelmstr. 124, 72074 Tübingen, Germany

Hardy, Colin A.
Loughborough University, Department of Physical Education, Sports Science and Recreation Management, Ashby Road, Loughborough, Leicestershire LE11 3TU, England

Hoberman, John
University of Texas at Austin, Department of Germanic Languages, E. P. Schoch Building 3, 102, Austin, Texas, 78712-1190, USA

Joch, Winfried
Westfälische Wilhelms-Universität, FB Sportwissenschaft, Horstmarer Landweg 62b, 48149 Münster, Germany

Kahila, Sinikka
University of Jyväskylä, Department of Physical Education, Seminaarink 15, P.O. Box 35, 40351 Jyväskylä, Finland

Lawson, Hal A.
Miami University, Department of Health and Sport Studies, 109 Phillips Hall, Oxford, OH 45056, USA

Lund, Jacalyn
University of Louisville, Department of Health Promotion, Physical Education, and Sport Studies, 211B Crawford Gym, Louisville, Kentucky 40292, USA

McLeod, Rosetta
Grampian Regional Council - Education Department Resources Service, Summerhill Education Centre, Stronsay Drive, Aberdeen AB2 6JA, Great Britain

McMorris, Terry
West Sussex Institute of Higher Education, College Lane, Chichester, W. Sussex PO19 4PE, England

Overdorf, Virginia
William Paterson College, Department of Exercise and Movement Sciences, 300 Pompton Road, Wayne, NJ 07470, USA

Peiser, Benny J.
Liverpool John Moores University, School of Human Sciences, Mountford Building, Byrom Street, Liverpool L3 3AF, England

Penney, Dawn
Loughborough University, Department of Physical Education, Sports Science and Recreation Management, Ashby Road, Leicestershire, LE11 3TU, England

Pettit, Anthony
Northern Territory University, Faculty of Education, 40146, Casuarina, 0810 Darwin, Australia

Rintala, Pauli
University of Jyväskylä, Department of Physical Education, P.O. Box 35, 40351 Jyväskylä, Finland

Sage, George
University of Northern Colorado, School of Kinesiology and Physical Education, Greeley, Colorado 80639, USA

Schempp, Paul
University of Georgia, Physical Education Building, Athens, GA 30602, USA

Sherrill, Claudine
Texas Woman's University, Department of Kinesiology, P.O. Box 23717, Denton, Texas, 76204-1717, USA

Sparkes, Andrew C.
University of Exeter, School of Education, Heavitree Road, Exeter EX1 2LU, England

Svoboda, Bohumil
Charles University, Faculty of Physical Education and Sport, J. Martího 31, Prague, Czech Republic

Tanguay, Élaine
Université de Sherbrooke, 2500 boulevard Université, Sherbrooke J1K 2R1, Québec, Canada

Telama, Risto
University of Jyväskylä, Department of Physical Education, P.O. Box 35, 40351 Jyväskylä, Finland

Van Veldhoven, Nicolette
Utrecht University, P.O. Box 80140, Heidelberglaan 1, 3584 CS Utrecht, The Netherlands

Waring, Michael
Loughborough University, Department of Physical Education, Sports Science and Recreation Management, Loughborough, LE11 3TU, England

Williams, Leslie R.T.
University of Otago, 46 Union Street, P.O. Box 56, Dunedin, New Zealand

Yang, Xiaolin
LIKES Research Center, Seminaarinkatu 15, 40100 Jyväskylä 10, Finland

Zaniboni, Carlyn
Boston University Academy, One University Road, Boston, MA 02215, USA

Zhu, Weimo
Wayne State University, HPR, 257 Matthaei Building, Detroit, MI 48202, USA

Zilberman, Victor
Vanier College, 821 Sainte Croix, St. Laurent, Québec, Canada

1. Political, Social and Cultural Changes: Their Impact on Sport and P.E.

George Sage

Global Intersections: Political Economy, Culture, and Physical Education and Sport

It is a great honor for me to be chosen to deliver the Jose Cagigal keynote address. I first met Jose Cagigal in 1968 in Washington, D. C. We were both attending the 2nd International Congress of Sports Psychology. He made two presentations during that congress. One was titled "Social Education Through Sport". I remember being deeply moved by his sincere humanistic commitment to the role of sport as a means of education for liberation and human development. Our paths didn't cross again but I followed his impressive career through various publications to which I subscribe. It was an extraordinarily productive career. The field of physical education and sport lost one of its greatest leaders of the 20th century with his untimely death. I congratulate AIESEP for keeping his name alive through this keynote lecture.

During the course of this conference, numerous papers will be presented dealing with specific aspects of research and practices within the field of physical education and sport. There are papers about motivation in sport, fitness, research methodology in sport science, student misbehavior in physical education classes, etc. These are all appropriate and useful to teachers and researchers in this field, but physical education and sport are not disconnected from the wider world. Every day in every way, this wider world impacts and influences our professional and scholarly endeavors. Noted American sociologist C. WRIGHT MILLS (1961) described what he called the sociological imagination as an attempt to historically situate our personal experiences while at the same time relating ourselves to the wider world in which we live. In a similar way a physical education imagination necessitates that we engage in a continuing quest to understand the broader historical, political, economic, and cultural realities in which physical education and sport are embedded.

In my career of some 30 years as a physical educator, I have taught at 10 institutions of higher education, either as a regular member of the faculty or as a visiting professor. Through those experiences, I have had many opportunities to observe physical educators at work close up and personal. What I have found is that most of our attention and professional work in physical education does not connect physical activity programs with the larger political, economic, and social milieu and its impact on our personal lives, or the lives of our students. We tend to have little awareness about how sport and other forms of physical activity, as well as our own professional lives, are linked to the social relations which underlie social class inequality, sexism, racism, and other forms of oppression and discrimination. Hierarchical and autocratic organization, so prevalent in physical education and sports organizations, seem not to be problematic to physical educators, nor do the wider social injustices and undemocratic traditions of contemporary society seem relevant. This is the case because our scholarship and professional practices, as well as most of the public discourse about physical education and sport, does not confront us with questions about political and economic power and ideology and their linkages to physical activities and sports.

This is unfortunate because unfamiliarity with the connections between human movement practices and the broader social world prevents us from recognizing how hegemonic political, economic, patriarchical, and particularized cultural interests shape and mold the values of our social world and how our human movement practices may reinforce and reproduce these same values. This has been one of the most persistent obstacles for us as professionals in forming meaningful interpretations about the linkages of our programs to the broader society - to how and why society works as it does, what its effects are, who benefits, who loses, who are left out, who are silenced, and what alternatives might exist.

Really understanding our role as human movement professionals in contemporary society requires that we move beyond perceptions of ourselves as isolated from the broader social order. As long as we confine our vision merely to what's going on in our profession, we will only be dealing with symptoms of much larger configurations. Sports and physical education are practices which are socially constructed, and any adequate account of them must be grounded in an understanding of power, privilege, inequality, oppression, and dominance within society.

Australian educator, Richard TINNING (1993) has noted that, "we have a responsibility to try to identify the ways in which our professional practice affects, and is affected by, social issues such as violence, sexism, or racism, and that with such identification comes a moral responsibility to attempt to change our practice to ensure it is socially responsible" (p. 3). The implication for such action is that if we become more active in the construction of our social world, we become active agents rather than merely the objects of socio-historical processes; we, as sociologist Richard FLACKS (1988) argues, make our own history by transforming social structures instead of being dominated by them. Again, TINNING argues, "sport is a very useful vehicle for deflecting national attention away from issues of the state and political processes... but [it also has the potential] to challenge the dominant ideologies which underpin violence, poverty, and oppression" (p. 3).

Following MILLS, I take physical education and sport to be rooted within the broader stream of political, economic, and social forces of which they are a part. So in this presentation I'm going to attempt to map out the present world conjuncture, to discern its essential features and trends. I am going to situate political, economic, cultural, and educational issues and connect them with the future of our field so that we might become more active in constructing a better future.

The Present World Conjuncture: The Globalized Social Order

The world is presently engaged in the most extraordinary era of transformation since the Industrial Revolution. We are all participants in one way or another in an unprecedented globalization of the political, economic, and cultural order. A transformation of this extent and scope quite obviously is bound to have a profound impact on the world's educational systems, and thus carry enormous implications for educators. Richard FALK, professor of international law at Princeton University, argues that two very different sorts of globalization are occurring. One he calls "globalization-from-above"; the other type of globalization Falk identifies as "globalization-from-below" (FALK, 1992, 1993). Other social analysts are now using this classification for the globalized social order.

Globalization-From-Above

Globalization-from-above corresponds to the widely acclaimed New World Order. It is spearheaded by a few hundred giant transnational corporations, many of them bigger than most sovereign nations. For example, Ford Motor Company's "economy is larger that Saudi Arabia's and Norway's. Philip Morris's annual sales exceed New Zealand's gross domestic product" (BARNET & CAVANAGH, 1994, 14). The combined assets of the top 300 transnational firms now make up nearly 25 percent of the productive assets in the world ("A survey of multinationals," 1993). Overall, transnational corporations control 40 per cent of the world's manufacturing assets. Thus, a few hundred corporations control the workforce, the capital, and the technology that are constructing the new global social order; and they have every intention of shaping and molding educational systems throughout the world to conform to their vision of the social order of the future.

We normally think of corporations as economic entities rather than political, private rather than public, but today's transnationals are positioning themselves to become the world empires of the twenty-first century. This is the case because the balance of power in world politics is shifting from territorially bound governments to corporations that roam the world. America's Secretary of Labor, Robert REICH (1991) has argued that transnationals "everywhere are becoming global webs with no particular connection to any single nation" (REICH, 1991, 131). Richard O'BRIEN (1992), in his provocative book *The End of Geography*, argues that global economic and financial integration, supported by information and communication technologies, makes the very notion of place spurious as far as transnational corporations are concerned. This is the case because the control and regulation of the flow of capital is moving away from nation-states and towards organizations created and controlled by the corporations themselves.

The World Trade Organization (WTO), arising out of the Uruguay Round of GATT negotiations, and the North American Free Trade Agreement are prime examples. The major purpose of both is to give more freedom of action to the transnational corporations and further limit the ability of nations to regulate corporate activities. A transnational regime of this sort suits transnational corporations because it constructs and merges a production and trade alliance that serves the interests of transnational corporations, while disenfranchising local and national governments, unions, and other groups which have sought to restrain runaway free market forces.

Thus, globalization-from-above erodes the power of national governments to control their own businesses and other social institutions, such as education. Gay W. SEIDMAN, professor of sociology at the University of Witwatersrand, Johannesburg and editor of the *South African Labour Bulletin*, notes: "Increased mobility of capital and new patterns of international investment have eroded nation-states' control over economic growth, reshaping economic linkages in ways we are only just beginning to understand" (SEIDMAN, 1993, 175).

As the influence of government shrinks almost everywhere, transnational "corporations are occupying public space and exerting a ... profound influence over the lives of ever larger numbers of people" (BARNET & CAVANAGH, 1994, 14). Their most ambitious project - deindustrialization of developed countries - is increasingly moving the national economies of their home country away from basic industries and transferring the labor-intensive phases of production to Third World nations (BERBEROGLU, 1987; GRUNWALD & FLAMM, 1985; HARRISON & BLUESTONE, 1988; STAUDOHAR & BROWN, 1987; "Who owns...", 1994). In the U. S. total domestic employment among the 500 largest industrial companies has fallen for 10 straight years; indeed, their share of the civilian labor force has slipped from 17 percent to less than 10 percent during that time (REICH, 1991).

For corporations, moving plants and operations to Third World countries is a way to boost profits. But for workers and their communities in developed countries the consequences have been grim. Workers faced with plant shutdowns lose much more than wages and benefits. Many lose their homes, their cars, and their savings. Increased rates of suicide, homicide, heart disease, alcoholism, mental illness, domestic violence, and family breakup have been linked to the stress of unemployment when plants are closed and productive operations moved to other countries. Schools deteriorate and educational opportunities are restricted or lost as corporations relocate in foreign countries (BARNET & CAVANAGH, 1994; BLUESTONE, 1988; DUDLEY, 1994; KAMEL, 1990; PERRUCCI, PERRUCCI, TARG, & TARG, 1988; STAUDOHAR & BROWN, 1987).

For workers in the Third World, there is overwhelming evidence that globalization-from-above via transnational investment in those countries carries with it some heavy burdens. Corporations are able to exploit the labor and resources of Third World countries. They are able to pay workers a fraction of what they would have to pay them at home, and they are able to work them longer hours under unsafe and unhealthy conditions; they are able to pollute the water, air, and soil; they are free to dump toxic chemicals, banned pesticides, and drugs that they are prevented from unloading at home (HERMAN, 1993; SLATER, 1991). Attempts to organize labor unions are often violently suppressed by government soldiers. Workplace democracy and worker rights are nonexistent. Finally, the education of children in these countries is ignored as millions of them are coerced into the workplace, and many others are left to the streets because of insufficient schools in the newly urbanized areas where export manufacturing takes place.

While the public discourse throughout the world is on the economic benefits of the globalized social order, in reality, the world is faced with a profound global problem: enormous global inequality. While the family income of the wealthiest Americans increased dramatically over the past 15 years, the number of full-time workers in the U. S. who are impoverished has increased by 50 percent; 18 percent of full-time workers now fall below the poverty line (SCHEER, 1994; SCHWARZ & VOLGY, 1992; "Who are the prisons for," 1994). Twenty-five percent of all children under age 6 live in poverty ("Study finds," 1994; SHAPIRO & GREENSTEIN, 1993).

In mid-1993 the unemployment rate of the 12 countries of the European Community was an distressing 10.3 percent (BARNET & CAVANAGH, 1994). According to the International Labor Organization some 30 percent of the world's active labor force - 820 million people - are currently unemployed or underemployed, and almost one quarter of the world's population, or 1.2 billion people, live in absolute poverty (EPSTEIN, GRAHAM, & NEMBHARD, 1993; PETERSON, 1994; World Bank, 1990; Worldwatch Institute, 1990). In the past 30 years the per capita income gap between the developed and underdeveloped countries has actually widened (ARRIGHI, 1991; Worldwatch Institute, 1990: 136-137).

This global inequality has a multitude of forms of misery it generates that are related to poverty (KLOBY, 1993; PHILLIPS, 1993). For example, the infant mortality rate, the best summary statistic of overall social development according to UNICEF, also reveals massive global inequality. Nineteen of the major industrial countries of the world have an infant mortality rate of less than 11 per 1,000 live births, while over 60 nations, with a total population of 2 billion, have infant mortality rates over 100 per 1,000 live births (UNICEF 1991). Similar inequalities are found in educational opportunities, literacy rates, life expectancy, access to clean air, safe water, and the like.

Globalization-From-Below

Globalization-from-above advances under the banner of a free-market economic liberalism promising economic prosperity; but it has delivered worldwide impoverishment and an unconscionable gap between the haves and have-nots, and between wealth for the few and lack of opportunities for the many. But globalization-from-above is not an independent force following a predestined path. Individuals, groups, organizations, and even nations have the capacity to oppose, resist, and fight back to shape globalization to match the needs of people throughout the world. In his book Explorations at the Edge of Time, FALK combines the concept of globalization-from-below with a model of a postmodern future.[1] In doing this, he argues that modernity has not turned out to be a force of human liberation but instead has become a conservative force limiting human freedom, obstructing progress, and hindering development of a humane basis for world social order. As a consequence, the political framework of modernity supporting the territoriality of the state and the reliance upon huge private corporations pursuing their own particular interests is in need of a major restructuring.

The postmodern image that animates FALK's (1992) explorations is quite different from the postmodernism that is found in literary and cultural discourses. FALK's postmodernism is "reconstructionist, optimistic, normative"; it "implies the human capacity to transcend the violence, poverty, ecological decay, oppression" and, injustices of the modern world (p. 6). FALK's model treats current trends advancing in postmodern directions as being formidable political and cultural attempts to transcend "the obsolescent constraints of modernist conceptions of the feasible" (FALK, 1992, 1). It is a direction that ought to favorably resonate with educators values and aspirations throughout the world.

Globalization-from-below and its accompanying postmodern perspective consists of numerous international social and cultural forces committed to human rights "and a vision of human community based on the unity of diverse cultures seeking an end to poverty, oppression, humiliation, and collective violence." It is an expression grounded in the spirit of "democracy without frontiers," mounting a challenge to the elitist and undemocratic tendencies of globalization-from-above. It is based on a notion of a "global civil society" which seeks "to extend ideas of moral, legal, and environmental accountability to those now acting on behalf of state, market, and media." (BRECHER, CHILDS, & CUTLER, 1993, p. ix). This approach is both humanistic and cosmopolitan, and it is also a celebration of plurality and the politics of race, gender, and the preservation of diversity (FALK, 1992).

Globalization-from-below combined with a postmodern model, in contrast to globalization-from-above, aspire to establish a voice and empowerment among people in communities throughout the world to develop their lives and environments to meet their needs; "to enhance the access of ordinary people to the resources they need; to democratize local, national, and transnational political institutions; and to impose pacification on conflicting power centers" (BRECHER, CHILDS, and CUTLER, 1993, p. xv; also see MOODY, 1994). Rector of the Central American University in Managua, Nicaragua, XABIER GOROSTIAGA (1993), notes that "international social subjects are sending out calls in different forms, in all parts of the world, through political, religious, union, and NGO [nongovernmental organizational] forums and, for the first time, they have begun to link up internationally" (p. 185).

Democratization at every level from the local to the global is a central goal of globalization-from-below. What presently exists at the global level is not the democratic expression of local and national concerns worldwide, but is instead "the imposition of a narrow group of interests from a handful of nations on a world scale, [so] democratizing of international interests is essential if genuine democracy is to exist at local and national levels" (SHIVA, 1993, 59). Evelina DAGNINO (1993), professor of political science at the University of Campinas in Brazil, notes that "the reestablishment of democratic regimes has been a widespread phenomenon in the past few years, sweeping the so-called Second and Third Worlds" (p. 239). She adds that social movements are creating an alternative definition of democracy based on an enlargement of the definition of democracy to include social and cultural practices not just the state. The consequence of this new conception of democracy is that the "struggle of the urban poor for housing, health, and education, of rural workers for land, of women, homosexuals, and blacks for equal rights, of all groups for environmental protection points in a single direction: the building of a truly worldwide democratic society, and the elimination of inequality in all its different forms. It also implies "the right to be different and the idea that difference shall not constitute a basis for inequality." This notion of citizenship constitutes "an elastic system of reference able to encompass different expressions and dimensions of inequality: economic, social, political, and cultural" (BRECHER, CHILDS, and CUTLER, 1993, p. xvii; see also FALK, 1992).

Economic rights are essential to this enlarged vision of democracy. SEIDMAN (1993) describes how the new labor unions that have emerged in newly industrialized countries "have expressed a vision of democratization that includes, beyond the right to vote, some kind of redistribution of resources and wealth" (p. 178). For them, democracy means more than just having the right to vote every few years; it includes the principle that citizens are entitled to a living wage, a decent standard of living, and basic social services such as food, housing, health care, and educational opportunities (WALLERSTEIN, 1994).

One of the most exciting aspects of globalization-from-below is that it represents a convergence of aspirations among people throughout the world. The director of the Mexico-American Border Program of the American Friends Service Committee, Primitivo RODRIGUEZ, states: "The globalization of capital, production, and communications has created the conditions in which the peoples of the world can come together across borders and barriers" (p. 298). What is created is the "opportunity for the convergence of 'world visions,' cultural experiences, and long-held aspirations whose dynamics can lead to a profound re-evaluation or revolution in our ways of thinking of and relating to ourselves and the universe around us" (p. 298). Today, as never before people in all walks of life, in countries throughout the world, are mapping out ways to empower themselves, to gain control over their destinies.

Peter BOHMER (1992) eloquently articulates the mission of their project. It is a project with a vision of a society that is equal and inclusionary, that respects the dignity of all people, and is environmentally sustainable, that is based on meeting human needs not greed, that is participatory economically and politically. This requires building grass roots movements working towards this evolving vision, participating in social movements and bold organizations which fight the exploitation of working people and against the oppression of women and people of color, and act in solidarity with those struggling for self-determination and social justice (p. 62).

Physical Education and Sports Leaders in the Globalized Social Order

And what about physical education and sports leaders - like all of you here - in the globalized social order? Those who are attempting to map out the future of globalization-from-below and a postmodern future are unanimous in their conviction that educators and intellectuals must play a vanguard role in this movement because, in spite of the many other cultural forces imposing upon the children and youth of today, educators will still, by the nature of their work, play an influential role in framing reality and shaping and molding attitudes, values, and behaviors of children and youth (ARONOWITZ & GIROUX, 1990; BARBER, 1992; TIERNEY, 1993).

Over 60 years ago American educator George COUNTS (1932) wrote a book titled Dare the School Build a New Social Order? His answer was "yes," but the educators of the 20th century have not been up to the challenge of social transformation and have, instead, been largely practioners of social reproduction. Will the educators of the 21st century be different? There are numerous ways in which physical education and sports leaders can be a part of social transformative movements in the future. But they must first come to an understanding of the consequences of the continuation of globalization-from-above and an understanding of the potential for a turn to globalization-from-below and postmodern images of human development. Once this is done, action can follow. This can begin at a personal level, with a personal inventory about how one's own actions may be contributing to various forms of inequality and injustice. Where such actions are occurring, a personal commitment to remedying them can be undertaken. One can also analyze the policies and procedures in the organizations of which one is a part. Where discrimination, oppression, and injustices are present, various forms of intervention and agency are possible. Finally, where social institutional inequalities, discrimination, and injustices exist in cultural norms and practices, intervention to change such practices can be undertaken in a variety of ways.

Finally, a major education battle is shaping up between globalization-from-above and globalization-from-below over education. On the one hand there are those who assert that schools are like business organizations and economic goals should drive education, and business models should be utilized to run the schools (KELLER,

1983). A globalization-from-below/postmodern view offers a dramatically different paradigm. Its premise is that educational organizations are not business organizations and educators must struggle against them becoming such. Schools are seen as communities and not markets. Human development rather than economic profit are the fundamental concerns. This view stresses connection, caring, and difference; it refuses to subordinate the purpose of education to narrowly defined economic and instrumental concerns. Educational leadership is geared less to "management" and "control" and more toward participation; educators function less as "masters of truth ... and more as creators of a space where those directly involved can act and speak on their own behalf" (p. 137, LATHER, 1991).

Concluding Comments

I cannot bring you a detailed plan for what you should do; I cannot offer specific prescriptions. Indeed, it would be a complete renunciation of my own theoretical stance if I did. However, I hope that what I have said today contributes to helping you to understand certain global trends and trajectories, and this that will cause you to think and reflect on their possible consequences, as well as your own potential to make history by intervening in and helping shape the future of your own life, as well as your students' lives. Perhaps in the next decade on two we will be able to point to exemplary actions among human movement professionals that made a difference toward a better world.

Social analyst Noam CHOMSKY (1993) noted: "If you assume that there's no hope, you guarantee that there will be no hope. If you assume that there... are opportunities to change things, there's a chance you may contribute to making a better world. That's your choice". But "If we relinquish the belief that we can make a difference, then the forces of [status quo and] greed will have won" (BRAUN, 1991, 283-284).

References

ARONOWITZ, S.; GIROUX, H.A.: Postmodern education: Politics, culture, and social criticism. Minneapolis: University of Minnesota Press 1991.

ARRIGHI, G.: World income inequalities and the future of socialism. In: New Left Review, 1991, September/October, 189, 39-65.

A survey of multinationals. In: Economist, 1993, March , 5-6.

BARBER, B.R.: An aristocracy of everyone. New York: Oxford University Press 1992.

BARNET, R.J.; CAVANAGH, J.: Global dreams: Imperial corporations and the new world order 1994.

BERBEROGLU, B.: The internationalization of capital: Imperialism and capitalist development on a world scale. New York: Praeger 1987.

BERBEROGLU, B.: Imperialism, capital accumulation, and class struggle in the Third World. In: B. BERBEROGLU: Critical perspectives in sociology. Dubuque, IA: Kendall/Hunt, 1993[2], 265-280.

BLUESTONE, B.: Deindustrialization and unemployment in America. In: Review of Black Political Economy, 1988, Fall, 17, 29-44.

BOHMER, P.: Continued stagnation, growing inequality. In: Z Magazine, 1992, September, 59-62.

BRAUN, D.: The rich get richer. Chicago: Nelson-Hall 1991.

BRECHER, J.: Global unemployment at 700 million. In: Z Magazine, 1993, November, 6, 45-48.

BRECHER, J.; CHILDS, J.B.; CUTLER, J.: Global visions: Beyond the new world order. Boston: South End Press 1993.

CHOMSKY, N.: Chronicles of Dissent. In: M.E. MONROE: Common Courage Press 1992.

COUNTS, G. S.: Dare the school build a new social order? New York: John Day Co. 1932.

DAGNINO, E.: An alternative world order and the meaning of democracy. In: J. BRECHER; J.B. CHILDS; J. CUTLER (Eds.): Global visions: Beyond the new world order. Boston: South End Press, 1993, 239-245.

DUDLEY, K.M.: The end of the line: Lost jobs, new lives in postindustrial America. Chicago: University of Chicago Press.

EPSTEIN, G.; GRAHAM, J.; NEMBHARD, J.: Creating a new world economy. Philadelphia: Temple University Press 1993.

FALK, R.: Explorations at the edge of time: The prospects for world order. Philadelphia: Temple University Press 1992.

FALK, R.: The making of global citizenship. In: J. BRECHER; J.B. CHILDS; J. CUTLER (Eds.): Global visions: Beyond the new world order. Boston: South End Press, 1993, 39-50.

FLACKS, R.: Making history. New York: Columbia University Press 1988.

GOROSTIAGA, X.: Latin America in the new world order. In: J. BRECHER; J.B. CHILDS; J. CUTLER (Eds.): Global visions: Beyond the new world order. Boston: South End Press, 1993, 67-86.

GRUNWALD, J.; FLAMM, K.: The global factory: Foreign assembly in international trade. Washington, D.C.: Brookings Institution 1985.

HALL, S.: The local and the global: Globalization and ethnicity. In: A.D. KING (Ed.): Culture, globalization and the world system. Binghamton, NY: Department of Art and Art History, SUNY at Binghamton, 1991, 19-39.

HARRISON, B.; BLUESTONE, B.: The great U-turn. New York: Basic Books 1988.

HAWKEN, P.: The ecology of commerce. New York: Harper Business 1993.

HERMAN, E.: The end of democracy? In: Z Magazine, 1993, September, 6, 57-62.

KAMEL, R.: The global factory: Analysis and action for a new economic era. Philadelphia: American Friends Service 1990.

KELLER, G.: Academic strategy. Baltimore: Johns Hopkins University Press 1983.

KLOBY, J. S.: Increasing class polarization in the United States: the growth of wealth and income inequality. In: B. BERBEROGLU (Ed.): Critical perspectives in sociology. Dubuque, IA: Kendall/Hunt, 1993², 27-42.

LATHER, P.: Getting smart: Feminist research and pedagogy with/in the postmodern. New York: Routledge 1991.

MILLS, C.W.: The sociological imagination. New York: Oxford University Press 1961.

MOODY, K.: If NAFTA don't get you... the GATT will. In: Labor Notes, 1994, February, 1, 12-13.

MOODY, K.; MCGINN, M.: Unions and free trade: Solidarity vs. competition. Detroit: Labor Notes 1992.

O'BRIEN, R.: Global financial integration: The end of geography. New York: Council on Foreign Relations Press 1992.

OGLE, G. E.: South Korea: Dissent within the economic miracle. Atlantic Highlands, NJ: Zed Books 1990.

PERRUCCI, C.C.; PERRUCCI, R.; TARG, D.B.; TARG, H.R.: Plant closings: International context and social costs. New York: Aldine De Gruyter 1988.

PETERSON, D.: Doing things right. In: Z Magazine, 1994, 7, 12-15.

PHILLIPS, K.: Boiling point: Democrats, Republicans and the decline of middle-class prosperity. New York: Harper Perennial 1993.

REICH, R.B.: The work of nations: Preparing ourselves for 21st century capitalism. New York: Knopf 1991. For another perspective on the globalized economy and the role of the nation state, see CARNOY, M.: Multinationals in a changing world economy: Whither the nation state? In: M. CARNOY; M. CASTELLS; S.S COHEN; F.H. CARDOSO: The new global economy in the information age. University Park: Pennsylvania State University Press, 1993, 45-96

RODRIGUEZ, P.: The uprooted from the land. In: J. BRECHER; J.B. CHILDS; J. CUTLER (Eds.): Global visions: Beyond the new world order. Boston: South End Press, 1993, 295-298.

SCHEER, R.:Welfare or work? The Nation. p.545, 1994, April 25.

SCHOR, J.B.: Global equity and environmental crisis: An argument for reducing working hours in the North. In: G. EPSTEIN; J. GRAHAM; J. NEMBHARD (Eds.): Creating a new world economy 183-198, Philadelphia: Temple University Press, 1993.

SCHWARZ, J.E.; VOLGY, T.J.: The forgotten Americans: Thirty million working poor in the land of opportunity. New York: W. W. Norton 1992.

SEIDMAN, G.W.: Facing the new international context of development. In: J. BRECHER; J.B. CHILDS; J. CUTLER (Eds.): Global visions: Beyond the new world order. Boston: South End Press, 1993, 175-189.

SHAPIRO, I.; GREENSTEIN, R.: Making work pay: The unfinished agenda. Washington, D.C.: Center on Budget and Policy Priorities 1993.

SHIVA, V.: The greening of the global reach. In: J.BRECHER, J.B. CHILDS, J. CUTLER (Eds.): Global visions: Beyond the new world order. Boston: South End Press, 1993, 53-60.

SLATER, P.: A Dream Deferred. Boston: Beacon 1991.

STAUDOHAR, P.D.; BROWN, H.E.: Deindustrialization and plan closure. Lexington, MA: D. C. Heath 1987.

Study finds millions of kids living in distressed neighborhoods. In: Rocky Mountain News, 1994, April 25, 3A.

TINNING, R.: We have ways of making you think. Or do we?: Reflections on 'training' in reflective thinking. In: Paper presented at the International Seminar on the Training of Teachers in Reflexive practice of Physical Education, Trois Rivieres, Quebec, Canada 1993.

UNICEF: The state of the world's children, 1991. Oxford: Oxford University Press 1991.

WALLERSTEIN, E.: The agonies of liberalism: What hope progress? In: New Left Review, 1994, February, 204, 3-17.

Who are the prisons for? In: The Progressive, 1994, June, 58, 10.

Who owns the world's assets and trade? In: Labor Notes, 1994, February, 12.

WORLD BANK: World development report 1990: Poverty. New York: Oxford University Press (for the World Bank) 1990.

World Commission on Environment and Development (WCED): Our common future. Oxford: Oxford University Press 1987.

Worldwatch Institute: State of the world 1990. New York: W. W. Norton 1990

Endnote

1. HALL, STUART (1991) has used the term "global post-modern“.

Hal A. Lawson

Economic, Political and Cultural Changes: Their Import for New Models for Practice

Introduction

"It was the best of times, it was the worst of times..." Charles DICKENS' (1975, 35) opening for **A Tale of Two Cities** also describes our world.

It is the best of times. For example, never before have so many people enjoyed such a high standard of living. We have created global networks of information age technologies, allowing instantaneous communication nearly everywhere in the world. We have built schools, sport institutes, and recreational complexes that were only dreams for previous generations. New hospitals and medical centers have been constructed around life-saving technologies. Democratic ideologies and political structures are pervasive. With the advent of what we call "global capitalism," a growing - and seemingly endless - array of consumer products increasingly is available nearly everywhere in the world.

Never before have so many people enjoyed the luxury of fashioning their own "lifestyles" around these consumer products, their behavioral preferences, and personal values. Our expanding culture of narcissism provides the psychological space needed for these choices: "You can do your thing, if I can do mine" is the rule of thumb. Different in identifiable ways around the world, we also can choose to be alike in our dress, eating habits, homes, work, and leisure pursuits. It's easy: Simply turn on the television, go to the movies, or read magazines to find an image; then make it a reality through planned purchases, friendships, and lifestyle choices. These and other heretofore unimaginable luxuries are characteristic of our times.

It also is the worst of times. With the growing culture of narcissism, our sense of community and the common good appear to be declining. We know that our natural resources are insufficient to support the earth's growing number of inhabitants, let alone the consumer-oriented lifestyles associated with "the good life."

Furthermore, gaps are growing between the nations, groups, and individuals who "have" and their counterparts who "have not." Although we may try to hide from these discrepancies, in today's world, we are unable to do so. The technologies and social conventions that make it possible for so many of us to ***thrive***, also present us with knowledge about the countless millions who strive to ***survive***. In the so-called "third world" and "post-industrial nations" around the world, children, youth and families literally are dying for our attention. So are many of our planet's most important environments and species.

Thus, at the same time that it is the best of times for some of us, it also is the worst of times for more of the world's people. The paradoxes or our era begin here, and there are others. As a members of a world community, we are similar, yet different; united, yet divided; peaceful, yet warlike; independent, yet interdependent. Worldwide there is evidence of crises in traditional value systems and the social institutions (e.g., the family, education, religion, sport) for which they are foundational.

These paradoxes and crises are symptoms of dramatic and rapid change. Uncertain about our futures, and positioned at the intersection of the past and present, we must decide what to preserve, revise and create. In an era of increasingly uncertainty, complexity and change, we must prepare ourselves to think, talk and act differently.

Today I hope to make a modest contribution to needed international dialogue about the ways in which we might begin to think, talk and act differently. I will sketch in the brief time allotted new models for practice. I offer these models as points of departure for planning and action. I hope to make it clear that the lion's share of the work must be planned and evaluated in each unique context with its local cultures. In brief, the rule of thumb will be "Think globally, act locally," just as it is for environmental planning.

First a caution: I am a North American and my biases are predictable. On the other hand, with the changing face of the world - especially in today's Europe - the North American perspective may be instructive. Whether because of planned immigration or by virtue of unanticipated refugees, nations around the world are now experiencing the challenges once thought to be uniquely North American. Today, nations around the world face challenges of multiculturalism and its implications for our institutions. All of us face challenges to our values and policies. So, while our differences remain, we also may learn from each other as our similarities and interdependence become more evident. We may begin with the transition from a traditional planning and action frame to a new one, a transition made in response to growing social problems involving children, youth and families.

Two Approaches to Planning and Action

In most parts of the world, pressures are mounting for all systems serving children and families to invent more effective policies, programs and supports. Poor outcomes involving growing school drop out rates, crime, teen pregnancy, substance abuse, mental health problems, teen suicide, gangs, drug dealing, illiteracy, and poverty, are like sirens in an early warning system. The question is, how shall we frame these problems and plan appropriate action strategies?

Categorical Thinking and Planning

We have a history of viewing each of these problems as separate. For each separate problem or need, a specialized profession, agency, and funding stream has been designed. In brief, categories of problems and needs have been matched by categories of professions, agencies and funding streams. As Figure 1 indicates, we have structured a specialized profession for every part of a human being, using the root metaphor of the machine (LAWSON, 1992). We call this approach to framing, identifying and solving needs and problems a ***categorical approach***. Similarly, funding streams in support of this work are called *categorical* (or *categorized*).

Figure 1 see appendix

Benefits of categorical approaches notwithstanding, it is timely to examine them critically. Similarly, we need to examine our language. In short, if we want to plan and act differently, then we will have to learn to talk differently. Otherwise we are likely to find ourselves constrained as we attempt to solve today's complex problem's with yesterday's words and planning. A new approach is required.

Relational Thinking and Planning

Whether in our everyday observations or in research, we see that undesirable outcomes such as teen pregnancy, school drop-outs, mental health problems and poverty are related, not separate. Yet, our categorical approaches have assumed that they are separate. And, because this assumption and others like it have been accepted, many of our systems have been flawed, despite the good intentions of the people working in them. These flaws are evident not only in what we have done, but what we have not done.

For example, some of our children, youth and families may have as many as 14 different professionals trying to met their needs and solve their problems. Rather than joining forces, these professionals often are engaged in a silent competition, at times under-cutting each other's efforts. Clearly, this situation is not conducive to high-impact programs and support services, nor is it cost-effective. These flawed systems are not just costly in dollars, but in their effects on the everyday lives of children, youth, families and service providers. It is time to think and talk differently.

Recognizing that the needs and problems of children, youth and families are, in the majority of cases, *related*, and furthermore, that we must join together to solve them, gives rise to a ***relational approach*** to problem-framing, -labeling and -solving. (Sometimes this also is called "an ecological approach" because it takes into account the related situations and contexts for children and families.)

For example, as indicated in Figure 2, a low birthweight child (less than 5.5 lbs.) "tracks" into other problems, needs and costs (after BRUNER, 1993). Preventing low birthweight babies thus helps prevent other problems, costs and needs. In the same vein, given that the needs and problems of "low birthweight children and youth" are related, strategies intended to solve one (e.g., school problems) must simultaneously address the others (e.g., substance abuse, delinquency). This is relational problem-setting and -solving in action.

Figure 2 see appendix

Relational thinking, planning, and action strategies give us reason to see ourselves and work differently. They compel us to look for interdependent symptoms and action strategies. They permit us to escape patterns of blame and maltreatment as we accept the fact that all of us are either part of the solution or part of the problem. They allow us to think about conservation, especially conserving our energy and human resources as we attempt to support the development and capacities of children and families. They force us to return to basic questions about our profession's moral foundations and purposes, questions of problem-setting (LAWSON, 1984). Who are we serving, how and with what outcomes? Who are we not serving, why, and with what outcomes?

A Time for Reappraisal

Beyond Performance Efficiency and Effectiveness

Our profession began as a child- and youth-serving enterprise. Initially, the majority of us worked in schools. Today, we have expanded to serve persons across the life cycle in a variety of public and private organizations. Our program specialization's in universities have expanded accordingly, and professionals in our field have invented a variety of new names for themselves. Regardless of where, and with whom, we work, we fancy ourselves as being experts in exercise, sport, and their relationship. As expert professionals, we diagnose and prescribe for others. We assume responsibility for exercise and sport; whatever else people may need or want is some other profession's responsibility. When it comes to exercise and sport - our "turf" - we feel justified in regulating people's lives (LAWSON, 1993b), confident that we know what others want and need. We believe that our values and purposes ought to become theirs.

We have dedicated ourselves to enhancing performance efficiency and effectiveness. Reflect for a moment on the dominant conceptions of our field's knowledge base and the kinds of research specialization's we have fostered. The labels "exercise and sport sciences" and "sport pedagogy" reveal a performance enhancement bias (BRETTSCHNEIDER, 1991; TINNING, 1993). Where performance is concerned, we assume that more is better. While the many persons want to know the least amount of exercise they need for health and well-being, in our view, more is better. Since there is always room for improvement, people's needs for our specialized expertise never ends.

Implicit in our work ideologies and approaches are labels and beliefs that affect others and their well-being. For example, one's performance characteristics determines one's identity - "athlete" or not; "fit" or fat; "motivated" or lazy; "healthy" or "at risk;" "moral" or "immoral, " leader or "outsider." Identity-signs also are connected to social affiliations such as youth sub-cultures and lifestyles (e.g., BRETTSCHNEIDER, 1992; WEXLER, 1992). In brief, there is more complexity to our work than our ideologies, technologies and language have allowed us to perceive.

With such a singular focus upon performance efficiency and effectiveness, we have worked with two kinds of "client groups:" (1) Captive audiences in schools, i.e., children and youth required to complete sport and exercise instructional programs; (2) Elite athletes and performance-conscious adults who are able to pay for our expertise and services. Our service technologies, ideologies and language have been developed accordingly. We have, in essence, two kinds of technologies, each with their supportive ideologies and language: (1) Those for captive children and youth in school programs; (2) Those seeking our services in fee-for-service settings. In both cases, we have assumed that we, as professionals, know what is best and appropriate for clients. In both, we have wanted to believe that "one size fits all" as we have tinkered with people's bodies and performance abilities. In both cases, ***a*** way of thinking about and performing work has become ***the*** way. An identifiable pattern of problem-setting and -solving is in place, and our occupational socialization processes maintain it (e.g., LAWSON, 1988; LAWSON & STROOT, 1993).

Many of our leaders take justifiable pride in our collective achievements. They suggest that we are accomplishing our missions. For example, performance records in sport fall regularly. Increasingly only licensed teachers and coaches may work with children and youth. Wealthy adults are becoming more physically fit, in part because of our programs and services. As a consequence of these and other achievements, some leaders claim that our profession's recognition and status may be growing.

In short, some of us may claim that it is the best of times. By surveying only our success stories and achievements, we can arrive at the same conclusion.

Are We Part of the Problem or Essential to Solutions?

On the other hand, in today's world, we cannot hide from the everyday realities that make ours "the worst of times." When it comes to exercise, sport, and people's well-being, "one size does not fit all." Nor can the needs, wants and problems manifested in a growing number of children, youth and families be delegated readily to some other profession. Already members of our profession are confronting challenges and experiencing crises. Predictably, our teachers and coaches working in required programs for children and youth in schools are among the first to do so. They are encountering limitations in our traditional ways of defining ourselves and our work. Cultural diversity and change are, at times, overwhelming these teachers and coaches.

Nor can others in our profession escape from today's changing realities. Even if their work roles may not change, their personal lives are changing because of the needs and problems of "have not" children, youth, families, communities and entire nations. Social, fiscal and moral costs are exacted from all of us when these needs and problems remain unattended. In many parts of the world, health, education and welfare systems are in a state of crisis.

There is increasing recognition that, while some parts of our personal and professional lives may remain in tact, we also must begin to think, talk and act differently. Mechanistic conceptions of humans, together with their relationship with each other and their environments, have out-lived their usefulness. Unable to continue thinking and planning categorically, our work now must be framed relationally and ecologically. Seeing relationships and ecologies requires an understanding of connections, of interdependent systems. Mindful of our interdependence with others, we can work toward new partnerships for change.

Expanded Partnerships Among the Professions: New Service and Support Systems for Children, Youth and Families

Interprofessional Collaboration and Service Integration

Heretofore discrete, even competing, professions thus are beginning work together. Initially cooperating, they seek to collaborate around shared visions, goals and resources. These newly-forged partnerships represent a new strategy called ***interprofessional collaboration.*** Entirely new to many professions, only the label is new to some of us. In our work with elite athletes, we know how a sport psychologist, biomechanist, physiologist, coach, and physician must all work together to enhance the performance efficiency and effectiveness of an athlete. Now all of us must gain the requisite sensitivities, skills and abilities for interprofessional collaboration. Just as a team of sport specialists "wraps around" an elite athlete, so must each of us learn how to work as an interprofessional team, which "wraps around" the needs, problems and aspirations of children, youth and families.

Accompanying collaboration is a related strategy called ***service integration***. Integrating programs, services and supports requires a departure from machine- and assembly-line approaches to framing and solving problems. Service integration involves the creation of "seamless systems" of education, health and social services. It is an effort to envelope children, youth and families in communities of caring and concern. Instead of asking these persons to come to professions offering "one size fits all" programs, supports and services, the idea is to tailor supports for diverse kinds of people. For this to occur, integration must be planned to occur simultaneously at five levels: (1) client; (2) professional provider; (3) program; (4)

organization; (5) policy (after KAGAN, 1993). "Wrap-around strategies" for service integration thus involve blending heretofore separate and competing policies, professionals, programs and supports into a coherent, cohesive, culturally-responsive, and context-sensitive framework.

Here, in short, professions like ours cease self-serving initiatives in which they make people fit their offerings. Instead, they serve people by tailoring their offerings to the problems, needs and aspirations of children, youth, families and communities.

With Katharine HOOPER-BRIAR, I have described elsewhere aspects and implications of interprofessional collaboration and service integration (HOOPER-BRIAR & LAWSON, 1994; LAWSON & HOOPER-BRIAR, 1994). In the brief discussion that follows, I sketch a few possibilities and their implications.

For example, in North America, there are five emergent models for interprofessional collaboration and service integration. There is considerable variation among and between them; we liken these models to "the prevailing winds." Examples appear in Table 1.

Table 1 Five Emergent Models for Service Integration and Interprofessional Collaborations

Home & Neighborhood-Based: e.g., Store front services, a family resource center in a home, a service strategy offered out of the home of one of the neighbors, a collaborative located in urban "projects".

Community-Base: e.g. Services can be offered in a variety of settings that support families such as a public health clinic, a multiservice center, a settlement house, a shopping mall, a public social service office.

School-Linked*: Services targeting children and families by means of referrals from persons at school. Although not housed at the school, families in the school's "catchment area" are defined as the population needed to be served. Working agreements are developed among school and agency personnel, new accountability structures and criteria are developed, and information-sharing and management are prioritized.

School-Based*: Services are located at the school as service providers from various agencies recognize that schools already may have as many as eight caseloads, warranting relocation because the population needing to be served is at, or near, the school; and, access to children and families is increased; and, improved access and quality of services for children can also be tied to beneficial classroom and school outcomes.

> ***Co-location of Services:*** Here, providers and services are merely moved to school sites, providing the opportunities for cooperation and collaboration.
>
> ***Schools as Hubs of Family Support Villages:*** Here, providers join with school professionals, community leaders, parents, and others to build school-community consortia aimed at the simultaneous development of children, families and communities.

Saturation-Oriented: A combination of the above models, together with a vision for child-focused, family-centered, community development.

*Community schools (and the community school movement) are examples of school-linked or school-based models; or, community schools may be a combination of both.

Interprofessional collaboration and service integration are not ends or goals in their own right. Rather, they are part of a larger vision for social development, one aimed at improving outcomes for children, youth, families, communities and nations.

A Focus Upon Children and Youth

"The world we inhabit is loaned to us by our children." The wisdom inherent in this popular saying is part of the heritage of our field. Children and youth remain central to our profession's missions and goals. With other professions--especially health education, recreation and social work--we can join forces in a three-pronged strategy aimed at enhancing the well-being and lives of children and youth.

For the highest risk or most vulnerable children and youth, ***crisis-oriented remediation strategies*** will be needed. At the same time, ***early intervention and primary prevention*** strategies need to be initiated. These two strategies are aimed at the needs and problems of children and youth. A third builds from their aspirations, their hopes and dreams. ***Educative and promotive strategies*** are predicated upon a build-from-strength philosophy. Instead of seeing children and youth as "walking clusters of needs and problems for professionals to diagnose and solve, professionals seek to enable these young persons to help themselves and one another.

The three strategies are related in three ways. First, efforts are aimed at moving dollars and resources from deep-end crises to front-end preventive, promotive and educative work. Second, all three are aimed at building the capacities of children and youth. Third, all are grounded in a broader vision for not only ***child welfare*** (LAWSON, under review), but ***social development***.

Toward a New Vision for Social Development

Family-Centered Supports and Practices

1994 is the United Nations' International Year of the Family. This is a timely reminder that, while a guiding vision for social development begins with children and youth, it does not end here. After all, the learning, development and well-being of children hinge in large part upon their families. For this reason and others listed in Table 2, we recommend a shift from child- and youth-centered to family-centered practices.

Table 2 Why Family-Centered Practice? Selected Reasons

- Families already perform up to 90 percent of the health care, education, counselling and other kinds of service provision, even though they have not received formal preparation or resources for this important work. When families fail in their duties, parents are blamed, and children are victimized.
- Children usually become what they see and experience, and families are the most powerful determinants of both.
- Family coping styles and intergenerational problem-solving abilities predict resiliency in children.
- Data from family functioning help predict the capacities, needs and developmental support requirements for children.
- Of some 26 identifiable risk factors for the health and well-being of children and youth, 19 either are located in the families, or shape their abilities to educate, nurture and support children.
- There never will be enough professionals such as nurses, social workers, health care workers, and police to address all of the needs, problems, and aspirations of children. Family support is the most direct way to aid children; the state does not make a good parent.
- Institution-building takes decades; building the capacities of families can take place immediately and bring results quickly.
- Strength-based service strategies for children must be grounded in the cultural diversity and heritage of their families.
- Many services do not reach those in need on a timely basis or when help comes it may reflect a sense of the deficits that exist e.g. suspension, child protection services, detention.
- Many families inadvertently are unable to follow through with case plans whether they are homework-lesson plan for the child, a

medical regimen or course of treatment, a caseplan that may be court order or part of a caseworkers case plan. Sometimes, the non follow-through is because there is not consensus about the problems or the solutions. When those we serve do not share our view of the problem and the solution, there may be failed outcomes.

- Much waste may occur when providers do not coordinate or when they work at cross-purposes. For example, a child who is to be reunified with once abusive parents may be seen to be at risk by a nurse or a teacher who may be unaware of the permanency planning or family preservation work which is federal law. Thus, these efforts may be seen as counter to the child's interest and may even result in an intervention that undercuts reunification or visitation plans some of the promising models that are being crafted are consumer guided so that families themselves aid not only with service design but in service delivery and ongoing feedback on needed changes.
- Families do not have the luxury of saying "we only do nursing, we only teach, we only do counseling etc." They are expected to perform all these functions without training or aid and them are blamed when children manifest needs and problems. To give them the tools is such a relatively low cost investment.
- There is a "domino effect" - Healthy, functioning families help themselves and other families. Healthy families involved in mutual aid and assistance networks facilitate community development initiatives and institutional redesign.

Here, I must emphasize that we need to talk about a *child-focused, family-centered* vision. It is not a matter of attending to the family at the expense of the child or youth. Both are targeted simultaneously, along with two other facets of this guiding vision.

Consumer-Guided Programs, Services and Strategies

One is an alternative to our time-withstanding efforts to regulate and control the lives of others. In contrast to efforts aimed at regulating lives, professional assistance can involve power- and knowledge-sharing, aimed at developing the capacities and independence of "clients." How can today's client become a partner (?) is one guiding question for what many called empowerment. Another guiding question is: At what point will the person no longer need professional assistance, and what is the plan for getting there? In other words, what capacity-building initiatives are mounted in support of children and families?

Questions like these are integral to consumer-guided and -delivered programs, supports and services. Here, the roles of children, youth, families and adults are recast; they move from "clients" to "partners." Selected benefits of consumer-guided services and supports are presented in Table 3.

Table 3 Seleceted Benefits of Consumer-Guided Services

Definition:
Consumer-guided services are provided by groups, which function as mutual aid societies; they provide information, direct assistance and referrals in helping stations conveniently located in a neighborhood or village. They are a basis for CONSENSUS-BASED PRACTICES.

Benefits include:

- Increasing cost-effectiveness and efficiency.
- Increasing appropriate impacts on needy persons and families through informal networking; with professionals, they add to the "saturation" of services of densely-populated areas of need and concern.
- Assisting professional service providers in problem-need identification and solving.

- Helping to insure contextual and cultural awareness and sensitivity.
- Improving accountability processes and measures.
- Facilitating cross-training for professional collaborations, especially the shift from child- to family-centered practice.
- Facilitating appropriate service delivery strategies because they have insider knowledge about "paths of help-seeking".

In brief, all technologies and service strategies are aimed at building the capacities of persons once viewed as dependent clients.

Capacity building involves, for example, creating mutual aid and assistance networks wherein children, youth and families help each other. It also involves nurturing the development of ***educational communities***, i.e., planned and unplanned, formal and informal, networks that facilitate the learning, development and well-being of children, youth and families. Clearly, the family itself is an educational community. Community organizations that support and strengthen the family (e.g., churches, community centers, voluntary associations) also have the capacity to create and maintain other educational communities that do the same. What HUIZINGA (1956) called "play communities" are essential kinds of educative communities, and we have vital roles in creating and sustaining them. Interprofessional collaboration involves planning with others for these educative and promotive opportunities for children, youth and families.

The Community Development Component

Planning for mutual aid and assistance networks and educational communities starts with children and families and connects them to community development initiatives. This community development component is a reminder that social, health and educational services and supports are crucial, but insufficient, for children youth and families. They also need safe and health-promoting homes and neighborhoods, along with good jobs and support systems. This

community development perspective is essential to a guiding vision for social development.
In this community development perspective, many of the presenting needs and problems of children, youth and families - e.g., teen pregnancy, dropping out of school, delinquency, substance abuse - are the equivalent of symptoms. Granting the importance of initiatives addressing each "symptom," long-term prevention requires attention to what we call their ***root causes***. Chief among these root causes are unemployment, poverty, homelessness, crime, abuse, hopelessness and despair.

With children and families guiding services, these root causes become evident. They talk about the need to create meaningful employment opportunities, including what we call ***microenterprises***. These are small businesses run by youth and families. Parents talk about the lack of faith that many children have in their futures, including the contributions of schooling to productive lives and lifestyles. They know the impact of relocation and dislocation caused by housing problems and needs. The list goes on. The point is, community development work, aimed at root causes of many presenting problems and needs, is an essential part of a guiding vision for interprofessional collaboration and service integration.

To summarize, interprofessional collaboration and service integration may proceed with a guiding vision described as ***child-focused, family-centered, consumer-guided, and community development-oriented***. This is a vision that gives life to the African proverb, "It takes a whole village to raise a child." It builds upon the capacities of children and families, alongside professionals. It attends to community-based, root causes of presenting problems and needs. Beyond these needs and problems are the hopes, dreams and aspirations of children, youth and families, inviting educative and promotive strategies facilitating mutual support and assistance networks. This is a vision based upon relational planning and action strategies. It suggests ways in which we might change ourselves, work roles, organizations and societies as a new Century approaches.

Space and time do not permit a detailed analysis of all of the possible changes. Two related examples will have to suffice: (1) Changes in professional preparation programs; (2) New Work Roles.

Interprofessional Education and Practice

Simultaneous Changes in Universities and Communities

Interprofessional collaboration and service integration, framed around a guiding vision for children youth, families and communities, represent products of a re-invention and re-vitalization process. It is not a coincidence that the first exemplars for this work occurred in schools and related health and human services agencies for vulnerable and poor children, youth and families. Nor is it surprising that it took crises involving children and professionals alike to cause us to think and plan differently. Fresh visions of healthy children, families, schools and communities fostered new missions for interprofessional collaboration and service integration. Based upon these visions and missions, new conceptions of competent practice were derived, involving collaborative relationships among heretofore competing professions, programs and service strategies.

Colleges and universities, especially their professional departments, schools and colleges, now face the same challenge of commitment, and accompanying changes in their visions, missions and conceptions of competent practice. As indicated in Table 4, there are analogs that may facilitate joint planning with practitioners in communities. For example, interprofessional collaboration in communities must be matched by its counterpart in higher education called ***interprofessional education***. This preparation provides a common denominator of knowledge, language, values, sensitivities and skills for all of the human services professions. Ideally, it includes collaborative teaching and learning experiences for students and faculty alike (GOODSELL et al., 1992). Similarly, service integration in communities requires, as its counterpart, knowledge integration and academically-oriented in universities. Cross-professional and disciplinary partnerships in higher education must be joined to those in communities. These are components in a plan for synchronized, conjoint changes in higher education and in the world of practice.

Table 4 Comparable Elements in Higher Education Institutions and Their School-Community Partners

School-Communities	Higher Education Institutions
Interprofessional Collaboration	Interprofessional Education
Service Integration	Cross- and Inter-Disciplinary Knowledge Frameworks
Interagency Agreements & Role Release	Inter-Departmental Agreements & Role Changes
Congruence Across Schools & Agencies in the Same Feeder Pattern	Congruence and consistent messages across programs and departments
Theory of Social Development	Theory of Program

Having spent the better part of a Century establishing competing programs of study that reinforce their professional borders, today planners in human services fields committed to interprofessional collaboration and service integration must think and act differently. Mindful of differences borne out of necessary specialization, planners need to emphasize similarities, commonalties, and complementarities. If practitioners are to collaborate and integrate, they must receive preparation for both. Courses and experiences designed to provide social workers, nurses, health promotion specialists, educators, recreationists, and others (e.g., criminal-juvenile justice, public administration) a common denominator of knowledge, values, sensitivities, skills and language for collaboration and integration are called interprofessional education programs. Like the preparation provided foreign nationals who will enter a new country with its unfamiliar cultures, traditions and language, interprofessional education prepares human services professionals for "border crossings."

In the present era of economic insecurity, the idea of professionals from other fields crossing one's borders and entering once-exclusive professional terrain can be threatening. In this perspective, interprofessional education is perceived inaccurately as a social movement aimed at reducing the number of specialized professions by preparing students to perform more than one role. This is not the case. Interprofessional education is not the beginning of the end for specialized professions. Rather, it changes the parameters of specialization.

Responsive, Practice-Oriented Interprofessional Education

We believe that interprofessional education and practice are inseparable. That is, it makes little sense to design interprofessional coursework in colleges and universities in the absence of interprofessional collaborations and service integration initiatives in nearby communities. Disciplinary study apart from practice settings and first hand experiences is not the best alternative for interprofessional education. Joining forces means firm partnerships between higher education institutions and innovative settings in communities. The aim is the simultaneous renewal of organizations, faculty, practitioners and students (after GOODLAD, 1990) with the intent of better serving children, youth and families.

Planning for interprofessional education and practice should therefore proceed conjointly, involving partnerships among faculty, students and administrators from higher education and practitioners, supervisors, children and families in schools and community agencies. All parties are equally empowered in this kind of collaborative. All are, in this sense, consumer-guided because each is a kind of consumer of what the others want and need.

Thought of in this fashion, interprofessional education and practice are the equivalent of mutual aid and assistance networks - educative communities. Each party contributes to the learning and well-being of the others. Each learns from, evolves with, the others. This kind of planned interdependence, a symbiotic relationship, constitutes a core principle for planning interprofessional education and practice.

Another is to honor cultural diversity, while responding to community needs and priorities. My colleague, Katharine Hooper-Briar, offers a brief checklist (LAWSON & HOOPER-BRIAR, 1994) by means of which we can begin to assess the cultural- and community-responsiveness of our higher education curricula.

(1) Make a list of the needs, problems and community concerns that appear repeatedly.
(2) Now make a list of the root causes of these needs, problems, and concerns as you can best determine them.
(3) Now examine the course titles and descriptions listed for your department, school or college with an eye toward the needs and problems of children and families and the concerns of the community. What percentage of these courses address the needs and problems of children and families? The community's concerns?
(4) Next, examine the resumes of faculty. What percentage of their publications andpresentations address the needs and problems of children and families? The community's concerns?
(5) Now review the external service records of faculty? How many are actively involved with the needs and problems of children and families? With the community's concerns? Who defines the service commitments that faculty accept?
(6) Finally, examine the accountability structures used in evaluating faculty, programs, departments, schools and colleges. What percentage is assigned to work activities involving children and families? The community's concerns? What role is assigned to cultural competency?

(7) Now total your percentages. If your relevancy score is under 50 percent, what steps need to be initiated?

This is one way to begin dialogue aimed at reinvention and revitalization of faculty, programs, departments, schools and colleges. It helps set the stage for discussions about our collective needs to become more, not only more responsive, but more cohesive and congruent by means of interprofessional education.

Core Values, Content and Competencies?

Interprofessional education is not only a new approach to pre-service and professional development programs. It signals new knowledge bases for practice. Note the plural knowledge ***bases***; our era is the beginning of the end for "one size fits all" thinking, knowledge bases and technologies. The interplay among local cultures, contexts and biographies spawns multiple realities and conceptions of knowledge.

Avoiding the quest for a one best model for interprofessional education is one thing. Neglecting common denominators in these programs is quite another. Without a common vision there is little promise of congruence and cohesion across professions, organizations and settings. There are few standards against which to assess practices. Standards serve as planning guides and help insure quality control. When the lives of children, youth and families are at stake, we can ill-afford to fail when we could have avoided it.

To be an educated person and professional is to be adaptable, and adaptability in new and experienced practitioners is essential if they are to change with their service systems. What values, content and competencies help comprise this adaptability? At a minimum, we need to prepare persons to think critically, understand contexts, engage authentically with other learners, and both reflect and act prudently. These are the abilities of liberally educated individuals who may act as professional leaders.

So, it is timely to accelerate an international dialogue on recommended values, content and competencies that are required for successful work in interprofessional collaboration and service integration initiatives. How, by whom, under what conditions, when and why these values, content and competencies are disseminated and learned will vary among colleges and universities.

Interprofessional education must be tied to a guiding vision for social development. Mindful of our child-focused, family-centered, consumer-guided, community-development-oriented vision, the following content areas merit consideration for inclusion in interprofessional education programs.

- Child-focused, family-centered, consumer-guided, community-development service strategies.
- Relational versus categorical analysis, policies, and service designs
- Assessment frames and methods for child-family risks, needs, strengths and capacities for resiliency.
- The special characteristics (needs, problems, wants, aspirations, and strengths) of vulnerable children, youth and families.
- Culturally-responsive and congruent service strategies, program designs, and language.
- Consumer-guided and -delivered programs and services, including the roles "clients" may play as partners and paraprofessionals.
- The multiple forms and functions of families, including ways to build upon and assess their capacities.
- Child and adolescent health and development, with special emphasis upon youth subcultures and value systems, influences of the mass media, and addictive behaviors (both beneficial and harmful).
- Circular causality, especially relationships among teen pregnancy, success in school, delinquency, child abuse, indices of mental health, substance abuse, poverty, un-employment and under-employment, and interventions that proceed beyond single-problem, -profession, and-organization to address these and other relationships.

- o The import of occupational and economic development initiatives in re-vitalizing communities and families, while helping and supporting children and youth.
- o Empowerment and strength-based service strategies using consensus-based practice principles (in which clients become partners).
- o Practice-oriented, developmental designs for research, evaluation and assessment, which are built-in to renewal efforts.
- o Indicators of children and youth in crisis, together approaches to referral.
- o Wrap-around service strategies.
- o Five levels of service integration (policy, organization, program, provider, and client-consumer), which each involves and requires, together with relationships among them.
- o Knowledge, sensitivities and skills for collaboration, including consensus-building, compromise tactics, barrier-busting strategies and conflict resolution approaches.
- o Ethical-moral principles and codes of conduct, which unite professionals and citizens in collaboratives.
- o Conditions conducive to beneficial interprofessional collaboration and service integration, including conditions under which collaboration and integration may have unintended and adverse consequences.

Here, then, is a starter list intended to elicit reactions and catalyze further dialogue.

Together with discussions of core values, principles and content, it also is timely to initiate dialogue about recommended teaching-learning processes and related experiences. After all, the conditions under which learning occurs affects the character and quality of learning. And, when it comes to interprofessional collaboration and service integration, the amount that might be learned is nearly overwhelming. Here, strategies for self-directed, continuing learning will prove invaluable to future practitioners. Group-based problem-solving and learning strategies are at the heart of successful collaborations; they merit emphasis, too.

Toward New Career Opportunities and Roles

Interprofessional collaboration and service integration initiatives, launched simultaneously in communities and universities and aimed at a guiding vision for child-focused, family-centered, community development-oriented enhancement, usher in a host of related changes. Some of these changes have been identified here, while others are implicit. Changes in career opportunities and roles can be added to the list.

Changes in Schools and Teachers' Roles

For example, there are changes in schools and teachers' roles. Schools, instead of being stand-alone institutions concerned only with the cognitive-academic development of children and youth, become concerned with children's learning, development, and well-being. Teachers, instead of being asked to "do it all and alone," work collaboratively with health and human service providers, families and community leaders. In our guiding vision, it becomes possible to talk about, and plan for, healthy learners, schools and communities (LAWSON, 1994). In these schools, everyone is a health educator (LAWSON, 1994), with attendant implications for the relationship between physical and health education as well as related subjects such as science education (LAWSON, 1993a).

With our guiding vision, schools can become, in KATHARINE HOOPER-BRIAR's terms, "Hubs of Family Support Villages." Here, there are firm reminders that education involves more than schooling, and that interprofessional collaborations need to be mindful not only of educative communities, but of ***miseducative communities*** (e.g., drug trafficking, crime-related economic networks). The list of opportunities involving sport, exercise and games in such a school-community network is nearly endless. Here are areas in which we can thrive at the same time we serve others.

For example, a recent report (Carnegie Council for Adolescent Development, 1992) reminds us of the importance of children's and youth's out-of-school time. Up to 60 percent of this time is not only discretionary, but with changing family demographics, many young people are home alone. There is need for programs, support and services for children and youth, opportunities that combine education, recreation, and health promotion.

So called "midnight basketball leagues" are one example of a response to these needs. Here, sports and games sponsored by communities are offered at non-traditional hours for youth otherwise prone to violence, crime and abusive behaviors. The results are promising, and they suggest needs for more expansive programming and supports for high risk adolescents.

New Careers

Figure 3 identifies the ways in which interprofessional education provides the foundation for four related kinds of careers. With appropriate preparation, there is good reason to believe that persons from our profession can perform at least three of them; with joint preparation in social work, family advocate roles also are possible.

Figure 3 see appendix

Interprofessional education alone will not prepare us to perform these roles.

We need to revisit our work ideologies, technologies and language with an eye toward not only interprofessional collaboration and service integration, but the changing faces of today's world. We need to prepare ourselves and our colleagues for cultural pluralism and complexity. Pluralism requires an enriched understanding of diverse cultures and local contexts. Complexity requires us to examine more thoroughly the targets for, and implications of, our work.

For example, BRETTSCHNEIDER (1991) has urged us to consider "a radical rethinking" of sport and, in turn, sport pedagogy. TINNING (1993) has recommended a critical posture about the role of science and its offspring, technology, in our fields. And my colleague Alan Ingham (work in progress) is mapping new ways to study and change relationships among the body, self, psyche, social structure and culture in sport, exercise and health-related contexts. These and other leading thinkers are pointing toward not only expanded conceptions of ourselves and our work, but transformational agendas to meet future challenges and needs. Implicit in their work are criticisms of media-generated images and lifestyles, followed by productive visions for improved outcomes for children, youth, adults, families, communities and societies.

An International Agenda for Renewal and Change

In the United States, a popular poster has the following caption: "Just when I thought that I had all of life's answers, they changed the questions!" So it is with so many of us. Sensing accomplishment in "the best of times," we now confront anew the prospects of change. As we contemplate both the process and the substance of change, it is important that we come to terms with the fact that, in today's and tomorrow's world, change, uncertainty and complexity will not vanish. Individuals, groups, professions, and organizations thus face needs for the kinds of learning and development that allow renewal. There is growing international awareness of the need to prepare self-renewing people, professions, organizations, and communities. We need to participate in this dialogue and take it to center stage in our profession's communications.

Human Rights and Moral Responsibilities

Renewal and change, in this perspective, are moral obligations. Here, one's role as a citizen cannot be isolated from one's role as a professional. Who I am and what I do must become merged, henceforth seen as interdependent. Our work roles and organizations must change to accommodate such a unified identity and moral purpose. Such a sense of authenticity is a human right; creating and sustaining conditions for it is a moral responsibility. Joined by a shared vision for the common good--for human and societal betterment--human rights and responsibilities are like opposite sides of the same coin. They are aimed at changing worst of times into the best of times for a greater number of the world's people.

Relationships With Democratic Structures and Traditions

Think globally, act locally. Become part of the solution or remain part of the problem. Recognize that the democratic structures must themselves become self-renewing, grounded in vibrant ideals of civic community. As Robert PUTNAM (1993) has argued so brilliantly, democracy rests upon civic community, and civic community depends upon four related components:

- o Solidarity, trust and tolerance made possible by virtuous citizens who value diversity and differences of opinion.
- o Associations for cooperation, especially those that are indigenous, participatory and voluntary (like the educative communities I discussed earlier).
- o Civic engagement by all citizens, combining enlightened self-interest with care for the commons.
- o Political equality, borne out of both rights and responsibilities, and expressed in horizontal relationships supported by norms of reciprocity and trust.

PUTNAM (1993) also has reminded us that:

- o Social context and history profoundly condition the effectiveness of our institutions.
- o When we change our institutions (and professions) we can change political practice.
- o Where institution-building and -changing our concerned, time is measured in decades.

PUTNAM's work is, in fact, a kind of wake-up call for all of us.

New Beginnings

Framed in this way, our paths toward renewal and change become clearer. As individuals, we also are part of something larger than any of us. Empowered as citizen-professionals, we are forced to abandon self-interested, profession-specific frames of reference. Instead, we are compelled to think about the ways in which our profession must be revitalized for renewal and change, to earn the title ***Human Services Profession***. Mindful of our differences, there are also reminders of the ways in which we are identical, similar, and complementary. Living in separate parts of the world, we are compelled to think about our relationships with, and responsibilities to, each another. New to some of us, the agenda is also a familiar one, reminiscent of what those of us who have enjoyed the benefits of democracy are in danger of losing.

Ours is a time for new beginnings. We have the opportunity to renew and change, to invent and create. More than any of us can do alone, this is something we must plan together. The future of our children, and their children, hinges upon our moral courage and willingness to act now.

References

BRETTSCHNEIDER, W.: The many faces of sport as a challenge for sport pedagogy and physical education. The Cagigal Memorial Lecture, AIESEP World Congress, Atlanta, Georgia 1991, January.

BRETTSCHNEIDER, W.: Adolescents, leisure, sport and lifestyle. In: T. WILLIAMS; L. ALMOND; A. SPARKES (Eds.): Sport and physical activity: Moving toward excellence. London: E & FN Spon, 1992, 536-550.

BRUNER, C.: Examining the costs of failure. Unpublished materials, Center for Social Policy, Washington, D. C 1993.

DICKENS, C.: A tale of two cities. London: Penguin Classics. Carnegie Council for Adolescent Development (1992). A matter of time: Risk and opportunity during the non-school hours. New York: Author 1975.

GOODLAD, J.: Teachers for our nation's schools. San Francisco, Jossey-Bass 1990.

GOODSELL, A.; MAHER, M.; TINTO,V.; SMITH, B.; MACGREGOR, J.: Collaborative learning: A source book for higher education. University Park: PA.: National Center on Postsecondary Teaching, Learning and Assessment 1992.

HOOPER-BRIAR, K.; LAWSON, H.: Serving children, youth, families and communities: A resource guide for interprofessional collaboration and service integration. St. Louis, MO., The Danforth Foundation 1994.

HUIZINGA, J.: Homo ludens: A study of the play element in culture. Boston, Beacon Press 1956.

INGHAM, A.: (work in progress) Miami University, Oxford, OH., USA.

KAGAN, L.: Integrating human services: Understanding the past to shape the future. New Haven, CT., Yale University Press 1993.

LAWSON, H.: Problem-setting for physical education and sport. Quest, 1984, 36, 46-60.

LAWSON, H.: Occupational socialization, cultural studies and the physical education curriculum. Journal of Teaching in Physical Education, 1988, 7, 265-288.

LAWSON, H.: Toward a socio-ecological conception of health. Quest, 1992, 44 (1), 105-121.

LAWSON, H.: School reform, families and health in the national agenda for social and economic improvement: Implications. Quest, 1993a, 45, 289-307.

LAWSON, H.: After the regulated life. Quest, 1993b, 45, 523-545.

LAWSON, H.: Toward healthy learners, schools and communities. Journal of Teacher Education, 1994, 45 (1), 62-70.

LAWSON, H.: (Under review). Schools and educational communities in a new agenda for child welfare. Journal of Adjusting and Caring Education.

LAWSON, H.; HOOPER-BRIAR, K.: Expanding partnerships: Involving colleges and universities in interprofessional collaboration and service integration. St. Louis, MO.: The Danforth Foundation 1994.

LAWSON, H.; STROOT, S.: Footprints and signposts: Perspectives on socialization research. Journal of Teaching in Physical Education, 1993, 12, 437-446.

PUTNAM, R.: Making democracy work. Princeton, NJ: Princeton University Press 1993.

TINNING, R.: Physical education and the sciences of physical activity and sport: Symbiotic or adversarial knowledge fields? Keynote address, Congreso Mundial de Ciencias de la Activitdad Fisica y el Deporte, Granada, Spain 1993, November.

WEXLER, P.: Becoming somebody: The social psychology of school. London: Taylor & Francis 1992.

*Keynote address, AIESEP World Congress, Berlin, Germany, July, 1994. Parts of the paper are borrowed from Hooper-Briar & Lawson (1994) and Lawson & Hooper-Briar (1994).

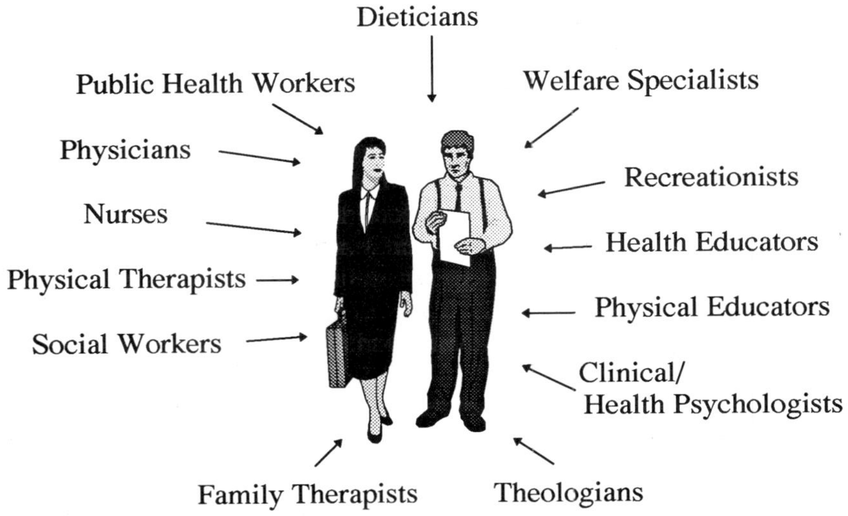

Figure 1. Fragmented Persons and Specialized Professions

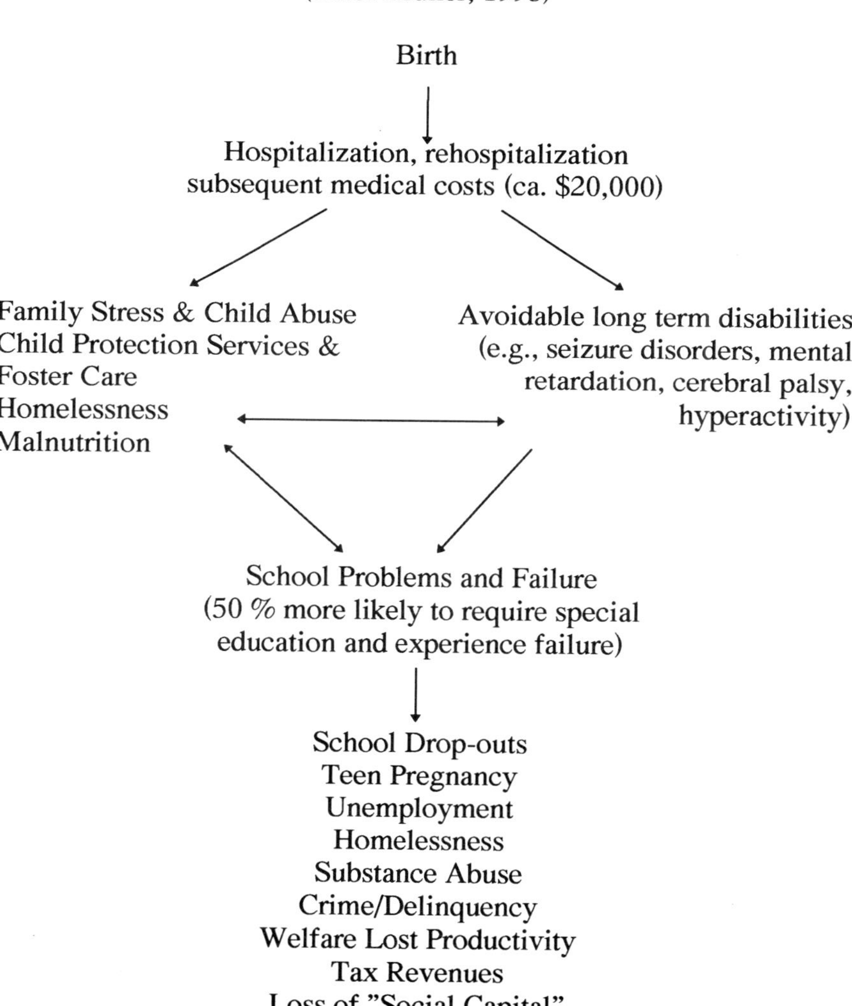
A LOW BIRTHRATE CHILD
TRACKING COSTS OF FAILURE
(After Bruner, 1993)
Birth
Hospitalization, rehospitalization
subsequent medical costs (ca. $20,000)
Family Stress & Child Abuse
Child Protection Services &
Foster Care
Homelessness
Malnutrition
Avoidable long term disabilities
(e.g., seizure disorders, mental
retardation, cerebral palsy,
hyperactivity)
School Problems and Failure
(50 % more likely to require special
education and experience failure)
School Drop-outs
Teen Pregnancy
Unemployment
Homelessness
Substance Abuse
Crime/Delinquency
Welfare Lost Productivity
Tax Revenues
Loss of "Social Capital"

Figure 2

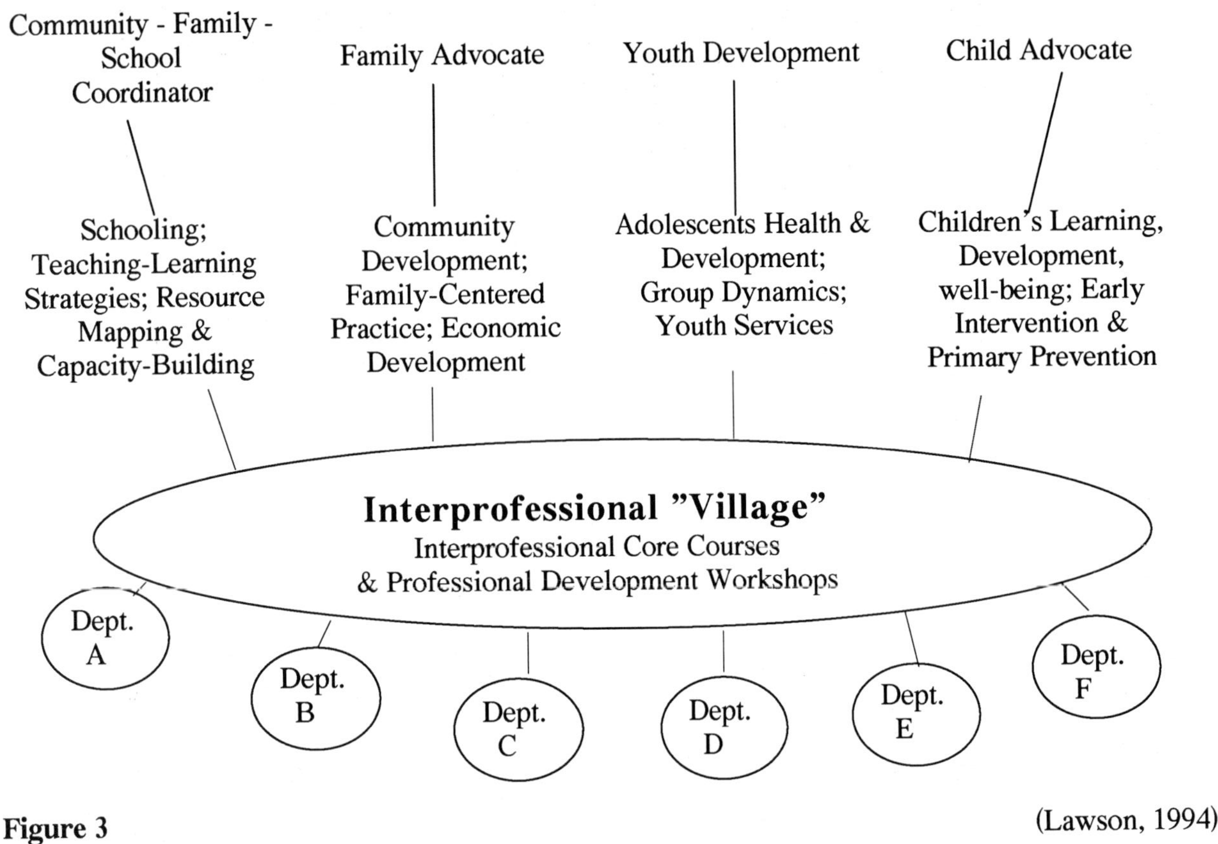
Community - Family - School Coordinator
Family Advocate
Youth Development
Child Advocate
Schooling; Teaching-Learning Strategies; Resource Mapping & Capacity-Building
Community Development; Family-Centered Practice; Economic Development
Adolescents Health & Development; Group Dynamics; Youth Services
Children's Learning, Development, well-being; Early Intervention & Primary Prevention
Interprofessional "Village"
Interprofessional Core Courses
& Professional Development Workshops
Dept. A
Dept. B
Dept. C
Dept. D
Dept. E
Dept. F
(Lawson, 1994)

Figure 3

John Hoberman

Democratizing the Athletic Body - Everyman as High Performer

My topic this afternoon is the commingling of elite and ordinary experience that has become an everyday occurrence in our media-dominated world, and how this social process has produced what I have termed the democratizing of the athletic body in modern societies. In order to introduce this mixing and fusing of the extraordinary and the ordinary - "Spitzenleute und Alltagsleute" - I would like to begin by analyzing some advertisements that appear in the June 1994 issue of **Runner's World**, a publication that has succeeded in marketing an elite athletic ethos to a vast number of athletically ordinary people. The fact that we are analyzing the mechanism of a *market* is of primary importance, because the democratizing of the athletic body exists primarily as a commercial project. For this reason, we should keep in mind that advertising experts have become the unelected, and too often unrecognized, legislators of the modern imagination. Their appropriation of the sportsworld for marketing purposes is only one example of their enormous and essentially unregulated power.

Those of us who are familiar with the advertising strategy aimed at establishing the existence of a "Planet Reebok" will understand that much advertising targeted at runners aims at evoking both a special state of mind and a sense of inclusion in a closed community of initiates into a way of life. This combination of subjective feeling and membership makes it possible for an unlimited number of people to feel that this special status is distinctive of them as individuals. This paradoxical fusing of individual and mass experience is, of course, a basic principle of modern advertising and is easily adapted to any marketing scheme that can present elite performers as role models to the masses.

This emphasis on the private experiential world of the individual consumer is one of the two dominant themes of the many advertisements for performance-linked products such as athletic shoes and dietary supplements that crowd the pages of **Runner's World**. The other, as we will see, is the power of science and technology to make dreams of athletic performance come true.

How do advertisers appropriate the athletic aspirations and intimate thoughts of ordinary people for whom running is a way of life? There are, in fact, first-, second-, and third-person narrative strategies to address the ordinary person's intimate thoughts about his or her state of fitness and how fitness itself can transform everyday life. The first-person strategy offers us the private voice of Everyman or Everywoman: "Sometimes when I run," says a woman pictured in an Adidas ad, "I'll get into this zone where an hour will pass but it'll feel like a minute. It's this amazing mind groove." Here is naive (and therefore compelling) testimony that running makes possible extraordinary experiences for ordinary athletes.

The second-person variation on this technique assumes an authoritative tone and is thus both more intrusive and more instructive in a pedagogical sense. Here, for example, is the introductory text for a PowerBar ad: "3:30 p.m. You feel *flat*. Motivation for tasks at hand lapses. Lunch is a distant memory and you have much more to accomplish before heading home. The energy lag you're experiencing at work is not much different than how you may feel 30 or 40 minutes into your Sunday run." The crucial point here is the effortless merger of work and sport, of labor and leisure, ostensibly separate realms that coalesce under the aegis of the performance principle that rules the modern world. The solution is nutritional technology or, in the manufacturer's words, "Fuel for optimum performance." Another ad promoting "the science of Gatorade" takes the same approach, installing its own voice inside the mind of Everyman and planting a crucial physiological doubt in the process: "Your training is on schedule. You feel prepared. But how well is your sports drink preparing you?" Here, too, the solution lies in a purported science of energy metabolism. A third second-person strategy employed in an Asics shoe ad abstains from offering expertise but rather flatters the potential customer's emotional stability: "Intense? Stubborn? Need some space? Have we got the shoe for you."

A third-person narration can also flatter the perseverance or fanaticism of amateur runners: "Tens of thousands of loyal runners can't be wrong. Obsessive, perhaps. But not wrong" says a Saucony ad, which continues: "Almost all [runners] actually enjoy pushing themselves to physical exhaustion." It is certainly a sign of the times that the exemplary figure whose picture appears in every one of these ads is a woman. A Saucony ad that appeared in the May 1994 issue of **Runner's World** praises the same kind of fanaticism but in this case features not an amateur but a male "World-Class Triathlete." The text reads: "A bit of rational technology for those prone to irrational behavior." These ads cleverly promote the idea that membership in the athletic elite depends less on talent than on a state of mind.

This continual celebration of the emotional intensity of the anonymous athlete - a mental condition that both mimics and is shared with the elite performer - is only one example of the democratizing process I referred to above. I think once again of an advertising slogan I saw some years ago in a German newspaper: "Der Wille zur Leistung führt bis ans Ende der Welt" - The will to performance reaches to the ends of the earth. Today I want to argue that the democratizing of the athletic body has resulted from this ubiquity of "performance" as a cultural ideal and its apparently limitless charisma in an age of technology. And how interesting it is that the paean to the performance principle quoted above was given perfect expression not by a poet but by a copywriter.

Another major factor in this democratizing process is the popular scientific approach to fitness and training for the masses. The constant stress on products offering scientific solutions to self-styled athletes, whether this means the "FASTBURN Technology" of the PR*Bar or the "Artificial Intelligence Techniques" that plan training regimens at home, dissolves the traditional boundary separating the ordinary from the elite by making everyone participants in the drama of high-stress physiology. This leveling process means that the psychophysiological realm of "peak performance" is where Everyman and the Olympic athlete live out their own (and essentially equal) versions of athletic stress. The novel factor here is that the nature of the athletic drama as it is imagined in advertising has changed in a radical way. My survey of advertising that incorporates sportive themes shows that Everyman's subjective experiences now predominate over the traditional athletic role model. Here is powerful evidence that a kind of physiological democracy based on the shared features of *all* stressed-out human bodies has marginalized the elite athlete as a cultural standard-bearer. The eagerness of advertisers to pay homage to the emotional life of anonymous runners reflects as well the rise of the consumer as a participant in cultural norm-setting.

The democratization of athletic emotion points in the direction of a democratization of human potential both inside and outside the sphere of sport, the idea that Everyman can participate in the ethos of high-performance that creates "stars" by developing his or her latent or neglected abilities in a systematic or "scientific" manner - whence the popularity of sophisticated exercise machines that automate fitness in an "elite" fashion for the athletic nonelite. The commercial success of this technology confirms that style is, as Stuart Ewen points out, "a realm of being 'exceptional' within the constraints of conformity."

The fixation on the ordinary person's relationship to the exceptional is evident in many advertisements that employ athletic body images in contemporary advertising. One important strategy promotes the ideal of the self-absorbed Everyman who can be a high performer, in a more than merely vicarious sense, by entrusting the development of his body to a machine in a determined and systematic way. From a thematic standpoint, it is clear that the will to embark upon this developmental journey vastly outweighs in importance any physical performance it might make possible. It is understood that Everyman will never approach Olympic standards. Given the irrelevance of his own individual performances, it is clear that the "high-performance Everyman" is participating in a personal conditioning process that reproduces on the microcosmic scale of his life a vast cultural process: the technologizing of human effort and thus the ongoing "experiment" being carried out on the human organism that has been endowed with an aura of power and prestige. The identification of the individual with a process rather than a person renders superfluous the athlete who, in a diminishing number of advertisements, is presented as a role model for children and adolescents, those individuals who are not yet "performing" in their own careers.

"Body by Design" is one of many advertisements that hold out the promise of using muscle-building technology to transform the body into a private, self-styled utopia. The postmodernity of this technology is not to be found in the role of electricity; on the contrary, a variety of pseudoscientific treatments based on the idea of electrical therapy flourished in the United States throughout the nineteenth century. Similarly, promoting the ambition to develop greater muscularity has existed as a commercial strategy for most of the twentieth century. What makes this scheme thematically different from so many similar ones preceding it is the fact that it is not a therapeutic treatment at all. Electrical muscle stimulation - a controversial technique that is used by some elite athletes - is offered here as a painless, passive, and risk-free way to stylize an already healthy body. The aura of scientific progress, traditionally associated with healing, now plays a postmedical role by "treating" the disease-free human body to satisfy the desires of its "owner." The extreme plasticity of the body claimed in the advertisement is simply a hyperbolic accommodation to the narcissistic needs of consumers who want to acquire sportive-dynamic bodies of their own without having to endure "agonizing exercise." A more recent advertisement for an exercise machine in **Runner's World** (October 1993) reiterates the themes of passivity by promising "continuous motivational feedback" as ersatz willpower and unlimited plasticity of form ("you can immediately start to resculpt your physique and reveal the sleek and hard body you want"). It is clear that this type of dynamic body has no manifest sportive role to play since it is primarily an accouterment of style.

Such self-transforming techniques are rooted in the ideal of the scientifically conditioned body. At least in a symbolic sense, they reproduce the experience of the elite athlete under controlled conditions within the private sphere of the consumer. This form of vicarious participation in the charismatic ideal of high performance can even be seen as a rudimentary antecedent of the "virtual reality" experiences that are now becoming a mass entertainment. Let us note, however, that what one writer has called "exercise as a cosmetic science" comes in two forms, and that the crucial variable here is pain and stress. The triumph of the consumer is once again evident in the fact that, in contrast to the ethos of "no pain, no gain" associated with some exercise machines, this apparatus and others offer an ostensibly stress-free affiliation with the ethos of high performance. The illusory nature of this promise is evident in the pathologies that grow out of this obsession with the body, including anorexia, drug abuse, and the narcissistic character disorders associated with bodybuilding.

The democratization of the athletic body also involves stretching and metaphorizing the idea of athleticism so that it encompasses activities that lie well outside the traditional definition of sport. This elastic definition of athleticism prominently includes the performances of corporate "bodies" such as multinationals that depend on the efforts of countless "ordinary" people.

This democratizing process is represented by the nonathlete who earnestly embraces the high-performance ideal in pursuit of a corporate goal. For example, a serious-faced, middle-aged jogger is presented in an advertisement for a savings bank in the *Frankfurter Allgemeine Zeitung* (September 1989). "I am proud of my savings bank," he declares in the headline. "Performance and success are what count here." The devoted functionary goes on to athleticize his service to the company: "I love the challenge of jumping over hurdles - both private and professional," he says, erasing the boundary between personal and corporate effort and thereby anthropomorphizing the business operation he represents. While it demands much of the man and his colleagues, the driven character of this enterprise is tempered by the civilizing touch of sport: "Our motto is fairness." The company man is presented full-face and in full stride because we are meant to see his willpower and what it means to his company. It is just as well that his unimpressive torso is covered by a parka, for it is his determination, not the forty-year-old body, that symbolizes efficient force. Here, in short, is Everymanager as high performer.

A further step toward the elastic definition of athleticism is achieved by shifting the emphasis from athletic performance to corporate performance while retaining an association with high-performance sport. This can be done by showing how the corporation contributes technological infrastructures to a highly complex sports festival. One example is a full-page advertisement for the 3M Corporation that appeared in Munich's *Zeitmagazin* (July 1992). Under the deadline, "We sponsor the Olympic Games - and take part in them," appear eight color photographs: a male skier schussing down a hill; a male cyclist on a high-tech racing cycle and adorned in high-tech clothing and futuristic helmet; a computerized scoreboard for reporting the results of Olympic competitions; a multi-screened media control room for broadcasting the Games to the world; a tower emblazoned with the design symbols of the Barcelona Olympiad; an athletic shoe being tied; a robotic figure in black piloting a bobsled down the ice; and a piece of adhesive notepaper affixed to a surface next to a spiked running shoe. The unifying theme behind these Olympic scenes is the fact that every one of them displays 3M technology at work. Rather than a single body we are presented with commingled images of technological devices and athletes' bodies covered with the most advanced fabrics or plastic gear. The bodies of half-naked divers have been replaced by bodies that merge with equipment. The dominant theme is the ubiquitous technological innovations that make an Olympiad and its athletic performances possible. This is a crucial shift of emphasis because the most impressive performance is now organizational rather than athletic. This celebration of organization's triumph over complexity means that the charismatic potential of the athlete's body must be diffused by covering it with high-tech products and presenting it in the context of other competing images of technological achievement.

The shift of emphasis from athletic to corporate achievement is attended by the gradual disappearance of the body itself. This trend is taken further in a full-page advertisement for IBM found in the Norwegian newspaper *Aftenposten* (September 1993): the page is dominated by a color picture of Gerhard Heiberg, the manager of the 1994 Lillehammer Winter Olympic Games, who is holding an apple by its stem about half a meter above the floor. The point of this demonstration, as explained in the accompanying text, is that the IBM equipment monitoring the results of these Olympic competitions can process information and transmit it over 400 kilometers faster than the apple could drop to the floor. At this point the shift from athletic to electronic performance is complete. The body of the athlete -- whose performances underlie the entire enterprise - has now disappeared entirely as a visual presence. The sponsoring corporation appropriates athletic efficiency, at one remove, as it were, incarnating it in the manager of an Olympiad whose organizational feats - like those of the athletes he administers - take on an aura of wonder. Managerial "athleticism" basks, however obliquely, in the glow of the real athletes it puts on stage.

The role of technology in dissolving the boundary between the ordinary and the elite athlete is evident in a full-page color advertisement for an athletic show that appeared in September 1993 in **Runner's World**. Above the shoe and its high-tech slogan ("HydroFlow"), a male runner appears against the complex circuitry of a greatly magnified computer chip: "We put the world's leading technology at your feet." The ad absorbs the shoe into the more glamorous world of high-powered computing and its exacting technical standards. Its human protagonist - an Everyman figure rather than an elite athlete - has no special appeal. On the contrary, his role is dependent on technological expertise. The striking juxtaposition of electronic pathways and the body makes it clear that it is circuitry rather than muscle that exemplifies the ideal of high performance. The body is no longer the principal site of productivity, and this shift is one more sign of the elite athlete's ironic marginality given how productivity is imagined within the modern order of technology.

Endless sloganeering by businessmen and management experts about "high performance" organizations and "world-class" standards has established an imaginary norm of "excellence" that has invaded every type of human effort, and high-performance sport has provided advertisers with a limitless supply of images that can serve this myth of continuous ultimate striving. Small wonder that advertisers and the mass media have cultivated the image of dynamic health and a thoroughly romantic view of human potential. Journalistic pandering to the fantasy of limitless powers that supposedly dwell within us occasionally appears on the covers of the world's leading newsmagazines. The honorable exception in this regard has been *Der Spiegel*, whose 1984 Summer Olympic cover warned of "giants, dwarves and monsters" in the age of the "computer athlete." The more conventional romantic view appeared on the covers of two other mass-circulation magazines just before the 1992 Barcelona Olympic Games. The cover of the August 3, 1992 *U.S. News & World Report* offers the prospect of high performance for Everyman: "Mind & Body: The New Science of Performing at Your Peak." Superimposed upon the strenuously concentrated brain is an image of the athletic performance that mental focus has made possible. Now it is the brain that through the superimposed image contains the body. Mind rules over muscle and anything becomes possible for anyone.

A similar exercise in the mythologizing of human potential appeared simultaneously on the cover of *L'Express* (31 July and 6 August 1992): "Sport, Medicine and Science: Man Without Limits." Inside the magazine the obligatory sports psychologist recites the fashionable thesis that barriers to setting records are actually psychological rather than physical. Yet the evidence of the past decade, during which many record-setting performances were made possible only by the illicit use of drugs, suggests otherwise: our physiological limitations are quite real. Some prominent sports physicians have flatly stated that the human body cannot support the stress that certain events now inflict on joints and tendons. It has become axiomatic among high-performance athletes and their trainers that some forms of training cannot be intensified or prolonged past certain limits without the use of anabolic steroids. In conformity with the myth of vanquished limits, *L'Express* exaggerates the powers of science to boost athletic performance, a ploy made possible by public ignorance about the topic. "There is a widespread perception," the prominent sports scientist Carl FOSTER wrote in 1989, "that contemporary technologic capabilities, including physiologic testing, can contribute to improved performance in athletes." In fact, his assessment of what these procedures actually do will disappoint those who assume that applied science (excluding some drugs) can boost human athletic performance: "There is a continual quest for the correct or optimal way to train. Unfortunately, we know so little about the quantitative aspects of adaptation to training that it's hard even to ask the right questions."

Given these sobering realities about human limits, why does it still pay to claim that human minds and bodies can do things no one has believed possible? It would appear that the hyperbolic interpretation of human potential is a kind of necessary falsehood required to sustain a myth of constantly expanding possibilities, a myth that is, to be sure, grounded in certain realities as well as in utopian fantasies about science. We are, in short, addicted to the sense of excitement that attends diverse technological performances, and especially to those that offer the sensation of speed or force. Everyman's vicarious participation in the adventure of "high performance" is now a marketable commodity, while the democratization of human potential is an ideology that appears to be a natural consequence of technological progress. What is more, the romantic doctrine of man-without-limits has been embraced by at least one of history's great runners. When asked in 1994 about the future of the record for the mile run, Herb ELLIOTT replied: "Although there is no basis of logic to make this statement, I think we're only on the border of understanding the interface between mind, spirit, and body. I believe there is a quantum leap somewhere in the equation that we have yet to discover. There are all sorts of things that are possible."

Dawn Penney, John Evans

The Expression of Change: Towards an Understanding

Acknowledgements

This paper draws on data from research funded by the Sports Council, Economic and Social Research Council (Project No. ROO 23 3629) and the Leverhulme Trust. We are grateful to these organisations for their support.

Introduction

Not only in physical education but education as a whole, the 'gap' between 'policy' and 'practice' is a much talked about but under researched phenomenon. This paper reports on research that specifically aimed to explore and understand the relationship between changes in 'policy' and the 'practice' arising in schools*1. In this instance 'policy' refers to legislation instituted by central government and specifically, to the National Curriculum for Physical Education (NCPE) in England and Wales. However, as we discuss below, the view of 'policy' that has informed and guided our research is far broader. In our view how we conceptualise 'policy' has direct implications for how we research it. In researching the 'making' and 'implementation' of the NCPE our concern was to explore not only what changes occurred in PE in schools, but also how and why they arose. In this paper we try to illustrate how our theoretical and methodological stances have shaped our research and furthered our understanding of 'policy' and 'practice' in PE.

Policy as a Process

An important starting point for our research was the conceptualisation of **policy as a process**. This involved the deconstruction of the divide between policy 'making' and 'implementation'. We anticipated that the 'making' of a NCPE would not end with the production of a policy text by central government. Rather, adaptation, adoption, contestation and modification would continue throughout subsequent 'implementation'. In BOWE and BALL with GOLD's (1992) terms, there would be "slippage" throughout the policy process. Our view acknowledged that on the one hand many 'sites' and individuals (including Local Education Authorities (LEAs), LEA officers, headteachers, heads of PE departments and PE teachers) would be involved to various degrees in 'implementation', and on the other that in 'implementation' the NCPE would enter and interact with a variety of different contexts in which at the same time, other policies were being 'implemented'. Inherent in this conceptualisation is an acknowledgement of the complexities of '**texts**'; that is representations of 'policy' "...which are encoded in complex ways (via struggles, compromises, authoritative public interpretations and reinterpretations)..." and "decoded" in equally complex ways (BALL, 1993, 11). Our research illustrated that texts (in PE) contain a variety of (often competing) discourses and in the policy process these interact with other discourses; discourses become embedded in discourses (see EVANS, DAVIES & PENNEY, 1994; PENNEY, 1994). From this perspective, relationships both between sites and between policies can be expected to be significant in shaping how government 'policy' will be expressed in 'practice' in schools.

This conceptualisation of policy directly informed our methodology and research design. Critically we considered that an investigation of *only* schools would give at best a 'partial' and potentially a distorted 'picture' of the policy process. We regarded the investigation of micro, macro and "meso" (HARGREAVES, 1986) 'levels' as critical to gaining an understanding of the policy process 'as a whole'; of why individuals at any one site acted as they did. In our view cross-site investigation has a key role to play in our exploration and understanding of the actions arising at any single site and our research therefore encompassed multiple sites and multiple policies.

Given that we were exploring an 'emerging picture'(with the NCPE still in its design stages when the research commenced and uncertainty surrounding what the effects of other aspects of the Education Reform Act (ERA) (1988) (see below) would be in the context of PE (see PENNEY & EVANS, 1991; PENNEY, 1994)), we stressed the flexible and developmental nature of our research, in terms of both focus and design. In this respect ethnographic principles (LUTZ, 1986) were central to our research. We anticipated that a range of research procedures*2 would be needed to explore the variety of sites and issues that would be addressed in the research, and regarded quantitative and qualitative procedures*2 as "complementary tools" in the research process (BURGESS, 1984).

Policy Texts : Establishing Boundaries to and Opportunities for Change

Whilst anticipating important 'slippage' in the policy process accompanying the 'implementation' of the NCPE, we were also aware that the government text defining what was to comprise the NCPE would nevertheless play a vital part in shaping the future provision of PE in schools. In addressing policy texts BERNSTEIN's (1971, 1990) work prompted us to look 'beyond' texts themselves, to what 'underlay' their form and content, to the processes of their 'production' and the ways and means by which particular discourses were included, excluded, privileged, subordinated in and from texts. Our participant observation (at both a 'national' 'level' and within the LEA) and semi-structured interviews with policy 'makers' showed that the issues of who is entitled to speak, when and with what authority in the policy process (BALL, 1993) are of vital importance in understanding changes in 'policy' and 'practice' in PE. Critically, the texts produced by central government (and the group established to advise it; see EVANS & PENNEY with BRYANT, 1993; EVANS, DAVIES & PENNEY, 1994) defined physical education in a particular way; as comprising a set of essentially separate and different areas of activity; games, dance, gymnastic activities, athletic activities, outdoor adventurous activities and swimming. It thereby established a particular principle of classification (BERNSTEIN, 1990) for the PE curriculum, and in emphasising the distinction between the different areas of activity, reinforced strong classification of the curriculum (ibid, 1990). There was little space or opportunity for the development or expression of integrated curricula (or curricula expressing "integrated codes" (BERNSTEIN, 1990)), for example a curriculum organised around the principle of health related exercise. In the development of the NCPE discourses privileging health, or other 'alternative' definitions of (and thus structures for) PE, were increasingly subordinated in or excluded from policy texts and accompanying debates (see EVANS, DAVIES & PENNEY, 1994; PENNEY 1994).

Certainly the NCPE texts reflected the wider context (and changes occurring in this) in which they were being 'made'. Political, ideological and economic pressures were reflected in how PE was defined and what was included, omitted, privileged and subordinated in the NCPE (see EVANS, DAVIES & Penney, 1994). Specifically we saw a progressive privileging of games over and above the other areas of activity and an increasing emphasis of the need for "flexibility" in requirements so that they could accommodate the very varied school contexts in which 'implementation' was to occur. This "flexibility" meant that many important decisions regarding the design of the NCPE, such as the areas of activity to be included in PE and the attention to be devoted to different areas, were to be made by schools and the teachers within them. It appeared that much was still to be 'made' in 'implementation'; that "slippage" (BOWE et al., 1992) was set to occur in the policy process. However, we also need to consider the questions of "slippage from what?" and "within what boundaries?". Throughout the 'making' and 'implementation' of the NCPE we saw that the principle of classification (BERNSTEIN, 1990) and curriculum structure privileged by the government were progressively reinforced rather then challenged. The NCPE texts established strong discursive frames (LUNDGREN, 1977; PENNEY, 1994) within which the policy process occurred, defining both the thinkable and unthinkable in terms of what was to constitute a NCPE. In the policy process particular discourses were embedded in texts and legitimated, and others were omitted or subordinated (see EVANS, DAVIES & PENNEY, 1994; PENNEY, 1994).

From 'Policy' to 'Practice'

In both the LEA and schools the NCPE texts 'entered' and interacted with new contexts and other discourses that were critical in determining how 'policy' was expressed in 'practice'. Economic issues were again a primary concern and their influence in the policy process illustrated both the interaction between policies and between policy sites. Specifically, we saw that the NCPE was 'implemented' within contextual constraints arising from and/or reinforced by other policies within the Education Reform Act (ERA); notably Local Management of Schools (LMS)*3, Open Enrolment*4 and the introduction of the National Curriculum (NC) in other subject areas. Specifically, the Local Education Authority's LMS scheme (see DES, 1988) was critical in determining the resources that were available for distribution within schools and schools were variously advantaged or disadvantaged in these terms. We also saw considerable variation in the fortunes of different subjects within schools. Qualitative data from both headteachers and heads of PE highlighted that subjects are not equally placed to 'play by market rules' post-ERA. Our research (and in particular the combination and integration of quantitative and qualitative data) showed the subtlety of the introduction of market principles to education and their implications for curriculum planning in PE. In many instances the feared 'direct' cuts in staffing, funding and time for PE (see PENNEY & EVANS, 1991; PENNEY, 1994) were not in evidence. Rather, PE, like other subjects, was feeling the effects of new pressures within schools (in particular to minimise expenditure on staffing and to 'fit'

the NC into an overcrowded timetable), and there was some evidence to suggest that PE disadvantaged relative to other subjects. Certainly in some schools 'implementation' of the NCPE occurred within significant constraints (of increasing non-specialist teaching of PE and timetabling arrangements and budgetary constraints precluding the use of off-site facilities) that were inevitably reflected in the breadth and balance of the PE curriculum and the quality of teaching and learning in schools (see EVANS, PENNEY & BRYANT, 1993; PENNEY, 1994).

In addressing the position and fortunes of PE in the 'internal market' (see PENNEY & EVANS, 1995), our attention was again drawn to the importance of inter-relationships between policies in policy 'implementation'. Specifically, the position of PE 'late' in the phased programme of developing and introducing the NC (see DES, 1989) was reflected in resource allocations in some schools, with PE being disadvantaged in comparison to (higher status) subjects introduced earlier. Qualitative data showed that the NC and PE's 'position' within this had further influences in and on the 'implementation' of the NCPE. The NC in particular was associated with an unprecedented administrative workload for teachers and in addition, teachers felt largely excluded from the development of the curriculum that they were charged to 'deliver'. In the light of experience in other subject areas, PE teachers also anticipated that the texts they received would change again. Not surprisingly in this climate, many PE teachers were less than enthusiastic about the 'arrival' of the NCPE and were notably hesitant in making any response to the texts they received (see PENNEY, 1994). Ultimately, the time that was 'left' before 'implementation' was due to commence was insufficient to encourage or enable comprehensive curriculum review and development in PE. We saw that the 'gaps' in the text of the NCPE could be 'explored' not only in terms of facilitating curriculum change; they also enabled the NCPE to be largely accommodated within present practice. In many schools it seemed that a change in 'policy' would not signal changes in 'practice'. *Accommodation* was the response encouraged by both the *text and the context* in which many PE teachers were working.

Invariably, present practice matched all too well the definition of PE and the games bias inherent in the text. Meanwhile, school contexts post-ERA, typified by pressures on time, staffing and finance, did not lend themselves to this curriculum design and emphasis being contested. In the 'implementation' of the NCPE there was "slippage" (BOWE et al., 1992), with curriculum planning invariably mirroring the different resources and different interests present in different schools. However, at the same time there was important continuity in curriculum design and 'delivery' in PE. The "slippage" did not challenge the principle of classification (BERNSTEIN, 1990) established by central government. Rather, existing practice and responses to the NCPE further legitimated this definition of PE and the biases and inequalities inherent in present curricula. In our view it therefore remains highly questionable whether the stated aim of the NC, to provide a broad and balanced curriculum for *all* pupils (see MARTIN, 1988; DES, 1989), will be met in the context of PE in schools in England and Wales.

Conclusion

This research has highlighted that understanding why 'changes in policy' give rise to particular 'practice' demands that we address a complex process. Not only the 'policy' but how it is 'made' and how it then interacts with other policies and practices in the course of its 'implementation' are factors to consider. If we are to avoid explanations of 'change' that are 'incomplete' and therefore of little use to those who are concerned with advancing PE in schools, the complexity of the policy process has to be addressed in the methodology and research design adopted in policy studies in physical education. We must explore the influence of many individuals, interests and other policies in the policy process. In our experience a variety of research procedures will be required and flexibility and the active integration of empirical, theoretical and methodological matters are key features of such research.

Endnotes

*1 Professor John Evans and Dr. Dawn Penney are co-directors of an ongoing research project entitled "The Impact of the Education Reform Act (1988) on the Provision of PE and Sport in State Schools" and supported by the Sports Council (1990-1993), the Economic and Social Research Council (Project No. ROO 23 3629) (1992-1994) and the Leverhulme Trust (from 1994).

*2 Following Ellen (1984) we take methodology to mean "an articulated, theoretically informed approach to the production of data"; method to refer to "... a general mode of yielding data", e.g. interviews, and technique the "specific means of making particular methods effective, e.g. questionnaires, shorthand, kinship notations. "Methods" and "techniques" together constitute "research procedures"" (ibid, 1984, p. 9).

*3 Local Management of Schools made fundamental changes to the financial and management structure of education in England and Wales. LEA budgets for education were allocated to schools via a process called "formula funding", which linked school finance directly to pupil intakes. "Delegated management" made school governing bodies responsible for the management of their delegated budget (see DES, 1988).

*4 Open Enrolment removed LEA control of school intakes by requiring schools to accept pupils up to their intake in 1979 when intakes for all schools were at a peak.

References

BALL, S.J.: What is Policy? Texts, Trajectories and Toolboxes. Discourse, 1993, Vol.13, No.1, April 1993, 10-17.

BERNSTEIN, B.: On the Classification and Framing of Educational Knowledge. In: M.F.D. YOUNG (Ed.) Knowledge and Control. New Directions for the Sociology of Education. London: Collier Macmillan 1971.

BERNSTEIN, B.: The Structuring of Pedagogic Discourse. Volume IV Class, Codes and Control. London: Routledge 1990.

BOWE, R.; BALL, S.J.; GOLD, A.: Reforming Education and Changing Schools. Case Studies in Policy Sociology. London: Routledge 1992.

BURGESS, R.G.: In the Field: An Introduction to Field Research. London: Unwin Hyman 1984.

DES, E.R.A.: L.M.S. Circular No.7/88 DES 1988.

DES, National Curriculum - From Policy to Practice DES 1989.

ELLEN, R.F. (Ed.): Ethnographic Research. A guide to general conduct. London: Academic Press Inc. Ltd. 1984.

EVANS, J.; PENNEY, D.; BRYANT, A.: Improving the Quality of Physical Education? The Education Reform Act, 1988 and Physical Education in England and Wales. Quest, 1993, 45, 3, 321-338.

EVANS, J.; DAVIES, B.; PENNEY, D.: Whatever happened to the Subject and the State in Policy Research in Education? Discourse, Australian Journal of Educational Studies 1994, 14, 2, 57-64.

HARGREAVES, A.: The Macro-Micro Problem in the Sociology of Education. In: M. HAMMERSLEY (Ed.): Controversies in Classroom Research. Milton Keynes: Open University Press 1986.

LUNDGREN, U.P.: Model Analysis of Pedagogical Processes. Stockholm Institute of Education: CWK Gleerup 1977.

LUTZ, F.W.: Ethnography: The Holistic Approach to Understanding Schooling. In: M. HAMMERSLEY (Ed.): Controversies in Classroom Research. Milton Keynes: Open University Press 1986.

MARTIN, C.: Schools Now. Oxford: Lion Paperbacks 1988.

PENNEY, D.; EVANS, J.: The Impact of the Education Reform Act (ERA) on the Provision of Physical Education and Sport in the 5-16 Curriculum of State Schools. British Journal of Physical Education 1991, Vol. 22, No.1, 38-42.

PENNEY, D.; EVANS, J.: Changing Structures: Changing Rules: The Development of the 'Internal Market'. School Organisation 1995, (in press).

PENNEY, D.: No Change in a New Era?: The Impact of the Education Reform Act (1988) on the Provision of PE and Sport in State Schools. Thesis submitted for Doctor of Philosophy, University of Southampton, March 1994.

Victor Zilberman

The Changing Face of International Sport under the New World Order

International sport, in the 1990s has been affected by the political and social reforms in Eastern Europe, local wars and the struggle for independence. Moreover, sport is transforming due to the growing number of events, television ratings and corporate sponsorships, decreased government financing, migration of athletes and coaches and the escalating costs of organizing major sport events.

Transformation of Eastern Europe Sport Organization

Prior the political turbulence in the late 1980s the communist countries firmly established themselves as front runners of international amateur athletics. Unlimited financial resources allocated by the respective governments resulted in the development of powerful sport organizations which consistently dominated the international sport arena. The most accomplished in sport, the Soviet Union and East Germany, claimed two of the top three places in every Winter and Summer Olympic Games in which they participated since 1972 (ZILBERMAN, 1994).

In its 75 years of existence, Soviet sport, under the totalitarian regime, progressed to a giant sport delivery system. The number of sport participants increased from 40,000 in 1917, to 87 million in the mid 1980s. Recognition and promotion of coaching as a profession resulted in the growth of the number of paid coaches from 6,000 in 1921, to 136,336 in 1986. Meanwhile the organizational effectiveness was carried out by 336,000 full time professionals (ZILBERMAN, 1990).

Political, social and economic reforms in the former USSR transformed the unified and regimented sport delivery system to a decentralized western model of sport organization. Decreased government financing, decline in the number and worsening conditions of sport facilities, substantial loss of youth programs and the exodus abroad of the best athletes and coaches negatively affected mass sport participation and high performance athletics.

East Germany, which had established itself as a leading world sport power, fully blossomed in the 1970s and 80's. Entirely financed by the State, athletes were provided all the necessities to become top performers expected to focus on training and competing. Striving for international recognition through sport, East German authorities rewarded their top athletes for major accomplishments with the highest state honours and monetary prizes. The reunification process brought wide-ranging reforms in GDR sport. Changes welcomed by the general population resulted in a reduction in financial support, an uncertain future and worsening training conditions for athletes, loss of facilities and youth programs. The strongest attributes of East German sport, its highly qualified coaching force, was faced with financial cuts and loss of employment. In track and field, for example, only 20 out of 592 full time coaches were still employed as of September 1990 (Sovetskiy Sport, Sept. 23, 1990).

The other European communist states went through a comparable society transformation with changes in values and priorities. The importance of high performance sport as a tool to promote their political system and ideology has been diminished. A worsening economic situation and political instability consequently led to decreased financing and attention to sport from both the government and the population.

Analysis of International Sport Performances

The transformation of renown sport systems of the Eastern European countries resulted in the decline in their international sport performances which meant foremost increasing number of medals for the western world athletes. In 1992 when the former Soviet republics competed as one unit under the CIS, and in 1993 when they participated independently, their international sport output overall and specifically in the category of team titles, gold medals, consistency and proficiency have significantly fallen in comparison to the quality of USSR sport performances.

In Albertville, for example, the Unified team won a total of 23 medals in comparison to 29 in the Calgary Olympics (which is considerably less in view of the expansion of sport events). Meanwhile, in the final "Cold War" 92 Barcelona Games the CIS, composed of its multi republic counterparts, collected 20 medals less (112) than the Soviet Union in the 1988 Seoul Olympics (132) (USA Today, Aug. 10, 1992, Sportivnaya Jizn Rossii, 1992).

In the major tournaments of 1993 the United States, Germany and China emerged as the major international sport organizations. The United States, which won the 1993 University Games with an overall 75 medals (30-24-21), had 75 per cent of its athletes competing for the first time in such an international event. Russia, which inherited the bulk of the Soviet population, coaches, athletes, and facilities placed 15th in total medal count (7) without a single gold medal. China, with 28 medals (17-6-5) placed second (Sovetskiy Sport, July 20, 1993). At the 1993 World Games in Holland, Germany placed first accumulating 60 medals (24-21-15), and the USA second with 46 (16-15-15). Russia placed ninth with 20 medals (7-8-5) (Sovetskiy Sport, Aug. 7, 1993).

In track and field political changes in Eastern Europe have significantly affected the medal distribution and team standings as illustrated in Tables 1 and 2. Track and field changes in the medal and gold medal distribution at the outdoor World Championship is reflective of the changes in most sports. Table 3 lists the results at the 1988 and 1992 Summer Olympics which also reflect the changes in medal distribution.

Table 1: Change in medal distribution at the outdoor Track & Field World Championships among leading countries.

COUNTRY	1983	1987	1991	1993
USA	24 (8-9-7)	19 (9-5-5)	26 (10-8-8)	26 (13-7-6)
USSR	23 (6-6-11)	25 (7-12-6)	28 (9-9-10)	
Russia				16 (3-8-5)
E. Germany	22 (10-7-5)	31 (10-1110)		
Unified Germany			17 (5-4-8)	
China				8 (4-2-2)

(Sovetskiy Sport, Sept. 3, 1991, Sept. 8, 1987; Physical Culture in School, N. 8, 1985, 37.)

Table 2: Track and Field Outdoor World Championship medal distribution.

YEAR	OVERALL MEDAL DISRIBUTION	GOLD MEDAL DISTRIBUTION
1983	25 Countries	14 Countries
1987	27	14
1991	29	16
1993	35	19

(Sovetskiy Sport, Sept. 3, 1991; Aug. 23, 1993.)

Table 3: Olympic Track and Field medal distribution among leading countries.

COUNTRIES	SEOUL 1988 OLYMPICS	BARCELONA 1992 OLYMPICS
USA	26 (13-7-6)	30 (12-8-10)
USSR/Unified Team	25 (9-6-10)	21 (7-11-3)
GDR/United Germany	27 (6-11-10)	10 (4-1-5)
China	1 (0-0-1)	4 (1-1-2)

(Sport Life of Russia, N. 12, 6-7, 1988; Montreal Gazette, Aug. 10, 1992)

East German speed skating exemplifies the decline of former communist countries' successful sport programs. The 1980 Olympics marked the beginning of their speed skating success with two gold medal wins. In the 1984 and 1988 Winter Olympics they won three gold in each Games. The epitome of East German speed skating was the 1990 Worlds' when J. Boerner won GDR's ninth consecutive all-around World Championship and in the 1992 Olympics, products of the East German sport system won five gold medals. The total medal win in the last three Olympics indicates the decline in the powerful speed skating organization: 1988 Olympics 13 medals overall (3-6-4), 1992 11 Medals (5-3-3) and 1994 6 (1-2-3) (Sportivnaya Jizn Rossii, 1992; Sovetskiy Sport, April 14, 1988; Montreal Gazette, Feb. 28, 1994). Similarly in swimming, while at the 1986 World Championship East Germany won 30 medals including 14 gold; at the 1991 worlds the United German team won only 22 medals, including 4 gold (Sport Abroad, Oct. 1986; Montreal Gazette, Jan. 14, 1991).

The distribution of Olympic medals, 1988-1992, for the top countries, as seen in Table 4, exemplifies the transformation of international performances in swimming.

Table 4: 1988-1992 Olympic medal distribution in swimming among leading countries.

COUNTRIES	1988 SEOUL	1992 BARCELONA
GDR/Unified Germany	28 (11-8-9)	11 (1-3-7)
USA	16 (8-5-3)	27 (11-8-8)
USSR/Unified Team	9 (2-1-6)	10 (6-3-1)
China	4 (0-3-1)	9 (4-5-0)

(Sport Life of Russia, N. 12, 6-7, 1988; Montreal Gazette, Aug. 10, 1992)

Leader of the former USSR, Russia, as well as CIS countries in total, have fallen significantly in major international competitions. In sports such as freestyle wrestling, rhythmic gymnastics, canoe and kayak, rowing, swimming, weightlifting, handball, judo, volleyball and basketball, Russia and CIS countries lost or are rapidly losing their leading positions. Wins and performances of the Russian men's handball, Greco-Roman wrestling, biathlon, and hockey teams at the 1993 World Championships were a shadow of the former Soviet sport superiority. Best performances of Russian and CIS athletes in 1993 were accomplished in the junior age category. Former head of the USSR State Sport Committee, N. Russak, in predicting the future, stated that Russia will need 8 to 10 years to be competitive with the new leaders in summer sports - the United States, Germany and China (Sovetskiy Sport, July 28, 1992).

Extensive changes in sport and the new distribution of medals resulted in unprecedented performances by individual athletes, teams and countries in the 1990s. Miriam Bedard gave Canada its first unexpected international biathlon victory by winning the women's 7.5 kilometre 1993 World Championship and then two gold medals at the 1994 Winter Olympics. British cyclist, Chris Boardman, won the gold medal at the 1992 Barcelona Olympics in individual pursuit, the first gold medal for British cycling in the last 72 years. Similarly, Spain, at the 92 Barcelona Games won its first gold medal in 72 years in soccer (Sovetskiy Sport, Dec. 5, 1992).

The performance by the Canadian women - winning four out of six Olympic class events at the 1991 World Championship - rocked the rowing establishment. Since women's rowing became a part of the World Championships in 1974 Eastern European nations have dominated the heavyweight division winning all but one gold medal (Montreal Gazette, Aug. 26, 1991).

Among new performances are France's premier win of the 1993 European basketball championship by the Limoges Club, and their female biathlon team in the 15 km relay at the 1993 World Championship. J. Evanshine became the first American male to win a gold medal at the 1991 world cycling championship since G. LeMond in 1979 and T. Dubnicoff became the first Canadian women in a century to win a Cycling World Championship gold medal in 1993.

Changes in the world of sport contributed to the new performances of the Italian gymnasts. In 1993 Yuri Checki won the first ever gold medal in the World Championships for Italy (Sports Weekend, TV Show, May 2, 1993). The rise in the level of proficiency of Italian gymnastics was exemplified as well by its team victory at the 1993 World University Games.

Major changes are experienced also in the women's gymnastic, whereby a new leader, the USA, has been gaining performance consistency with the win of the overall titles in 1991, 1993 and 1994 Worlds.

In team competitions there is a growing trend of changes as well. At the 1993 European freestyle wrestling championship Turkey won the team title for the first time in 26 years. At the 1993 world freestyle wrestling championship the United States won the team standing. Russia, who placed second with one point ahead of Turkey lost the team title at the world's or Olympics for the first time since 1970 (Novoe Russkoye Slovo, May 19, 1993).

In ice hockey, Sweden won the first ever Olympics in Lillehammer, while Canada won the 1994 World Championship - the first in 33 years. The world team chess championship, dominated by the USSR for decades, in 1993 was won by the United States.

The disintegration of the East European sport systems made it possible for many nations to challenge the first spots in team standing. Due to the break up of the USSR, however, many former republics who are still in possession of many top-athletes and especially in junior competition made it difficult for many athletes of other countries to compete for a medal. In figure skating, for example, the Russians, Belorussians, Uzbeks and Ukrainians - six out of 21 teams who skated in the 1993 World Championship pairs competitions were from what used to be the Soviet Union. In chess, at the 1993 World Team Chess championship, among the top 10 teams, five were the republics of former USSR (Sovetskiy Sport, Nov. 4, 1993; Edmonton Journal, March 10, 1993).

The evolvement of the Summer Olympics is predominantly effected by the expansion of sport competitions and by the international political events. While at the 1980 Olympics 203 sets of medals were awarded, in Los Angeles the number of events grew to 221, in Seoul 1988 to 237 and in 1992 Barcelona to 257 (Sovetskiy Sport, June 8, 1990).

Analysis of the non-boycotted 1988 and 1992 Summer Olympics show that the number of former and present communist countries in the top eleven has decreased from six in 1988 to four in 1992. Moreover the number of countries winning medals in the Olympics increased from 52 in 1988 to 64 in 1992. Meanwhile the geography of gold medal winners has also grown from 32 countries in 1988 to 37 in 1992.

Political reforms in Eastern Europe resulted in a change in the government's priorities and economic hardship which by far prevailed the need for sport. Faced with indifferent attitudes towards sport from the government, media and the population at large, East European athletes and coaches, on a mass scale, began pursuing contracts with foreign clubs and teams.

Ten-time world and three-time Olympic champion in figure skating, I. Rodnina coaches in the USA. Head coach of Russia's ski team, N. Lapukhov, moved to work in South Korea. The most successful coach in Soviet volleyball, V. Platonov, coaches the Finnish National Team and the most accomplished gymnastics coach, Bela Koroli of Romania, produces world class athletes in Houston (USA) where he took permanent residence. Former East German coaches work for sport federations in China, New Zealand, South Korea, Australia and Italy to name a few. Chinese coaches successfully produce gymnasts in France and divers in Canada (Sovetskiy Sport, July 27, 1993; Sport Express, Aug. 4, 1993).

For the 40 years prior 1990, according to the Belgrade Press Agency, nearly 800 athletes from East European countries moved west (predominantly from Romania). In the 1990s the number of athletes and coaches relocating to different countries has been rising by the thousands (Sovetskiy Sport, Jan. 10, 1990). In the beginning of the open door policy, in 1989-1990, Soviet coaches and athletes became the largest migrating expertise in international sport, and could be found in every corner of the globe. In hockey, departure from the CIS has been immense. By 1991, 106 top players moved to compete abroad, 11 to North America and 95 to European clubs (Fizkultura i Sport, 1991). In the 1992 NHL draft, 46 out of 264 players were selected from the CIS. (Only Canada had more players drafted; 133) (Sovetskiy Sport, August 15, 1992).

Among other sports, a large scale exodus has been witnessed by the top chess players. The number of ex-Soviets competing in European tournaments became so high that the International Federation has been considering limiting former Soviet players participation to 30 per cent. At the 1992 tournament in Radjo-Emiliya, Italy, for example, 9 out of ten players were representatives of the former USSR (Sovetskiy Sport, Jan. 14, 1992).

Ex-Soviet athletes moved west in such numbers and of such a high calibre that in some countries national federations began restricting immigrants from competing for their new home country (Sovetskiy Sport, Aug. 15, 1992; ZILBERMAN, 1994). Moreover, international federations had to impose specific rules dealing with immigrating athletes. In badminton players are not permitted to compete for their new country for six years. In gymnastics, athletes without a country were allowed to compete as independents at the 1993 worlds. According to FILA rules, in wrestling an athlete cannot compete in the World Championship without a passport of the new country. While immigrants to Turkey, Israel or the former Soviet republics are given immigrant citizenship-passport expediently, in Canada those athletes have to wait three years and in the US five.

Migration abroad has not been only typical of East European countries. Athletes competing for countries other than their place of birth in the Lillehammer Games represented a growing trend in international sport. Peter Medved, born in the Czech Republic, after lengthy negotiations with the International Hockey Federation competed for the Canadian team which won a silver medal. Canada's Jimmy Camazzola, who played for Italy in 1992 Olympics played again for Italy in 1994 (Calgary Herald, Feb. 14, 1994). Antonina Ordina who won the Olympic Games for USSR in Lillehammer competed for Sweden (where she has lived for three years), placing in the top ten in the 10 and 15 km races (Sovetskiy Sport, Feb. 17, 1994). Hockey player, Benoit Doucet of Montreal who once played for the Canadian national team was Team Captain for Germany. The French team, "which is the hockey equivalent of the French Foreign Legion", had a Swedish coach, a Finnish goalie and seven players who have called Quebec home at some point in their lives. Eric LeMarque, who was born in France and grew up in Los Angeles, played Junior hockey in Detroit and attended Northern Michigan University on a hockey scholarship played for France as well (USA Today, Feb. 15, 1994; Montreal Gazette, Feb. 14, 1994; ZILBERMAN, 1994).

1994 Olympics and New Trends in Winter Sports

The Lillehammer Olympics, primarily due to political changes in Eastern Europe (USSR, East Germany, Czechoslovakia, Yugoslavia) became the first Winter Games, since 1956, where athletes have competed on a level field. Moreover, the 1994 Olympic Games have been affected by the inclusion of new sports, contradictory officiating, media and violence, to name a few.

Olympic competition in Lillehammer was representative of a growing problem of substandard and subjective officiating in international sport. With the sport encountering record television ratings worldwide rarely has figure skating and its judges been watched more widely. Participation of professional skaters, the Harding-Kerrigan turmoil, rivalry between medallists and the media attention made circumstances surrounding the skaters and the event unusual for this level of competition (USA Today, Feb. 23, 1994; Ottawa Citizen, Feb. 14, 1994; Montreal Gazette, Feb. 27, 1994).

Even though Olympic competition had the best judges available their subjective and questionable scoring was on the rise. Extensive debate after the figure skating competition revolved around gold medallists; whether the best Russian pair won, whether Elvis Stoiko should have been placed ahead of Alexei Urmanov, whether Torvill and Dean out-danced the Russians, and whether Oksana Baiul won or Nancy Kerrigan was deprived. The dissimilitude in the performances between gold and silver medallists was minimum. It was the judge's personal preference that made a difference between first and second placing. The female competition officiating, for instance, was effected by the Harding-Kerrigan incident, and the on-ice collision between world champion Oksana Baiul (Ukraine) and Tanja Szewczenko (Germany) during their training session. Baiul's practice crash and the publicity of having lost her parents at an early age made Oksana the sentimental favourite in the minds of the judges and media (Ottawa Citizen, Feb. 25, 1994; Montreal Gazette, Feb. 27, 1994).

Dissatisfaction with the referees and competition rules adversely affected the athletes and spectators in the short track speed skating and hockey events. Violence and uncertainty of which athletes broke the rules created a negative image of short track speed skating. Meanwhile, the shootout in the final match between the Canadian and Swedish hockey teams brought out extensive debate whether a shutout is an appropriate way to decide the gold medal team. Ironically, a few weeks later Canada, who lost the Olympic gold to Sweden, won its first World Championship in 33 years over Finland, also in a shootout.

The Lillehammer Olympics, referred to as the most successful Winter Games ever, had a few controversies; i.e. judging in figure skating, violent and unsportmanship behaviour in figure skating and short track speed skating and the number of falls and collisions. The accident issue and safety were first raised prior the Games when two-time world super-G champion, Austrian, Ulrike Maier, died in a downhill race crash at the World Cup event in February 1994. Most falls and collisions in Lillehammer occurred in figure skating involving experienced skaters such as B. Boitano, K. Browning, J. Chouinard, O. Baiul and T. Szewczenko, and ice dancers J. Swallow and E. Punsalan. Germany's pair M. Woetzel and I. Steuer, after a fall, could not continue competing due to injury. In speed skating, G. Niemann and D. Jansen fell in their strongest 3,000m and 500m distance. Accidents are rare in Olympic calibre luge racing, however Duncan Kennedy of the US, three-time Olympian favoured to win, lost control of his sled and crashed. A similar accident occurred with US bobsledder B. Shimer.The number of falls of top athletes indicates a decline in consistent performance in major international events. Olympic and world figure skating championship represent the growing tendency of inconsistent performances and change of winners (USA Today, Feb. 15, 1994; New York Daily News, Feb. 28, 1994).

Negative incidents which have occurred prior to and at the Olympics have largely contributed to an enormous media blitz. One of the most sensationalized stories in Olympic history was the unsportsmanship and violent attack on Nancy Kerrigan. The anticipation of the competition between Harding-Kerrigan was the major event of the Games. More than 750 journalists were on hand to watch Tonya Harding and Nancy Kerrigan on the ice together to practice for the first time in more than a year (Montreal Gazette, Feb. 18, 1994).

Short track speed skating which at Lillehammer was surrounded by personnel conflicts, controversial medal presentation (China's Y. Zhang), athlete dissatisfaction with refereeing, poor sportsmanship, charges of underhanded tactics on the track and threatening letters through the Olympic E-mail system all made short track speed skating the least attended and popular event at the 94 Winter Olympics (Montreal Gazette, Feb. 28, 1994; Calgary Herald, Feb. 27, 1994).

The Lillehammer Games will be remembered for the records that were broken for Olympic competitions. It began with an unprecedented number of countries participating - 69. With regards to attendance, more than 1.2 million tickets were sold for the Lillehammer events, 88 per cent of the total capacity surpassed all previous Winter Olympics. More than 8,000 accredited media created another Winter Olympic record and over a billion television viewers, worldwide, tuned into the Lillehammer Games with the highest number of countries watching, 100, in comparison to 86 at the 92 Olympics (Maclean's, Feb. 14, 1994, 42; Sovetskiy Sport, Feb. 12, 1994; USA Today, Feb. 11, 1994).

The 94 Games, like no other event, exemplified wide population support and love for winter sports and the Olympic spirit. Two million spectators watched athletes from around the world compete in 12 events for 61 sets of medals. The number of fans, especially for outdoor events, were massive. Some 106,000 people turned out to stand in the cold for a cross-country skiing relay race. And, in the Nordic event an estimated 150,000 people were watching the competition (Globe & Mail, Feb. 26, 1994; New York Daily News, Feb. 28, 1994; USA Today, March 1, 1994).

Lillehammer were the Games where professional figure skaters were allowed back in to compete with amateurs. But the highest profile professional singles skaters, Brian Boitano, Katarina Witt and Victor Petrenko were not able to step back into the amateur world and win medals.

At the 1994 Games for the first time in the last 11 Olympics Russia/USSR did not place in the medals in hockey (4th). The Soviets who won eight of the last 10 gold medals, had seven players from the 1993 Russian World Championship team competing in Lillehammer (Sovetskiy Sport, March 5, 1994; The Toronto Star, Feb. 27, 1994).

Among other reversals at the Games was the United States, which staged a surprise when T. Moe earned gold in the downhill, and a silver in the super-giant slalom; and D. Roffe won the women's super giant slalom. Meanwhile, the Austrians and Swiss, with their long legacy as powers on the hill, did not take a single alpine gold (Globe & Mail, Feb. 26, 1994).

The Russians came into Lillehammer predicting no higher than third place in the overall medals table. They surpassed other countries in the gold medal column 11, however, placing behind Norway and Germany with a total of 23 medals (Globe & Mail, Feb. 26, 1994). The gold medal performance of Russia in Lillehammer was surpassed by the USSR only in the 1976 Innsbruck Olympics, 13 (USA Today, 28.11.94, Nov. 28, 1994).

Norway's performance in the 94 Winter Olympics was stupendous. With a population of 4.3 million, they won the overall team standing; a total of 26 medals. Norway's accomplishment was magnified by the fact that in 1988 they only won five medals, and placed as a team progressing to 20 medals and overall place in the 1992 Olympics (USA Today, Feb. 28, 1994). Due to the transformation to a new organization of sport in East Europe, as well as the expansion of Olympic events, countries such as the USA, Canada, Italy, South Korea and China showed a record number of medal performances and moved up in the team standings.

Besides changes in team standings and the unexpected performance of Russia's hockey team, a number of top athletes performed below their expectations marking a new era in international sport, where the difference between athletes proficiency is minimum and a group of few can challenge medal positions. Heavily favoured Norway's Vegard Ulvang, triple gold medallist in the '92 Albertville Olympics in cross country skiing, failed to win a single medal in individual events (only silver in relay). Four time world champion figure skater Kurt Browning fell in his technical program placing only fifth overall. In speed skating, leaders G. Niemann and D. Jansen, failed to win a medal in their strongest events. Among other experienced performers who lost the Olympics were D. Kennedy, 1988, 1992 Olympic Champion A. Tomba and six-time World Champion Speed Skater I. Zjelezovski (Sovetskiy Sport, April 21, 1994). The independence movement and the fall of communism in Eastern Europe contributed to a record number of countries competing, a more levelled playing field, and a greater distribution of medals among the participating countries (effected as well by the introduction of new sports). The number of events in the Winter Olympics were increased from 14 in 1932 to 57 in 1992 and 61 medal events in the 1994 Games (Globe & Mail, Feb. 26, 1994).

The Lillehammer Olympic competition marked a growing trend of medal distribution. While in Calgary 88 Olympics 17 countries won medals, in 92 Albertville the number of countries winning medals increased to 20. In Lillehammer 22 countries won medals. The expansion of the new sports resulted in the rise in team standings. South Korea which in 1988 in Calgary did not win a single medal due to short track speed skating moved to the tenth position in Albertville and improved to place in Lillehammer with 6 medals in total (4-1-1). The break-up of USSR helped Norway to place first (26) and Germany second (24), however, in total republics of former USSR have taken a greater share of medals in the short term. Duplication of some athletes on those teams brought the CIS a total of 31 medals (14-12-5).

Conclusion

International sport in the 1990s has been going through immense transformation marked by changes in medal leaders in individual performances, teams and countries. Political changes and levelling of the playing field have contributed to a growing geographical spread of medals and growing participation in major sport events.

The disintegration of the renown East European sport systems resulted in the emergence of new sport powers. Instead of the USSR (Unified Team) and East Germany it appears that in the summer sports it is the United States, Germany and China who are becoming the dominant forces, and Norway, Germany and Russia in winter sports.

The analysis of international sport performances in the 1990s indicate a growing trend of changes in the winners of World and Olympic events.

References

Calgary Herald, 1994, Feb. 14, Feb. 27, Calgary, Canada.

Edmonton Journal, 1993, March 10.

Fizkultura i Sport (Journal), Physical Culture and Sport, Moscow, 1991, 7, 8.

Globe & Mail , Toronto, Canada, 1994, Feb. 26.

Maclean's Magazine, 1994, Feb. 14, 42.

Montreal Gazette ,Montreal, Canada, 1994, Feb. 14, 18, 27, 28; 1991, Jan. 14, Aug. 26,.

New York Daily News, New York, 1994, Feb. 28.

Novoe Russkoye Slovo, New York, 1993, May 19.

Ottawa Citizen, Ottawa, Canada, 1994, Feb. 14, 25.

Physical Culture in School, Moscow, 1985, N. 8, 37.

Sovetskiy Sport, Moscow, 1994, Feb. 12, 17; March 5; April 21; 1993, July 20, 27; Aug. 7, 23; Nov., 4; 1992, Jan. 14; July 28, Aug. 15; Dec. 5; 1991, Sept. 3; 1990, Jan. 10; June 8, Sept. 23; 1988, April 14; 1987, Sept. 8.

Sport Abroad (Journal), Moscow, 1986, Oct., 19, 2.

Sport Express, Moscow, 1993, Aug. 4.

Sportivnaya Jizn Rossii (Journal), Moscow, 1992, 5-6, 9, 10, 11. (Sport Life of Russia).

Sports Weekend, 1993, TV Show, May 2.

Toronto Star, Toronto, Canada, 1994, Feb. 27.

USA Today 1994, Feb. 11, 15, 23, 28; March 1; 1992, Aug. 10.

ZILBERMAN, V.: Physical Education and Sport for Children and Youth in the USSR (1969-1989). Unpublished Doctoral Dissertation, Université de Montreal 1990.

ZILBERMAN, V.: Break-up of the Soviet State and Disintegration of the Renown Sport System. International Council for Health Physical Education, Recreation, Sport, and Dance (ICHPERD), Reston, Virginia, Spring 1994, No. 3, Vol. XXX, 33-42.

2. Changes in Sport: Their Impact on Sport Pedagogy, Teacher Education and School P.E.

- Sport Pedagogy

- Teacher Education

- School P.E.

- Fair Play in Sport - Fair Play in P.E.

Bart Crum

Changes in Movement Culture: A Challenge for Sport Pedagogy

Introductory Remarks

"Changes and Challenges", the conference theme here in Berlin. This combination of theme and site is not by chance. For, almost five years ago, this city was the site where the end of the cold war was sealed by the demolition of the wall between East and West. A tremendous change, which raised hopes and challenges for a better world. "Changes and challenges" - in the days preparing this paper, Nelson Mandela has been inaugurated as president of South Africa, Bill Clinton, the president of the state which 50 years ago led the way in the last battle against European fascism, dined with some neo-fascist members of the new Italian government, almost all television stations broadcasted the commemoration ceremonies of D-Day, in Ruanda the massacre continued and in the Bosnian ethnic war the umpteenth cease fire was announced and violated. When placed in such a frame, the changes and challenges, that are in the focus of this congress, have the importance of peanuts.

Although a relativization of the weight of our conference work may be in place, it is also appropriate to realize that peanut-problems are important if you are in the peanut-business. Therefore, I dare to state without reserve, that 'changes in movement culture' are important to the field of physical education (PE) and that they entail challenges for the theory and practice of sport pedagogy.

Yet, at least one caveat should be made. Focusing on 'changes in movement culture', we are faced with sweeping cross-cultural discontinuities. By comparison movement cultures (and their changeability) in the affluent West or North European democracies are quite different from movement cultures in the new democracies of Eastern Europe, not to mention the fact that there are still many countries in this world, where matters of movement culture and PE are pushed below the horizon by survival problems. For that reason, I think it necessary to underline, that my reflections are very much determined by the perspective of a scholar who lives and works in the affluent, peaceful, liberal and relatively postmaterialistic society of the Netherlands.

With that reservation in mind, I will undertake three things. First, I will explain, why I view changes in movement culture as a major challenge for sport pedagogy. Therefore, I need to give a concise explication of my PE conception. Second, I will describe changes in movement culture that can be observed in West European societies. Third, I will reflect on the consequences of the changes in movement culture for the PE curriculum.

1 Movement Culture as the Point of Reference for Physical Education

Schools can be viewed as society's answer to the problem of juvenile development in a culture with growing complexity. Their main mission is to qualify youngsters for future participation in social-cultural life (in labor as well as in leisure situations). School education should also open opportunities for personal development. In my view, however, this personal development aspect of the task of the school is a derivative of the qualification task. Facing the growing number of subjects that claim room in the time table, the school should concentrate on subjects that are emancipating because they prepare youngsters for a relevant, humane and independent participation in social-cultural life.

Movement culture - an umbrella concept which comprises all leisure actions in which the human moving act is the essence - can be viewed as society's reaction to the retreat of the experience of embodiment and moving from the domains of labor and transportation (due to the advancement of technology). In modern societies the number of people who highlight their embodied existence by engagement in movement culture is growing.

By their active participation in movement culture they unfold a rather central aspect of their being and gather experiences of self-realization, vitality, health and recreation. Therefore this participation contributes importantly to the quality of their lives.

In my view, today the main rationale to include PE in the school curriculum lies in its potential to qualify youngsters for an emancipated, satisfying and lasting participation in movement culture. I think that PE, like the other school subjects, should be a teaching-learning enterprise. Just like the subject English has the assignment to qualify for and to introduce into a language culture and arithmetics should introduce into the world of numbers and calculations, so is it PE's assignment to introduce youngsters into movement culture in order to qualify them for participation. Holding this view of PE's mission, the conclusion is obvious: the movement culture is a paramount point of reference for the arrangement of PE classes with utility value.

Much more could be said concerning PE's legitimation in contemporary schools and its desirable learning outcomes (cp. CRUM, 1989, 1993b). I waive that because of time limitations. However, there are two points that I better underline in order to avoid misinterpretations. Firstly, that PE should be arranged in view of learning with utility value for the movement culture outside the school, does not mean that the compass needle should only be oriented to future participation. Besides relevance for the future ("Zukunftsbedeutung"), PE should also have relevance for the present ("Gegenwartsbedeutung"). Consequently not only future, adult, movement-cultural modes, but also the present, juvenile movement culture should be a point of reference. Secondly, following Seneca's "non scholae, sed vitae discimus", PE should be arranged in view of learning with utility value for the movement culture outside the school. Nevertheless, PE programs (including the intra- and interscholastic sport) should also offer opportunities for exciting and joyful experiences in the here and now. In this respect, the compulsory classes and the optional school sport could be arranged as mutual complements. On the one hand, the arrangement of PE classes as real teaching-learning situations constitutes the heart of the PE enterprise. Because, only by didactic transformations of movement culture - in other words: by holding exercise, play and sport at arm's length - students are invited to transcend the level of just doing exercise or sport or just playing, and only then they can learn to understand movement culture as socially constructed and changeable, and only then they can systematically acquire the technomotor and sociomotor skills needed for a satisfying engagement. On the other hand, the decontextualization caused by the didactic preparation of exercise, play and sport, brings also the risk of boredom and lack of interest. Therefore, the trick of the trade is, on the one hand, not to neglect the pleasure and joy in the learning oriented classes, and on the other hand, to make sure that the optional school sport activities offer opportunities for relevant learning besides the central experiences of excitement, fun, celebration, competition and achievement.

2 Changes in Movement Culture

'Changes in movement culture': where are we talking about? Until the middle of the sixties in West European countries such as Germany, the Netherlands and Belgium 'sport' was a clearly defined and neatly arranged domain. 'Sport' was pre-eminently a matter of competition, of winning and loosing, of league tables and records. It is true, also other motives, such as fun, togetherness, fitness, recreation and adventure, played a role in this traditional sport. However, they were overshadowed by the achievement motive. The sport of those days was organized in civil clubs, which preferably accommodated vital, competitive, skilled, young people, in particular males.

During the past decades, the movement-cultural landscape has drastically changed. The generic social criticism induced criticism of the excessive achievement orientation within competitive sports and led to fervent pleas in favour of a relativization of traditional sports conventions and to the emergence of the 'sport for all' ideology. Consequently, 'sport' is no longer an exclusive activity for young and skilled people, but an activity for young and old, men and women, skilled and less skilled, handicapped and non-handicapped. 'Sport' is no longer only club sport, but offered by different agencies on different markets. Not only the number of participants increased spectacularly, but also a striking qualitative differentiation occurred. 'Sport' has developed into a multiform domain. Multiform qua movement problem and movement task, qua participation motive, qua context, qua characteristics of participants, qua degree of organization, qua function and qua effect. Consequently, the term 'sport' has been increasingly eroded, in particular in German 'sport' is used in an inflated way.

These roughly sketched movement-cultural developments can better be understood by placing them in the light of postmodern value orientations, the re-discovery of the body and the feeling towards life that emerges in postmaterialist societies.

The postmodern era is characterized by a parting of the values, views and lifestyles which were formed according to the traditions of enlightenment, rationalism and industrial revolution. Time is too short to present a detailed description of postmodernity. I confine myself to putting forward those generic cultural shifts which can directly be connected to the issue under discussion.

INGLEHART (1977) found in Western societies empirical shifts in value orientation. He placed these shifts on a line from materialism to postmaterialism. Examples of such shifts are: from a social order by command to a social order by negotiation, from strictly defined gender roles to egalitarian roles, from a readiness to conform and to discipline, obedience and fidelity to a craving for emancipation, creativity and self-realization, from emphasis on work and work ethic to emphasis on leisure, from ascesis to hedonism, from domination over nature to ecological awareness, from confidence in scientific progress to scepticism about rationality and science.

These shifts undeniably have dimensions that are directly relevant to movement culture. This is in particular so for the shift from work ethic values to values related to leisure, quality of life and self-realization. Seven years ago in this same congress center, LÜBBE, a Swiss social philosopher, called 'self-realization' "a radiant star of the modern attitude to life" (LÜBBE, 1988). He argued that modern people in fact do not have any other possibility than to choose the pathway to self-realization, because of the many degrees of freedom because of the increase of free time and money. He argued that individuals try to practise and to improve their capacity for self-realization and that this can be done particularly by participation in such action contexts in which one is closely connected with others and can experience their support. Movement culture is not the only context that comes up to this criterion. However, in modern societies there is no cultural domain which is more accessible as a medium for the experience and training of self-determination and self-realization for so many people, irrespective their sex, age, social class and level of education. This fact is reflected in the increasing numbers of sport participants.

The trend of individualization, another characteristic of our time, can be seen as a counterpart of the craving for self-realization. 'Individualization' stands for the complex process of the retreat of old ideologies, traditional certainties and binding norms, and the resulting disintegration of the society. Traditional collectivities, such as the church, the social class, the labor union, the family and civil clubs, are suffering from a substantial decrease of their function and status. This affects also the domain of sport, in particular the traditional club sport. The increase of sport participants on the one hand is associated with a growing lack of interest in conventional sport roles and traditional sport institutions on the other. The average sports club member has now a weaker identification with the club than before and the number of members with a consumerist attitude is rapidly growing.

There is still another influencing socio-cultural factor. That is what the German sport scientist Karl-Heinz BETTE has labelled as 'the paradoxical simultaneity of the denial of the body on the one hand and the rediscovery and upgrading of the body on the other' (BETTE, 1989). What does this mean? In our daily life the denial of the body advances due to the development of modern technology. The demand made to the body has largely disappeared as a result of the use of machines, engines, robots and computers in work and transportation. While in former days trading and finance were directly related to the physical presence of the business partners, it are nowadays abstract acts which are stripped from all physical involvement. The inventions of telephone, television and telefax ensure that more and more people communicate at increasingly larger distances without being physically close. The gentechnology opens the possibility of procreation without physical intercourse between a man and a woman. Obviously, in a society that is controlled by modern technology, the experience of embodiment is neglected. However, the human body does not accept this. It protests and takes revenge with stress symptoms, psycho-somatic problems and cardio-vascular diseases. In turn the society reacts to these self-generated symptoms, problems and diseases by an explicit thematization of embodiment. The body is rediscovered and all kind of body-processing agencies experience a boom. Think of the growing health business, the spectacular growth of body- and movement-oriented psychotherapy and also of the growth of the movement culture.

Together, the shift towards postmaterialist values, the craving for self-realization, the trend to individualization and the rediscovery of the body have procured a process, that can be labelled as 'the sportification of the society' (cp. CACHAY, 1990; DIGEL, 1990; GRUPE, 1988).

This 'sportification' can, for example, be noticed in the spoken language. While in former days the Dutch language was full of metaphors derived from the Bible and sailing, now the world of sport becomes an important source. Another indication of the general sportification can be found in the advancing of the Nikes, the New Balances, the Reeboks and the training suits in non-sport contexts.

Apart from the sportification of language and clothing, the 'sportification of the society' also comes forward in the domain of sport itself. The emergence of the 'sport for all' idea invited or seduced the traditional sport system to extend its own borders, to play along with new needs and expectations and to try to fulfill a range of new functions. Moreover, it was not only the traditional sport agencies, associations and clubs, that tried to play along with the differentiation of needs and expectations of sport consumers. New sport-offering agencies, most of them with a commercial orientation, shot up like mushrooms. Although the traditional sport club is for the majority still the place to do sport, it has lost its original position of monopoly.

The sportification of the society did not only cause the traditional sport organizations to give up their monopoly, it also induced the socialization of sport as the other side of the coin. This socialization of sport led to a kind of dilution of the 'real' sport. The more sport is instrumentalized, that is: used for objectives outside the sport itself, the more its traditional social values and characteristics will be blurred.

The 'sportification of the society' and the socialization of sport resulted in a striking process of internal differentiation of sport; a differentiation process characterized by on the one hand the 'sportification of sport' and on the other hand the 'de-sportification of sport'.

First a few words concerning the 'sportification of sport'. This label is used to indicate the process in which the original characteristics of sport, namely achievement and competition, are radicalized. This process has been started off by the cold war politicalization of sport and is continued by the commercialization, the mediazation and the scientization of sport, which interact as cogwheels. In many countries the 'sportification of sport' resulted in a by state and/or business financed elite sport system. Excesses, such as child labor, doping and injurious training methods, are intrinsic to this sport mode. In this media covered, sometimes extremely high payed but often outrageously low payed, elite sport, glorification of the body and body-hostile exploitation go hand in hand.

The 'de-sportification of sport' can be interpreted as a counter-move. Due to the 'sport for all' idea thresholds to sport participation have been lowered. This was done by shading the achievement orientation and by emphasizing motives such as pleasure, fun, togetherness, communication, recreation and health. This trend boomed on the up-current of postmodern values as self-realization and health and the related narcism and hedonism. Alternative sport modes (for which here in Germany the paradoxical label 'non-sportive sport' is used), in which pleasure, enjoyment, adventure, body sensation, fitness and appearance are in the foreground, have developed. These modes are mostly organized in commercial settings.

In conclusion: in particular under influence of the 'sportification of the society' and the 'de-sportification' of the traditional sport, the once relative homogeneous sport system has differentiated into a rather heterogeneous movement culture. Movement-cultural sub-systems develop beside each other as different shops with different assortments and different internal rules for different clients, who have different needs and expectations. For the time being, the following heuristic classification of sportive sub-systems, each of them part of a different social convention, could be useful (CRUM, 1992):
(1) Elite sport - The dominant motives are: absolute achievement, status, money. This sport mode is often commercialized and requires (semi-)professional participation.

(2) Competitive club sport - Here the dominant motive is a cocktail of the excitement of competition, pursuit of subjective achievement, relaxation and social contact.
(3) Recreation sport - Dominant motives are: relaxation, health and togetherness. Recreation sport is offered by sport clubs as well as by local authorities; often it is privately arranged.
(4) Fitness sport - The dominant, even isolated, motive is: physical fitness. This mode is mostly offered by commercial agencies and also privately staged (e.g. jogging).
(5) Risk and adventure sport - Adventure and thrill are the dominant motives. Think of the mostly commercially organized, expensive activities such as Himalaya trekking, helicopter skiing, hang-gliding, scubadiving, rafting and parachuting.
(6) Lust sport - Hedonism, exclusive pleasure is here the focus. Think of the commercially organized (often in combination with tourism) S-sport (sun, sea, sand, snow, sex, speed and satisfaction).
(7) Cosmetic sport - Focus on the model-appearance. Think of the commercially organized narcism of body-building, -styling and -shaping, with a 'warming up' or a 'cooling down' on the sunbed.

Finally in this paragraph, a brief outlook at some peculiarities of contemporay, juvenile movement-cultural subcultures seems to be in place.

Youngsters in a postmaterialistic culture are increasingly children of what can be called an 'excitement-society' ("Erlebnisgesellschaft", cp. SCHULZE, 1992). The German sociologist SCHULZE coined this concept as distinguished from the traditional, materialistic 'Überlebensgesellschaft' ('survival society'). While in the 'survival society' scarcity was pre-dominant, the 'excitement society' is characterized by an abundance of possibilities. An abundance in every respect: fruits, vegetables, breads, wines, beers, clothes, shoes, cd's, tv channels, holiday resorts and also sport scenes. People start, so to say, to suffer from the enormous offer of possibilities. Under the pressure of the imperative "live and look for excitement in your life", the main problem is not a problem of means, but the difficulty of making choices. The abundance of exciting experience options causes that modern people "amuse themselves to death" (POSTMAN, 1985). Different from the 'survival society', in which people had to cope with a material crisis, members of the 'excitement society' have to cope with a crisis of meaning, a crisis of orientation. For that reason a considerable number of youngsters do not view their youth as an unqualified pleasure. They have problems in finding orientations and producing their own biography. This causes uncertainty and hampers the formation of identity.

The youth of today forms a heterogeneous category. So generalizations are dangerous. Nevertheless, the following phenomena are striking. The majority of secondary school students (in my country even more than 60 %) are still engaged in more or less traditional sport club activities. Yet, for many of them the mode of club engagement is changing. Because they have so many options for leisure in general and for sport in particular, easily the idea comes up that a clear choice for one option implies the missing of another. Consequently, an increasing number of youngsters prefer to zap along the spectrum of sport clubs and other leisure options like they zap along the tv channels. There social-cultural life has staccato-character.

Another category of youngsters did not enter any sport club or definitively dropped out because they do not feel that regulated competition in a ball game or running between two lines or exercising on gymnastic apparatus give fun or excitement. Insofar they are physically active, they may engage in quite different sportive subcultures. There is, for example, a group that stresses its own distinctive features in the narcistic body-styling and body-building scene. A second group prefers to emphasize the expression dimension of moving and tries to find identity in the skateboard scene around the half-pipe or in the streetball scene with its trendy outfit, which is highly pushed by the sellers of sport commodities and their infectious tv ads. Other examples are the subcultures of the mountain-bikers, the inline skaters and the windsurfers (cp.

BRETTSCHNEIDER, 1990; BRETTSCHNEIDER & BRÄUTIGAM, 1990; BRINKHOFF, 1992).

3 Challenge for Sport Pedagogy: The Need of a Pedagogical Evaluation and Didactic Filters

Generally spoken, the changes in movement culture and the fashionable trends of juvenile movement scenes did not really penetrate to the practice of PE. There are considerable discrepancies between what is going on in PE classes and what is going on in the movement culture outside the school. Starting from the conception that 'introduction into movement culture' should be the heart of the PE matter, this state of affairs must be judged as problematic. The discrepancies might be a basic cause for the crisis in secondary school PE, a paramount reason for students' judgment that PE is boring. I think, that sport pedagogy should face this problem. Consequently, sport pedagogy is obliged (a) to set pedagogical criteria for an evaluation of present trends in movement culture, (b) to develop didactic filters for drawing consequences for the PE curriculum. Please, do not expect that I am going to present final solutions. That is not only beyond the time limits set, but also far beyond my expertise. I will use the last five minutes of my presentation for some initial considerations.

My first consideration focuses on pedagogical-ethical aspects of the problem. Some postmodern scholars - not only scholars - have developed an attitude in which relativization, irony and cynicism are important ingredients. The adagium is then: long life to normative relativism, everything goes. Such an attitude gives the mental flexibility to cope with social pluralism and relativism, with lack of orientation, with "the end of history" (FUKUYAMA) and with the misery that we daily get dished up by the media. It is my firm belief, however, that pedagogues cannot allow themselves such an attitude. If they do so, they commit an intellectual treason and become accessary to the lack of orientation to life of the upgrowi generation.

Some decades ago, PE in this country was inclined to turn into the direction of a mere reproduction of the content and methods of competitive sports; the so-called 'realistic turn' ("realistische Wende"). For a part of the sport pedagogical community this turn gave cause to a clear critical stance. Starting from the viewpoint that sport is a domain of human action, which is historically situated and socially constructed, an uncritical taking over of the achievement orientation of the organized sport was dismissed. Dismissed on the basis of the insight, that 'achievement' is a social construct and that the achievement benchmarks of competitive sport and the related skill teaching methodology would enhance inequity and implicit exclusion of students and restrict the development of a personal movement identity. In that period sport pedagogy produced lenses for a critical evaluation of competitive sports.

Sometimes I have the sneaking feeling that sport pedagogues, who have been (or still are) rather critical towards competitive sport (the 'real' sport), are much more tolerant in judging the 'alternative', 'non-sportive' movement-cultural modes. If that is true, they don't see the pitfall of trying to exorcize the devil with Beelzebub. For, it is really naive to think that in the alternative sport modes embodiment and human moving would not serve as sites for social struggle and would not reflect social relationships in which social control and oppression dominates individual development.

Sport pedagogues should feel responsible for an introduction in movement culture in which respect for the subjectivity of the individual (keyword: emancipation), respect for the fellow human (keyword: solidarity) and respect for the nature environment are leading values. Therefore, sport pedagogy should review and evaluate the alternative sport modes in the light of these values.
...r example become evident that:
...ıtalization of the body-machine, which takes often ... setting of the fitness sport, violates the integrity of ...ıbodiment;

* the narcistic obsession with mesomorphy in the cosmetic sport reflects a macho ideology;
* the hedonism in the lust sport runs the risk of going for own fun and satisfaction at the cost of others;
* many forms of risk and adventure sport imply severe ecological damage.

My second consideration concerns the question, which modern movement-cultural forms should be represented in the PE curriculum and how they can be didactically transformed. (By the way: it might be appropriate to underline that this paragraph particularly focuses on PE at the secondary level). Reflecting on a PE program that prepares todays kids for participation in movement culture in 2022, Dieter BRODTMANN (1992) asks, whether it makes sense to try to prognosticate activities that will be characteristic for the movement culture of 2022. His answer is that the responsibility for the development and the future lifes of the students let no choice. In his view, sport pedagogues have a calling to predict the unpredictable and to plan that what cannot be planned. I have a different opinion. I prefer to stick to the wisdom of the Arabic saying, that "prediction is hard, in particular when the future is at stake". I remember the visions Aldous HUXLEY (1932) had about people's play in the "Brave New World": Riemann-surface tennis, electro-magnetic golf, obstacle golf and escalator-squash, and I know that it did not come true. Therefore, I think we better waive the waste of time of trying to predict the unpredictable.

Moreover, the prediction of future activity types is not that important, because it is not a particular movement activity as such that is decisive in a PE class but the thematization of that activity (that is the didactical transformation of that activity in the light of the objectives). For that reason it is worthwhile to return to the objective-question. Earlier in this paper I have set the following objective: "to qualify youngsters for an emancipated, satisfying and lasting participation in movement culture". Taking into consideration (a) that movement culture in itself is continuously in change, and (b) that because of the aging process the meaning of sport for an individual is changing, so that his or her sport participation will be differently staged throughout life, it may become obvious that "qualification for an emancipated, satisfying and lasting participation" implies at least the following aspects:

(1) basic competency to solve technomotor and sociomotor problems (if you want you can call this 'skills'), and
(2) a thorough understanding of the social making of the movement culture.

I think that the first aspect will meet full agreement. I am not sure that the second will meet the same. For that reason I underline why this understanding is important. If students understand the rule character of sport and the conventions of movement culture, then

(a) they are able to change rules if that is appropriate in the situation,
(b) they are able to value and to organize exercise for fitness and health,
(c) they can act as critical consumers on the market of sport, health and happiness, and
(d) they are able to keep distance from the often misleading messages about sport that are spread out by the mass media.

The realization of a basic technomotor and sociomotor competency and a thorough understanding of sport requires reflective teachers, who arrange their classes in such a way that students are invited to reflective learning (cp. CRUM, 1993a). Reflective PE teachers will avoid to fall into didactic actualism when making decisions on the movement activities that are going to be thematized in their classes. They do not view the present hitlist of juvenile sport activities as the first point of reference, neither do they make holy cows of traditional forms. They judge the value that a particular movement activity or sport form has for a relevant teaching-learning process much more important than the fun and excitement value of that activity. They are ready to adopt a methodology of displaying the social making of movement culture (cp. DIETRICH, 1992; EHNI, 1993). They are not afraid of a school PE curriculum that gives students possibilities to choose. Sport pedagogy is called to accept the challenge of developing, testing and evaluating such curriculums and methodologies.

References

BETTE, K.H.: Körperspuren; Zur Semantik und Paradoxie moderner Körperlichkeit. Berlin/New York: Walter de Gruyter, 1989.

BRETTSCHNEIDER, W.-D.: Adolescents, leisure, sport and lifestyle. In: T. WILLIAMS, L. ALMOND, A. SPARKES (Eds.): Sport and physical activity: Moving towards excellence. London: E & FN Spon, 1990, 536-551.

BRETTSCHNEIDER, W.-D.; BRÄUTIGAM, M.: Sport in der Alltagswelt von Jugendlichen. Frechen: Ritterbach, 1990.

BRINKHOFF, K.-P.: Zwischen Verein und Vereinzelung; Jugend und Sport im Individualisierungsprozess. Schorndorf: Hofmann, 1992.

BRODTMANN, D.: Schulsport für das Jahr 2022. Sportpädagogik, 1992, 16, 6, 5-7.

CACHAY, K.: Versportlichung der Gesellschaft und Entsportung des Sports - Systemtheoretische Anmerkungen zu einem gesellschaftlichen Phänomen. In: H. GABLER, U. GÖHNER (Hrsg.): Für einen besseren Sport ....Schorndorf: Hofmann, 1990, 97-113.

CRUM, B.J.: Zwischen Anpassung und Kritik - über das Verhältnis der Schule zur Bewegungskultur. In: H. BINNEWIES, J. DESSAU, B. THIEME (Hrsg.): Freizeit und Breitensport '88. Ahrensburg: Czwalina, 1989, 375-393.

CRUM, B.J.: Over de Versporting van de Samenleving. Haarlem: De Vrieseborch, 1992.

CRUM, B.J.: The urgent need for reflective teaching in PE. Keynote presented at the International AIESEP Seminar, University of Quebec at Trois-Rivières, July 1993.

CRUM, B.J.: A Critical Review of Competing PE Concepts. In: J. MESTER (Ed.): Sport Sciences in Europe 1993 - Current and Future Perspectives, Aachen: Meyer & Meyer, 1994, 516-533.

DIETRICH, K.: Der Sport ändert sich, brauchen wir ein neues Sportcurriculum? In: R. ERDMANN (Hrsg.): Alte Fragen neu gestellt. Schorndorf: Hofmann, 1992, 111-122.

DIGEL, H.: Die Versportlichung unserer Kultur und deren Folgen für den Sport - ein Beitrag zur Uneigentlichkeit des Sports. In: H. GABLER; U. GÖHNER (Hrsg.): Für einen besseren Sport .... Schorndorf: Hofmann, 1990, 73-96.

EHNI, H.: Das Elementare in der Sportpädagogik - Sieben Fragen zur Thematik. Vortrag Tagung der Kommission Sportpädagogik der DGfEW, Heidelberg, Dezember 1993.

GRUPE, O.: Menschen im Sport 2000. Von der Verantwortung der Person und der Verpflichtung der Organisation. In: K.-H. GIESELER, O. GRUPE; K. HEINEMANN (Hrsg.): Dokumentation des Kongresses 'Menschen im Sport 2000'. Schorndorf: Hofmann, 1988, 44-67.

HUXLEY, A.: Brave New World. Harmondsworth: Penguin, 1932.

INGLEHART, R.: The Silent Revolution: Changing Values and Political Styles among Western Publics. Princeton, 1977.

LÜBBE, H.: Menschen im Jahr 2000. Rahmenbedingungen für die künftige Entwicklung des Sports. In: K.-H. GIESELER, O. GRUPE, K. HEINEMANN (Hrsg.): Dokumentation des Kongresses 'Menschen im Sport 2000'. Schorndorf: Hofmann, 1988, 32-43.

POSTMAN, N.: Amusing ourselves to death: Public discourse in the age of show business. New York: Penguin, 1985.

SCHULZE, G.: Die Erlebnisgesellschaft. Frankfurt/New York: Campus, 1992.

Paul G. Schempp

A Study of Pedagogical Knowledge in Physical Education

Professionals are called into service because they bring a unique understanding and critical insight to a situation. It is the body of professional knowledge that explains what those in a particular occupation do and why (SCHON, 1983). The body of knowledge currently used in a profession is, therefore, of major concern to those practicing the profession and preparing future practitioners. Contemporary literature on teaching lacks substantive information on the knowledge base teachers use in their professional practice. There has been, however, a growing recognition in teacher education that the understanding of the knowledge used by teachers will lead to a better understanding of pedagogical practice (SHULMAN, 1986).

Within the last decade, educational researchers have studied rules and principles used in teacher thinking (ELBAZ, 1983), teachers' classroom images (CLANDININ, 1985), subject matter expertise (LEINHARDT & SMITH, 1985), and pedagogical content knowledge (GROSSMAN, 1989). These studies, and other similar work, represent the start of a trend in research into what teachers know and how they use that knowledge in their classrooms. This study continues that line of inquiry by offering a glimpse into the world of an experienced high school physical education teacher. Specifically, this case study examines the criteria one teacher employed in acquiring the knowledge he found necessary for his professional practice.

Method

Teacher and Setting

Robert Halstop has taught high school physical education for the past 14 years at Hillcrest High School (HHS). Over those years, Bob has coached many sports and been involved in numerous school clubs, groups, and projects. At the time of this study, he was coaching the girls' varsity basketball team. Besides teaching and coaching, he performed normal student counseling activities and other school duties assigned by the administrators. Bob's school day officially began at 7:30 a.m. and ended at 3:30 p.m., but he was usually in school much earlier and it was common for him to stay later. Bob was assigned six classes, one planning period, and a lunch break.

Hillcrest High School, where Bob taught, enrolled approximately 470 students and was located in a small, rural community. Two years before this study, HHS received an educational excellence award from the United States Department of Education. All first year students were required to take physical education for one year and could elect physical education after that. The freshman physical education classes were separated by gender and were taught as a survey course to cover many subject areas. The other physical education classes were co-educational and defined by student interest (e.g., recreational sports, weight training). HHS had two physical education teachers; one for boys (Bob) and one for girls (Kathy).

Data Collection and Analysis

Data were collected and analyzed using participant observation, artifact and document analyses, stimulated recall using videotaped classes, and both formal and informal interviews. Data collection began two days before the start of school and officially ended just before the Christmas break. Data analysis involved summarizing data into themes and categories using procedures recommended by GOETZ and LECOMPTE (1984) and PATTON (1980). The construction of these categories was influenced by SHULMAN's (1987) theory of a knowledge base for teaching. Four of SHULMAN's seven categories were used to describe the forms of knowledge Bob acquired in pursuit of his professional practice: subject matter, general pedagogical (renamed teaching behavior), pedagogical content, and context (renamed external conditions). Classroom organization and operation was a category constructed independent of SHULMAN's theory as it appeared to better describe a dominant form of Bob's knowledge.

The themes and categories identified forms of knowledge as well as the criteria Bob used in acquiring pedagogical knowledge. The first step was to review the collected data to determine tentative categories. Next, the data were coded using the tentative scheme. The category scheme underwent revisions until the data were able to be classified within the scheme with no redundancy of categories. The constant comparison method of analysis (GLASER & STRAUSS, 1967) was used to identify these patterns and relationships. The final step of the analytic procedure was to present a copy of the report to Bob so that he could: (a) check the accuracy of the data, and (b) validate the findings of the report. This procedure was considered a critical component for establishing the validity and trustworthiness of the study's findings (LATHER, 1986).

Findings

Bob's knowledge was classified in five domains: (a) classroom organization, (b) teaching behavior, (c) subject matter, (d) pedagogical content knowledge, and (e) external conditions.

Class Organization and Operation

Like many teachers, classroom order and control were predominant concerns for Bob. The concern for classroom organization and controlled operation rose from Bob's belief that if order was not established, and the classroom not operated in the manner he needed, little could be accomplished. Although he had spent much time formulating, writing and explaining his operational policies and procedures, the complex and fluid nature of his classes required constant interpretation and reevaluation of the codes of operation and organization. The variety of students with varying levels of interest, responsibilities, motivations, and attitudes demanded adaptations in the organization and management of the class. Similarly, different subject matter, teaching stations, or equipment would also signal a change in class organization and operation. Bob, like many teachers (CLANDININ, 1985), relied on practical rules and principles, routines, and habits to guide classroom operation rather than inflexible standards or absolute rules. He perceived the ability to manage a class to be the foundation of good teaching.

Bob could set all the rules he cared to set. There were no formal guidelines or recommendations. How he enforced those rules was another matter. Parents and administrators took a strong interest in the consequences Bob dealt students for misbehavior. Bob explained:

> You've gotta have the right administration, the administrator that is willing to go along with what you see as important, what your values are, a disciplined structured program, and back you up on that. Because if you don't, ... the kids are going to start complaining, which in turn, the parents start complaining. Parents are going to the administration.

Teaching Behavior

A significant portion of Bob's everyday actions and activities were devoted to the task of instructing students. Knowledge for meeting these demands was classified by SHULMAN (1987) as general pedagogical knowledge, for this knowledge transcended a particular subject content. Much of Bob's teaching behavior was characterized by well rehearsed, time-worn rituals. Every class began with student-led exercises while Bob took attendance. Then Bob informed the students of the day's activities. A brief skill demonstration or explanation was followed by a drill. Most classes closed with a game or culminating activity. Sometimes, a game was played for the entire class. The practices that defined Bob's teaching behavior were largely composed of comfortable habits and familiar routines. Comfort in crafting a teaching style appears to be an common criterion among teachers (LANGE & BURROUGHS-LANGE, 1994; RUSSELL & JOHNSTON, 1988).

Bob did not actively pursue knowledge that directly affected his instructional practices. The roots of this perspective can be traced to his undergraduate days. "When I was going through college," he said, "they didn't have any methods classes, none. Zero." The fundamental criteria used to determine the success of a lesson was, therefore, not so much what students learned, but rather their level of enjoyment. During one interview Bob told me that "they really seem to enjoy it (the activity). They develop certain skills. The more skill they develop, the more they seem to enjoy it."

Bob's teaching behavior was a non-issue with almost everybody in the school. The structure of the school provided him with no feedback on his teaching behavior, nor was their visible encouragement for him to stimulate greater student achievement. Students, for example, appeared to have little regard for their learning in physical education. Upon seeing Bob before class, students would invariably ask "what are we gonna play?", "do we have to dress down?", or "are we gonna do anything today?" No student ever thanked Bob for something they learned or requested to learn a particular skill or concept.

The immediate and multiple demands placed on Bob's time in school often relegated the learning of his approximately 130 students to the back-burner of his priorities. Time that could be used to evaluate and improve his instructional practices is consumed by the competing requirements of his coaching responsibilities and the many mundane activities he continually has to attend to (e.g., lost locks, attendance records, clean towel supply, field preparation, equipment maintenance). His work environment conspired to inform Bob that the operation of the school as a system took precedent over student learning in physical education.

Additionally, there was little incentive for Bob to improve his teaching behavior to stimulate increases in student learning. Administrators held a greater concern for the operation of the school than they did for achievement of students in physical education. Parents were more concerned with how their children were treated than what they learned. Students wanted to play; not learn. Whether students learned in his class or not was a concern that was, from my observations, held only by Bob. And because of the lack of concern from others, it was often not even at the forefront of Bob's concerns. He received no rewards if learning was increased and there were no consequences for a lack of student achievement.

Subject Matter

The content of Bob's classes was described and detailed in a curriculum guide he had compiled. Objectives for each program were identified and the policies used to conduct the program were also described. The largest portion of the guide was composed of the specific subject matter units. When asked about the resources used to complete the guide, Bob told me that most of the units came for an undergraduate curriculum course assignment. He has added to the guide from materials and resources gathered at in-service programs.

Although the guide was a 148-page document and included an outline of each subject taught, it was used sparingly. Over the course of my time with Bob, I observed him using the guide perhaps a half dozen times, mostly to review teaching points for an upcoming lesson or remind himself of game rules. The guide did not hold the majority of subject matter Bob taught, for experience has taught him that he must "keep most of the (subject matter) knowledge organized in my head and I can't write it down because everything is situation-specific."

Bob acquired new subject matter knowledge based upon these criteria: (a) perceptions of his own competence in teaching the subject, (b) personal interest in the subject matter, c) perceptions of student interest, (d) actual student demand as demonstrated by elective class enrollments, (e) time investment necessary to teach or prepare to teach the subject, (f) the novelty of the subject, and (g) facility and equipment constraints. Bob reported that gymnastics and outdoor education were two content areas recently dropped. Gymnastics was no longer offered because Bob did not like teaching it and had a concern for liability. Outdoor education was no longer part of the curriculum because the individual who taught the course had left the school and Bob did not want to give up his weekends for the activities. Weight training was a new subject added to the course offerings because of student demand, Bob's personal interest in teaching the subject, and the availability of an adequate facility. Personal understanding and significance play an important role in Bob's acquisition and use of content knowledge. Teachers in other subject areas also appear to rely on personal understanding in selecting content (WILSON & WINEBURG, 1988).

Pedagogical Content Knowledge

SHULMAN (1987) defines pedagogical content knowledge as content knowledge "which goes beyond knowledge of subject matter per se to the dimension of subject matter for teaching" (p. 9). Years of experience have forged a mode of operation, a routine, which frames the knowledge Bob imparts to his students. Bob seeks curricular content that fits his teaching style. In pedagogical practice, he teaches an activity in terms of its essential skills by giving brief explanations and sometimes demonstrations, then has students practice these skills through drills, and after varying amounts of practice the students are then given the rules and play the game. These procedures have been used for years by Bob with all varieties of subject matter. He is, therefore, more inclined to select new activities that fit his mode of operation than he is to look for new ways to teach old subject matter. Further, Bob was less likely to teach subject matter in depth and more likely to teach many activities at the "introductory" level. The more conveniently new information fit into familiar routines, the more likely would be incorporated.

External Conditions

Conditions originating outside the classroom, and removed from Bob's immediate control, came to bear on several pedagogical decisions. These conditions include local regulations and requirements that were imposed by the administration and school board as well as regulations and laws handed down from state and federal agencies. Therefore, the wishes and demands of administrators, students, parents, and state agencies factored into Bob's procurement of knowledge. The influence of administrators, parents, and students on Bob's knowledge was discussed above. School and state regulations also influenced him, but to a far lesser degree. External conditions were only a minor consideration in Bob's acquisition of knowledge.

Conclusion

Classroom order and operation held the highest priority in Bob's pedagogical knowledge. Subject matter that fit his personal interests, workplace conditions, and would result in student enjoyment had the greatest chance of penetrating the curriculum. And new knowledge that conformed to his well-worn classroom practices passed Bob's test of valued professional knowledge. He acknowledged a lack of information regarding effective teaching behavior, and given his workplace conditions, this situation appears to have little chance to change. Will Bob ever change? He is, in fact, always changing as new information comes to him and is incorporated into his professional knowledge base. In the final analysis, however, Bob's time in service has made him well aware of who he is, what he does, why it does it, and what knowledge is required for him to meet the demands of teaching in a public school.

References

CLANDININ, D.J.: Personal practical knowledge: A study of teachers' classroom images. Curriculum Inquiry, 1985, 15, 361-385.

CLANDININ, D.J.; CONNELLY, F.M.: Rhythms in teaching: The narrative study of teachers' personal practical knowledge of classrooms. Teaching and Teacher Education, 1986, 2, 377-387.

ELBAZ, F.: Teacher thinking: A study of practical knowledge. London: Croom Helm 1983.

GLASER, B.; STRAUSS, A.: The discovery of grounded theory: Strategies for qualitative research. Chicago: Aldine 1967.

GOETZ, J.P.; LECOMPTE, M.D.: Ethnography and qualitative design in educational research. Orlando: Academic Press 1984.

GROSSMAN, P.: A study of contrast: Sources of pedagogical content knowledge for secondary English. Journal of Teacher Education, 1989, 40, 24-32.

LANGE, J.; BURROUGHS-LANGE, S.: Professional uncertainty and professional growth: A case study of experienced teachers. Teaching and Teacher Education, 1994, 10, 617-631.

LATHER, P.: Issues of validity in openly ideological research: Between a rock and a soft place. Interchange, 1986, 17, 63-84.

LEINHARDT, G.; SMITH, D.A.: Expertise in mathematics instruction: Subject matter knowledge. Journal of Educational Psychology, 1985, 77, 247-271.

PATTON, M.: Qualitative evaluation methods. Beverly Hills: Sage Publications 1980.

RUSSELL, T.; JOHNSTON, P.: Teachers' learning from experiences of teaching: Analysis based on metaphor and reflection. Paper presented at the annual meeting of the American Education Research Association, New Orleans, LA. 1988, April.

SCHON, D.A.: The reflective practitioner. New York: Basic Books 1983.

SHULMAN, L.S.: Knowledge and teaching: Foundations of the new reform. Harvard Educational Review, 1987, 57, 1-22.

WILSON, S.; WINEBURG, S.: Peering at history through different lenses: The role of disciplinary perspectives in teaching history. Teachers' College Record, 1988, 89, 525-539.

Gary T. Barrette

Physical Education Teacher Education Design and Research: Studying Curricular Intents and Outcomes

As I began to outline and organize this paper I was reminded of an educational philosophy lecture I heard as an undergraduate student over thirty years ago. As I recall, the topic of the lecture was reality and education, and the professor quoted Alfred NORTH WHITEHEAD (1949) from his then reasonably contemporary text, Aims of Education. He wrote:

> I emphasize the point that our only exact data as to the physical world are our sensible perceptions. We must not slip into the fallacy of assuming that we are comparing a given world with given perceptions of it. The physical world is, in some general sense of the term, a deduced concept. Our problem is, in fact, to fit the world to our perceptions and not our perceptions to the world. (157-158).

This admonition lends support to the idea that one of the primary functions of any educational system is to find the ways and means to promote innovative thought and its subsequent translation into effective praxis. In this sense, individuals guiding any education system, regardless of level, must be aware of their responsibility to constantly question and thoughtfully examine program intentions and outcomes.

The purpose of this paper is to relate how we as teacher educators can fit the world into our perceptions of teacher education by 1.) identifying some critical issues regarding program intentions and outcomes, 2.) provide a couple of theoretical perspectives, 3.) share a conceptual system and action framework designed to bring theory into practice, and 4.) explain how some teacher educators have organized the study of the effectiveness of teacher education design including the instructional inventions and processes which were devised.

Although research on PETE programs has been limited, recent works (BARRETT, ALLISON & BELL, 1987; BELKA, 1988; and GRAHAM, HOHN, WEINER & WOODS, 1993) have indicated that "apprenticeship of observation" effects have had a substantially greater role than formalized teacher education in influencing preservice and inservice teacher's views of teaching. Views expressed by CRUM (1993), DODDS (1989), and LAWSON (1983), commonly point to the absence of a salient programmatic view of teaching (what I call program convergency and congruency) within the PETE program itself, as the most cogent reason for the failure of teacher education to effectively translate hopeful intentions into achieved outcomes.

DODDS' (1989, 97) analysis of this issue states that "when primary socializing agents neither share nor value a common teaching perspective, and when differences among professors may be even greater than those between one professor and cooperating teacher, than the prospective teachers views of teaching will be shaped by random influences rather than by coordinated messages reiterating a familiar programmatic teaching perspective". CRUM (1993, 349) underscores, this point by stating that "it is high time for PETE program Directors to check how far their conceptual needles point in the same Direction". Similarly, (BARRETTE, 1990), I have argued that strong leadership, regular faculty dialogue and a collective commitment to PETE staff development regarding program congruence and convergence were needed in order to accomplish conceptual cohesiveness, and clear direction in PETE programs.

However, the question of exactly what the intentions (objectives) of teacher education programs should be, how PETE programs are designed and work, and how PETE faculty interact to achieve teacher development outcomes has not been adequately addressed. Teacher educators have tended to describe their programs in terms related to course titles, course requirements and syllabi and have eschewed the critical analysis and in-depth discussion of theory-based programmatic underpinnings and the interaction dynamics of professors, students, and subject-matter. We need better or at least more creative models and theories which can be useful metaphors for naming, framing and understanding our teacher education designs and practices and the related educational intentions they seek to achieve in terms of teacher development outcomes.

O'HANLEN and WANZILAK (1980) have characterized the problems in physical education teacher education (PETE) as follows:

> In particular there are no planned relationships among learning in various subdisciplines nor are there any between them and what is included about teaching methodology. Students are expected to pull together what they are learning into a meaningful whole even though college faculty have not done this in designing the teacher education program. (54)

The need for strategies which combat curricular fragmentation and faculty dissociation; and which promote convergent strategies of planned integration connected to the real work of teachers in long overdue. If we are to move forward in our own work as teacher educators we must study our program theories, models and designs (curricular structures and processes) for achieving outcomes and scrutinize these outcomes in relation to the intentions we have selected at the outset.

Teacher education may be expressed as a congruent design model. Figure 1 provides a schematic representation of this concept.

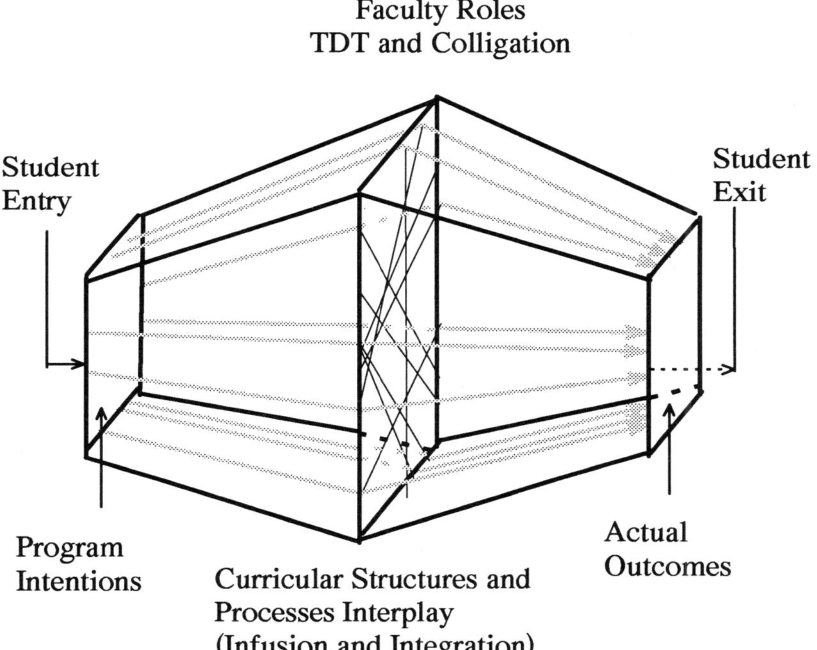

Key - —— Curriculum Framework
Curricular Intentions/Outcomes
— Curriculum Structures (Course) and Processes (Infusion and Integration

Figure 1 - Congruency Model Linking Theoretical Intentions to Actual Outcomes in Teacher Education Through Curricular Structurs and Processes

In this model, theoretical program intentions are linked to actual program outcomes through the curricula structures and processes, which are the planned translatory mechanisms intended to achieve the match (congruency) between intentions and outcomes. This is represented by the equal square planes at either end of the model. The larger square plane represents the context in which intentions are set and then sought and includes the curriculum structure (course) and processes as well as the interplay between and among faculty in collaborating for the benefit of the students. Visually it suggests that the pursuit of intentions (objectives) can be achieved in a variety of ways within the teacher education context, and that ultimately this fanning out strategy, augmented by the colligation process (binding together) effectively achieves the transformance of intentions to actual outcomes in student performance.

I have also borrowed from MCDONALD's (1965) longstanding but persuasive "systems" conception in developing the notion of convergence in the teacher education process itself. Figure 2 is a graphic representation of the four systems which comprise the teacher education process, and the distinctions which can be made. Teaching is a personality system, including unique values, previous experiences and idiosyncracies which teachers act out. Learning is also a personality system which includes perceptions, previous experiences and other conditions of the learner. The instructional system is a social system which represents the teaching-learning transaction. It is comprised of a professor, a learning site (classroom, gymnasium, pool, public school, etc.), students, materials and social norms. The curriculum system consists of professionals or persons who are part of the social system which results in a written curriculum, including objectives content and assessment and delivery system variable. Since each system theoretically has its own boundaries it excludes the possibility of any of four areas being totally included within any other system.

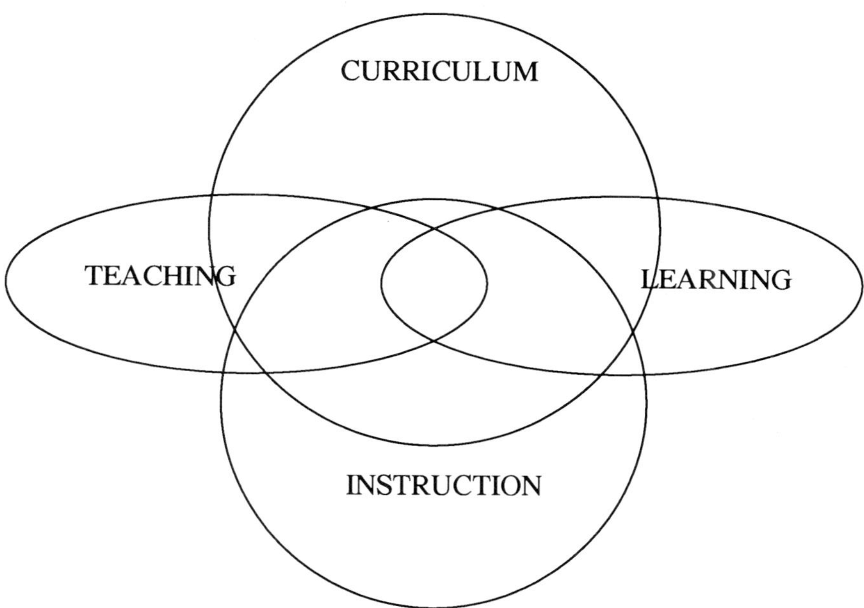

Figure 2. A convergent system model applied to physical education teacher education (adapted from J.B. MACDONALD's, action space of four systems; curriculum, instruction, teaching, learning, 1965, 4).

Note, however, that the four systems overlap. Each shares some space with each other, some space with two others, and one space with all others. Theoretically, this small shadowed space represents that ideal point of convergence where curriculum intentions are actually in operation in the instructional setting through effective teaching actions as evidenced by student outcomes which match programmatic intentions. Accepting that this space could be larger or smaller depending upon a myriad of conditions which affect these systems and those who interact within them, provides the challenge for teacher education program design and research.

Theory into Practice: An Exemplar of PETE Program Redesign

We began in 1989 with the basic notion that teacher development is essentially a process which is transformative in nature, and that instruction would necessarily be directed at developing student "know how", if we were to be able to move toward the goal of "authentic assessment"; that is, assessing student performances grounded in the reality of teacher work. This required that we focus especially on the instructional system, that space previously referred to, which we have often passed over or included as part of either the teaching or curriculum systems. One of our major objectives was to redesign the instructional system in order to achieve instructional dynamics which would indeed help students not only know about teaching, but "know how to teach". We call this concept "authentic instruction"; that is, instruction which is interactive and experiential, and which seeks to facilitate (1) higher order thinking; (2) professionalization of attitudes and values; (3) depth of knowledge: (4) connectedness with the world beyond the university classroom; (5) substantive conversation with and among students; and (6) social and professional support for student achievement.

These objectives, we believe, are the means by which students can be helped to develop more sophisticated "pedagogical schemata", a concept advanced by POSNER (1985), SHULMAN (1986) and TAMIR (1988). These schemata have been defined as ... "the complex cognitive structures that include both theoretical and practical knowledge and an understanding of the interrelatedness of these knowledge sources for informing judgement and action. (BARNES, 1987, 7). Consequently, it logically followed that teachers with more fully developed schemata would have a better understanding of the teaching-learning transaction and are therefore more likely to be effective. We further agreed that the instructional process from the outset must be one which was interdisciplinary, team-based and non-linear, reflecting as much as possible the broadest range of interdisciplinary expertise.

The major assumption which explicitly guided our work called for a more unified faculty team approach to teacher development at Adelphi. Consequently, the Teacher Development Team (TDT) was created and we named the overarching internal collaborative process we sought to achieve, "colligation"; literally meaning to tie or bind together. The team (a mechanism for building consensus) is comprised of eight full-time faculty members, with specialized training representing the sub-disciplines of human movement, who collectively are also content/method experts in dozens of physical activity areas. The team meets weekly or bi-weekly focusing on curricular, instructional, and assessment issues related to the development of preservice and inservice teachers. The far right column in Table 1 (see appendix) depicts the continuous team-oriented approach, which anchors the teacher development process.

Table 1 also provides a summary of the conceptual framework for the present program, and includes selected course composites and key program features and components. The TDT developed and organized the program framework around four interdependent and complimentary program components underscored in the second column from the right. Taken together the components express a systemic view of, and attention to the means by which the goals of professional teacher development may be attained. These components reflect the Teacher Development Team's concern for addressing issues of socialization effects as a function of the instruction system, using infusion and integration strategies for achieving programmatic outcomes linked to our intentions to develop teaching competence, and reflective teaching as an on-going professional process.

We are now engaged in our own programmatic research process, and are collecting data with respect to the effects of our systemic efforts especially as it pertains to the six "authentic instruction" related objectives discussed earlier. Unpublished studies by two Adelphi colleagues have provided some interesting data regarding our teacher education intentions at adelphi and the outcomes which seem to have been achieved. We are now fully committed to this type of on-going programmatic research since it provides us with data for analytic review and new insights which may help us to better do our work.

References

BARNES, H.O.: The conceptual basis for thematic teacher education programs. In: Journal of Teacher Education, 1987, 38 (4), 13-18.

BARRETT, K.R.; ALLISON, P.D.; BELL, R.: What preservice physical education teachers see in an unguided field experience: A follow-up study. In: Journal of Teaching in Physical Education, 1987, 7, 12-21.

BARRETTE, G.T.: Discipline profession gridlock in physical education: Implications for teacher education reform. In: D. ELDAR; U. SIMIRI (Eds.): Integration or Diversification of Physical Education and Sport Studies. Wingate Israel: Emmanuel Gill Publishing House, 1990, 147-156.

BELKA, D.: What preservice physical educators observe about lessons in progressive field experiences. In: Journal of Teaching in Physical Education, 1988, 7, 311-326.

CRUM, B.: Conventional thought and practice in physical education: Problems of teaching and implications for change. In: Quest, 1993, 32 (1), 54.

DODDS, P.: Trainees field experiences and socialization into teaching. In: T.J. TEMPLIN; P.G. SCHEMPP (Eds.): Socialization into Physical Education: Learning to Teach. Indianapolis: Benchmark Press, 1989, 81-104.

FIORENTINO, L.H.: Dimensions of programmatic effects: Qualitative analysis of student perceptions. Presented at AIESEP World

Congress Physical Education and Sport '94 Changes and Challenges 24-28 June 1994, Berlin.

GRAHAM, K.C.; HOHN, R.C.; WEINER, P.H.; WOODS, A.M.: Prospective pete students, pete student teachers and clinical model teachers in a university teacher education program. In: Journal of Teaching in Physical Education, 1993, 12 (2), 161-179.

KOWALSKI, E.M.: A comparative analysis of preservice students's attitudes towards teaching individuals with disabilities. Presented at AIESEP World Congress Physical Education and Sport '94 Changes and Challenges 24-28 June 1994, Berlin.

LAWSON, H.: Toward a model of teacher socialization in physical education: The subjective warrant, recruitment and teacher education. In: Journal of Teaching in Physical Education, 1983, 2(3), 1-16.

MACDONALD, J.B.: Educational models for instruction. In: J.B. MACDONALD, R.R. LEEPER (Eds.): Theories of Instruction, Washington, D.C.: Association for Supervision and Curriculum Development, 1965, 1-7.

O'HANLEN, J.; WANZILAK: Physical education: A professional field. In: Quest, 1980, 32 (1), 512-59.

POSNER, G.J.: Field experiences: A guide to reflective teaching. New York: Longman 1985.

SHULMAN, L.S.: Those who understand: Knowledge growth in teaching. In: Educational Researcher, 1986, 5 (2), 1-14.

TAMIR, P.: Subject matter and related pedagogical knowledge in teacher education. In: Teaching and Teacher Education, 1988, 4, 99-110.

WHITEHEAD, A.N.: Aim of Education. A Mentor Book. New York: The New American Library, 1949, 157-158.

Table 1. Physical Education Teacher Preparation Program Framework
The Development of Identity and Career

Professional induction socialization begins in workplace

- Student exits from program - program socialization process ends

	PROGRAM COURSE COMPOSITE	KEY PROGRAM FEATURE	KEY PROGRAM FOCUS	COLLIGATION PROCESS
year 4 ↑	Core values & actions course, student teaching professional seminar	Support-PE (collaboration with practitioners in school districts-PETE advisory board)	**INDUCTION** (pre-induction phase) into the profession application of knowledge and reflection on teaching	TDT COLLABORATION
year 3 ↑	University core and education sequence, PE curriculum and teaching courses, PE theory and practicum	Support-PE (collaboration with practitioners in school districts-PETE advisory board)	**INTEGRATION** of theoretical and practical knowledge and reflection on teaching	TDT COORDINATION

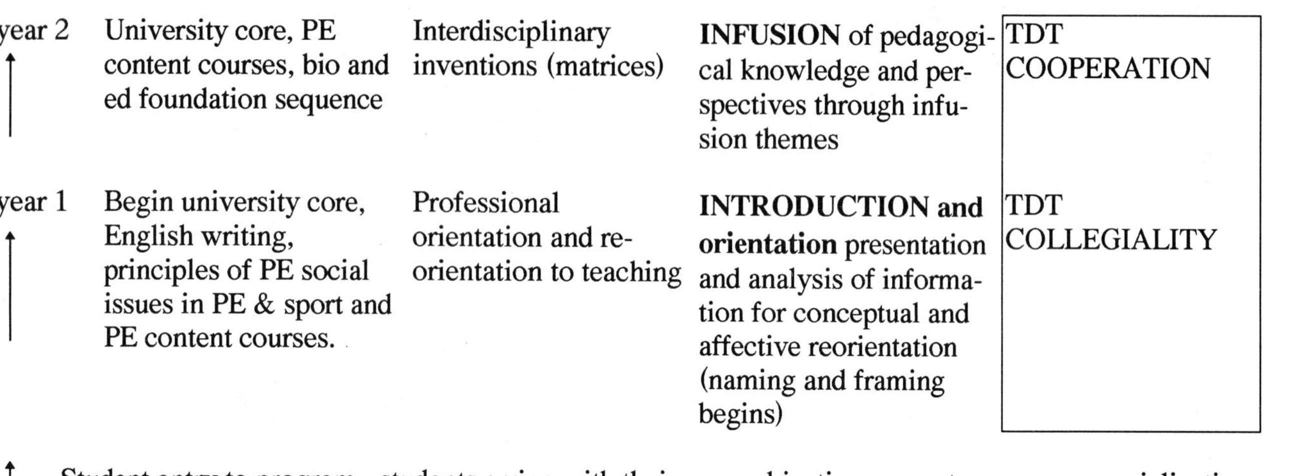

year 2 ↑	University core, PE content courses, bio and ed foundation sequence	Interdisciplinary inventions (matrices)	**INFUSION** of pedagogical knowledge and perspectives through infusion themes	TDT COOPERATION
year 1 ↑	Begin university core, English writing, principles of PE social issues in PE & sport and PE content courses.	Professional orientation and re-orientation to teaching	**INTRODUCTION and orientation** presentation and analysis of information for conceptual and affective reorientation (naming and framing begins)	TDT COLLEGIALITY

↑ Student entry to program - students arrive with their own subjective warrants - program socialization process begins

↑ socialization experience in physical education - apprenticeship of observation (elementary, middle school and high school)

Susan Capel

The Impact of a Changing External Environment on Physical Education Teacher Training

This paper is more about what we are not doing than about what we are doing. It looks at the influence of the wider environment on physical education (PE) and what is likely to happen if we do not consider this in what we are doing on a day-to-day basis. It focuses on England and Wales, although I hope people from other countries can relate to what is being said. It provides a context for the challenge facing the profession into the year 2000 and beyond. We need to organise to meet this challenge. Does it provoke thought about challenges facing you, and how can you organise to meet these challenges?

Introduction

There has been some dissatisfaction with the outcomes of schooling in England and Wales in recent years, and this is no doubt the same in many other countries. There are many reasons for this dissatisfaction, but perhaps one of the major ones is the inability of schools and education to adapt quickly enough to keep up with the rapidly changing demands of society, particularly at a time of rapid environmental change. Teachers and the quality of teaching are convenient targets for criticism for the perceived failings of schooling. It follows that if teachers are criticised and the quality of teaching is questioned, there is also criticism about the quality of teacher education. This paper considers the impact of some aspects of a changing external environment in the 1990s on PE Initial Teacher Training (ITT) in England and Wales.

Factors Influencing Change in Education

Social Versus Political Change

The external environment is generally described as social, technological, economic and political environments. In the long term, social changes are likely to be the most influential factors, offering the greatest opportunities but also posing the greatest threats. However, political changes, often with accompanying economic changes, tend to have the greatest impact in the short term. The political influence on education is especially important because much of the funding for education is from public funds. Higher Education in England and Wales has become subject to greater control by government as more of its funding has been received from government. Thus, the influence of the government as a stakeholder in education, including higher education and ITT, is very important.

Stakeholders

All education institutions are accountable to a number of internal and external stakeholders, including students, parents, employers, government, and society itself. The interests of these different and often competing stakeholders have to be balanced. However, some stakeholders, e.g., powerful external stakeholders such as the government, have a greater influence than others, e.g., less powerful internal stakeholders such as staff and students in an institution. This influence results in institutions reacting in specific ways, and perhaps even ignoring the needs of some stakeholders.

The JARRETT report (1985) noted that 'despite the constitutional autonomy of universities, their freedom of action is significantly limited in practice', and this includes freedom over ITT. This limit on action comes largely from Government legislation. Political and economic developments continue to reduce freedom to act even further and today politicians have a greater influence over what happens in education. It seems most likely that this trend will continue because, and I quote, 'the Government is determined to keep educational reform at the top of the political agenda' (The Economist, 1991).

Political Influences

So, what are these specific political factors affecting education in England and Wales? There are obviously too many to include in a presentation of this length, but three of those that are considered to be most influential will be looked at here. These are:

Funding
Accountability
Managerialism

Obviously the specific detail of these is unique in England and Wales, but they may help you identify appropriate issues in your own country. Each of these will be considered briefly in turn.

Funding

Throughout the 1980s and into the 1990s there has been a planned campaign to reduce public expenditure, and funding for education in general and higher education in particular has not been spared in this. In the later part of this period this has coincided with a period of recession throughout industrial society. This has resulted in a climate in which Ministers and government departments have to vigorously justify and defend their spending requirements and more carefully account for public money. Value for money is an integral part of this funding regime. This has led to educational institutions also having to demonstrate efficiency and value for money.

One area where government has long tried to control spending is in trying to train only the number of different types of teachers it projects will be needed to meet the needs of the education system. This system has been criticised because projections have often been inaccurate, but also because it appears that there has been so much concern with the number of teachers to be trained, that the content of the training, its effectiveness and its position within higher education in general have been forgotten (WARNOCK, 1989, 100).

The debate about methods of teacher training, for example, the difference between four year concurrent training (the Bachelor of Education (BEd) degree or BA/BSc and Qualified Teacher Status (QTS)) or a three year degree course plus a one (or two) year Post Graduate Certificate in Education (PGCE) training is heightened in the current climate of funding with its focus on efficiency and value for money, and therefore on the costs of different methods of ITT. The PGCE course is seen to have several advantages for the government. It allows numbers of teachers in training to be altered more easily to meet the changing demand for teachers and is also considered to be a cheaper method of training teachers. The number of students following this route is therefore likely to increase.
But what of four year concurrent courses which to date have trained the majority of primary teachers and many PE teachers? PE is one of only a few Secondary subjects in which teachers are trained through a BEd or BA/BSc plus QTS route.

There are those who feel that in this climate four year concurrent courses are dead, especially for practical subjects such as PE which have heavy resource demands. However, the general perception is that concurrent training is likely to survive, at least for primary teacher training. It is, however, very likely that four year courses will be reduced to three years, within which there must be more time than on present courses spent in school. This has implications for PE ITT at both secondary and primary levels. For courses training teachers for the secondary age range the debate is whether institutions will adopt three year courses or whether they will stop concurrent training, concentrating instead on the PGCE route. Some institutions with a long history of four year Secondary PE teacher training are opting already to stop such training. This decision is not being taken by physical educators but by departments of education and/or senior management who see four year courses as expensive or with an uncertain future, therefore want to move resources into other less expensive or more certain areas. Such decisions do not take account of the effectiveness of different routes of training teachers. Often sport science degree courses are very theoretical, therefore students following a sport science degree, plus a one year PGCE course have little time in the teacher training year to develop underpinning knowledge and understanding of practical aspects of the subject. They rely on their own experience as participants and coaches, and coaching qualifications gained. They, thus, focus on their areas of interest and lack knowledge and understanding in other areas. Their experience and interest is usually in one or more games, and the lack of knowledge and understanding is often in dance, gymnastics, swimming, outdoor and adventurous activities, and athletics, all an integral part of the national curriculum in physical education. As yet there has been little national debate about appropriate routes through sport science degree courses for those wishing to go into teacher training.

Within primary ITT the debate is focusing on how to prepare teachers to teach the ten (eleven in Wales, including Welsh) subjects in the national curriculum within the available time and resources. A statutory number of hours are required in training teachers to teach the core national curriculum subjects of English, Maths and Science (100 each). When the remaining time is divided between the other seven subjects there seems to be little recognition that account should be taken of different demands on students of different subjects, e.g. common teaching methods that could be used to teach Geography and History, and the safety implications of PE. In many institutions students are expected to be qualified to teach the six national curriculum areas of activity included in PE (athletics, dance, games, gymnastics, outdoor and adventurous activities, and swimming), having undertaken a course of a total of 30 hours or less in their ITT course. The current proposal that a primary four year ITT course be reduced to three years, with a greater proportion of time being spent in school, is likely to exacerbate this situation further. Questions about whether teachers will be adequately prepared even to take a class safely, let alone be able to teach pupils anything worthwhile over a period of time, must be asked. This could have tremendous implications for the teaching of PE in primary schools. It could, for example, lead to PE being taken out of the compulsory curriculum, or to coaches being used to teach sports within curriculum time, both of which beg the question, at what cost to attitudes and the health of our children?

Changes in funding of education, other than teacher education, also have an impact. For example, the Government policy of Local Management of Schools, in which schools are allocated their own budget, and its policy to allow schools to leave local authority control and become grant maintained, with their funding coming directly from central government, has given schools control over their own budgets. School managers therefore look very carefully at how the money is spent to ensure efficiency and value for money. Again, decisions in many schools affecting PE are not being taken by physical educators but by senior management. Decisions made by management, as opposed to decisions made by subject specialists, therefore tend to assume greater importance. For example, it is cheaper to employ a number of different coaches, each to teach their own sport within the PE programme, than it is to employ a full-time PE teacher. Some schools are therefore taking this option. In such situations, PE teachers may spend less time teaching classes themselves than managing the diverse range of people being employed in the school. Staff may need staff development to acquire the necessary management skills. Tthey may also need to undertake joint development activities with the coaches to enable them to develop a shared philosophy for teaching a sport in a PE lesson. This impacts on ITT because teachers require a diverse range of skills, including management and negotiating skills. Several institutions now are changing, or considering changing, from having a traditional second teaching subject such as English or Mathematics to support PE as a main subject, to introducing options such as Community or Recreation Management, and Coach Education.

Accountability

All areas of education are becoming increasingly more accountable. This has implications for PE, e.g., accountability of schools. Local Education Authority (LEA) Advisers are increasingly taking on an inspectorial role. LEAs have reduced considerably the number of Advisers who were able, in the past, to help teachers by providing inservice education and training (INSET), either through courses or through visiting individual schools. This INSET helped new primary teachers overcome deficiencies not addressed in ITT, where they had very few hours in their ITT course devoted to PE. Inspectors do not have the remit to provide this professional development, therefore creating less opportunities for deficiencies remaining from ITT to be addressed.

Towards the end of the 1980s and in the 1990s the Council for the Accreditation of Teacher Education (CATE) indicated that institutional and professional autonomy had taken second place to accountability and central control (TAYLOR, 1989). Performance indicators, external audits etc. have been introduced to provide greater accountability, particularly to ensure that institutions demonstrate value for money in the use of resources. These have led to a further reduction in freedom of operation. Performance indicators as a means of accountability mostly measure output rather than outcome (e.g., how many people are dealt with rather than how good the teaching is), as efficiency in use of resources is easier to measure than whether stated objectives have been effectively achieved. For example, league tables are compiled of schools performance on National Curriculum tests set at ages 7, 11, 14 and 16, or of their truancy rates, or of graduation rates from Higher Education Institutions (HEIs). Further, increasing emphasis on accountability, through performance indicators, external audits etc., with a corresponding decreasing emphasis on the curriculum, could mean these define quality, therefore the definition of quality may become based on factors which are not purely educational.

As institutions become increasingly accountable to government for their funding, greater pressure is exerted on them to spend less, to reduce unit costs in order to be more efficient, and to maximise the use of scarce resources in order to be more cost-effective. Management in some institutions is putting pressure on some colleagues teaching PE in ITT because their courses are deemed to be expensive. In such instances the requirements for large spaces such as fields, gymnasiums and dance studies, as well as laboratory space for physiology and biomechanics, and for expensive equipment, along with high maintenance costs, are questioned, as management calculates how many students can be put into a space such as a gymnasium if it were to be converted into, say, a lecture theatre, and how much could be saved by introducing a course such as business studies which does not have such high resourcing costs. Thus, it appears that some HEIs are beginning to question the cost and viability of continuing to offer a PE ITT course.

Managerialism

The environment produced by the need for greater efficiency, value for money, and accountability has led to growing managerialism in British education. Some people in education have felt that this has been pushed from the outside by government ideology alongside a perceived distrust of educators as professional experts which is driving current educational policy. The result has been pressure to replace, or at least subordinate, professional and collegial values that have always been important in education, thereby modifying the values of educational institutions. This has resulted in professional responsibility being replaced by concepts of line management.

This ideology and perceived distrust of educators can be exemplified by the relatively recent involvement of the government in the curriculum as well as the funding of education. The school curriculum has become more determined by Government since the introduction of the national curriculum. This political input by the government has a significant impact on a subject such as PE as ministers and members of the public do not necessarily understand the different aims of PE and sport. When the national teams are not doing well (which seems to be a frequent occurrence these days!), the blame is laid at the door of PE teachers. However, when the national teams are doing well, PE teachers never get any of the credit. Thus, the influence by the government is overt in PE, where the Minister for Sport lobbied for the inclusion of team games in all schools, especially those sports for which the results of the national teams are of concern, including, cricket, hockey, netball, rugby and soccer, without seemingly understanding the difference between PE and sport.

At present ITT must meet certain criteria but has flexibility over how it does this and what else to include in the curriculum. As debate about the curriculum in schools is being exhausted, at least for a while, with the review of the national curriculum (DEARING Report, 1994), it is likely that the debate will focus more forcefully on ITT to ensure that newly qualified teachers can teach the national curriculum. The governments proposal for the Teacher Training Agency (TTA), to have oversight of ITT, is currently going through Parliament. This is generally felt to be one way for government to increase its control over ITT, through funding and influence over the curriculum.

Another recent development of ITT in England and Wales is the promotion of school based training, both by increasing the amount of time students spend in school, and by allowing a range of providers other than HEIs to be involved in ITT. These are perceived to be due to government ideology and the perceived distrust of educators, designed to break down the perceived monopoly or ideologies held by staff involved in ITT and decrease the influence of such staff on students. Schools, local authority advisers, the Open University, industry, private groups and other agencies (e.g., the Sports Council), can provide ITT courses, either in partnership with an HEI or 'by going it alone'. This will result in many different models of provision and have implications for such things as freedom over the design of courses and the curriculum, and ensuring the quality of courses.

There is a particular problem with school based ITT in subjects such as PE, where a wide range of different activities are taught. This is especially acute on one year courses. Students only experience what is being offered in the school at the time they are on teaching practice. Therefore, as different activities tend to operate at specific times of year, it is possible that students will not be able to teach or observe the full range of national curriculum areas of activity during their training year. Further, much of the practice in schools is very traditional, therefore students may see a limited range of teaching styles and good practice in such a system of training.

What can the PE profession do about this?

Thus, political influences impact on PE in a number of ways. The government are already heavily involved in education, including ITT, and are likely to become more involved if we allow them to. The teaching profession, including PE, is losing control over aspects of education, partly because of our own action, or put more correctly, inaction. This trend must be reversed. This can only be done by working on several different fronts at the same time, both in ITT in general and PE in particular.

First, it is important that the public perception of the teaching profession is raised. This, in turn, would help to raise the public perception of ITT. It is not enough for people within the profession to perceive that the quality of teachers or the quality of the training they have received has remained good and has been effective in producing teachers who are able to meet the demands of schools today. So far, we seem to have failed to convince others of this. We must work on trying to change these perceptions.

In order to do this, the teaching profession must be seen as one which can be trusted with its great responsibility. The values which underpin teachers professionalism should be made explicit and be open to scrutiny (WARNOCK, 1989). She went on to say that 'it is essential that teachers should unite in a common professional enterprise, and impose on themselves common professional standards by forming a General Teaching Council. If a General Teaching Council were to be set up, its first task would be to establish criteria for good practice. .... : It would thus have a strong influence on the training of teachers and would, indeed, be empowered to lay down a common curriculum for this training' (132-133).

Generally, neither teacher trainers nor the PE profession have been involved in political debate. As they have been busy getting on with the job at hand, ignoring the external environment, and particularly the political environment, the Government has been able to influence the education system without much discussion with the profession. It is difficult to be proactive in a highly politicised climate because the uncertain nature of political change demands a reaction in order to survive. This is not to say that we should not be proactive. Quite the reverse is, in fact, the case. It is essential for the PE profession and people involved in PE ITT to become more political, and more proactive, politicking to try to influence Government policy and legislation about education directly, but also about other elements of the external environment which influence education. It is not enough to just be aware of the impact of political changes and respond appropriately, we must take the initiative and become an external environment for the Government.

It is no good ITT courses only producing students who can teach well. It is important that PE teachers understand the external environment in which they work, including the political environment, to enable them to operate most effectively in a changing role in a rapidly changing environment. In order for them to do this successfully it is important that during their ITT course students are made aware of the changing external environment and begin to develop the skills, including political skills, they will need to survive in it.

The government appears to have been deliberately trying to break up the system of ITT, and the influence of HEIs on ITT, for example, by increasing funding to encourage other/new providers of ITT. In order to counter this trend, and to develop effective schemes for training teacher, there must be an effective partnership between an HEI and schools at a local level, in all aspects of the planning and delivery of courses. This will enable higher education, school tutors and mentors, and any other professionals involved in the training of PE teachers to become well-trained for their particular role as they understand and agree on what they are trying to achieve, and develop a shared philosophy about teaching PE. This model may eventually also be applicable to the induction of beginning teachers and inservice education and training. This requires the sharing of ideas rather than 'we know best' attitudes. This may require staff development. Up to now partnerships may not have been entered into as whole-heartedly and fully as is needed. This must change as full partnership is required for the effective development of courses.

Finally, a range of strategies, focusing both internally and externally, have to be used to resist and change environmental demands. Any strategies, tactics, programmes, procedures and processes developed by educational administrators and physical educators to respond to, and manage, the environment must be based on a broad view of the external environment, the general as well as the specific.

To conclude:

> 'Tensions between contribution and control, autonomy and accountability, are not new phenomena. The universities today are facing dilemmas which are not dissimilar in nature to those which confronted the ancient medieval universities. It is the extent of the problem and the sophistication of the society in which they find themselves that are new' (SHINN, 1989, 19).

Thus, problems that PE ITT in England and Wales is facing in the 1990s are not new, but are perhaps larger and more complex than in the past. This is in part the result of the changing social environment. As I indicated at the beginning of this paper, the social environment is likely to have the biggest influence on PE ITT in the long term. Therefore, we should not forget the social environment in our attempts to be proactive and, at the same time, to respond to the changing external environment, particularly the political environment, in which we are currently operating.

The challenge is clear in England and Wales. We need to organise to meet this challenge. Is the challenge for you clear, are you organised to meet the challenge, or how can you organise to meet it?

References

DEARING, R.: The national curriculum and its assessment: The final report (The Dearing Report). London: HMSO 1994.

JARRETT: Report of the Steering Committee for Efficiency Studies in Universities (The Jarrett Report). London: HMSO 1985.

SHINN, C.: Whose university? In: STEPHENS, M.D.: Universities, education and the national economy. London: Routledge 1989.

TAYLOR, W. Education and the economy. In: STEPHENS, M.D.: Universities, education and the national economy. London: Routledge 1989.

'Teenager's Charter'. The Economist, 18 May 1991, Volume 319.

WARNOCK, M.: A common policy for education. Oxford: Oxford University Press 1989.

Anthony G.J. Pettit

Teacher-Student-With-Students-Teachers: Justice, Compassion and Interrelatedness for a New Age of Physical Education Teacher Education

> 'Grade three is going out for physical education, the teacher has three large balls, three skipping ropes and three hoops. I watch with interest to see the creative use of these articles, but no - first the balls, then the hoops and finally the ropes are used for relay races - three teams, ten children per team. I am tempted to start my stop-clock to test the waiting time both during each activity, and as each 'race' finishes, while winners are announced, and teams 'stand straight' and 'quiet'.

The vignette above depicts a situation that is not only an everyday occurrence within Northern Territory primary schools, but worse, this same situation is regarded as 'normal' by students entering EDN 311 which is a compulsory five credit point unit in first semester of the third year of a three year diploma of teaching course at the Northern Territory University.

This paper reports on aspects of a much larger study (PETTIT, 1994) which attempted to change teaching and learning within a physical education methodology class and develop a "New Age Pedagogy" which would increase student awareness of these issues while at the same time introduce them to ways of knowing, ways of teaching that foreground these same issues. In broad terms, the study was about the need for change in physical education teacher education (PETE) if future graduates are to be effective in preparing citizens of the future.

With increased scientisation of physical education and a reliance on sport education and fitness education as models of curriculum,

teachers are failing to produce 'physically literate' students as the stated aims of physical education suggest that they should As lecturers in (PETE) we have compunded the problem by failing to see the need for change, and I believe that it is our responsibility to convince pre-service teachers of the need to be involved in key social issues such as freedom, justice and equality.
Given that the experience depicted in the vignette is accepted as 'normal', and the fact that for many students, EDN 311 is the first unit of physical education they have had to enrol in during their study for the diploma, many arrive with attitudes related to physical activity and how it should be conducted in schools, that are the antithesis of these notions of justice, freedom and equality. In spite of this however, most students are receptive to alternate approaches which they perceive as being a means whereby the children they will teach can have the opportunity for more positive experiences than they (the students) have experienced.

In developing a new pedagogical vision, this study posits the view that critical theory provides a framework for understanding a number of educational traditions which can act as discourses of critical pedagogy and as such provide lenses for viewing a New Age pedagogy. To operationalize these discourses however, we require new ways of knowing and in particular new teaching strategies that allow for the formation of a different relationship between teacher and student.

An important aspect of the study therefore was to model teaching strategies that are well to the right of a teaching continuum (REINSMITH, 1992) and were more facilitative and elicitive rather than transmissive as is the traditional model of university teaching. In doing so, it was hypothesised that a feminization of the teaching act would occur (REINSMITH, 1992) and this would have positive outcomes for the majority of students in terms of demonstrating an ethic of care. To this end, I intentionally set out as part of the project to create and demonstrate 'counter-patriarchic practices' as proposed in the feminist literature (for example LEWIS & SIMON, 1986).

In adopting a post-structural view of research, the study does not make claims or provide objective categories, but rather seeks to tell the story of teaching a New Age pedagogy as students experience it. This is done through 'narratives of experience' which provide a number of inferences about teaching future PETE students. These narratives were based on the portfolios, interviews and anecdotal evidence of current students, as well as reflections on data that had been distributed back to students who had recently completed EDN 311 and a number of ex-students.

Three perspectives, the person I am, the person I hope to be, and the changing me, were considered at a number of levels (adapted from LATHER, 1991), so that students could create their own meaning from the data based on their experience within the unit. These levels are:- an idealist view, my own interpretations of the data which consciously or unconsciously highlight aspects I consider the most important; a reflective view - a reading of, and reaction to my idealist view by current students; and a deconstructive view - a reaction to the raw data by a group of students who have completed the unit The three levels are reported on here, but in the interests of space only one aspect of the narratives is considered viz. the response to more facilitative types of teaching and an ethic of care.

1. In obtaining an idealist view, students share their biographies as a stepping stone to a consideration of 'alternatives', the relationship aspect of teaching and learning is brought to the surface as students remember in terms of how they were treated rather than the activities.

> 'For some reason whenever school P.E. is mentioned, my mind thinks of 'softball'. My teacher was a keen softball player herself, and on Fridays (P.E. day) I often found myself lining up behind one of two captains, whoever was the least reluctant to choose me. ... suffice to say I dreaded Fridays'. Audrey.

When students try a more facilitative method of teaching themselves and practice giving a little control rather than taking all of it, they are often amazed at the results

> 'At After School Care today I had the opportunity to put some dance teaching into practice. ... I suggested that they (the children) may like to devise their own dances. The response that followed was overwhelming! They became so enthusiastic, ran inside and raided the dress-up box for costumes. They said they wanted it to "be real". ... I was really pleased (although very surprised) because the boys actually dressed up too! I was astounded when they came back in dresses and put together their own dance sequences. Although I was aiming to encourage them to form their own dances, I certainly didn't expect them to "dress-up". I am hooked on this way of teaching!'
>
> Gail.

As well as coming to terms with these new ways of knowing and new ways of teaching, students indicate that they feel empowered to look critically at the methods and actions of the teachers they work with in schools and make comparisons with their own biographies and what they are learning in EDN 311.

> 'My recent prac opened my eyes to two of the problems we had been discussing in class - the use of PE for reward and organisation so that all participate. ... We were to play a modified cricket. 50 children - four teams. Team 1 fielded while team 2 batted then they swapped at "half-time" so that team 2 fielded and team 1 batted. Teams 3 and 4 sat and watched - becoming increasingly frustrated as time went on. I noticed numerous things. Firstly, bowlers were rotated, but "good" bowlers got more bowls than "not-so-good". Secondly a couple of children fielding spent more time looking around as they were not able to field - a couple of good cricketers did all the fielding. Thirdly, children in teams 3 and 4 were chastised repeatedly for restlessness. After sitting for 35mins, they went on to play - for 10 mins - with the promise that they would play first next week. I was horrified and tried to suggest that two separate activities be organised - No, two teachers were needed to supervise the game! - I am a better teacher than this already!'
>
> Carol.

For many students, such comparisons entail a struggle to determine the person they are in relation to new methodology and how this impinges upon their experiences and their 'taken-for-granted' ways of doing things. By struggling with themselves in this way, a certain frustration is also apparent in that students have to come to terms with 'ways of knowing' that overturn the view they have accepted as 'truth'.

> 'Why is the earth round? Why is the sky blue? What is the difference between PE and Sport? Is there a difference? ... We were all trying to get inside your mind and say the things you were thinking. But to think for ourselves, not just re-gurgitate what we thought you wanted to hear, Oh this is a (sic) admirable goal. So why does it still make me agro when I think about this week's tutorial? I could hazard a statement that it is what I have been conditioned "socialised" to expect through all of my education--- The teacher has the right answer and I'm not right until I say what the teacher believes is right. The teacher will keep plugging away until we get it right. I know why I feel this way, it's because of fear. Fear that my opinion may be wrong or devalued. I have to take a *risk!* ... I never realised what it would feel like to be on the receiving end of a teaching strategy that encourages thinking for yourself. I will be aware now of how good that can make you feel'
>
> Naomi.

If students can overcome their initial feelings of negativity toward the area of physical education, they begin to see possibilities for 'changing the system'. This development takes place either as a reaction to what they have already seen in schools as part of their practice teaching, or they see the possibilities of giving children in their care better experiences than they had themselves.

> 'One thing I particularly noticed about the dance session was the emphasis that was put on allowing us (the children) to explore rather than inflicting teacher ideas on us. Working in small groups allowed for creativity, group co-operation and inter-relationships. ... I've noticed that the lecturer tends to stand back and observe, rather than hovering over each group and demanding results or inflicting

his ideas on the group. This had a lot to do with the success of the session' Genevieve.

In the example below Micky relates how the attitudes about physical education which she is picking up from the class sessions, are motivating her to change what she has seen during practice teaching and which she thinks should not be happening.

'Wow! Today's PE workshop has left me with very positive feelings about opening new doors in school PE. I feel that yes I can make a difference about how children will react to, and feel about, participating in physical activities. I was beginning to feel that this area of the curriculum was neglected. But I feel as though I've just been kick started into realising that attitudes about PE can be changed. ... For example whilst on my last prac ... I noticed that PE was not an integral part of the daily (or weekly) curriculum, but rather something that is put up as a "bribe". The teacher would say something like "If you all work very hard and very quiet all day we will play basketball this afternoon. To me PE should be part of every day, not used as a reward system' Micky.

Almost all students completing this unit say or demonstrate that they have changed in some way. For some, as in the first two examples this change is related to how they will teach the activities of physical education:

a) 'From this unit, I have come to believe that a child's ability to cope adequately as an adult, has much to do with their learning environment. I firmly believe that a child must gradually be taught to think for themselves, a teacher can aid this process by giving students a choice of a variety of tasks or responses. ... I agree with the unit philosophy that children should be excited about what they have learned and what they are doing. ... In this way basic movement skills ... can be acquired then used in routines and challenging problem solving situations. My lessons in movement will I hope now be - not definite steps or directions, but open ended statements calling for indefinite responses' Genevieve.

b) 'I am at the point where to me it seems that the crucial element of a successful physical activity program, especially at school level, is therefore not necessarily *what* particular physical activity events the children are exposed to, but the *manner* in which that exposure occurs. That manner is best defined as the quality of interpersonal relationships and sensitivity to others' feelings, abilities and limitations that unfolds within the event, enabling each child to feel inwardly comfortable. ... Positive relationships developed in the physical domain will impact upon children's confidence and ability in all other life pursuits' Rhonda.

For other students, the 'changing me' is represented by their philosophy, how they feel they have become empowered as agents of change, or the methodological changes they have established in their own teaching of physical activity or coaching.

'Last Thursday I began a different class ... I ran through a few movements and then asked them what else they could do. The girls were quite shocked that I had actually asked them ... they were not used to being asked ... shocked once again when I put on a tape ... and asked which piece of music they preferred. They were ecstatic ... and ideas began pouring fourth (sic) ... their excitement was certainly infectious and I am hoping that because the girls had the opportunity to contribute, and will continue to have, they will take great pride in what they are doing. It was not until this tutorial that I really thought about why the girls were so enthusiastic ... I had handed over control' Katherine.

'(This unit) ... has made me realise the great need for a teacher to be a researcher, to improve one's teaching style. While reading, I have come across examples of things that I have experienced, but previously did not have an answer for' Hannah.

'Since commencing this unit, ... my perspective of physical education and working with peers and children has changed. The teachers in a school all teach different subjects, however the underlying rationale must necessarily apply across the board. That rationale is based on respect for each child as an individual, acknowledgement of his (sic) capacities and an unflagging encouragement to succeed. As a consequence it is clear that what a teacher teaches, is by no means as important as how he teaches it. ... my concept has changed considerably - and so has my philosophy. I now accept that physical education is another subject in the core curriculum. I now also accept that the teacher ... (of PE) ... has the same responsibilities as any other teacher - the students come first...'

Ira.

2. To obtain a 'reflected view' of the data students who had completed EDN 311 in semester 1 and then during semester 2 were asked to reflect on what I had written about them, and how I had used aspects of their portfolio writing and quotes. Within their reflections students acknowledge that the unit and the teaching and learning strategies are different, and that they feel they have the power to 'change the system'.

'We can become too theorised if not given the opportunity to reflect and keep in touch with our own thoughts and interpretations of what we read or what a lecturer is putting forward. As I said in my portfolio, I found it hard at times and emotionally draining trying to come to terms with my own ways of learning and knowing. I hadn't realised how restrictive my formal ways of learning had been until I was challenged in this unit and then attempted to learn something for myself. I realised in this unit that no-one judges you except yourself. You pick up on your own attitudes and feelings when you reflect on your actions. You are then able to branch out and see things in hopefully a wider and richer perspective - that is what I think I have gained most from EDN 311'

Zeena.

'As an ex student of EDN 311, I am able to state with full conviction that the unit altered drastically two thought processes or conditioned beliefs like no other unit has done during my three years at university. The first relates to a style of lecturing and teaching that needs to become more prevalent in universities, schools and other educational institutions, and the second relates to an altered view of teaching physical education. ... Carla.

'EDN 311 provided many opportunities for me to really think and be able to reflect on that thinking. There was no need to think about what you (the lecturer) was thinking and even if there was a felt need by some students, you very cleverly disguised exactly what you were thinking at any one point in time and you stood back and viewed our participation (you certainly demonstrated your phrase 'teacher-off-centre')' Maria.

'On reading these chapters I believe that one of the aspects of the unit which makes it so appealing is that we are able to discuss what and how we feel and are then challenged to support our feelings. How many other units really give us the chance to do this? How many other units really give us the opportunity to get down to the nitty gritty, to challenge assumptions and to end the unit with a feeling of accomplishment' Peter.

'I found it quite easy to reflect in my portfolio because you really handed tutorials over to us and although we often left with mixed feelings, or feelings of confusion we quickly realized that we really could give our own ideas and there really wasn't just one answer that the lecturer expected us to arrive at sooner or later. ... so much knowledge 'came out' of each student (just like your 'mid-wife' model of teaching) as you very cleverly chose the content of the readings and lectures to challenge what we thought' Katherine.

3. In seeking to provide a 'deconstructive view' of the study, the aim has been to take an approach 'where both researcher and researched become, ... "the changer and the changed" (LATHER, 1991, 56). To obtain such a view, students who had completed the unit prior to this study were asked to read the raw data and react to it. The following is a small section of a playlet constructed from the words of these students and collected through individual writings, conversations, and from a taped discussion session.

DB: Shall we move on to the next question which is about the students feeling that they have the power to bring about change?

S: I want to say something about L's comment. You know they may be thinking about how to change the status quo, but be too scared to actually do it. One student talked about prac in her journal and said she was observing a very structured authoritarian PE lesson but when she said something to the teacher she was shunned because she was only a 'prac' student. I think that if they feel Tony is encouraging them and supporting them - like I said before, they will make changes when they can, even if it is not straight away.

L: OK, but they have to feel that they really do have the power to make change. I want to refer to a piece of writing that really demonstrates this aspect. This particular student did not enter the unit with the attitude that the way she did things in physical education was right and anyone else's ideas were wrong. Rather, right from her very first entry, she was reflective and open to questioning her own philosophy. This student is a coach of a sport that encourages children to strive to be the best. As the student has been involved in this sport from a very young age, this aspect was something she did not question. However, when reading her portfolio, it was obvious that the issues raised in the unit caused some questions to be asked. By the end of the semester, the student had progressed through an on-going battle within herself as to whether all students should receive recognition for their efforts within the sport or whether only the ones who had excelled should be recognized. We finally saw her pose this question to higher 'authorities' within the sport and how the problem was eventually solved. Because she learnt that sensitivity to the needs of every child is important she discovered the power to bring about change that emphasized moral, ethical and political dimensions.

Where am I now? I began this project in the hope that I could model a pedagogy of justice and compassion and together with my students look at alternatives for the teaching of physical education in terms of 'what's worth knowing and what's worth doing' (HELLISON and TEMPLIN, 1991). I believe that there is an increased awareness of the problematic nature of teaching from the way students talk about and view teaching in schools. Importantly my own perspective has shifted also in that I see, through student eyes, more of the difficulties under which teachers work, their lack of opportunity to have in-service education and the lack of opportunity they have to experiment with new ideas.

An important outcome is that I believe students feel they are learning something of value and can relate to me as a teacher. This was demonstrated by the fact that along with several staff members, student representatives from EDN 311 nominated me for the 1993 Northern Territory University Teaching Excellence Award. In doing so, I believe students and staff are indicating a belief in the merits of 'New Age' pedagogy and to develop this I want to attend even more to teaching that gives justice, emancipation and an ethic of care. This in turn will lead to furthering of the notion of 'relationship' with students In that we (my students and myself) can really work toward a 'teaching presence' and a demonstated desire on my part to move well to the right of the continuum of teaching forms. In this way my goal remains -

> 'Through dialogue, the teacher-of-the-student and the student-of-the-teacher cease to exist and a new term emerges; teacher-student-with-students-teachers' (FREIRE, 1974, 67).

References

FREIRE, P.: Pedagogy of the Oppressed. New York: Seabury Press 1974.

HELLISON, D.; TEMPLIN, T.: A Reflective Approach to Teaching Physical Education. Champaign, Illinois: Human Kinetics 1991.

LATHER, P.: Getting Smart: Feminist Research and Pedagogy Within the Postmodern. New York: Routledge 1991.

LEWIS, M.; SIMON, R.I.: A discourse not intended for her: Learning and teaching within patriarchy. Harvard Educational Review, 1986, 56 (4), 457-472.

PETTIT, A.: A New Age Pedagogy in Teacher Education: Justice and Compassion as an Alternate Discourse in Pre-Service Physical Education. Unpublished PhD dissertation. Deakin University 1994.

REINSMITH, W.A.: Archetypal Forms in Teaching: A Continuum. Westport, Connecticut: Greenwood Press 1992.

Leslie R.T. Williams

Science in Physical Education and Sport in New Zealand: Changes and Challenges

As you know New Zealand is quite a small country situated about 1200 miles East of Australia. Its size is 268,100 square kilometres and the total population is about 3.5 million. There are six main university centres and the total number of students is 90,900.

Table 1. New Zealand University courses in Physical Education, Leisure, Recreation & Related Areas: Student Numbers and Percentages[a] (1994)

	All	PE Related Areas	
		Number	Per Cent
Auckland University	23,300	49	3.3
Waikato University	10,100	166	11.3
Massey University	28,300	Proposed	--
Victoria University	11,300	24	1.6
Lincoln University	3,400	289	19.6
University of Otago	14,500	944	64.1
Totals	90,900	1,472	--

[a] Per cent of the PE-related total (1,472)

The distribution among the universities as shown in Table 1 along with the distribution of those enroled in physical education, recreation, leisure and related areas. It can be seen that the School of Physical Education at the University of Otago has the highest absolute number of students and the highest percentage of specialist students, while the smallest programme is at the Tamaki campus of the University of Auckland where a new programme has just begun this year. A small programme is being proposed by Massey. So the oldest is the biggest and the youngest is the smallest.

In reviewing the state of scientific activity in sport and physical education in New Zealand, it is necessary to describe the formal programmes of study that are to be found. In doing so, a broad view is taken by initially including reference to recreation, leisure and sports medicine. A summary of the undergraduate and graduate programmes in the six main centres is given in Table 2.

Table 2. New Zealand University Courses in Physical Education, Leisure, Recreation and Related Areas

University	Course	Length	Majors
Auckland (1994)	BSc (Sports Science) BSc (Hons) Dip. Sport Medicine (proposed)	4 yrs 1 yr	Sports Science; Sport Psychology Sports Medicine
Waikato (1993)	Bachelor of Leisure Studies	3 yrs	Physical Education; Leisure Management; Sport Studies
Massey (Proposed)	Dip. sport Bachelor Business Studies (proposed)	1 yr 3 yrs	Sport Management; Coaching; Sport Management; Coaching
Victoria (1976)	MA (Applied)	2 yrs	Recreation & Leisure Studies

Lincoln (1987)	Bachelor of Parks & Recreation Management Bachelor of Parks & Rec. Management (Hons) PG Dip. Parks, Recreation & Tourism Masters of Parks & Recreation Management	3 yrs 4 yrs 1 yr 2 yrs or 1 year thesis	Ecology, Recreation Ecology, Recreation Ecology, Recreation, Tourism Ecology, Recreation; Tourism
Otago (1948)	Dip. Sports Studies BPhEd BPhEd (Hons) PG Dip. MPhEd PhD	2 yrs 4 yrs 1 yr 2 yrs or 1 yr thesis 3 yrs	Sports Studies, Fitness Management Kinesiology; Sport & Leisure Studies Professional Studies Kinesiology; Sport & Leisure Studies Kinesiology; Sport & Leisure Studies Kinesiology; Sport & Leisure Studies

In beginning with Auckland, we note that it is a new programme that is being established this year and that the qualification is not a full specialist one but is a set of selected papers forming one of the options for the Bachelor of Science degree. They have just begun with 10 papers and are entering a strong developmental and growth phase over the next few years.

The focus of the curriculum at Auckland is likely to remain on sport science with offerings in technology, business, psychology, management, administration and research.

Table 3. Comparison of Courses at Auckland and Otago

Proposed Courses at Auckland	Notes	Equivalent Courses at Otago
T711.101 Introductory Sports Science Technology	Similar to ..	PHSE 211 Biomechanics 1
T72.120 Sport, Business & Society	At Otago, there are 5 papers dealing with the topics listed in the one paper ..	PHSE 214 History of Sport 1 PHSE 216 Sociology of Sport 1 PHSE 314 History of Sport 2 PHSE 316 Sociology of Sport 2 PHSE 328 Women, Sport and Leisure
T711.201 Sports Science Technology 2A	This material is dealt with under ...	PHSE 211 Biomechanics 1 PHSE 213 Exercise Prescription 1 PHSE 223 Principles of Exercise
T711.202 Sports Science Technology 2B	This material and more is dealt with by ..	PHSE 211 Biomechanics 1 PHSE 213 Exercise Physiology 1 PHSE 221 Motor Learning & Disability PHSE 223 Principles of Exercise PHSE 232 Physical Education Practice
T711.301 Sports Science Technology 3A	Material is covered by ..	PHSE 311 Biomechanics 2 PHSE 313 Exercise Physiology 2 PHSE 312 Motor Learning and Control 2 PHSE 321 Exercise Prescription PHSE 323 Motor Disorders PHSE 324 Sport Pedagogy PHSE 326 Sports Coaching
T711.302 Sports Science Technology 3B	Biomechanics and some ergonomics covered by ..	PHSE 313 Exercise Physiology PHSE 321 Exercise Prescription
T32.2xx Sport Psychology	At Otago there are two papers ..	PHSE 215 Psychology of Sport 1 PHSE 315 Psychology of Sport 2

Txx.yyy Sports Administration & Management	Material is covered by ..	PHSE 327 Sports Management
T711.401 Advanced Sports Science	This one paper includes material which is included in a number of Otago papers, including ..	PHSE 221 Motor Learning & Disability PHSE 225 Exercise & Sport: Medical Aspects PHSE 216 Sociology of Sport 1 PHSE 316 Sociology of Sport 2
T711.403 Project and Dissertation	This obviously has its equivalent at Otago where it also has a value of two papers.	PHSE 491 Dissertation

Table 3 lists the present proposed courses and makes a brief comparison with related courses at Otago. It is clear that considerable curriculum development is required and that the challenge for Auckland is to develop a focus that will be complimentary to other programmes in the country and one that provides a unique contribution. At present, the emphasis is on direct application to sport, however, if proper standards are to be met, there will need to be closer attention to the fundamental academic discipline of human movement. The Auckland area is important because the greater city has the largest population of the country and this programme will be important for helping to meet the needs of that population.

It is also worth noting that there are two medical schools in N.Z., one is at Auckland and the other is at Otago. The current proposal for a postgraduate diploma for Sport Medicine at Auckland is long overdue and is likely to be followed by a similar development through the Medical School at Otago. In the meantime, we at the School of Physical Education will continue with our undergraduate courses in Exercise and Sport Medicine, Exercise Prescription and Management as well as our Clinical programmes in these areas.

At the University of Waikato which is in the city of Hamilton, the major university course is the Bachelor of Leisure Studies. This degree is made up of a combination of papers on leisure topics taught by the university and physical education and sport papers that are taught by the Waikato Polytechnic. This programme is in its early developmental phase and its strengths are likely to be the concentration on leisure. The strong demand for courses in sport and physical education is being recognised and the challenge will be to ensure that high standards of teaching and research are attained.

The more formal involvement of polytechnics in university qualifications is a recent development in N.Z. and while this is good for the integration of academic, professional and vocational courses between tertiary institutions, it will be some years before proper integration reaches maturity. A danger is that academic and research standards are not met; which could create a two-tier system of tertiary level education. Of course that need not be a problem as long as true quality remains recognised.

At Massey University which is in the city of Palmerston North, the present course is a one-year diploma in sport that is centred on six papers involving leisure, management, coaching and recreation. It is housed in the Faculty of Business Studies and cannot be regarded as a strong specialist course. At present, they have a proposal to establish a major of the Bachelor of Business Studies (BBS) degree in sport management and coaching. The extent of the papers would be similar in time commitment to a one-year undergraduate programme with the level of study reaching a typical second-year in a 4-year specialist programme.

The Masters degree at the Victoria University of Wellington is an excellent programme that was established in 1976. It specialises in the applied study of recreation and leisure studies with emphasis on areas such as public management, public economics, public policy and social inquiry with strong practicum and research components.

Lincoln University is near Christchurch and is closely linked with Canterbury University. Its Department of Parks, Recreation and

Tourism has an excellent range of programmes in ecology, tourism and recreation management. The first of these was introduced in 1987. Currently, there are 39 graduate students including six at PhD level. Similarly, Victoria provides excellent opportunities for students with a broad undergraduate background in physical education to specialise at advanced levels in the wide discipline of recreation.

The School of Physical Education at Otago has the advantage of being the oldest programme. It began in 1948 with a 3-year undergraduate Diploma and for several decades was the only university course in the subject. The School has the broadest programme with the highest level of specialisation in physical education and sport. The 4-year bachelors degree (BPhEd) was added in 1975, the masters (MPhEd) and doctoral (PhD) degrees came four years later and more recently, the Honours course was established. The original diploma was phased out and group of qualifications (Diploma in Sport Studies, Certificate of Sport Studies, Certificate of Fitness Management) were introduced in 1990. These diplomas and certificates are below bachelors degree level and are designed for external students who are taught at a distance using telecommunication. In 1994 we added the postgraduate diploma which has the same requirements as a masters degree except that there is no thesis.

The annual intake for the undergraduate degree programme at Otago has grown steadily from 50 students in 1981 to 200. The staff has doubled in size over the same period to reach 63 (academic and general staff). The School's total number of students (944) is made up of 685 (BPhEd), 230 (Diploma and Certificates) and 29 graduate students (PG Dip, MPhEd, PhD).

The range of subjects for the degrees are now very broad in scope and are grouped generally into the three areas (kinesiology, sport and leisure studies, professional studies). However, it is important to point out that these groupings are not divisive and that many of our courses overlap groups. Currently, we have 50 different lecture courses and we offer over 100 different practical courses. Naturally, we continue to try to improve the curriculum and to keep pace with new academic and professional needs. At present we are seeking four new lectureships in History, Dance, Gender Issues, and Pedagogy; with a replacement position in Movement Development. It is beyond the scope of this address to discuss the Otago programme in more detail but I would be pleased to have discussions at another time.

So far in this overview, we have considered the types of courses available for tertiary level study in physical education, sport, recreation and related areas. I now turn to a general overview of scientific activity. It may be taken that the programmes at Victoria and Lincoln are active in research and play a leading role in the area of recreation management. Researchers at Lincoln's Department of Parks, Recreation and Tourism for example have been very productive over the past year in publishing four books, 19 chapters in books and 18 articles in refereed journals. The programmes at Auckland and Waikato have not been established long enough to make an impact; and Massey's programme is still in a developmental stage. The major producer in the field of physical education and sport therefore is the School at Otago.

To give an idea of research activity I first refer to the funding outcomes from the N.Z. Sport Science Technology Board (NZSSTB). This agency is given governmental funds to support research in sport throughout N.Z.

Table 4 shows the distribution according to sport and we find that rugby, swimming, tennis, turf culture, cycling, cricket and netball have some consistency of research funding.

Table 4. NZSSTB: Annual Grants by Sport

SPORT	1990/91	1991/92	1992/93	1993/94	TOTALS
Auto Cycle Union					
Archery					
Athletics	1,800	4,500	3,200		9,500
Badminton			2,000		2,000
Bowls		6,500	10,800		17,300
Canoeing	13,306				13,306
Coaching			4,985	11,320	16,305
Cycling	9,044	15,000		15,000	39,044
Cricket	8,500	11,200		8,500	28,200
Equestrian				7,000	7,000
Fencing		19,641			19,641
Golf			7,000	6,500	13,500
Gymnastics		10,440			10,400
Hockey		11,500			11,500
Ice Racing	5,300				5,300
Medicine		13,500		15,375	28,875
Netball	10,214	21,000	5,000		36,214
Orienteering			3,250		3,250
Paraplegic Ass.		6,582	2,300		8,882
Rowing		15,453		4,471	19,924
Rugby	17,014	21,000	5,000		43,014
Squash			13,100		13,100
Swimming	2,500	12,600	23,280	8,500	46,880
Surf Riding			1,256	3,438	4,694
Shooting		11,490			11,490
Table Tennis			13,641		13,641
Tennis	2,500		13,100	24,175	39,775
Trampoline	8,886				8,886
Triathlon	5,000				5,000
Turf Culture	6,800	6,500		15,500	28,800
Under Water Hockey			4,000		4,000

Water Polo				5,950	5,950
Yachting				14,883	14,883
No Sport				4,300	4,300
Totals	90,864	186,906	111,912	144,912	534,594

When these grants are arranged by discipline (Table 5) the distribution of funding shows that exercise physiology and biomechanics are dominant with turf culture, psychology and motor learning also being significant.

Table 5. NZSSTB: Annual Grants by Discipline

DISCIPLINE	1990/1	1991/2	1992/3	1993/4	Totals
Exercise Physiology	21,144	28,785	24,450	40,049	114,428
Design Engineering		12,750	4,985	15,000	32,735
Biochemistry					--
Nutrition					--
Telemetry			5,000		5,000
Biomechanics	24,692	34,530	24,680	20,500	104,402
Medicine		13,500			13,500
Education					--
Psychology	12,714	21,000	1,256	17,888	52,858
Recreational Plan.					--
Turf	15,300	29,200	17,800	15,500	77,800
Sociology				4,300	4,300
Vision			2,000		2,000
Motor Learning		19,641	13,641		33,282
Talent Identification				16,175	16,175
Totals	73,850	159,406	93,812	129,412	456,480

A comparison of the funding according to institution (Table 6) shows that in the 1990-1994 period, over 50 % of the grants were made to the School of Physical Education at Otago and the next largest category was turf culture.

Table 6. NZSSTB: Annual Grants by Institution

INSTITUTION	1990/91	1991/92	1992/93	1993/94	TOTALS
Otago University	45,750	122,191	51,927	39,134	259,001
ATI			13,100	14,000	27,100
Auckland University				31,058	31,058
Turf Culture	6,800	18,000	17,800	15,500	58,100
Canterbury University	10,300			4,471	14,771
CIT			4,000		4,000
Wanganui Sport Education		6,465			6,465
DSIR Grasslands	8,500				8,500
Individuals	2,500	12,750	6,985	25,250	47,485
Totals	73,850	159,406	93,812	129,412	456,4802

It is necessary now to assess the research output in terms of published papers and conference presentations. Unfortunately, I do not have ready access to all details from the other institutions so the data presented here are incomplete. Nevertheless, it should be useful to give an idea of research productivity in sport and physical education.

Workers at the School of Physical Education at Otago have published 40 papers in the international and national literature over the past 18 months. The major output has been in sociology of sport with 15 papers, followed by motor learning and control with 8 papers. Publications on health topics from our Life in N.Z. Research Unit are prominent with 7 and the other representatives are: sport psychology (4), biomechanics (3), pedagogy (2) and exercise prescription (1). The lack of output in exercise physiology is because a key staff

member has left us and there are at least 8 papers currently under review. The paper output of staff at the School is matched by their conference presentations which total 68 for the same period.
Another source of evidence of research activity is in the three journals of the national associations for physical education, sports medicine and coaching. Each journal is published four times a year and although the primary motivation is not to publish basic research, it is useful to see that such publication does occur. An analysis for the past three years for example, shows that a total of 17 research articles involving data and theoretical issues were published (Table 7).

Table 7. A General Classification of Articles, and the Number Published in Three Selected New Zealand Journals

Type of Article	Journal of Physical Education New Zealand	New Zealand Coach	New Zealand Journal of Sports Medicine
Research	10	0	7
Views, reviews, reports	52	43	123
Professional practice	17	44	21

In addition to these articles, a substantial amount of research activity is funded by Government agencies in areas of health, recreation, education and welfare. Much of this is aimed at producing reports that are used for the guidance of action by committees and groups. While it represents a source of knowledge that is potentially important, it is a disadvantage that it has a relatively restricted circulation and a significant amount does not reach the international literature.

An example of this type of activity is given in Table 8 where the Accident Compensation Corporation (ACC) has targeted injury from sport and other contexts for priority of research.

Table 8. Accident Compensation Corporation research priorities for both injury prevention and rehabilitation (1994/95)

For 1994/95 the ACC will concentrate its research efforts, in both injury prevention and rehabilitation, in the following areas:

- Farming
- Forestry
- Sawmills
- Meat Industry
- Building and Construction Industry
- Sports Injury (specifically rugby, rugby league and soccer)
- Back Injury
- Road Traffic Safety
- Community Interventions
- Falls in the Elderly
- Criminal Injuries
- Domestic Violence

Nevertheless, the future holds much promise because the Government has recently established a very broad programme to fund research in New Zealand and provides for collaboration with other countries. This is the Public Good Science Fund (PGSF) which has NZ$ 250 million allocated for research in 40 output categories. One of the difficulties for sport and physical education is that usually the research topics cut across several categories and it is difficult to gain the most appropriate fit that maximises the likely impact and contribution of the research for the public good. Nevertheless, it is a challenge that needs to be faced because the potential support is substantial.

One of the major benefits of the PGSF and other similar programmes is that they are strongly encouraging collaboration between areas and institutions. I believe that this is a major challenge for the discipline of physical education and sport to face over the coming decade. However, there are two aspects to that challenge. One is the obvious need to expand our inter-disciplinary links in research so that we can strengthen and coordinate the different kinds of expertise and knowledge on human movement.

The other aspect of challenge is to develop stronger intra-disciplinary links. At least that is the case in New Zealand. We have seen sub-disciplines working very hard at establishing their own areas of study and research as part of the formal programmes in our universities and while this has been a necessary step, it is now time to integrate more of our work. For example, I remain struck by the lack of confluence of subjects like biomechanics, energetics, ergonomics, learning, transfer and the principles of motor control at advanced levels of study in our undergraduate programmes.

The explosion of information and technology has benefited our understanding of human movement but we are obliged to control that expansion so that the fundamentals are taught in a manner that is more integrated in content and our teaching approaches. Therefore, we should be moving towards new groupings and new schema for curriculum development as well as taking a more coalitional approach to our research.

Indeed, the coalitional approach is especially important in New Zealand because we are small in number and geographic space. A challenge for our tertiary institutions to plan and work more together so that we establish a more harmonious balance between diversity and commonality. In this manner we can take advantage of the special strengths of different institutions and expand the range of opportunities for people who wish to study the very broad discipline of physical education and sport.

As always, the key elements of development are:

- the orientation of the institution;
- its administrative policies;
- the constraints of facilities, equipment, staff and support services;
- and the intentions of teaching staff.

In summing up therefore, I have attempted to describe the nature of university-based programmes in sport and physical education in New Zealand. It was noted that we have several new programmes that are developing curricula and research activity and some older courses that are more established. I have also described some of the scientific activity that characterises New Zealand. In considering our future needs, I am sure we echo many of the same themes that apply to European and other countries of the academic world when we recommend a stronger coalitional approach at both inter- and intra-disciplinary levels. The fundamental challenge for the future is, as always, to try to do the very best we can.

Acknowledgements

I am grateful to the following colleagues for providing information on their programmes:

Professor R. Meyer, University of Auckland at Tamaki
Associate Professor B. Grant, University of Waikato
Professor G. Cushman, Lincoln University
Mr A. Laidler, Victoria University
Dr B. Wilson and Mr I. Ansell, N.Z. Sport Science Technology Board of the Hillary Commission.

Sinikka Kahila

Cooperation in Physical Education as a Teaching Method in Learning Social Behavior and Making Friends

1 Introduction

1.1 Premises and Goals for Social Education

Two important goals and expectations for the school education imposed by the surrounding society are to promote the individuality of the pupils and to develop the capability of cooperation i.e. social-ethical behavior. The educational methods used in school are supposed to give the opportunity to learn those positive social skills an individual needs when interacting with other people. That means to give psychological support, to care about others, to take others into consideration and to give concrete assistance like giving advice and help and correct errors (HUSEN et al., 1985; KAHILA, 1993).

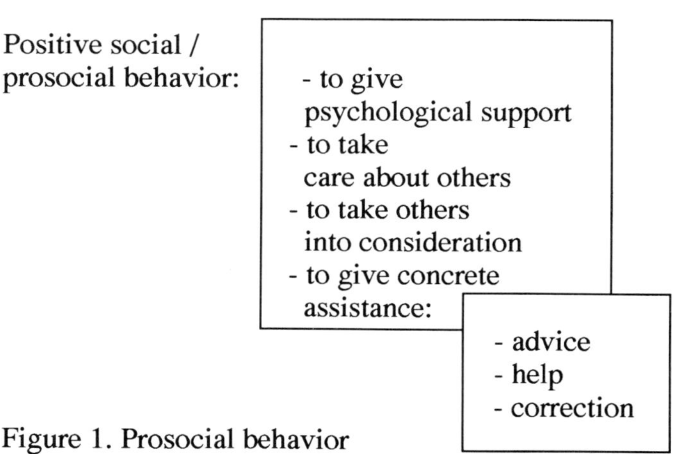

Figure 1. Prosocial behavior

Cooperation with many different individuals gives the opportunity to create new contacts and make friends. The reasons why people choose certain friends are that those people are seen as generous, cooperative and skilled helpers (RAVIV et al., 1980).

Physical education can be seen as a very remarkable socializing environment because it has some meaningful characteristics which can be used as educational instruments. First of all many kinds of actions in physical education produce interactive situations not only on the verbal level but also on the level of concrete physical action and therefore provide an opportunity to learn and practize prosocial skills (KAHILA, 1993; TELAMA, 1992). By interacting with each other pupils learn to understand and to internalize social skills needed for working together with other people (DELINE, 1991).

The old belief that only participating in physical activities without any guidance will promote social development and good characteristics is not necessarily true (COAKLEY, 1987; SAGE, 1986). Without any guidance aggressive or selfish behavior, so called negative social behavior can be as usual as prosocial behavior (SHERIF, 1967; TELAMA, 1992).

2 Purpose of the Study

The aim of this study was to demonstrate that social behavior, in this case social skills needed for prosocial i.e. helping behavior, can be taught in physical lessons at school, by means of a cooperative teaching method. In this study social skills needed for prosocial behavior were total helping tendency, teacher dependency or initiative, caring about others and number of friends. The more contact an individual has with other people, the greater are that individual's opportunities for learning to show consideration to other people and for creating new friendly relations. For this reason it was expected, that friendly relations would proliferate in a group, in which members worked cooperatively with a variety of different individuals.

3 Research Methods

In this study the pupils in all four groups were fifth-form girls about 11 years of age. The experiment lasted nine months in 1989-1990. The cooperative teaching style was used, in two different ways.

In group 1 (n=20) using the cooperative teaching style, pupil pairs were changed regularly at intervals of three weeks. The great difference from group 2 (n=24), which also used the cooperative teaching method, was that the pupils chose their partners themselves at the beginning of each lesson three times a week. That meant of course that everybody chose her best friend if she had one. In a third group (n=27) the teaching content was the same but the teaching method was that of working independently according to the instructions and criteria given by the teacher; it was the so-called task style. The point is that in group 3 there was no real interaction between the pupils. The study also included a control group (n=24) in which no requirements were laid down regarding either teaching content or teaching methods. The method actually used in the control group turned out to be doing a task simultaneously with the teacher or first observing a demonstration by the teacher and then copying it, perhaps in a small group but not as a group. Like the task style this style gave very little room for interaction between the pupils. This very common style was labelled the conventional teaching style.

Prosocial behavior was assessed by means of a questionnaire on total helping tendency, teacher dependency, number of friends and caring about others. To discover the degree to which a pupil was accepted by other members of the group, the numbers of each pupil's friends and the structure of the group as a whole, sociometric measures were used. As many choices and rejections as they wanted to make were allowed.

4 Results

The pre-test measurements showed no significant differences between the groups in prosocial behavior. In the sociometric measurements group 2 showed more choices than other groups ($p< 0.05$).

In the final measurements group 1 differed from three other groups in total helping behavior, in teacher dependency and in caring about others. The differences were statistically significant ($p<0.01$). Group 3 (working with task teaching style) was more dependent on the teacher than group 2. The difference was significant ($p< 0.01$). (Figure 2 A, B, C see appendix)

Group 1 has many more friends than group 3 and group 4. The difference was statistically significant ($p< 0.01$). (Figure 3, see appendix)

There was no statistical difference between group 1 and 2 in number of friends determined by means of the questionnaire. In the questionnaire pupils were asked about number of all friends even outside the school.

In the sociometric measurement the choices (to want somebody to be one's working partner) made in the classroom showed that in group 1 more different pairs of girls were significantly more often accepted than in any other group ($p< 0.01$). There were also significantly more choices in group 2 than in group 3 ($p< 0.01$) and a close to significant difference the control group ($p< 0.05$). (Figure 4, see appendix)

But at the same time group 2 showed significantly more rejections (don't want somebody to be one's working partner) than group 1 ($p<0.01$) and significantly more rejections than the control group ($p<0.05$). There were no other differences between the four groups in rejections. (Figure 5, see appendix)

On the final measurement the number of choices made during physical education lessons had risen by 84 % in group 1 compared to from the final measurement with those from the pre-measurement. The difference is statistically significant (p<0.001) In group 2 the rise in the choices was 14 %, the difference is statistically significant (p<0.01). In the control group there was a significant difference (p<0.05) whit a rise of 23 %. In group 3 no significant difference at all occurred between the results. In percentage the rise was 9. (Table 1; figure 6, see appendix)

Table 1 Rise of the Choices

	Pretest FR	Final Test FR	Rise %	p
Group 1	75	138	84	0.001
Group 2	94	107	14	0.01
Group 3	86	94	9	NS
Control Group	68	84	23	0.05

The results of the sociometric measurements during the break were parallel with results from the lessons.

5 Conclusion

The study showed that prosocial behavior can be learned by practice in situations specially designed for that purpose and that concrete inter-active relations are essential preconditions for learning social skills, such as giving psychological support, caring about other people, taking others into consideration, giving concrete assistance like verbal and physical help, advice and corrections. In addition to coping with new psychological-concrete situations also presenting the girls in group 1 with challenging, motivating activity, taught them to see where help was needed. It also led them to carry out concrete actions on the basis of their aroused motivation to act prosocially. The situation of acquiring a new partner created the basis for working at the active level and by so doing also created the conditions at the social level for interaction and prosocial behavior.

Results from the final sociometric measurement showed that choices in every group had increased in number but also rejections had increased in all groups except group 1. The results probably meant that some kind of "cliques" were formed in groups 2 and 3 and in the control group.

The results show that even the ability to help and advise would not appear to be as dependant on physical abilities and skills as is generally thought. This is shown by the results of the sociometric measurements obtained in group 1. As mentioned earlier the number of choices had risen by 84 % in group 1 as against a range of 8-19 per cent in the other three groups. Since activity in group 1 was based on helping and advising different pupils of differing abilities, it can be assumed that choices were made on the basis of the ability to cooperate, to help and advise rather than physical skills. In particular, a situation in which a physically less skilled pupil is able to help and advise successfully a more skilled pupil is an invaluable boost to that pupil's sense of self-esteem and can help to strengthen, to keep or to change this pupil's attitude to physical education and sport in a positive way.

In group 2 social interaction with several pupils in cooperative learning tended to be on a minimum level and restricted to a single "best friend". The lack of a best friend and the resulting situation of "left-over" pairs may have induced a sense of anxiety or distress or even aggression. For this reason pupils in group 2 were caring much less about each other and had a greater number of rejections than group 1.

Ball games in physical education have traditionally been regarded as a useful way of promoting social interaction, cooperation and making new friends. The control group played games for 25 % more lessons than e.g. group 1. However, the prosocial behavior results and sociometric results of the control group were poorer than results of group 1. It would appear that the right teaching method chosen for the special aims is at least as important as curricular questions of teaching hours or teaching content.

Preconditions for success in social interaction and working cooperatively are first of all caring about other people but also having a sense of responsibility. By working cooperatively with changing partners every pupil can interact and be a working partner with many other pupils. Success in working cooperatively requires both partners to respect each other, to accept each other as a working partner and to accept each other's level of performance and opinions. Cooperation also requires giving and receiving help, advice and feedback. By showing empathy and by learning to accept other people it is possible to remove prejudices between people and promote new friendships to spring up.

References

COAKLEY, J.J.: Children and the sport socialization process. In: D. GOULD, M.R. WEISS (eds.): Advances in pediatric. Pediatri sport sciences 2: behavioral issues, Human Kinetics, Champaign Ill, 1987, 43-60.

DELINE, J.: Why...Can't they get along? Journal of Physical Education, Recreation and Dance 1991, 1:21-26.

HUSEN, T.; POSTLETHWAITE, T.N.: International encyclopedia of education, vol. 1. Pergamon Press, New York 1985.

KAHILA, S.: The role of teaching method in prosocial learning - developing helping behavior by means of the cooperative teaching method in physical education. Studies in sport, physical education and health 29. University of Jyväskylä 1993.

RAVIV, A.; BAR-TAL, D.; AYALON, H.; RAVIV, A.: Perception of giving and receiving help. Representative Research in Social Psychology 1980, 11:140-151.

SAGE, G.H.: Social development. In: V. SEEFELDT (ed.): Physical activity and well-being, RESTON, V.A., American Alliance for Health, Physical Education, Recreation and Dance, 1986, 343-371

SHERIF, M.: Group conflict and co-operation. Routledge & Kegan Paul, London 1967.

TELAMA, R.: Children's sport as an educational environment. Paper presented at the Olympic Congress in Malaga. Department of Physical Education, University of Jyväskylä 1992.

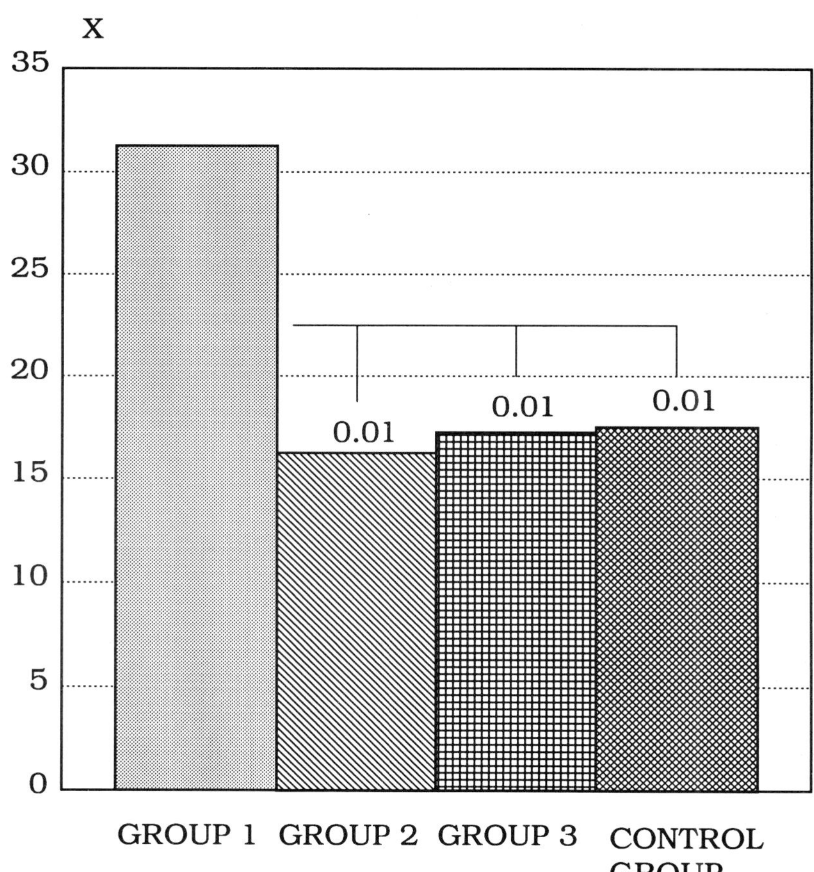

Figure 2A. Helping behavior: differences between the groups

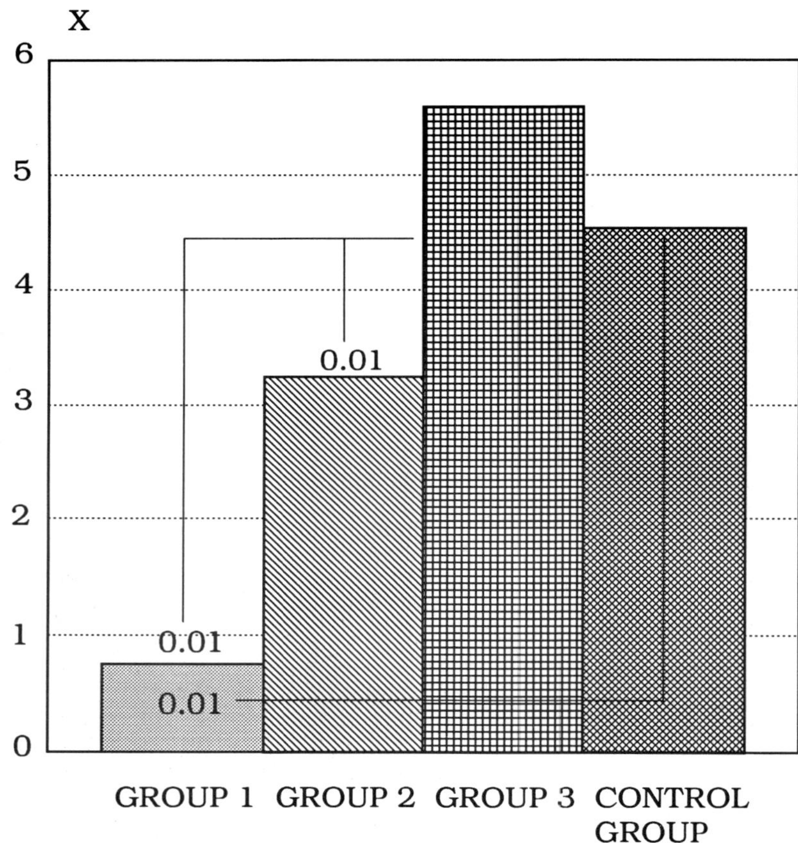

Figure 2B. Teacher dependency: differences between the groups

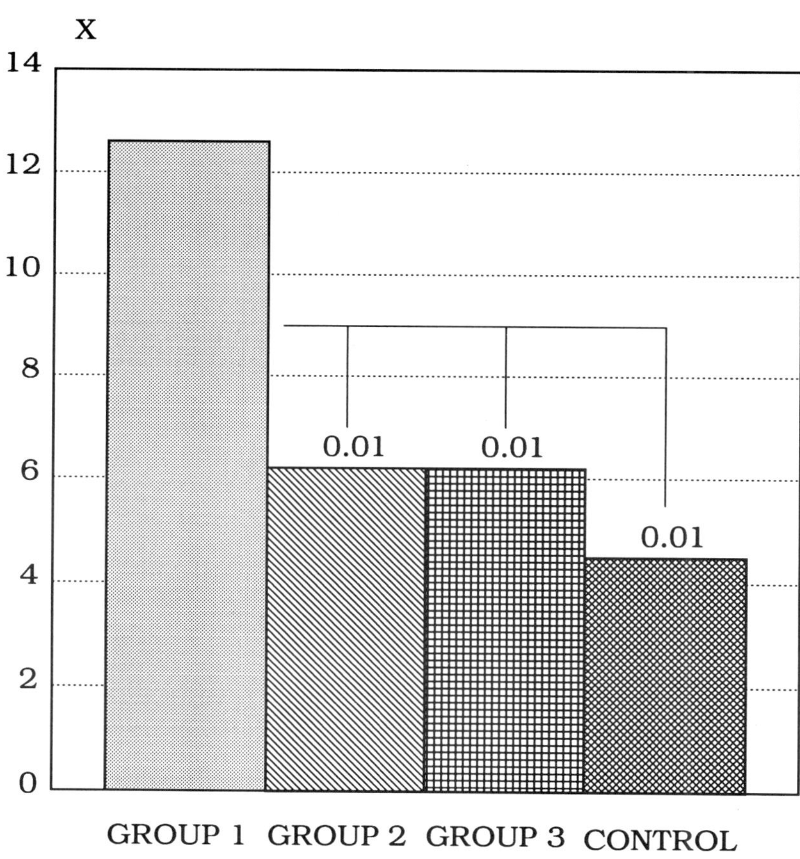

Figure 2C. Caring about others: differences between the groups

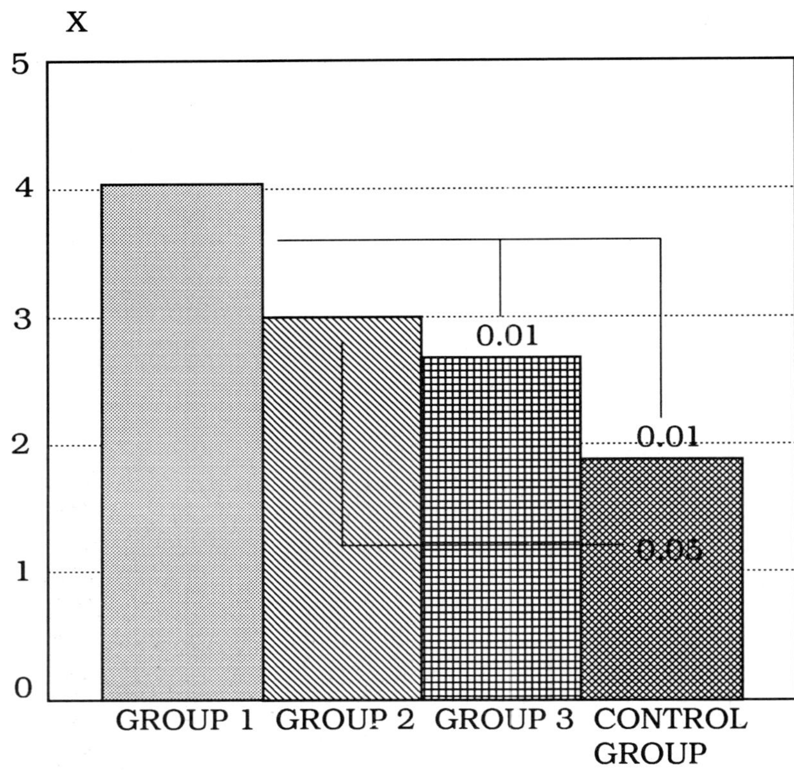

Figure 3. Number of friends: differences between the groups

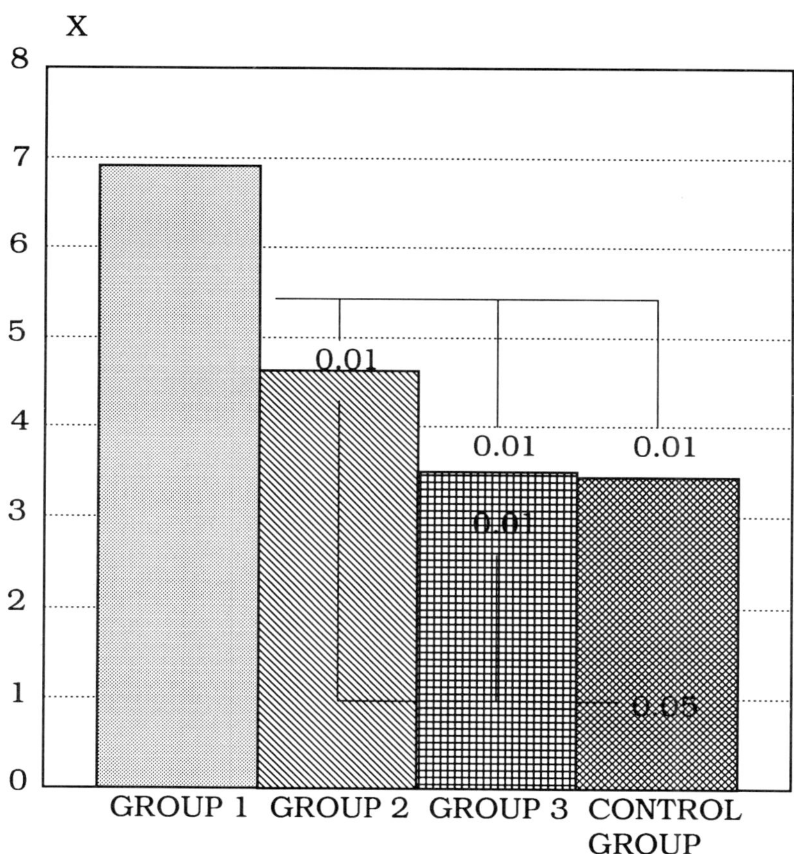

Figure 4. Choices: differences between the groups

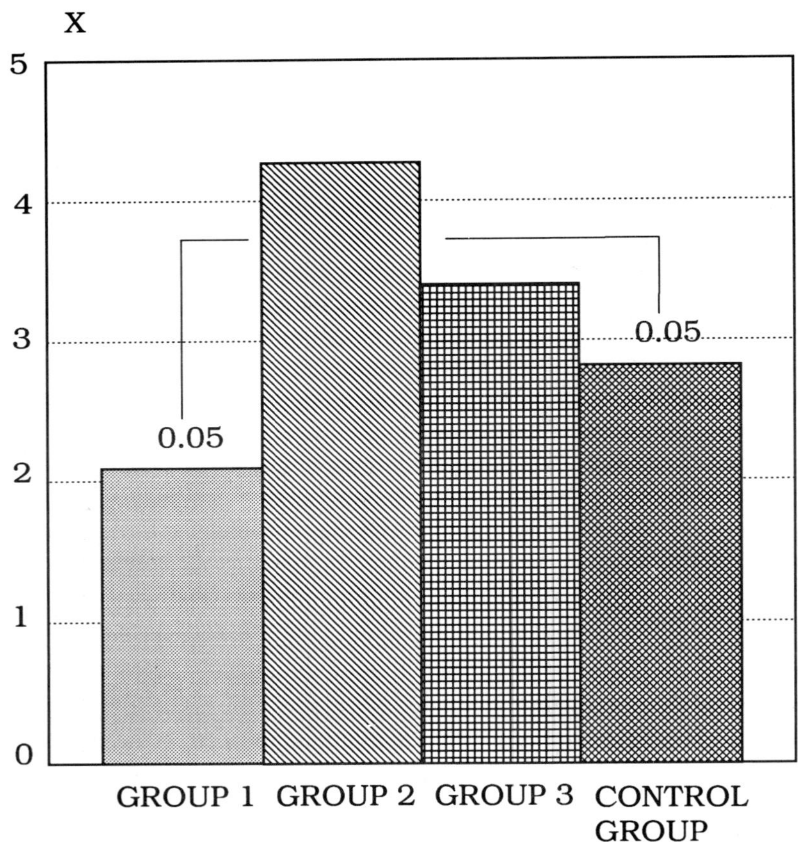

Figure 5. Rejections: differences between the groups

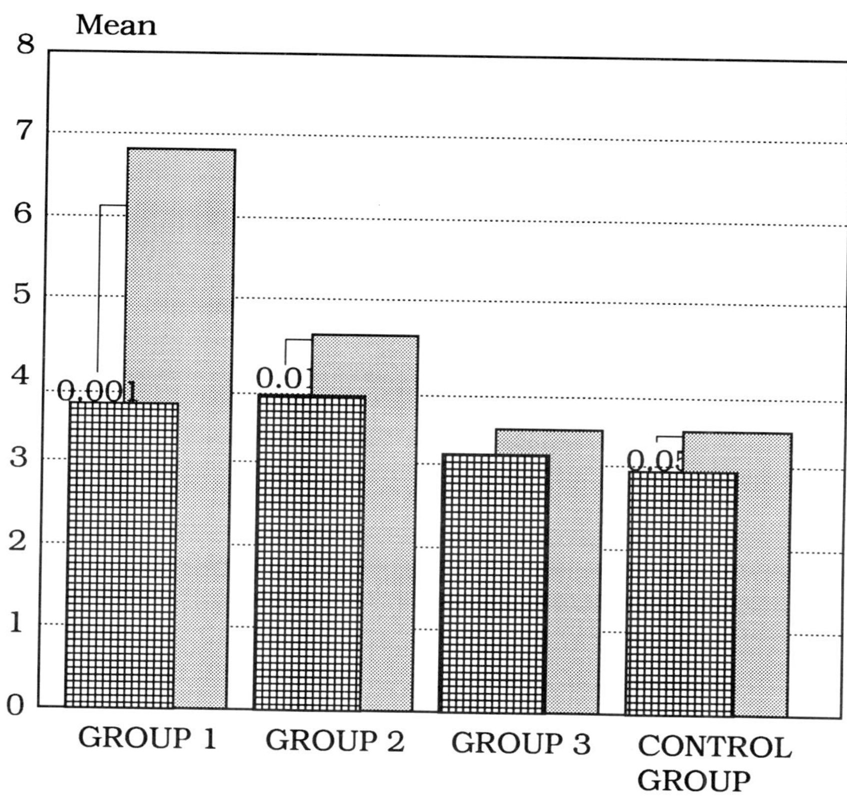

Figure 6. Rise of the choices

Colin A. Hardy, Charlotte E. Hardy

Male and Female Teachers' Responses to Student Misbehaviour in Mixed-Sex Physical Education Classes

1. Introduction

Misbehaviour of pupils in the educational setting has been a major concern not only of pre-service teachers but of experienced teachers, principals and parents for as long as schools have existed (BORKO, LALIK and TOMCHIN, 1987; CAIRNS, 1987; TENOSCHOK, 1985; VEENMAN, 1984). Publications on control and discipline are common in educational literature (GRAHAM, 1992; HENKEL, 1989) with much of the research focused on ways of dealing with discipline problems (BROPHY, 1987; LEACH and RAYBOULD, 1977). However, there is very little research data on how effective teachers respond specifically to the misconduct of pupils in particular situations (REYNOLDS, 1992).

Definition of Terms

Pupil misbehaviour: in the present study an incident is only recorded as an incident when the teacher refers to the problem.
Teacher response: this is defined as how a teacher reacts to a pupil misbehaviour incident.
Experienced teacher: an experienced teacher is a teacher who has been in the profession for five years or more.

2. Null Hypotheses

(i) Null hypothesis: there will be no significant difference in the frequency of pupil misbehaviour incidents per lesson committed by males and by females in secondary school mixed-sex physical education lessons.

(ii) Null hypothesis: there will be no significant difference in the types of pupil misbehaviour incidents in secondary school mixed-sex physical education lessons between lessons taken by experienced male and female physical education teachers.

(iii) Null hypothesis: there will be no signifcant difference between the experienced male and female physical education teachers' responses to pupil misbehaviour incidents in secondary school mixed-sex physical education lessons.

3. Methodology

Ten schools were randomly selected from forty-five co-educational secondary schools within a twenty-five mile radius of the University. The total number of morning (n=69) and afternoon (n=50) classes observed was 119 in fourteen activities with sixty-two of the lessons being taken by male teachers and fifty-seven by female teachers. All intact classes involved males (n=1359) and females (n=1309) with no class showing a difference between the sexes of more than four pupils. As the school physical education programmes focused more on the younger age groups, most of the lessons observed were from years seven, eight and nine (81.51 %) with years ten and eleven accounting for the remainder of the lessons (18.49 %).

The number of intact classes observed in each school ranged from ten to fourteen with the length of the lesson ranging from twenty-five to seventy minutes ($\underline{M}$ = 50.6 minutes) and the class size varying between sixteen and thirty-one pupils ($\underline{M}$ = 22.4 pupils). The number of teachers involved in each school varied from two to four. The data was collected using the instrument constructed by HARDY (1992).

4. Results

The coders recorded 593 misbehaviour incidents in the 119 observed lessons with the number of misbehaviour incidents in each lesson ranging from nought to eleven.

4.1 Frequency of student misbehaviour incidents according to sex (Table 1.1; null hypothesis i).
There was a significant difference (p<.01) in the frequency of pupil misbehaviour incidents committed by males and by females in secondary school mixed-sex physical education lessons in that males committed more incidents.

4.2 Types of pupil misbehaviour incidents according to teacher sex (Table 1.2; null hypothesis ii).
There was a significant difference (p<.05) in the types of pupil misbehaviour incidents in secondary school mixed-sex physical education lessons taken by male and female teachers in that the former group had more disruption between pupils but less incidents during their instruction than the latter group.

4.3 Male and female responses to student misbehaviour incidents (Tables 1.3, 1.4, 1.5, 1.6, 1.7, 1.8: null hypothesis iii).
There were significant differences in the responses of male and female teachers to pupil misbehaviour incidents in secondary school mixed-sex physical education lessons in the method of communication (p<.05), the public or private nature of the reaction (p<.05) and in the manner (p<.01), but no significant differences in the focus, the time taken to deal with the incidents and the final action taken. In the method of communication (Table 1.3) male teachers made less verbal but more non-verbal responses than female teachers, they gave more private and less public reactions (Table 1.5) and they were more controlled and firm and less emotional and threatening in their manner (Table 1.6).
The focus for both male and female teachers was more on the behaviours than on the pupils (Table 1.4), the majority of their responses lasted for less than thirty seconds (Table 1.7) and, in

most cases, they allowed the misbehaving pupils to remain in the class (Table 1.8).

5. Discussion of Results

The significantly greater number of pupil misbehaviour incidents committed by males (Table 1.1)[1] may not only reflect teachers' expectations of the behaviour of the sexes (CAIRNS, 1987), but it also sets the scene for teacher responses in mixed-sex physical education lessons. In the types of pupil misbehaviour experienced by male and female physical education teachers the former group had less incidents during their class instruction but more disruption between pupils than the latter group ($P<.05$). As it has been noted that male teachers tend to be more direct and subject-centred and female teachers tend to be more indirect and pupil-centred (MIFSUD, 1993), it is possible that male teachers deal with formal class situations slightly more effectively whereas female teachers tend to have more control of group situations where the disruption of others mainly tended to occur. In addition, as it has been noted that female teachers spend more time explaining lesson content (VARSTALA, PAUKKU and TELAMA, 1983), it is possible that long class instructions give rise to more fidgety pupils and more misbehaviour incidents. However, the general profile of pupil misbehaviour incidents according to the sex of the teacher (Table 1.2) does not show any great variations, and the difference noted between the teachers' responses could have been affected by pupils' reactions to the nature and conditions of the lessons (e.g. activity taught, length of lesson). SPACKMAN (1986) noted that male and female physical education teachers across all activities and age groups did not show any significant differences in their managerial and teaching behaviours, whereas the present study reported differences in responding to pupil misbehaviour incidents in three areas. Firstly, male teachers tended to respond more frequently in a non-verbal way but less frequently verbally than female teachers. This difference could be explained by the leadership styles of male

[1] This is part of a wider study in which male and female pupils' behavior is examined in detail.

and of female teachers; the more direct and dominant style of male teachers in classrooms (Adams and Biddle, 1970) and the more relaxed and 'disposed towards discussion' style of female teachers (Good, Sikes and Brophy, 1972) could result in more posturing and gesturing by males and more explanations from females. Secondly, although the vast majority of both male and female teachers' responses were in public, the former group was more likely than the latter to respond privately ($p<.05$). However, as more of the misbehaviour incidents in classes taught by females were during the teachers' instructions (57.24 %), this could be expected. Thirdly, the difference in the manner of responses between male and female physical education teachers ($p<.01$) perhaps reflects the authoritarian leadership style of male teachers (Griffin, 1972) and the warmer, more nurturant style of female teachers (Dunkin, 1987) in classrooms. The style that encourages discussion and greater tolerance of misbehaviour (Good et al., 1972) may allow pupils to go beyond acceptable standards of behaviour and can result in situations that cause teachers to show more frustration in their responses.

In the focus of responses, the time taken to deal with the responses and in the final actions taken, there were no significant differences between male and female physical education teachers' responses. Such similarities are not unexpected when it is noted that much of the literature on dealing with behaviour problems suggests focusing on the behaviour and not the pupil (Docking, 1987, Henderson and French, 1990), dealing with the misbehaviour incident quickly in order to avoid interrupting the lesson flow (Emmer, 1987) and using techniques that keep pupils in the lessons (Rink, 1993).

The differences and similarities reported between male and female physical education teachers in the present study are also reflected in the general education literature. Whereas some researchers have reported differences in styles (Adams and Biddle, 1970; Good et al., 1972; Griffin, 1972) other researchers have concluded that there are no differences (Spackman, 1986). Nevertheless, it is suggested by Dunkin (1987) that as males are brought up differently from females, and with differences in physical and physiological attributes, it would be surprising if there were not differences in teacher behaviours between the sexes.

6. Conclusions and Implications

The differences noted in the types of pupil misbehaviour incidents in lessons taught by male and female teachers and the differences in some of the teachers' responses suggest that perceptions of and reaction to pupil misbehaviour may vary according to the teachers' sex. In addition, as male pupils misbehave more frequently than female pupils, the teachers' responses may be influenced by their expectations of male behaviours. The implication of the present study for physical education teachers is that some leadership styles may be more effective than others in dealing with problem behaviour in mixed-sex physical education lessons.

7. References

ADAMS, R.S.; BIDDLE, B.J.: Realities of teaching: Explorations with video tape. New York: Holt 1970.

BORKO, H.; LALIK, R.; TOMCHIN, E.: Student teachers' understandings of successful and unsuccessful teaching. Teaching and Teacher Education, 1987, 3 (2), 77-90.

BROPHY, J.E.: Educating teachers about managing classrooms and students (Occasional Paper No. 115). E. Lansing, MI: Michigan State University, Institute for Research on Teaching 1987.

CAIRNS, L.G.: Behaviour problems. In: M.J. DUNKIN (Ed.): The international encyclopedia of teaching and teacher education Oxford: Pergamon Press 1987, 446-452.

DOCKING, J.W.: Control and discipline in schools. London: Harper and Row 1987.

DUNKIN, M.J.: Teachers' sex. In: M.J. DUNKIN (Ed.): The international encyclopedia of teaching and teacher education. Oxford: Pergamon Press 1987, 606-608.

EMMER, E.T.: Classroom management. In: M.J. DUNKIN (Ed.): The international encyclopedia of teaching and teacher education. Oxford: Pergamon Press 1987, 437-446.

GOOD, T.L.; SIKES, J.N.; BROPHY, J.E.: Effects of teacher sex and student sex and student achievement on classroom interaction. Technical Report No 61, Centre for Research in Social Behaviour, University of Missouri at Columbia, Missouri 1972.

GRAHAM, G.: Teaching children physical education: Becoming a master teacher. Champaign, IL: Human Kinetics 1992.

GRIFFIN, J.: Influence strategies: theory and research. A study of teacher behaviour. (Unpublished doctoral dissertation, University of Missouri at Columbia, Missouri 1972.) Dissertation Abstracts International, 1973, 34 : 13,73A University Microfilms No. 73-21, 424.

HARDY, C.A.: Pupil misbehaviour during physical education lessons. Bulletin of Physical Education, 1992, 28 (2), 59-67.

HENDERSON, H.L.; French, R.: How to use verbal reprimands in a positive manner. Physical Educator, 1991, 47 (4), 193-196.

HENKEL, S.A.: The teacher's edge to pupil control. Journal of Physical Education, Recreation and Dance, 1989, 60 (1), 60-64.

LEACH, D.J.; RAYBOULD, E.C.: Learning and behaviour difficulties in schools. London: Open Books 1977.

MIFSUD, C.: Gender differentials in the classroom. Research in Education, 1993, 49, 11-22.

REYNOLDS, A.: What is competent beginning teaching? A review of the literature. Review of Educational Research, 1992, 62 (1), 1-35.

RINK, J.: Teaching physical education for learning. St. Louis: Mosby - Year Book, Inc. 1993, 2nd Ed.

SPACKMAN, L.: The systematic observation of teacher behaviour in physical education. Physical Education Review, 1986, 9 (2), 118-134.

TENOSCHOK, M.: Handling problems in discipline: some guidelines for success. Journal of Physical Education, Recreation and Dance, 1985, 56 (2), 29-30.

VARSTALA, V.; PAUKKU, P.; TELAMA, R.: Teacher and pupil behaviour in physical education classes. In: R. TELAMA; V. VARSTALA; J. TIAINEN; L. LAAKSO; T. HAAJANEN (Eds.): Research in school physical education. Jyväskylä: The Foundation for Promotion of Physical Culture and Health, 1983, 47-57.

VEENMAN, S.: Perceived problems of beginning teachers. Review of Educational Research, 1984, 54 (2), 143-178.

Table 1.1: Frequency of pupil misbehaviour incidents committed by males and females per lesson in secondary school mixed-sex physical education lessons*

SEX OF PUPIL	Number of physical education lessons	Number of misbehaviour incidents	MEAN	SD
MALE	119	319	2.681	1.995
FEMALE	119	160	1.345	1.575

$t(118) = 5.733$, $p<.01$^

There is strong evidence ($p<.01$) to reject the H_0

* Group and class misbehaviour incidents where both males and females were involved are excluded (n=114).

Table 1.2: Types of pupil misbehaviour incidents in secondary school mixed-sex physical education lessons in lessons taken by experienced male and female physical education teachers

SEX OF TEACHER	Not paying attention during teachers' instructions	Not carrying out teachers' instructions	Disrupting others	Not carrying out the policy procedures	Wishing to be the centre of attraction	Refusing to take part in the lesson
MALE (Number of incidents = 303)	154 (50.83%)	82 (27.06%)	32 (10.56%)	13 (4.29%)	11 (3.63%)	11 (3.63%)
FEMALE (Number of incidents = 290)	166 (57.24%)	72 (24.83%)	13 (4.48%)	20 (6.90%)	14 (4.83%)	5 (1.72%)

X^2 (df = 5, N = 593) = 12.93, p<.05

Table 1.3: Communication responses given by experienced male and female physical education teachers in dealing with pupil misbehaviour incidents in secondary school mixed-sex physical education lessons

SEX OF TEACHER	VERBAL	NON-VERBAL	VERBAL AND NON-VERBAL	IGNORED
MALE (Number of responses = 303)	226 (74.59%)	28 (9.24%)	36 (11.88%)	13 (4.29%)
FEMALE (Number of responses = 290)	231 (79.66%)	8 (2.76%)	39 (13.45%)	12 (4.14%)

X^2 (df = 3, N = 593) = 11.046, p<.05

Table 1.4: Focus of the responses of experienced male and female physical education teachers in dealing with pupil misbehaviour incidents in secondary school mixed-sex physical education lessons*

SEX OF TEACHER	Emphasizes what is to be done	Emphasizes dislike of the behaviour	Makes pupil feel guilty or foolish	Withdraws respect, showing little concern for the pupil as a person
MALE (Number of responses = 290)	62 (21.38%)	161 (55.52%)	57 (19.66%)	10 (3.45%)
FEMALE (Number of responses = 278)	61 (21.94%)	156 (56.12%)	54 (19.42%)	7 (2.52%)

X^2 (df = 3, N = 568) = 0.444, NS

* The twenty-five incidents that were ignored are excluded

Table 1.5: Reaction responses given by experienced male and female physical education teachers in dealing with pupil misbehaviour incidents in secondary school mixed-sex physical education lessons*

SEX OF TEACHER	PUBLIC	PRIVATE
MALE (Number of resposes = 290)	265 (91.38%)	25 (8.62%)
FEMALE (Number of responses = 278)	269 (96.76%)	9 (3.24%)

X^2 (df = 1, N = 568) = 6.384, p<.05

* The twenty-five incidents that were ignored are excluded

Table 1.6: Manner of responses shown by experienced male and female physical education teachers in dealing with pupil misbehaviour incidents in secondary school mixed-sex physical education lessons*

SEX OF TEACHER	CONTROLLED/FIRM	EMOTIONAL/THREATENING
MALE (Number of responses = 290)	279 (96.21%)	11 (3.79%)
FEMALE (Number of responses = 278)	240 (86.33%)	38 (13.67%)

X^2 (df = 1, N = 568) = 16.332, p<.01

* The twenty-five incidents that were ignored are excluded

Table 1.7: Time taken by experienced male and female physical education teachers in dealing with pupil misbehaviour incidents in secondary school mixed-sex physical education lessons

SEX OF TEACHER	15 Seconds and less	16 to 30 seconds	31 to 45 seconds	Over 45 seconds
MALE (Number of responses = 303)	255 (84.16%)	29 (9.57%)	10 (3.30%)	9 (2.97%)
FEMALE (Number of responses = 290)	249 (85.86%)	26 (8.97%)	6 (2.07%)	9 (3.10%)

X^2 (df = 3, N = 593) = 0.951, NS

Table 1.8: Final action taken by experienced male and female physical education teachers in dealing with pupil misbehaviour incidents in secondary school mixed-sex physical education lessons*

SEX OF TEACHER	Pupil(s) continues in the group/class	Pupil (s) is taken out of the group/class
MALE (Number of responses = 290)	271 (93.45%)	19 (6.55%)
FEMALE (Number of responses = 278)	272 (97.84%)	6 (2.16%)

X^2 (df = 1, N = 568) = 5.509, NS

* The twenty-five incidents that were ignored are excluded

Bohumil Svoboda, Peter Jansa, Jan Kocourek, Tom Peric

Emotional Reactions of Pupils to School Physical Education

Introduction

In our country (Czechoslovakia, now Czech Republic) the attention was formerly not paid very much to psychic response of pupils to school physical education. The directive style of teaching was prevailing.

Therefore, we decided to follow that question. Very soon we found that diagnostic tools were the greatest problem in any investigation. We had to construct original questionnaires when trying to follow the dependence **of emotional reactions** (which may be regarded as basic for supporting the formation of positive attitudes to physical activity) on general intrinsic motivation, family influence and body mass index.

Purpose

This paper refers to one and the most important questionnaire from the three constructed quests. The purpose in that case was to compile a questionnaire which would disclose both positive and negative emotions originating during the school physical education in boys and girls.

Methods

In the third version (after procedures like especially item analysis, factor analysis) the questionnaire called DEMOR includes 60 items on 10 factors scored 0 to 6 points each. Four positive and four

negative emotions are followed and also positive and negative attitudes as well.
We administered that questionnaire to boys and girls aged 14 until 16 years, since that age is regarded as most problematic for a creation of positive attitude to physical activity. We selected groups in 5, respectively 6 (girls) schools in different parts of the Czech Republic.

Results

The following procedures were employed: descriptive characteristics in total numbers and in individual groups (schools); correlation matrices of all results; and ANOVA (Duncan) in groups.

1. Total basic **characteristics** are in table 1. The means in individual factors indicate in both boys and girls the ambivalence of emotions experienced in physical education, nevertheless, higher figures in all positive factors than in negative ones and expressively higher positive attitude than negative one. Relaxation is considered to be the most favourite aspect of physical exercises, and unpleasant sensation of incompetency the least important in negative factors. Experience of anxiety and anger are highest in negative emotions which coincides with the lowest mean of risk taking in both sexes. Typical is also the finding that with only one exception all positive emotions are higher and all negative factors lower in boys than in girls. Individual results see tables 2 and 3.

Table 1 Total basic descriptive characters

	Boys, N=158		Girls, N=265	
Emotional reactions	M	SD	M	SD
F1 Energy	3.82	1.53	3.52	1.43
F2 Risk taking	3.58	1.76	2.96	1.74
F3 Relaxation	4.56	1.46	4.42	1.54
F4 Competence	4.39	1.39	3.92	1.53
F5 Positive attitude	4.09	1.99	3.82	1.90
F6 Fatigue	2.17	1.47	2.37	1.25
F7 Anxiety	2.81	1.68	3.60	1.61
F8 Anger	3.22	1.40	3.19	1.37
F9 Unpleasant	1.98	1.25	2.46	1.29
F10 Negative attitude	1.57	1.63	1.43	1.42

Table 2 Basic descriptive characteristics in individual schools

	Nymburk N=22		Olomouc N=32		Praha A N=22		Praha B N=24		Brno N=58	
Boys:	M	SD	M	SD	M	SD	M	SD	M	SD
F1	4.04	1.4	4.15	1.2	1.86	1.5	4.00	1.3	4.8	2.0
F2	4.13	1.3	3.59	1.6	3.13	1.2	3.83	1.5	4.0	2.0
F3	5.04	0.9	4.65	1.4	3.18	1.5	4.95	1.1	4.7	1.5
F4	5.09	1.0	4.81	1.2	2.40	1.8	4.58	1.2	4.3	1.3
F5	5.13	1.3	4.28	1.9	3.18	1.4	4.41	2.1	4.1	1.9
F6	1.6	1.2	2.37	1.5	3.33	2.0	1.92	1.3	2.12	1.5
F7	3.23	1.8	2.69	1.6	3.46	1.3	2.71	1.3	2.61	1.6
F8	2.87	1.4	3.41	1.2	2.82	1.3	3.21	1.2	3.1	1.5
F9	1.41	1.2	2.00	1.3	3.32	1.9	1.73	1.0	2.0	1.1
F10	0.60	0.7	1.64	1.6	3.36	1.5	1.35	1.2	1.41	1.4

F1 Energy; F2 Risk taking; F3 Relaxation; F4 Competence; F5 Positive attitude; F6 Fatigue; F7 Anxiety; F8 Anger; F9 Unpleasant; F10 Negative Attitude

Table 3 Basic descriptive characteristics in individual schools

	Nymburk N=32		Olomouc N=69		Praha A N=22		Praha B N=38		Praha C N=49		Brno N=55	
Girls	M	SD	M	SD	M	SD	M	SD	M	SD	M	SD
F1	3.90	1.3	4.18	1.1	2.13	1.4	2.97	1.6	3.42	1.2	4.0	1.0
F2	3.06	1.7	3.17	1.7	1.27	1.3	2.65	1.7	3.36	1.4	3.0	2.0
F3	4.90	1.1	4.55	1.3	2.63	1.9	3.94	2.0	4.83	0.7	4.7	1.5
F4	4.21	1.5	4.08	1.5	2.90	1.6	3.39	1.5	4.32	1.1	4.0	1.6
F5	4.21	1.7	4.56	1.2	1.45	1.9	3.18	2.1	4.42	1.1	3.5	2.0
F6	2.00	0.9	2.40	1.2	2.60	1.2	2.72	1.6	2.32	1.0	2.5	1.5
F7	2.40	3.6	3.66	1.6	3.37	1.8	3.37	1.7	4.00	1.3	3.6	1.6
F8	3.15	2.8	3.37	1.3	3.10	1.4	2.98	1.7	3.68	1.1	3.0	1.3
F9	4.09	1.9	2.57	1.3	3.11	1.4	2.53	1.5	2.88	1.0	2.2	1.2
F10	1.00	1.1	1.28	1.1	2.91	2.3	1.98	1.8	0.93	0.5	1.5	1.5

2. **Correlations** of total results show the following (table 4): very high and all significant correlations in boys, positive among themselves in positive factors and negative among negative factors; the same trend may be found in girls, though here are the coefficients a little lower with only few not significant statistically. But the results as a whole seem to speak for the validity of our conception of the diagnostic means.

Table 4 Correlation matrices

Boys: F1	F2	F3	F4	F5	F6	F7	F8	F9	F10
F1									
F2	63								
F3	61	64							
F4	61	67	60						
F5	65	62	74	65					
F6	-54	-52	-45	-54	-58				
F7	-41	-41	-25	-31	-29	45			
F8	-36	-32	-24	-22	-23	37	32		
F9	-45	-40	-41	-46	-44	47	33	33	
F10	-58	-57	-66	-58	-74	56	22	20	42

Girls: F1	F2	F3	F4	F5	F6	F7	F8	F9	F10
F1									
F2	45								
F3	55	49							
F4	54	55	57						
F5	62	54	66	61					
F6	-50	-32	-39	-38	-41				
F7	-30	-33	-18	-36	-26	44			
F8	-22	-14	-14	-13	-18	40	34		
F9	-41	-37	-30	-40	-37	44	44	51	
F10	-51	-42	-61	-52	-68	48	20	33	46

Significance: alpha=0.05 r=0.195 alpha=0.01 r=0.254

3. ANOVA (Duncan) very clearly indicated the differences between groups. Specially one group (Praha A) was found to be significantly differing from the others (example see table 5). It was true both in boys and girls. Evidently this group influenced to some extent the total results, as we found in the negative direction (higher negative and lower positive emotions). We therefore investigated the reasons for such results. Since we also followed the teachers and the facilities for physical education we easily disclosed the season. The school has poor facilities for physical education (no gym of its own, using a small gym of the lower grade school, asphalt playground). The two very young teachers evidently did not succeed in facing fully the situation.

Table 5 Analysis of variance (Duncan), example of one factor

Boys

F1		A	B	C	D	E
A (3)	2,72	-	S	S	S	S
B (5)	3,91	S		-	-	-
C (4)	4	S	-	-	-	-
D (1)	4,04	S	-	-	-	-
E (2)	4,15	S	-	-	-	-

1 Nymburk, 2 Olomouc, 3 Praha A, 4 Praha B, 5 Brno

Discussion and Conclusion

There are many other factors influencing the pupils in experiencing different emotions in physical education lessons. So e. g. the contents of the lessons; although the curriculum should be followed everywhere, teachers differ in laying stress on their favourite sport and exercises. We tried to find out the most appreciated activities (games in both boys and girls), but for that a much wider sample should be investigated. We could of course observe the lessons in the questioned groups, but our intention was different; we wanted to compile a diagnostics that would help to make later on a more extensive research.

Our first experience with this questionnaire is acceptable. That may be e. g. also documented so, that when we counted the ten best in positive emotions we found in those quests also very low negative scores and vice versa. Naturally, there are also individuals who are very high in athletics and dislike some school activities. To conclude we may say that our data bring relatively fair proof for our questionnaire, although the validization process cannot be regarded as finished.

Hartmut Gabler

Motivation for Fairness in Sports - Psychological Considerations as a Basis for Pedagogical Consequences

"Fair geht vor" - "fairness comes first" is the motto of an extensive current campaign of German sport, namely the "Fair-Play-Initiative". This initiative was first introduced in 1987 and has been widely accepted since. Recently, as a result of the "Fair-Play-Initiative", the discussion of fair play has also reached the realm of sport science. This initiative and its sport scientific discussion is led based on the assumption that a virtual or an actual given increase in aggressiveness (unfairness) in sports exists.
Taking a look at the literature relevant to the theme of fairness, one realizes that few attempts have been made to operationalize fairness and also that little empirical research exists which could help to test and develop further theoretical assumptions. This is the case especially for the empirical discussion regarding fairness-**motivation**. If it is a special task of the Fair-Play-Initiative to "make young people aware of the idea of Fair-Play and to make them understand that this is also an attitude for other situations in life" (Fair-Play-Initiative of German sport 1990), then it is necessary to ask young people about their existing attitude and motivation towards fairness in sports, and it is also necessary to take this into account for the pedagogical efforts, especially in schools and sportclubs. This article is divided into four parts:

1. First, a closer look will be taken at fairness in sports, because only on the basis of definitional clearness can moral evaluations and pedagogical measures be deduced.

2. Then the motivation for fair behavior will be analyzed from a theoretical point of view.

3. The preliminary results of a current research study will be presented which consists of a newly developed questionnaire for the measurement of fairness-motivation of about 1000 young people.

4. On the basis of this research and its theoretical base, pedagogical considerations for an education towards fairness in sports will finally be outlined.

What Does Fairness in Sports Mean?

The discussion in German speaking countries about the question of the meaning of fairness in sports is first of all considered with the question whether, in order to be fair, it would be sufficient not to be unfair (see HERINGER, 1993, 5a). The protagonist of this approach is HERINGER. His definition is: "1. Everything that is not unfair, is fair. 2. Anything that destroys the wit of the game is unfair. 3. The wit of the game is the common aim of the players. 4. The common aim is: To play and to win by playing"(1993, 58).

This definition presents two problems. On the one hand, it is not clearly determined what the meaning of unfair is and what then destroys the wit of the game; therefore, according to the definition it is unclear what it means to be fair. On the other hand, the question arises whether there are actions in sport that can neither be classified as fair nor as unfair. I would like to give an example; the referee of a tennis match decides that player A hit a ball beyond his opponent's baseline. Player B, however, due to his perception, thinks that the ball has touched the line.

- If player B does not correct the referee´s decision, this could have two reasons. He can be mistaken, which seems plausible, because you do not only have to see the ball while running for it, but must hit it back precisely. He can also stick to the common rule (This is a main condition of fairness for LENK (1993, 29)) and just accept the referee´s decision. He can do so with the assumption that in the course of the match the referee might be mistaken on both sides (and therefore equally). The decision not to correct the referee can, therefore, not be seen as fair; neither can it be seen as unfair.

- If, however, player B corrects the referee's decision to his own disadvantage, because due to his perception and his attitude he is not willing to take an unsuitable advantage to his favor, then this would usually be seen as a fair action.

This example shows that the whole range of actions cannot be regarded solely under the two categories of fair and unfair.

HERINGER's approach bears two problematic consequences:

1. If everything was fair that isn´t unfair, if fairness was only defined on the basis of unfairness then the concept of fairness would become so widened and ambiguous that it wouldn't have a meaning anymore. Then, e.g., a foul in a soccer game, which would be regarded as harmless by the players and the referee, could be defined as a "fair foul" (see LENK/PILZ, 1989) - a paradox. And if - as shown by GRUPE (1993) - sportsmanship spreads out into many social areas - that means: fairness is applied not only in traffic, but also in economy and politics - then fairness also mutes to a general, placative and inexact norm of behavior.

2. If everything was fair that isn't unfair, then laudable research would lead to fatal conclusions. PILZ asked young soccer players for their attitudes towards Fair-Play by having them judge certain actions in given situations. For example: "It's the last game of the championship and a victory would make you the regional champion. The score close to the end is 1:0. In this moment the following happens: Your opponent has overrun you and you stop him from running alone towards the goal by pulling his shirt" (1993, 190). For the evaluation of this item a scale from 1 to 5 was given. 1 means "fair", 5 means "unfair" and 3 is right in the middle and means therefore "neither nor". The categories 2 and 4 signify "less fair" and "a little bit unfair", in both cases a

> sentence is added: "necessary in the interest of victory"; "I am expected to do so". These inadmissible additional sentences suggest that unfair actions are necessary in the interest of victory and are expected and therefore legitimize "less fair" and "a little bit unfair" actions, so that it is no surprise that PILZ finds (which is inadmissible from a methodical point of view) that 57,6 % of the soccer players understand fairness in the sense of a fair foul (1993, 176). My opinion is that PILZ is not dealing with the theme of fairness but rather that of unfairness.

I believe that fairness cannot be determined on the background of unfairness and vice versa. Comparing publications of those authors who agree on this type of definition and looking for their smallest common denominator it becomes obvious that fairness is determinable as something **more** than obeying rules (see COURT, 1993; GABLER, 1990; GEBAUER, 1993; GERHARDT, 1993). Richard von Weizsäcker, former president of the Federal Republic of Germany, said: "Not only the formal fulfillment of the rules is demanded and never will written rules be able to replace the human attitude of Fair-Play. The sportsman who considers Fair-Play does not act according to the words, he acts according to the spirit of the rules"(1986, 107).

What then, is the spirit of the rules? Of what consists this "more than obeying rules"? First of all it has to be emphasized that rules regulate, e.g., the size of a soccer goal, how a game is started, and under what conditions a goal can be awarded by the referee. E. g., the rule that the sides of the playing field have to be changed after 45 minutes shows that the rules are supposed to guarantee equal opportunities, which are an important principle of fairness in sports (see also GERHARD, 1993, 15). But rules determine the actions of players only partially, and a moderate disobeying of rules, such as making-the-opponent-fall-down can be considered as normal and can - realistically - not be prevented. The spirit of the rules actually is constituted by the interpretation of these rules and their interpretation in situations which are not determined by the rules, mostly in conflict situations (see also GEBAUER, 1993, 110).

The aim of the spirit of the rules is that 1. a competition can be accomplished and maintained under well-regulated conditions and that 2. the competitors have the same conditions to win during the competiton and that 3. the intactness of the opponent player, without whom, e.g., a tennismatch can't be realized, is guaranteed. According to HERINGER (1993, 58) the opponent is not only necessarily needed to be able to win. Respect for the spirit of the rules "can even mean that rules have to be broken when my respect for the the opponent as a person represents the highest value" (COURT, 1993, 123). A fair action in this sense is given in the following situation: In a soccer game a team is in the last minutes of the game and down by 2 goals to 1. While team A is attacking a player of team B lies injured on the ground without the referee noticing it. The player who has the ball kicks the ball - not according to the rules - into the outfield, so that somebody can enter the field in order to examine the injured player. Mostly, team B will respond to this fair action with an equally fair - and not rule-conform - action (in the sense of equal opportunities) by throwing the ball after the short interruption back to team A.

Such actions exceed the rules. They constitute the spirit of the rules.

> Fairness can be found within the framework of sport competitions in the effort of the sportsmen to violate rarely and obey consequently(even under difficult conditions) the rules and - in the interest of equal opportunities - not to accept unsuitable advantages or to exploit unsuitable disadvantages of the opponent and to see and respect the opponent as a person and a partner, not as an enemy (see GABLER, 1990, 184).

This approach recommends not only to differentiate between fair actions and unfair actions, but to settle the "reality" of sports in fair and unfair. This means that it is necessary to distinguish between: actions which deviate from rules or norms (unfair), actions which deviate from rules but conform to norms, actions which conform to rules (neither fair nor unfair), actions which conform to norms (fair) (see also Figure 1 in appendix) In this sense fairness, above all, has to be understood as a guiding idea of sports.

Looking at my theme, two conclusions can be deduced from this definition:

If fairness consists of interpreting the spirit of the rules, then it means "to understand sport from the inside" (GERHARDT, 1993, 18). Sport, then, has to be determined from an **inner perspective**.

If fairness is shown in the effort of the player to act according to the spirit of the rules, then this shows that fair actions are connected to **attitudes, moral standpoints** and **motivations**. Hence, an education towards fairness also has to aim at the motivation to fairness.

Motivation to Fairness in Sport

The presented definition of fairness in sport leads to three possible motivational dimensions of fairness. After an examination of the relevant literature and an extensive questioning of different sport groups it turned out that the theoretical construct "fairness in sports" in a motivational-psychological perspective can be differentiated not only into 3 but rather 13 dimensions. These 13 dimensions can be subsumed into two categories depending on whether they belong either to an intrinsic or an extrinsic motivation.

Intrinsically motivated fair action exists when the fair action is realized for its own sake, if the action virtually represents the aim of the action.

Extrinsically motivated fair action exists when the fair action is instrumentally employed, e.g., for the sake of obtaining social acknowledgement.

A detailed description of the 13 dimension is given in the following (see also Figure 2 in appendix).

Intrinsic Fairness Motivation

Fairness as Internalized Concept of Acting

The idea of fairness as an internalised concept of acting proceeds from the assumption that the acting person has internalized certain patterns of behavior in its sport-socialization and that the person is keen on realizing this internalized concept whenever possible. In this connection it doesn't really matter in what kind of sport situation the acting person finds itself at the moment, because for the person the personal norms and values are valid for all situations.

Fairness Motivated by Conscience

This type of fairness has to be regarded in close connection with the idea of the internalized concept of acting, though with a different focus. The main intention of the acting person is to obtain a good conscience and to avoid a bad conscience.

Fairness due to superior social systems of values and norms

In this case the acting person understands fairness as a part of social norms and values which are relevant to itself and which represent a social duty. These moral demands have a fundamental and an interindividual validity. Therefore, it subordinates the system of the game and of the competition to superior, general and obligatory systems of value (e. g., Christian values).

Fairness as Instrument for an Ego-Boost

A characteristic for this category is that the acting person is trying to prove its fairness through its fair acting. This means that it receives a reinforcement by the contentedness with its own way of acting. The encouragement of acting thereby creates an opportunity for reward and reinforcement of the positive self-image.

Empathy as a Reason for Fairness

The fair action is directly motivated by the fact that the acting person puts itself in the situation of the opponent and therefore sympathetically anticipates how its acting would improve or wouldn't impair the condition of the opponent. E. g., if my opponent lost a match due to a false decision of the referee, I would correct this decision because I know how disappointing such a defeat can be.

Fairness as a Strive for Justice and Equal Opportunities

The action is motivated by a general striving for justice and equal opportunities. In a competition a player is - from his point of view - confronted with an inequality of opportunities and therefore tries to remedy these inequalities with an according behavior, e. g., by taking out a player of his own tug-of-war-team when the other team is lacking a player.

Extrinsic Fairness Motivation

Fairness as an Instrument for the Preservation of the Game

The acting person is interested in keeping the game/competition going and therefore avoids every action that could risk the positive atmosphere of the game. Fair behavior has in this sense become a means to preserve the game.

Fairness as an Instrument for Obtaining Social Acknowledgement

In contrast to fairness as an instrument for an ego-boost, this dimension of fairness is characterized by an acting person who receives reinforcement of its fair behavior by the recognition of other persons (opponents, spectators, publicity). The encouragement of acting in this case forms the chance for external reward.

Fairness in Order to Avoid Disapproval

According to the fore-mentioned aspect, in this case the acting person tries to avoid negative social consequences (e.g., through spectators, public opinion, relatives, friends) which it could be confronted with if it didn't behave in a fair manner.

Fairness as an Instrument to Reach Performance Goals

The acting person tries to influence the referee by acting conspicuously fair in order to reach a better judgment for his superior personal aims of performance in a future situation.

Reciprocal Fairness

In this case fair behavior is motivated by the “norm of mutuality” which has a general validity in the social interaction of persons and which can have two effects in sport. On the one hand, it is possible that an acting person has already been treated in a fair way by his opponent and therefore wants to return this fairness (reactively). On the other hand, a fair behavior (actively) could be motivated with the intention to oblige the opponent to act also fair.

Fairness as an Instrument to Reduce the Danger of Injury

This type of fairness only exists in disciplines with direct physical contact. The acting person tries to avoid an injury of his opponent by explicitly acting fair.

Fairness as an Instrument for the Preservation of Friendships

The acting person is interested in forming new friendships or doesn´t want to damage friendships that already exist. It signalizes this by acting in a fair way.

Results of a Research on Fairness Motivation of Young People

In order to record the attitudes and motivations for fairness of young people we are currently developing a questionnaire. In this questionnaire 35 situations are described, e.g., the situation in tennis that has already been mentioned above. The situation in this case is: “After a long and exciting rally in the decisive set the referee erroneously sees a ball as “out”. The player who would falsly get the point has seen that the ball has touched the line”. Now the following question is posed: “Would you as the beneficiary player correct the referee's decision to your own disfavor?” The probationers could choose between six possible answers from 1 to 6. 1 means “Yes, definitely”, 6 means “No, definitely not”. Afterwards different items are given. They can be related to the 13 dimensions of motivation that have been presented above, e. g.:

- If I corrected the decision, I would do so because I would like the applause of the spectators (this corresponds to the dimension "Fairness as an instrument for obtaining social acknowledgment"), or:
- If I corrected the decision, I would do so because I would hope that the referee might decide to my favor later on in the match (this corresponds to the dimension "Fairness as an instrument to reach performance goals").

The preliminary results of a study among 238 young people show the following tendencies:

1. Regarding the questions (which were put in a concrete form with examples) whether young people would act in certain situations in a certain (namely a fair) way and also regarding the possibilities of answers between the two poles "Yes, definitely" and "No, definitely not" on a scale from 1 to 6 (a scale with a central value of 3.5) the total fairness-score was 2.8, which means that young people are actually willing to act fair (see also Tabulation 1 in appendix).

   At the same time interesting differences can be found between individual subgroups. These differences correspond to theoretical assumptions. E.g., the following subgroups have a lower score (towards fairness):

- female subjects compared to male subjects.
- subjects under 18 years compared to subjects over 18 years.
- subjects without orientation towards competition compared to subjects that are oriented towards competition.
- subjects which are on low or middle level of performance compared to subjetcs on a high level of performance.

2. However, this positive picture gets darkened by the fact that the agreement with the corresponding actions relates mostly to those situation in which the opponent is treated in a fair manner **before** the competition, e.g., to lend an opponent goggles for swimming or wax for his cross-country skis. But if the questions address not

accepting unsuitable advantages or not exploiting unsuitable disadvantages of the opponent **while** the competition is going on, then the following tendency can be found:

- fail to correct the wrong decision of the referee to the disfavor of the opponent in a tennis match.
- not avoid a fake-fall after a "non-foul" in soccer.
- accept a goal that has been made with the help of the (hidden) hand in soccer.
- rather consider a physical attack which can be quiet dangerous for the opponent.

This applies even to a stronger degree for those subjects who are oriented towards competition.

It becomes evident that there is a willingness on the side of young people to act in a fair manner, but it can also be seen that this willingness decreases in situations of competition and it decreases even further the more important success becomes.

3. The summary of reasons for fair actions shows that the intrinsic motivation (total score of 2.70) is stronger than the extrinsic motivation (total score of 3.08). This applies especially for the two dimensions "Empathy as a reason for fairness" and "Fairness due to superior social systems of values and norms". In regard to extrinsic motivation the dimension "Fairness as an instrument to reduce the danger of injury" is rather strong, while the dimension "Fairness as an instrument to reach performance goals" is rather weak.

   Apparently, the attitude to influence other participants (e. g., the referee) by one's own fair actions in order to obtain a better result in future situations (in the interest of superior aims of performance) is not predominant especially since sometimes unfair actions can lead to immediate success.

Pedagogical Consequences

The theoretical approach and these part-results of the current research lead to schematic pedagogical considerations of an education towards fairness in sports. If fairness is constituted of taking decisions according to the "spirit of the rules" in situations that aren't exactly determinable and to act correspondingly, then the rules do not only need to be accepted but also have to be understood in their meaning. I want to depict three pedagogical consequences:

1. Besides the usually employed measures for a reduction of unfair actions (that means, especially the intensification of the sanctions for a reduction of actions that are not conform to the rules and the roll-calls and marketing-activities of the Fair-Play-Initiative), a pedagogically oriented education to fairness must begin with fairness as a concept (and not with unfairness).

2. Learning to understand this concept means to make concrete situations in which a fair attitude is an expected content of a physical education class (see GESSMANN, 1993 and KÄHLER, 1985). Above all, the pupils should talk about the possibilities they have to solve conflict situations and how those situations have to be evaluated from a point of view of sports and on a basis which morally considers general social systems of norms and values. This approach is close to KOHLBERG's (1976); in accordance with Piaget, he constructs a theory of developing morals based on the solving of moral conflict situations. On the highest level of this development of morals, moral judgments are made based on the ability to put oneself in the position of other persons, which is equal to empathy. Thereby the requisite for Kant´s categorical imperative is given: "Act in such a way that the maxime of your will could at the same time also function as a principle of general legislative".

   The more concrete a situation is and the more often pupils have experienced those situations themselves, the better they can learn to understand the possibilities for solving such conflict situations and the better they can develop a consciousness for the interpretation of rules in sports according to the "spirit of sports".

3. Based on his research KÄHLER (1985) found out that pupils are rarely praised for fair behavior in physical education classes.

Therefore, the demand has to be put forward that fair actions should be positively reinforced irrespective of success or failure. However, this reinforcement should not be directed too much towards extrinsic motivation. A moral education in physical education classes should reinforce mainly intrinsic motivation. This means (according to the definition of fairness presented earlier) to adhere consequently to the rules, to recognize the importance of equal opportunities, and to respect the opponent as a person and a partner. The reason for this focus on intrinsic motivation is that pupils learn to understand fairness from an inside perspective as an internalised concept of acting and therefore fair actions can contribute to a self-made reinforcement of their positive self-image.

An education to fairness oriented towards these intrinsic motivations aims for an attitude that is stable over time and over different situations as a central basis for fairness motivation.

References

COURT, I.: Als Frank Rijkaard Rudi Völler beleidigte - Bemerkungen zur formalistischen Deutung des Fair Play. In: V. GERHARDT,; M. LÄMMER (eds.): Fairneß und Fair play. Academia Sankt Augustin, 1993, 114-126.

GABLER, H.: Fair geht vor - Sport zwischen Aggression und Fairneß. In: O. GRUPE (ed.): Kulturgut oder Körperkult? Attempto Tübingen, 1990, 172-194.

GEBAUER, G.: Das Fortschrittsprinzip im Sport und Probleme einer Sportethik. In: V. GERHARD; M. LÄMMER (eds.): Fairneß und Fair play. Academia Sankt Augustin, 1993, 103-113.

GERHARDT, V.: Fairneß - Die Tugend des Sports. In: V. GERHARDT; M. LÄMMER (eds.): Fairneß und Fair play. Academia Sankt Augustin, 1993, 5-24.

GRUPE, O.: Kultureller Anspruch und moralische Legitimation des Sports. In: V. GERHARDT; M. LÄMMER (eds.): Fairneß und Fair play. Academia Sankt Augustin, 1993, 68-86.

HERINGER, H.J.: Fairneß und Moral. In: V. GERHARDT; M. LÄMMER (eds.): Fairneß und Fair play. Academia Sankt Augustin, 1993, 55-67.

KÄHLER, R.: Moralerziehung im Sportunterricht. Frankfurt/Thun 1985.

KOHLBERG: Moral stages und moralization. The cognitive-development-approach. In: T. LICKONA (ed.): Moral development and behavior. Holt/Rinehart/Winston, 1976, 31-53.

LENK, H.: Fairneß und Fair Play. In: V. GERHARDT; M. LÄMMER (eds.): Fairneß und Fair play. Academia Sankt Augustin, 1993, 25-40.

LENK, H.; PILZ, G.A.: Das Prinzip Fairneß. Edition Interfrom Zürich 1989.

PILZ, G.A.: Zum Problem struktureller Bedingungen für Unfairneß - Eine empirische Analyse. In: V. GERHARDT; M. LÄMMER (eds.): Fairneß und Fair play. Academia Sankt Augustin, 1993, 173-201.

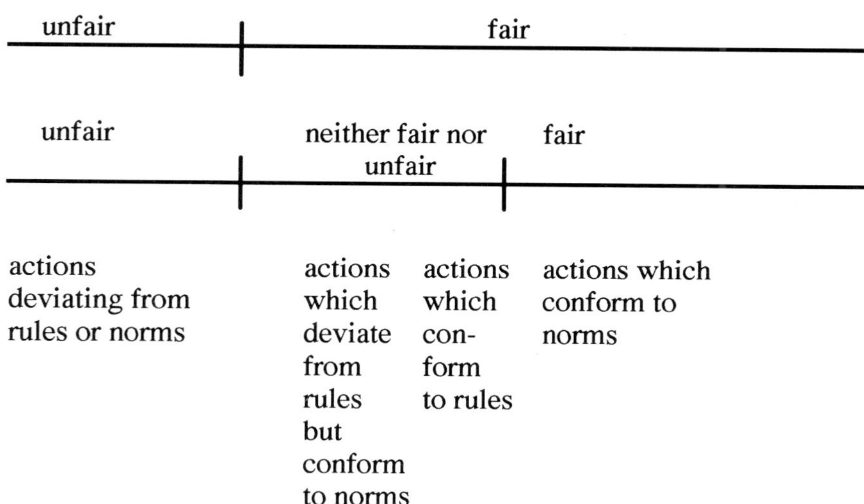

Figure 1: The "everyday life" of sport between fair and unfair

Table 1: Total fairness-score for the entire sample and the individual subgroups

SPOTCHECK	N	TOTAL FAIRNESS SCORE
1. Total	221	2,80
2. male	121	2,96
female	100	2,61
3. younger than 18	161	2,77
18 and older	60	2,89
4. oriented towards competition	152	2,86
not oriented towards competition	68	2,68
no statement	1	
5. Low and medium level	99	2,69
top performance level (state/national team)	122	2,89

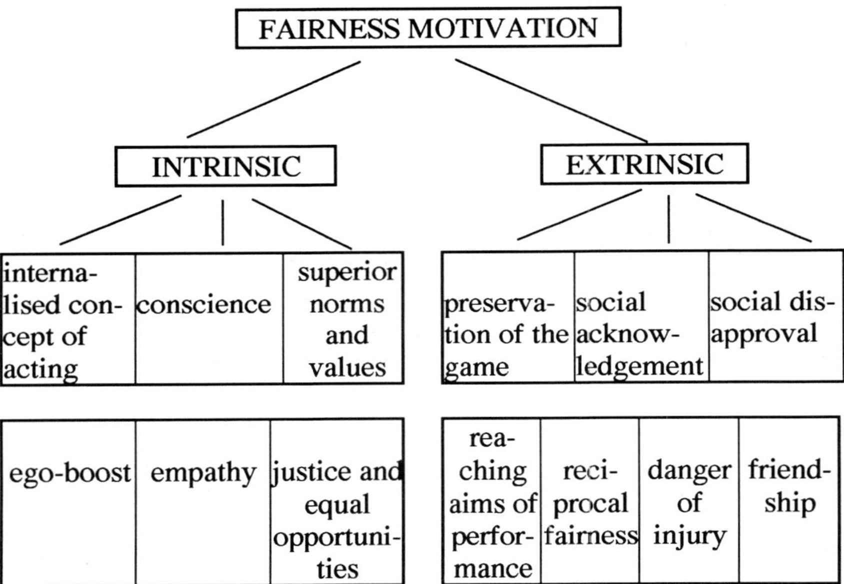

Figure 2: 13 dimensions of fairness motivation, arranged in intrinsic and extrinsic orientation

Benny J. Peiser

Sports and Moral Education
Fair Play and Aggression in Physical Education

Introduction

This paper discusses the issue of moral education, aggression and the idea of fair play in physical education (PE). I am particularly interested in issues which are related to forms of violence in PE. What does fair play mean in the contemporary sport lesson; how is it interpreted and legitimated from various standpoints and how do other try to emphasise its importance?

For more than 20 years the continuing increase of violence in sport and in physical education has caused great concern among both teachers and scholars. Up until now attempts to introduce fair play initiatives have neither resulted in progress nor have they eroded any of the problems. Why have these attempts failed and which measures would have been more appropriate in order to get the problem under control? The discussion of fair play has principally concentrated on moral behaviour of schoolchildren and athletes. It is the stated goal of all fair play initiatives to improve the moral consciousness of school children in order to establish fair sports.

I am, however, rather sceptical about attempts which try to establish fairness in sport and PE through moral awareness. It seems to me that the introduction of greater fairness in physical education lessons has to be carried out in a different way. Instead of simply waiting until schoolchildren learn moral behaviour in the PE lesson, which is even difficult to expect of average adults, certain fundamental rule changes could lead to a significant reduction of violence from the sport lessons.

Violence vs. Fair Play

Since the rise of spectator and player violence during the last 15 years, the European Governments have recognised violence in sport as a serious problem. After several years of effort on the Council of Europe, the European Ministers of Sport introduced the Code of Sports Ethics in May 1992. Among other things, school authorities are obliged to pay more attention to fair play in PE lessons. European Governments are requested not only to develop fair play education, but moreover to make it a focal point of the PE lesson. In order to implement this, research and pilot projects should be financed at the national and international levels.

Growing brutality, criminality and drug abuse among pupils and youth are often related to the decline of traditional moral values. On the other hand, it is expected from sport and physical education that they encourage the communication of moral values. This concept of the 19th century, that sports education should serve to encourage ethical and social behaviour, is still widespread among sport teachers. For more than 100 years the view has been represented in sport pedagogy that not only social behaviour can be encouraged, but also independence, altruism and fairness. Yet, professional sport is for a large part characterised by player and spectator violence, drug abuse and corruption scandals. There are, moreover, growing concerns about similar developments in the field of school sports.

The prescribed moral function which was once thought to have been played by sport has now backfired. This is increasingly apparent in the PE lesson. Instead of sport games and fitness exercise the more popular as well as considerably more dangerous contact sports are emerging. Violent behaviour, violation of rules and the use of steroids have become part of today's school sport. In reaction to the moral crisis of sport many fair play initiatives were established in different countries. These activities have for a long time showed no results. Yet the degree of aggressive behaviour in the PE lesson is still on the increase. Thus the question arises whether fair play initiatives are able to change anything with regard to this development?

A further topic has been pushing itself into the forefront of the discussion about moral and physical education for several years - the question whether competitive sports as such are responsible for increased violence. The supporter of the idea of competitive sports consider them to have a basic principle of personal and social success as well as the basis of socialisation into a competitive society. By contrast, aggression and violence are simply considered to be minor problems. Many are convinced that the acting out of aggression in school sports lead to an overall reduction of unsocial violence and criminal behaviour among youths.

The critics of the principle of competition, on the other hand, see it as a way of encouraging egoism and the rat race. Critics also maintain that those who teach schoolchildren competitive sports encourage a highly conscious moral behaviour that only affects the victors. Moreover, the competitive principle not only applicable in sport, but also leads to asocial behaviour on society in general. This criticism has remained distinctly in the background for the last few years. The economic and political collapse of the communist states has made it clear that a dynamic market economy is unobtainable without the pressure of competition.

Only cynics will conclude from this that the recognition of the principle of competition will simultaneously lead to the legitimisation of the inherent violence in sport. It is in fact quite the opposite. In spite of the dynamic competitive situation in sport there is a challenge to reduce this to a minimum. The more dynamic the competition, the more extreme the combat, the less likely that it is allowed to be resolved with physical violence. How is this possible?

For a long time sports teachers generally recognised that physical education encouraged not only moral education, but also that at the same time the dare to win was in the background. Modern sports is unthinkable without the desire to succeed. Sport and its global impact symbolises the victory of the competition-orientated society based on private ownership which is applicable in almost all parts of the world today. There should be, therefore, no moral objections against victory and success in sport.

But in spite of this, critics continuously maintain that the integration of types of combat sport in the PE lesson teach pupils how to achieve victory over others. I am unable to recognise the moral implications here since different pupils and different levels of competitiveness are present in all other school subjects too. Sport, here, is no different to any other area of education. One also wants to achieve success and awards in mathematics, the language lesson or in history. I also consider the problem of violating the rules of a game to be minimal, since most of the rules in sport are such that one can't help but break them.

The grave difference to other areas of education is that sport alone can successes can be achieved by means of violence. And in sport and the PE lesson alone is physical violence widely accepted. The most popular misconception regarding sport violence holds that aggressive behaviour in the PE lesson may serve as a social and individual safety-valve. According to the so-called catharsis theory of aggression, expressions of violence in school sports reduces the overall level of social aggression among youth. Aggression not acted out in sports will otherwise explode in a much worse form of unsocial or even criminal behaviour.

Consequently, aggression in school sport is widely regarded as a socially adequate means of discharging pent-up hostility and frustration, thereby improving the peaceful and lawful nature of society. Empirical research, however, shows unequivocally that violence in sport has quite the opposite effect. Far from reducing the level of aggression, it helps to reinforce aggressive impulses and leads to an increased likelihood of violent behaviour. Due to its inherent agonal structure and dynamics as a mock battle, many forms of sport create its own aggression. During the last twenty years, none of the major psychological studies on sport violence found any support for the catharsis theory. Furthermore, since aggression is an essential prerequisite of victory in sport, its catharsis is neither intended nor desired. The learning of a particular sport, in most cases, involves the learning of aggressive play. This is part of the socialisation process into sports and, in many cases, is encouraged by coaches, teachers and parents.

It is not the teaching of combat and contact sports per se, however, which poses as a moral problem in the PE lesson, but instead the seemingly increasing wave of violence among youth sport and PE. Before combat sports became legitimate, physical education of children and adolescents in past centuries was marked by aggressive and, in parts, by sadistic brutality. The traditional 'hardening' of children, in particular of boys, and the former military drill of physical education, included an even higher level of violence. Many modern team and combat sports, on the other hand, have in fact attempted to reduce physical contact and thus inherent violence.

Basketball is a particularly appropriate example of the development. Basketball was originally invented as a sport in which bodily contact and thus physical violence was reduced to an absolute minimum. Yet, as a result of the development of basketball into one of the fastest and most dynamic ballgames, bodily contact has increased over the course of the years. Today basketball counts as one of the toughest team sports, which is marked by a growing level of foul play and violence. This apparent regression, however, is not the result of more aggressive players today as there were previously. In my opinion, the responsible factor for the toughening of basketball has less to do with player attitudes. Instead it is primarily related to the liberal interpretation and punishment of rule violations. It seems that the governing bodies of basketball have widely bended according to the pressure of the public to allow more aggressive play. I am talking about a particularly delicate problem, with which sports organisations are confronted.

Most of the rules in modern sports have been formulated in order to hinder bodily violence. On the other hand, spectators, sponsors and, above all, the media, push for an increase of confrontation, aggression and attacks because this, inevitably, leads to higher levels of excitement among the audience therefore to increased popularity and higher revenues from broadcasting and advertising. Governing bodies in sport are thus confronted with a moral dilemma: They have to strike a balance between the social and moral interest to minimise violent behaviour in sport on the one hand and the interest of spectator, sponsors and the media, who prefer encased violence on the other.

Due to the public pressure of huge stadium crowds and fears of unpopular interruptions and the consequent slowing down of team sports, existing means of deterrence (i.e. free kicks, penalty kicks, cautions, sendings off, suspensions, etc.) are not used adequately. In other words: Violence in sport - above all in professional sport - could, at any time, be ruled out entirely, if only the governing bodies would take the initiative to tighten the rules accordingly.

Since these measures, although possible, are not introduced, PE teachers or pupils are confronted with existing rules and regulations which legitimise high levels of bodily contact. It is this legitimisation of certain forms of physical violence which makes fair play in the PE lesson difficult to achieve. This applies to an even greater extend when the rules of the game are unable to adequately prevent or deter unfair behaviour.

In most cases foul play is punished by simply with a free kick or with a warning. Only in rare cases it is punished with harsher measures. Since foul or violent behaviour in sport and PE is handled with inappropriate penalties, there seems to be little disadvantage of fouling. In most cases, fouling and violent acts by players result in advantages for the offender's team and disadvantages for the team of the victim. Moreover, fouls are not only inadequately penalised, but the free kick in itself is no adequate sanction of violent conduct. The advantages of foul play for the offending team heavily outweighs any benefits to be gained as a result of free kicks. As a result of this inherent deficiency, foul and aggressive play increases the overall chances of success.

Although free kicks are generally an inadequate means of deterring foul play, the degree of violent conduct in sport and PE significantly decreases after players have been cautioned or sent off. Effective punishment of unlawful conduct could, therefore, serve as a deterrent, both at the individual and general level. Consistent punishment of violent behaviour dissuades the individual offender from re-offending during a particular match. Furthermore, it would discourage other potential offenders. In other words, unfair behaviour and physical violence in sport seem to be worthwhile since the rules of the game are such that there are no appropriate discouraging factors. The real danger lies in the effects of habitual violence in sport and PE on the respect for the law. If one continues to deter and punish actual bodily harm and physical violence inadequately, pupils could eventually lose respect for the law.

PE teachers are faced with the problem of having to distance themselves from particularly popular sports if they want to prevent the inherent violence in these sports during their lessons. Violence in school sports can be significantly reduced if one tightens up particular rules in order to minimise bodily contact and to make unfair behaviour unattractive. At the same time, courage is necessary to independently alter some rules for different sports in the PE lesson in order that injurious play and painful collisions are avoided. In order to achieve this, it is necessary to undergo an intellectual reflection of the rules, their appropriateness and the possibility of change. Children and youth are able to recognise moral conflicts in sport if there was an appropriate framework and a morally consequent teacher present.

Risto Telama, Juha Heikkala, Lauri Laakso

Game Reasoning and Strategic Thinking in Sport: Attitudes among Young People toward Rules

Introduction

The ideals of fair play and sportsmanship can be considered to be the most important among the ethical principles of sport. These ideals are based on the traditional conception of sport being constructive for the character and valuable for the morals. The ideal of fair play incorporates unwritten norms such as consideration shown toward the opponent, a certain degree of altruism, and the requirement of being just. What is fundamentally important for the ideal of fair play, however, is the attitude toward rules. The rules are there to guarantee that the competition takes place on equal terms, which is an important condition for fair play. Rules have also been considered to be educationally valuable, because the observance of rules makes societal norms familiar and gives experience in cooperation.

We know from experience, and it is also confirmed by empirical research, that foul play is rather common at all levels of sport (HEINILÄ, 1984; JACKSON et al., 1985; MUSTONEN et al., 1987). Neither does empirical research confirm the idea that sport is educational in terms of the morals. On the contrary, it has been found out that among athletes moral thinking is at a lower level than it is among non-athletes, and the situations in sport are evaluated at a lower level than situations elsewhere (BREDEMEIER et al., 1984; BREDEMEIER et al., 1987; BREDEMEIER et al., 1987; GONCALVES, 1990).

The observations mentioned above support the conclusion that sport as such hardly develops moral thinking, but it is necessary to point out at the same time that sport as such cannot be considered to function without any morals either. The core of the problem lies in the nature of the interaction between individuals and various human factors governing such interaction as well as in the structural elements of sport itself. In this respect, sport can be analyzed in an interesting way on the basis of the theory of discourse ethics developed by HABERMAS (1992).

The central principle in discourse ethics, which is based on the theory of communicative action, is that "we can justify our choice of a norm" (HABERMAS, 1992, 66). The agreement on the norms and their justification takes place in communicative activity which is characteristically aimed at achievement of mutual understanding. Interaction is communicative "when actors are prepared to harmonize their plans of action through internal means, committing themselves to pursuing their goals only on the condition of an agreement - one that already exists or one to be negotiated - about definition of the situation and prospective outcomes" (134). HABERMAS makes a distinction between communicative action and strategic action, in which "one actor seeks to influence the behaviour of another by means of the threat of sanctions or the prospect of gratification in order to cause the interaction to continue as the first actor desires" (58). Strategic action is normally characteristic of behaviour that is solely aimed at the achievement of success and prospective outcomes of the activity, while communicative action is aimed at mutual understanding. Coordination between the actors in strategic action depends on the degree of agreement between self-centred calculations (133).

HABERMAS has also analyzed KOHLBERG's theory of the developmental levels of moral thinking in the light of discourse ethics. He says that "what KOHLBERG conceives as a constructive learning process operating at all levels is built into the transition (which has become routine for the adult) from norm-guided action to norm-testing discourse" (127). What is important then is the acquisition of communicative action and discussion of common norms. According to HABERMAS, it is the face-to-face situation that is crucial in interaction, and language plays a decisive role in it.

How can sport then be analyzed in terms of the conceptions of discourse ethics? Competitive sport is characteristically aimed at success, which means in a way that self-centredness is incorporated in it and accepted. Competitive sport could be seen to offer a good starting point for strategic action in particular, rather than for communicative action. Competition means an opposite to collaboration, and competitive situations do not involve a great deal of interaction that could make discourse possible. The structure of competition does not allow for communicative action as a usual form of activity in it.

It is however also true of sport that it involves a large number of dilemma situations which could in principle be solved by means of face-to-face discourse. The rules of sport and their observance as well as the ideal of fair play could also be regarded as communicative action as defined by HABERMAS, in which "actors are prepared to harmonize their plans of action through internal means, committing themselves to pursuing their goals only on the condition of an agreement - one that already exists or one to be negotiated - about definition of the situation and prospective outcomes" (134). What is important for the development of moral consciousness is the attitude toward rules. It is possible that rules are observed only because of the authority involved in them or in fear of sanctions, which refers to the lowest levels in the development of moral consciousness, but it is also possible that rules are regarded as part of communicative action and as an existing agreement on the conditions of action.

Earlier research has indicated that foul play and disregard of the ideal of fair play are stepped up with increased importance of competition (GRINESKI, 1989; SNOPPERS et al., 1986; LEE et al., 1990; SMITH et al., 1979; TELAMA et al., 1993). This may be in agreement with HABERMAS's observation that the probability of strategic action is increased, and that of communicative action is decreased, when the action is entirely devoted to achievement of success. This is why the level and importance of competition are factors that have a crucial impact on the attitudes toward rules. In addition to competition, subcultures with their unwritten practices found within various sports also influence the attitudes toward rules.

Purpose

The aim of the study reported here is to describe the attitudes of young athletes representing different age groups and types of sport toward foul play in general, rules, and the ideal of fair play at different types of competitive situations and to investigate the impact of the level and importance of the competition on the attitudes toward rules among them. The study is a part of the international comparative study on Ethical Values in Sport and Young People.

The Methods

Sixty 12-year-old and 16-year-old soccer players (boys and girls) and ten cross-country skiers (boys) were interviewed using a semi-structural method prepared by the Council of Europe research team under the leadership of Martin Lee (LEE, 1990). The subjects were asked to express their opinion and rationale for the opinions on a number of dilemma situations in sport. In addition, 327 ice hockey players, 128 biathlonists, and 51 wrestlers, all representing boys and the age groups from 10 to 16 years, were administered a multiple-choice questionnaire in which they were asked to take a stand toward a number of statements or dilemma situations in sport (HÄRKÖNEN et al., 1993; SORMUNEN et al., 1994; TIILIKAINEN, 1994). A number of examples of the questions are given in Appendix 1. The answers were used to calculate the summative values of fair play, foul play, and aggressiveness. The interview (soccer players and skiers) was used to investigate the importance of the level of competition by varying the dilemma situation (e.g. "what about a very important final?"). The ice hockey players, biathlonists, and wrestlers came from different levels.

The Results

In the questionnaire given to the biathlonists, wrestlers, and ice hockey players, one alternative was to be chosen from among three or four solutions to a dilemma situation. Among the alternatives at least one represented action conforming to the rules or the ideal of fair play, e.g. altruism. The majority of the answers were in accordance with this ideal alternative (biathlonists 70 %, wrestlers 66 %, ice hockey players 52 %). Action in accordance with the rules without any altruistic alternatives was even more common. In the interview, a total of 56 % of the answers by young soccer players were representative of behaviour in accordance with the ideal of fair play. Among the skiers interviewed this alternative was chosen by almost all. This means that the clear majority of young athletes are willing to observe the rules in ordinary competitions.

In types of sport which involve performance by individuals such as skiing or biathlon the importance of the rules is less crucial than it is in team sports, and there are fewer chances therefore to resort to foul. The possible forms of foul are taking a shortcut, forbidden change of skis, and mild aggressiveness towards fellow competitors or slight digression from sportsmanship. Answers that were indicative of actual transgression against the rules were very rare among skiers and biathlonists.

In combat sports such as wrestling, the rules are more important than they are in skiing. The types of foul that occur in wrestling are forbidden holds and causing injury to the opponent intentionally. A total of 23 % of the young wrestlers were inclined to use forbidden holds.

In team sports such as ice hockey and soccer, in which the opponents are regularly in physical contact with each other, the rules are highly significant. From among the young soccer players a total of 23 to 40 % were ready to commit an intentional foul at certain types of situations, and in ice hockey the proportion of clear transgression against the rules was about the same, but the inclination towards aggressiveness at the borderline of the rules was even greater.

The tendency towards foul play increased with age, and the inclination towards fair play decreased with ice hockey players and wrestlers. In addition, aggressiveness increased with age among the ice hockey players.

The importance of the level of competition was studied in the questionnaire data by dividing the athletes into two levels. The higher level consisted of wrestlers who had participated in Finnish championships and of ice hockey players who were members of teams that represented their clubs in junior leagues. The difference between the two levels was not significant for any variable.

The impact of the importance of the competition and the way in which the attitudes towards fair play and the rules were related to the situations concerned came up in the interviews. An example could be a situation of a 0 - 0 tie in soccer: team A is advancing and succeeds in passing the ball so that it goes past a defender of team B just above his head; behind the defender concerned there is nobody who could cut the pass, and it looks probable that the pass will result in a goal. Although almost all of the young people reacted to this situation the way the rules require, every fourth of them was ready to resort to action violating the rules when the nature of the situation was changed. For instance, 12-year-old boy (B 12); in the 1 - 0 situation the opponent should be tripped" or "G 16; tripping could be considered, since it is an important game". Many reasoned for behaviour in accordance with the rules by reference to fair play, but observance of the rules was also considered important for competitive strategy: "B 16; it may mean that you will be excluded from the game" and "B 12; you may end up having a penalty kick, which will almost certainly mean a goal".

The logic of competition is also visible in the answers by the skiers, but less often. For instance, skier A has got close to skier B, who started before him and is known to be good. A has asked him three times to give room for him to overtake but B has not accepted it. The trail is rather narrow. Most skiers were inclined to function in accordance with the rules, but only because of straightforward respect for the rules. "You may be excluded from the competition yourself, if you do something." Some were ready to hit the other competitor with the stick, and the reasoning behind such an action was the importance of the competition: "you lose your temper, and also valuable time, but I would not hit in practice competitions".

Altruism proper, that is, empathic concern for the other person, is not easily applicable to the idea of competition. For instance, in the situation of ice hockey "As an attacker you are trying to get hold of the puck at the opponent's end. Your stick hits your opponent's eyebrow accidentally, and at the same time you get the puck. What would you probably do?" As many as 56 % of the answers indicated that the players would go on playing towards the goal without paying any attention to what happened, 19 % would go on playing but would shout something to the referee, and 25 % would pass the puck elsewhere and check that the opponent is not injured. In skiing competitions also, most skiers would simply pass an injured fellow competitor, some of them without paying any attention, others trying to call for help. In the same way, at a situation in soccer in which an opponent seems to have been injured but the referee does not seem to have noticed it and a chance to make a goal is opening up, as many as 92 % of the players would like to make use of the situation and go on with the game. The reasoning that was said to be behind the unconcern was, among other things, the importance of the competition: "if you are skiing to beat the others, there is no time to stop and see how they are doing"; "the more important the competition is, the more certain it is that you just pass them". In soccer a mention was also made of the objectivization of the opponent: "It is no concern of mine, that's an opponent, and there is no reason why I should care".

At the above situation in soccer, a clear reference was also made to the rules and the task of the referee: "It is the referee's task to hold up the game"; "we have always been told that you go on playing until you hear the referee whistle".

Discussion

According to the information derived from the interviews and the questionnaire, the majority of the 10-to-16-year-old young athletes are inclined to observe the rules and the ideal of fair play, but the number of young athletes who are ready to resort to transgression against the rules and foul play is also large. The readiness to break the rules, to resort to unfair behaviour, or to be aggressive increases with age. This is in agreement with the results of earlier research (LEE et al., 1989; MCMORRIS et al., 1990; LIUKKONEN et al., 1992).

The change that takes place with age does not correlate well with the idea of there being cognitive development and development of moral consciousness behind moral thinking (KOHLBERG, 1975; PIAGET et al., 1977). Athletes certainly develop cognitively in the same way as other young people. It seems that they do not apply the moral facilities that develop in them to moral thinking in sport but rather to selfish strategic calculation required by the logic of competition. With age people learn to assess better what is worth doing to maximize the gain, for instance, resorting to foul purposefully when the penalty is considered to be a lesser risk than the gain achieved by means of the violation.

It is also possible that the fact that sport is regarded as an environment that is morally different from the rest of life is of some importance (BREDEMEIER & SHIELDS, 1985). Sport is either considered a moral world of its own or it is possible that decisions to be made in sport contexts are not regarded as moral problems at all. Sport is sport, game. Moral reasoning is replaced by game reasoning.

In the present data, the changes taking place with age as found among the ice hockey players are also due to the fact that players under 12 years of age apply rules that are different from those that are applied by older ones; for instance, tackle is entirely forbidden.

Some of the young people gave expression to a willingness to reach mutual understanding at certain types of situations. This came up as an emphatic adoption of a role or as an attempt to retain the meaningfulness of the game: "Nobody likes having legs kicked on", "It may be your turn some time", "Conning the referee makes the game silly", "What I want is good game", "Kicks on the legs make me lose all interest in the game". Answers like these were rather rare however. Reasoning that was concerned with maximizing the gain were much more common. Both fouls and observation of rules were argued for by reference to strategic thinking: at certain situations it makes sense to violate the rules, at others it does not.

In the study reported here no difference was found between competitors at different levels in the attitudes they had towards violation of rules or fair play. In this respect the results are in disagreement with several earlier studies (GRINESKI, 1989; LEE et al., 1990; SHUITEMAN et al., 1986; SMITH et al. & CURTIS, 1979; TELAMA et al., 1993). One reason may be that in the present study the difference between the levels was not big enough. The logic and structure of competition obviously functions the same way in all kinds of organized sport for young people. It is also probable that what is decisive is not the level of competition as such but the importance of a particular competition situationally and personally. The situational and personal importance of competition came up clearly in the interviews, where it was possible to vary the situations and the interviewees were able to argue for their choices. At less important competitions it is possible to observe the rules and even be altruistic, but when the importance of the competition is raised, such behaviour becomes less common. The influence of the personal importance of competition is also supported by the fact that competitive target orientation correlates with violation of rules and foul play (DUDA et al., 1991).

In young people's sport the influence of competition is also linked up with the impact of the way in which adults participate in the organization of their sport. Attention has earlier been called to the fact that young people observe the rules in their own games and plays better than in competitive sport organized by adults and the rules have a different function (MCINTOSH, 1988; TELAMA et al., 1993). In young people's own games, rules represent an agreement based on communicative action that is aimed at increased mutual understanding to make further action possible. Any disagreement there will be solved through interactional dialogue. It is the players themselves who determine the challenge and stress that relates to success. In sport organized by adults it is adults who take care of the observation of rules. In this way young people lose the chance of solving dilemmas by means of dialogue, which can be considered an important educational potential in sport. Moral decisions are in a sense delegated to referees, which results in the adoption of a strategic attitude toward rules.

At the highest levels of sport it seems to be rather difficult to accommodate the logic and self-centredness of competitive sport, on the one hand, and communicative action aimed at mutual understanding, on the other. At their best, the rules of sport could represent an agreement based on communicative action and mutual understanding. This requires however, as has been pointed out by HABERMAS, that face-to-face interactional discourse is possible and that the goals of action are not biased by achievement of success.

In conclusion, it could be suggested that in sport for young people the number of high-level competitions should be reduced and young people's own responsibility and interaction between them be increased.

References

BREDEMEIER, B.J.; SHIELDS, D.L.: Basketball players' and non-athletes' moral reasoning about life and sport. Paper presented in the Olympic Scientific Congress, Eugene, Oregon 1984.

BREDEMEIER, B.J.; SHIELDS, D.L.: Values and violence in sports today. The moral reasoning athletes use in their games and in their lives. Psychology Today, 1985, 19(10), 22-25, 28-29, 32.

BREDEMEIER, B.J.; SHIELDS, D.L.: Game reasoning and interactional morality. The Journal of Genetic Psychology, 1986, 147, 257-275.

BREDEMEIER, B.J.; WEISS, M.R.; SHIELDS, D.L.; COOPER, B.A.B.: The relationship between children's legitimacy judgements and their moral reasoning, aggression tendencies, and sport involvement. Sociology of Sport Journal, 1987, 4(1), 48-60.

DUDA, J.L.; OLSON, L.K.; TEMPLIN, T.J.: The relationship of task and ego orientation to sportmanship attitudes and the perceived legitimacy of injurious acts. Research Quarterly for Exercise and Sport, 1991, 62(1), 79-87.

GRINESKI, S.: Children, games and prosocial behavior. Insight and connections. Journal of Physical Education, Recreation and Dance, 1989, 20-25.

CONCALVES, C.: Fair play and youth sport participants. In: R. TELAMA; L. LAAKSO; M. PIERON; I. RUOPPILA; V. VIHKO (eds.): Physical education and life long physical activity. Jyväskylä. Reports of Physical Culture and Health, 1990, 73, 137-143.

HABERMAS, J.: Moral conciousness and communicative action. The MIT Press, Massachusetts, Cambridge 1990.

HÄRKÖNEN, A.; MIESTAMO, L.: Moraalikäsityksiä urheilussa sekä suoritusodotuksia ja -paineita jääkiekkoilevilla lapsilla ja heidän vanhemmillaan. Liikuntapedagogiikan pro gradu -tutkielma. Jyväskylän yliopisto, Jyväskylä 1993.

HEINILÄ, K.: Ethics of sport. University of Jyväskylä. Department of Sociology and planning for physical culture. Research reports, 1984, no. 30.

KNOPPERS, A.; SHUITEMAN, J.; LOVE, B.: Winning is not the only thing. Sociology of Sport Journal, 1986, (3), 43-56.

KOHLBERG, L.: The cognitive-developmental approach to moral education. Phi Delta Kappan, 1975, 56(10), 670-677.

LEE, M.: Experts group on Ethics in Sport and Young People. Summary of agreed interview procedures. Strasbourg, Council of Europe, DS-SR, 1990, (90) 22.

LEE, M.; COOK, C.: Review of the literature on fairplay with special reference to children's sport. Strasbourg, Council of Europe, DS-SR, 1990, (90) 10.

LIUKKONEN, J.; SALMINEN, S.; SAVONEN, L.: Reilu peli. Liikunta ja tiede, 1992, 2, 5-9.

MCINTOSH, P. C.: 41st European Teacher's Seminar on "Education against Violence" the Potential of Fair Play in Sport". Donaueschingen, 10-15 October. Council for Cultural Co-operation. Strasbourg 1988.

MCMORRIS, T.; MCGONAGLE, D.: Ethical values in sport - age group difference. In: R. TELAMA; L. LAAKSO; M. PIERON; I. RUOPPILA; V. VIHKO (eds.): Physical education and life-long physical activity, Jyväskylä, Reports of Physical Culture and Health, 1990, 73, 167-175.

MUSTONEN, P., LEHTINEN, I.; TAPANI, P.: Alakulttuurin vaikutus jääkiekkoväkivaltaan. Liikunta ja tiede 24, 1987, (3) 138-140.

PIAGET, J.; INHELDER, B.: Lapsen psykologia. Gummerus, Jyväskylä 1977.

SMITH, R.; SMOLL, F.; CURTIS, B.: Coach effectiveness training: a cognitive-behavioral approach to enhancing relationship skills in youth sport coaches. Journal of Sport Psychology, 1979, (1), 59-75.

SORMUNEN, H.; SUORANIEMI, M.: 10 - 17 -vuotiaiden painijoiden ja jääkiekkoilijoiden urheilumoraali ja urheiluun asennoituminen. Liikuntapedagogiikan pro gradu -tutkielma. Jyväskylän yliopisto, Jyväskylä 1994.

TELAMA, R.; HEIKKALA, J.; LAAKSO, L.: Conceptions about fair play and morals in sport among young finnish athletes. Paper presented at AIESEP Meeting of Experts. Ballarat, Australia, November 8-12, 1993.

TERRY, P.C.; JACKSON, J.J.: The determinants and control of violence in sport. Quest, 1985, 37 (1), 27-3.

TIILIKAINEN, H.: Urheilun moraali ja urheiluun asennoituminen 12 - 16 -vuotiailla ampumahiihtäjillä. Liikuntapedagogiikan pro gradu -tutkielma. Jyväskylän yliopisto, Jyväskylä 1994.

Appendix 1.

Examples of the dilemmas in questionnaire

Wrestling:

Your opponent has got you in a bridge and you can't get out of it. Probably...

1) I'll try to get out of the situation with all my strength
2) I'll accept my fate and see that I am powerless in the situation
3) I'll try to pull at his fingers without the referee noticing

You are leading by one point in the finals of the national championships and there are only 20 seconds left. Probably...

1) I'll begin to tie my shoelaces in order to gain some time to recover
2) I'll bluff the referee by pretending to be active
3) I'll try to increase my lead

Ice hockey:

You are tackled in a way which is against the rule (you think!) while you have the puck, but the referee doesn't whistle. Probably...

1) I'll finish the situation (don't care much)
2) When I get the opportunity I will tackle the player who tackled me
3) I stay on the ice and try to get the tackler a penalty

You are in the offensive line and you have just received the puck when you see that a player from the other side is lying hurt on the ice. Probably...

1) I keep on playing but tell the referee what has happened
2) I arrange an interruption of playing time (e.g. shoot the puck out of the rink)
3) I try to score in spite of what has happened

Biathlon

You have done your share in a relay race. The anchormen are on their way. Your team is leading, but your worst competitor has almost caught up with your team mate when his stick breaks in the forest close to where you are standing. There is no one else about. What do you do?

1) You turn away and pretend you did not see the whole thing
2) You laugh scornfully and wish him a happy race
3) You give him your own stick so that the winner of the relay race would be decided in a sporting manner.

3. Changes in Sport: A Challenge for Research

- Methodological Reflections

- Measurement in Sport

Andrew C. Sparkes

Multiple Voices and Visions: The Postmodern Challenge To Research in Physical Education and Sport

1 Introduction

At the 1990 AIESEP World Convention, as part of her keynote address, Linda BAIN (1990a) considered the immediate future for sport pedagogy and signalled that a collection of views labelled as postmodernism or poststructuralism might make a contribution to this future. Four years on, I believe this potential has yet to be fully realised. Consequently, my intention is to stimulate further debate, and I hope some action, in relation to research in physical education (PE) and sport by focusing upon the problems posed for researchers by postmodernist thinking with regard to issues of representation (also see SPARKES, 1995). In making this my focus I also hope to indicate how we might begin to meet the justifiable challenge put forward by BAIN (1990b) to the research community for a world spoken, and I would add written, from many sites in a way that celebrates ambiguity and competing discourses along with different voices and visions.

Postmodernism, according to TINNING (1991) is an intellectual position, a form of cultural criticism, and a response to an emerging set of social, cultural, and economic conditions that characterise an age of global capitalism and individualism. As such, it is about the changing nature of modern social thought and presents a radical challenge to our whole way of understanding the social world. MCLENNAN (1992, 328) notes, 'Post-modern theorists say that a changing social world requires an entirely different way of reflecting on our existence today. In other words, they argue that, just as social conditions change, so do the concepts and categories that we use to make sense of society'. As a consequence, researchers need to 'deconstruct' fundamentally the ways that they habitually look at the social world which entails examining, and perhaps even discarding, some of the sacred ideas and aspirations of social science that have their roots in the Enlightenment of the Eighteenth Century. The forms this deconstruction has taken is difficult to summarise. Indeed, it would seem that there are as many postmodernisms as there are authors who write about postmodernism! Given that this intellectual movement is so irritatingly illusive to define in any authoritative sense I will make no attempt to do so. My tactic will be to focus upon some recognisable features that provide a useful starting points for interrogating and reflecting upon the ways in which we represent ourselves as authors and Others in our written texts.

According to POOL (1991, 313) one of the most important characteristics of postmodernism is, 'the blurring of boundaries, not only those between the different arts, but also between science and art, fact and fiction, and between the different academic disciplines'. This blurring makes possible the uses of styles and genres which would have been considered inferior or non-literary in other schools of thought. An associated characteristic is postmodernism's focus upon the problematic nature of representation which opens up a host of questions regarding the creation of any text, and the relation between the text and the reader. For postmodernists representations do not mirror the world but are actively engaged in its production. All this leads to an increased sensibility regarding the social text and its claims to authority in an age in which the illusion of transparent 'objective' description is over as we enter the age of inscription. Here, according to DENZIN (1994, 505), 'Writers create their own situated, inscribed versions of the realities they describe'.

2 Research Texts as Persuasive Fiction

All scholarly or 'scientific' work must be written and read in accordance with some generic principles. There is no style-less or organization-less writing. The 'facts' of the case do not imprint themselves. Our experience of the world, both physical and cultural, is always mediated by conventions of enquiry, and that experience is equally mediated by conventions of writing. The ethnography is constituted by one collection of conventions, the paper in a scientific journal by another. The products themselves are very different in form and content, but are equally conventional (ATKINSON, 1990, 9).

When researchers of any paradigmatic persuasion write about their work, their findings, be it in the form of 'fact' or 'fiction', 'prose' or 'poetry', 'science' or 'literature', they all rely upon textual conventions and rhetorical methods. As ATKINSON (1992, 38) argues, 'Language is not a transparent medium through which the world may be experienced or expressed. Neither speech nor writing can furnish a privileged, neutral mechanism of representation'. Under the pervasive influence of postmodernism a host of questions have been raised regarding the creation of any text, and the relationship between the author, the text, and the reader. This new self-consciousness has led to what MARCUS and FISCHER (1986, 8) have called a crisis of representation that involves a reassessment of dominant ideas across the human sciences whereby, 'It is not just the ideas themselves that are coming under attack but the paradigmatic style in which they have been represented. The crisis arises from uncertainty about adequate means of describing social reality'. For RICHARDSON (1991, 2) this crisis means that the problem for social scientists is not simply just one of devising better techniques and instruments for apprehending social reality, 'since writing up what one has apprehended is itself a central theoretical and methodological problematic. How can we "write" (explain, describe, index) the social?'.

In recent years increased attention has been given to the process of writing as it transports the researcher from the 'context of discovery' to the 'context of presentation'. The product of inquiry is now under intense scrutiny. Language is now seen as a constitutive force that creates a particular view of reality which means that no textual staging can ever be innocent. That is, how we choose to write has profound implications not just for how readable the text is, but also how the people it portrays are 'read' and understood. Whose voices are included in the text, how they are given weight and interpreted, along with questions of priority and juxtaposition, are not just textual strategies but political concerns. As ATKINSON (1992, 7) makes clear, 'textual conventions do not merely raise technical or methodological issues: they have moral consequences'. This has led STRATHERN (1987) to talk of persuasive fictions which highlights new problems in the writer/reader/subject relationship and highlights issues to do with communication. Similarly, both YOUNG (1991) and TIERNEY (1993) argue that the conventions employed to construct ethnographic descriptions are at root fictive, and that in a postmodern period sensitive to multiple realities, the once comfortable distinctions between fact and fiction have begun to dissolve.

The notion of persuasive fiction is also important since it forces a recognition of the rhetorical features in any piece of writing as the author attempts to establish a relationship with the readers and convince them of the status of the 'findings'. It is now recognised that all researchers use writing and rhetorical devices as part of their methods and practices of persuasion (SPARKES, 1991, 1992a, 1995). With this in mind I will consider the dominant kind of tale told within the PE and sport research community, that is the scientific tale, and highlight some of its rhetorical features. Following this, I consider the realist tale which is the dominant tale told by interpretive researchers and suggest that while there are differences between this and the scientific tale, there are also striking similarities. These similarities might, once recognised, be a cause for concern for some researchers and stimulate them to tell their tales in different ways. Finally, to assist the process of reflection on representational issues a range of alternative tales are focused upon in order to encourage experimentation with different genres in the future.

3 Scientific Tales

According to ATKINSON (1990, 43), 'Conventionally, the scientific paper is self-effacing, in that its style and organization are not foregrounded'. The writing in such papers is a stripped-down, cool style that avoids ornamentation, often stating conclusions as propositions or formulae. However, the apparent absence of style is actually a rhetorical device in its own right. That is, the 'style of no-style' is the style of science. MULKAY (1991) sees this as a realist technique that allows the text to give the impression that its symbols are inert, neutral representations of the world that exist quite independently of the researchers interests and efforts. To this we must add the image of the researcher who is presented as a neutral and disengaged analyst. The language of identifying variables, measuring relationships between them, and describing events by using an abstracted, detached form of language with an impersonal voice that puts distance between language as written and the reality it represents. EISNER (1988) suggests that the purpose of writing in this way is to objectify through depersonalisation. Similarly, the use of propositions is a means to empty language of emotion and thereby convince the reader of the researcher's disengagement from the analysis.

RICHARDSON (1991) suggests that implicit metaphors orient and prefigure knowledge, and notes how in positivist-empiricist forms of research three metaphors are regularly used to remove the 'datum' from the temporal and human practices that produce it. In such a way human beings, both researcher and other, are metaphored out of this world.

First is the grammatical split between subject and object, a wholly unnoticed metaphor for the separation between "real" subjects and objects. The metaphor is particularly powerful because it is part of our language structure. Second, empiricism views language as a tool. The empiricist world is fixed and available for viewing through the instrumentality of language, downplaying that what we speak about is partly a function of how we speak. Third, empiricism uses a management metaphor. Data are "managed,", variables are "manipulated," research is "designed," time is "flow-charted," "tables" are "produced," and "model" (like toothpaste and cars) are "tested". The three metaphors work together to reify a radical separation between subject and object and to create a static world, fixed in time and space. In this world, the "knower" is estranged from the "known", intellectual inquiry becomes a matter of precise observation and measurement of what is "objectively" out there (8-9).

In WOOLGAR's (1988, 75) terms such metaphors are embedded in the 'style of no-style', an 'externalising device 'that emphasises the non-involvement of human agency whereby the discovered object is to be apprehended 'as neither the product nor the artful creation of scientists: scientists come upon these objects rather than creating them'. This textual strategy plays a crucial persuasive function within a research community that believes a major threat to the validity of any conclusion is likely to come from the writer's own bias. As WOOLGAR argues, 'The scientist needs to be the trusted teller of the tale but, at the same time, should not be seen as intruding upon the object' (ibid, 75). To create this impression a textual voice needs to be used that renders the actions of scientists passive and portrays entities like observations, results, and information as the prime movers. For the intended audience of peers to be convinced the scientist's contribution needs to be seen as essentially coincidental with the unfolding realisation about the objective state of the world. The impression is that any other scientist in the same situation would have been led to the same conclusion. Essentially, in keeping with positivistic assumptions regarding epistemology and ontology this form of language has to create the impression of knower and known as separate entities.

Without doubt, scientific tales constitute very powerful and persuasive fictions in western cultures and their value should not be underestimated. However, as indicated, they tend to provide what GEERTZ (1988) has called author-evacuated texts. The author is everywhere but nowhere and the voices of others tend to be present only in quantified form as, for example, when oral responses to questionnaires are translated into researcher categories for statistical analysis and presentation. Having said this, it is important to recognise that much that claims to be interpretive research (minus the emphasis upon quantified data) also draws upon the textual strategies outlined so far. To illustrate this point the following section focuses upon how realist tales are used in interpretive inquiry.

4 The Dominance of Realist Tales in Interpretive Inquiry

Given the different philosophical assumptions and sets of interest that undergird post-positivist, critical, and interpretive inquiry (see FAHLBERG & FAHLBERG, 1994; SCHEMPP & CHOI, 1994; SMITH, 1993; SPARKES, 1989, 1992b, 1992c), it would seem logical that researchers operating in the latter domain should call upon different rhetorical devises for reporting their work and constructing persuasive accounts - they should write about themselves and their subjects differently. This is particularly so in relation to the issue of 'voice(s)' in the text. For example, WOOLGAR (1988, 80) points out that the discourse of the natural sciences tends to deny it objects a voice, 'Although electrons, particles and so on are credited with various attributes, they are constituted as incapable of giving opinions, developing their own theories and, in particular for our purposes, producing their own representations. The natural science discourse thus constitutes its objects as quintessentially docile and can act upon them at will'. He adds, 'By contrast, various traditions in the social sciences wish to grant their objects a voice (and refer to them as 'subjects')' (ibid, 80). This generates difficulties for the rhetorical constitution of distance. In particular, in the discourse associated with interpretive social science, subjects/objects are granted the ability to talk back, have their own opinions and even to constitute their own representations. Furthermore, as ATKINSON (1990, 55) emphasises, just as with texts of biography, history or journalism, 'the ethnography claims factual status, not by eliminating the voice of the author... Rather, the ethnographic text is permeated by stylistic and rhetorical devices whereby the reader is persuaded to enter into a shared framework of facts, and interpretations, observations and reflections'.

In view of this, it is interesting to note the dominance of realist tales within interpretive inquiry and some of the similarities they have with scientific tales. In terms of voice and author positioning, COLE (1991) provides a useful summary of their location in realist tales.

Ethnographic realism corresponds to scientistic conventions that construct authority and objectivity through passive voice, obscuring and apparently distancing the author from the data. The writer's voice is set apart from the main text in prefaces, method sections, and footnotes as a device to indicate that a dispassionate observer "was there, saw, and knows," asserting a contradictory "disembodied" objective presence and "experiential" authority. The researcher constructs and positions him/herself as a conduit through which an "other" culture is seemingly symmetrically decoded and recoded (39).

VAN MAANEN (1988, 46) suggests that realist tales are characterised by various writing or representational conventions which include experiential author(ity) in which, 'the most striking characteristic of ethnographic realism is the almost complete absence of the author from the segments of the finished text. Only what members of the studied culture say and do and, presumably, think are visible in the text'. He notes that, once the fieldworker has finished the job of collecting the data, he/she simply vanishes. There is a marked absence of the narrator as a first-person presence in the text and the dominance of a 'scientific' narrator who is manifest only as a dispassionate, camera-like observer. Here, the collective and authoritative third person ("the X do this") replaces the more fallible first-person ("I saw the X do this").

Tellers of realist tales also go to great pains to produce the native's point of view. It is common to find extensive, closely edited quotations in the text that suggest to the reader that the views put forward are not those of the author but are the authentic and representative remarks of those people in the culture under study. This is closely linked to how the native's point of view is represented in the text, and the issue of interpretive omnipotence. Here, the author has the final word in realist ethnographies as to how the culture will be interpreted and how it will be presented. VAN MAANEN (1988) outlines several conventions of interpretive omnipotence. For example, often a cultural description is tied to a specific theoretical problem of interest to the researcher's disciplinary community. Then, field data, is put forward as facts marshalled in accordance with the light they shed on this topic of interest and the researcher's stand on the matter. The interpretation of the author is made compelling by the use of abstract definitions, axioms, and theorems that work logically to provide explanation. VAN MAANEN (1988, 51) notes that, 'Each element of the theory is carefully illustrated by empirical field data. The form is aseptic and impersonal, but it is convincing insofar as an audience is willing to grant power to the theory.

Another device for establishing interpretive credibility is where the researcher rests the case on what the members say and do themselves. The data are presented conventionally as the events of everyday life. These situations, along with a generalised rendition of the native's point of view are collapsed into explanatory constructs in such a way that the researcher's analysis overlaps with (if it does not become identical to), the terms and constructs used to describe the events. Here, as VAN MAANEN (1988) comments the author's authority is embellished by utilising the native's vernacular that suggests that the author is fully able to whistle native tunes. In summary, the stylistic conventions of realist tales operate together in a convincing manner. As COLE (1991) argues.

The account 'is given increased legitimacy through representations of actual subject voices selected and excluded based on their consistency with the author's "report". While a sense of authenticity and objectivity permeate the narrative, the ethnographer translates the voices and visions of local subjects into his/her own. The analysis (or view from above) is bounded and legitimised by monitoring incongruent voices or anomalous moments; thus, fixing and stabilising theory and limiting alternative interpretation by readers (40).

Therefore, while the voice of subjects are certainly present in realist tales they are usually orchestrated to serve the theoretical needs of an absent, disembodied author. As a consequence, there is often a tendency to produce texts which portray people as 'flat' unidimensional, highly stable and predictable characters, as opposed to multidimensional 'rounded' characters. Furthermore, as VAN MAANEN (1988, 53) recognises, the realist tale only offers one reading and culls its facts with care to support that reading, 'It is simply a matter of closing off or nailing down an interpretation without allowing alternative views to creep into view. The narrator speaks for the group studied as a passive observer who roams imperialistically across the setting to tell, of events that happen in this way or that'.

Therefore, while there are differences between realist and scientific tales, there are also some startling similarities particularly in terms of both being author-evacuated texts. As YOUNG (1991, 221-223) points out in relation to the conventions of realist writing this bodily withdrawal from the realm of events, or disembodiment in it, leaves behind the spoor of the voyeur, 'Though the body vanishes, its perceptual apparatus, especially the eyes remains. Ethnographic writing instantiates an invisible perceiver in a visible world...No vagaries of flesh compound perception...The text purports to become a transparency to the realm of events'. Perhaps, as GEERTZ (1988) suggests, realist tales may even be guilty of text positivism in which the problem is seen as simply one of getting the subjects to talk or write about their lives as carefully as possible, so that they can translated as faithfully as possible. Here, the ethnographer's role dissolves into that of honest broker passing on the substance of things with only the most trivial of transaction costs. For DENZIN (1991) such an agenda contains the traces of post-positivism/empiricism that often turns the subject into another whose thoughts are better understood by the observer than they are by the subject! Reflecting on these traces of post-empiricism, and the similarities between scientific tales and realist tales might lead us to consider how different tales might be told that are more suitable to the needs and interests of interpretive inquirers.

5 Taking the Next Steps: Telling Different Tales

GEERTZ (1988, 137) argues, 'The pervasive questioning of standard modes of text construction - and standard modes of reading - not only leaves realism less easy: it leaves it less persuasive'. If this is the case then perhaps interpretive and researchers might consider engaging in 'experimental writing' in the future. Initially, this might simply mean modifying realist tales to include the researcher-author's positioning in terms of the social categories to which they belong as these impact upon how we come to know, how we come to know it, and how we write about it. For example, I have drawn upon a modified realist tale, in order to highlight the experiences of oppression that a lesbian PE teacher, called Jessica, experienced in her daily working life in a secondary school in England. Given the power differentials that operated both in terms of our emerging relationship, and my own textual production, I felt it necessary to name in a separate section of the paper, the social categories that I belonged to in relation to Jessica, the participant in my paper, in order to signal not only the privileges that came with my membership of such categories as male and heterosexual, but to signal how these permeated the interpretation and the construction of the final text in relation to the participant as female and lesbian (see SPARKES, 1994a).

In constructed this text I was acutely aware of the issues of how voices are included or excluded in the act of writing, and ended up opting for a strategy that included theory at the beginning and end of the paper, with the middle section focusing completely upon selected moments from the life history of the Jessica that illuminated her experiences of homophobia and heterosexism in different contexts. That is, I only announced my authorial presence at various points in the text, and 'disappeared' once Jessica's voice was introduced. Of course my 'disappearance' is itself a textual illusion since I am ever present throughout the paper as its author whose guiding hand selects the quotations and shapes the story presented. Having acknowledged this, my disappearance needs to be seen as a textual strategy, a conscious decision, to focus attention upon the subjects words with a view to drawing the reader into the storyline of oppression and evoking a response. Essentially, I wanted the reader to feel Jessica's oppression and begin to locate themselves in this process. I wanted to evoke a response to her situation, and provide what Bel HOOKS (1991) called a 'narrative of struggle', a narrative in which the subjectivity of the oppressed individual reasserted itself. Whether or not this tactic works only the reader can tell. However, it does signal that realist tales can be used to serve a critical agenda by describing how the life-worlds of people who appear as strangers are shaped by particular webs of contingencies within a sociopolitical milieu, in such a way that the reader can achieve solidarity with them as fellow human beings.

6 Confessional Tales

The place of the author within realist and realist-critical tales can be variable depending upon the purposes of the creators of the text. In contrast, the confessional tale, as described by VAN MAANEN (1988, 78) is a highly personalised and self-absorbed mandate. It rests on a personalised author(ity) giving the fieldworkers point of view. It has naturalness 'despite all the bothersome problems exposed in the confessions'. In such tales the researcher tells us what 'really' happened during the fieldwork. As ATKINSON (1991, 170) comments, 'Ethnographers who have produced their realist accounts are frequently given to publishing autobiographical accounts in which the personal, the problematic, and the narrative elements are in the foreground'. Clearly, the confessional tale is different in many ways from realist tales. However, as VAN MAANEN (1988, 75) reminds us, 'Confessionals do not usually replace realist accounts. They typically stand beside them, elaborating extensively on the formal snippets of method description that decorate realist tales'. Indeed, he acknowledges that fieldwork confessions always almost end up supporting whatever realist writing the author may have done in the past. That is, whatever limitations are highlighted in the confessional tale it is unlikely that the author will conclude that he/she got it wrong. Furthermore, such tales are often produced separately from realist tales (usually by those who have already published realist accounts that are acceptable to a particular research community) in monographs, as journal articles, or book chapters devoted to fieldwork practices. In this sense, ATKINSON (1991, 170) suggests that the confessional tale is not really an alternative genre because 'it exists in a relation of complementarity rather than contrast with realist tales'. Furthermore, he notes the problematic relationship between the two in terms of their impact upon each other, 'To some extent, therefore, the separation of the "realist" and the "confessional" accounts leaves the former relatively uncontaminated by the contingencies reflected in the latter' (ibid, 170).

Of course, confessional tales need not always be produced after the realist tale. For example, I have constructed a confessional tale that provides insights into the ethical and political dilemmas embedded in my emerging relationship as a heterosexual, male, researcher with Jessica, a lesbian PE teacher in the context of a life history study (see SPARKES, 1994b). This text emerged simultaneously from an extended paper I wrote as an attempt to organise key themes, and gain some analytical purchase, on the data generated in over twenty hours of tape recorded interviews with Jessica. Once the draft of this paper was completed it became clear that two strands were intertwined. The confessional highlighted methodological issues with regard to the emerging relationship between myself and Jessica (the subject) and the ethical issues embedded both in this relationship that revolve around sharing stories, friendship, 'therapy', and trading points, plus my writing about Jessica's life as an 'author'. The realist tale of her life focused upon issues of oppression (SPARKES, 1994a). The confessional tale certainly exposes more of myself to the reader at a personal level both as a research and author, as well as giving some interesting insights into the process of life history work. However, as ATKINSON (1991) suggests both these tales act to complement each other in a symbiotic manner. Indeed, they work best when read one after the other.

7 Impressionist Tales

Impressionist tales are different. A good example of this genre is provided by WOLCOTT's (1990) tale of an emerging relationship between himself, a gay professor, and Brad, a young drifter who eventually attempted to murder him. This tale is even more startling and provocative given that it is provided as the central part of a chapter on the absurdity of validity in educational research. ATKINSON (1991) notes how such tales are 'permeated with a self-conscious deployment of the more "literary" resources. For FOLEY (1992, 42) this means that, 'Impressionist tales or documentary narratives have some obvious advantages over scientific ethnographies...such texts are usually much more dramatic and accessible'. The detachment of the realist genres is not sustained. The ethnography constructs a more explicitly vivid and metaphorical account'. Impressionist ethnographies attempt to startle their audience by the use of striking stories. Their medium is that of words, metaphors, phrasing, and imagery coupled with an expansive recall of field work experience. According to VAN MAANEN (1988, 102) 'Impressionist tales present the doing of fieldworker rather than simply the doer or the done...The story itself...is a representational means of cracking open the culture and the fieldworker's way of knowing it so that both can be jointly examined'.

In summary, impressionist tales as a form of representation attempt to provoke multiple and often contrasting interpretations that illustrate that coming to understand a culture is a continuous process of interpretation that involves learning to appreciate the world in different ways. As VAN MAANEN (1988, 19) comments, 'Knowing a culture, even our own, is a never-ending story'. Impressionist tales, therefore, are stories that are always unfinished. Their form and their dependence on the audience leads to more being discovered with each retelling as meanings are worked again and again. As tales, they are a recognition and a celebration of the more literary and metaphoric aspects of ethnographic writing. Consequently, they call upon literary skills to produce evocative tales and the difficulties of this task should not be underestimated.

8 Narratives of Self

Similar, but distinct from confessionals, and including elements of impressionist tales are narratives of the self as described by RICHARDSON (1994). The similarities are that both are forms of evocative writing that are highly personalised and revealing texts in which authors tell stories about their own lived experiences. Dramatic recall, strong metaphors, characters, unusual phrasings, and the holding back on interpretation are used to invite the reader to emotionally 'relive' the events with the author.

Narratives of the self do not read like traditional ethnography because they use the writing techniques of fiction. They are specific stories of particular events. Accuracy is not the issue; rather narratives of the self seek to meet literary criteria of coherence, verisimilitude, and interest. Because narratives of the self are staged as imaginative renderings, they allow the fieldworker to exaggerate, swagger, entertain, make a point without tedious documentation, relive the experiences, and say what might be unsayable in other circumstances. Writing these frankly subjective narratives, ethnographer's are somewhat relieved of the problems of speaking for the "Other", because they are the "Other" in their texts (RICHARDSON, 1994, 521).

Some examples of this genre are beginning to appear in the literature on PE & sport stimulated by a resurgence of interest in 'memory work' in Scandinavia. For example, TIIHONEN (1994) explores the social construction of male identity in Finland during the 1960s and 1970s by drawing upon memories of his own sporting involvement as they are shaped in relation to his experiences of asthma. SILVENNOINEN (1994) also utilises 'memory work' to write about himself as a way of bringing a personal and experimental voice to a story of how his own identity is constructed in relation to his childhood heroes. Likewise, KOSONEN (1993) adopts the same approach to explore the importance of her childhood bodily experiences of becoming a runner in terms of the formation of her self-identity. Finally, a book length narrative of the self is provided by FUSSELL (1991) regarding his journey in search of self into, and eventually out of, the world of hardcore bodybuilding.

In reading these accounts we are taken into the intimate world of the Other in a way that stimulates us to reflect upon our own lives in relation to theirs. As a reader, I assume that they have not deliberately fabricated details and have limited themselves to events they remember. However, as storytellers they are primarily concerned with evocation rather than 'true' representation. In their texts, 'learning about' integrates emotional and cognitive dimensions, and emphasises 'participating with' rather than 'describing for' the Other. As such, rather than the usual privileging of cognitive knowing and the 'spectator theory of knowledge' in which knowing is equated exclusively with observing from a distance, these authors incorporate feelings and participatory experience as dimensions of knowing. Finally, by acknowledging a potential for optional readings these authors give readers license to take part in an experience that can reveal to them not only how it was for the authors, but how it could be or once was for the reader.

9 Poetic Representations

Literary skills are also necessary for exploring other genres. This is particularly so with poetic representations such as those of RICHARDSON (1992) who has taken 36 pages of interview transcription and shaped it into a 3 page poem/transcript called Louisa May's Story of Her Life. In writing the poem, that used the words actually spoken by Louisa May, RICHARDSON (1992, 124), notes how she drew upon both scientific and literary criteria, 'The poem, therefore, had to build upon other poetic devices such as repetition, pauses, meter, rhymes and off rhymes. Without putting words into her mouth, which would violate my sociological sensibilities, I used her voice, diction and tone. I wrote her whole life - as she told it to me'. The writing of a sociological interview as a poem makes the reader constantly aware of the facticity of its constructiveness.

By violating the conventions of how sociological interviews are written up, those conventions are uncovered as choices authors make; not rules for writing truths. The poetic form, moreover, because it plays with connotive structures and literary devices to convey meaning, commends itself to open and multiple readings in ways that straight sociological prose does not. The poetic form of representation, therefore, has a greater likelihood of engaging readers in reflexive analyses of their own interpretive labors of my interpretive labors of Louisa May's interpretive labors. Knowledge is thus metaphored and experienced as prismatic, partial, and positional, rather than singular, total, and univocal (RICHARDSON, 1992, 25).

Since poetry constantly forces a recognition that the text has been constructed it helps to problematize issue of reliability, validity, and 'truth'. Equally, since when people talk their speech is closer to poetry that it is to sociological prose, RICHARDSON (1994) argues that writing up interviews as poems may actually be a better way to represent the speaker than the usual practice of quoting snippets in prose.and concludes that poetry is both a practical, and a powerful method for analysing social worlds.

10 Ethnographic Drama

Drama is a way of shaping an experience without losing the experience; it can blend realist, fictional, and poetic techniques; it can reconstruct the 'sense' of an event from multiple 'as-lived' perspectives; and it can give voice to what is unspoken' ...When the material to be displayed is intractable, unruly, multisited, and emotionally laden, drama is more likely to recapture the experience than is standard writing (RICHARDSON, 1994, 522).

An excellent example of ethnographic drama as an evocative genre is provided by ELLIS and BOCHNER (1992) who present a personal account of their lived experience of abortion narrated in both the female and male voices. Not surprisingly, during the time that these events took place ELLIS & BOCHNER were too engaged in what was happening to record their experiences. However, two months after the abortion they independently reconstructed a chronology of the events that took place, including the emotional dimensions of their decision making, turning points, coping strategies, the symbolic environment of the clinic, and the abortion procedure as it was experienced by them. These separate accounts were then transformed into a dialogic mode of narration that attempted to capture the processual and emotional details of what happened. They also got other people with whom they had consulted to write about their experiences during the decision-making process so that multiple voices were provided for telling the story.

The drama they present is offered as an experimental form of narrating personal experience that makes themselves experimental subjects and treats their own experiences as primary data. Their goal is to lead the reader through a journey in which they develop an experiential sense of the events and come away with a sense of 'what it must have felt like' to live through what happened.

Recognising that the literature rarely reflects the meanings and feelings embodied by the human side of abortion, we wanted to tell our story in a way that would avoid the risks of dissolving the lived experience in a solution of impersonal concepts and abstract theoretical schemes. We have tried to be faithful to our experience, but we understand that the order and wholeness we have brought to it through the narrative form is different than the disjointed and fragmented sense we had of it while it took place. Perhaps this is the way in which narrative constitutes an active and reflexive form of inquiry. Narrative express the values of narrators, who also construct, formulate and remake these values. A personal narrative, then, can be viewed as an 'experience of the experience' (98).

On the feelings that their work might evoke in the reader, ELLIS & BOCHNER (1992, 98) note that while identification and empathy are likely, but that these reactions are not the only nor necessarily the most desirable ones, 'Readers are put in the position of experiencing an experience that can reveal to them not only how it was for us but how it could be or once was for them. The are made aware of similarities and differences between their world and ours. It becomes possible for them to see the other in themselves or themselves in the other among other possibilities'. Accordingly, they conclude that their experiment in formulating narrative as a mode of inquiry should not be judged so much against the standards and practices of science as against the practical, emotional, and aesthetic demands of life.

11 Ethnographic Fiction

Literary skills and sensitivities are also important in constructing ethnographic fictions. A good example of this genre is provided by TIERNEY (1993, 314) who, disenchanted with traditional portrayals of organisational life, uses it to highlight the background and personalities of six people involved in significant changes undertaken at one institution in North America where, 'all the names, characters, and incidents are fictitious and any resemblance to actual persons or events is entirely coincidental'. Using fiction, the conflicts and personal struggles relating to a university's addition of a sexual orientation clause to its statement of nondiscrimination are explored to illuminate the conflicting nature of reality, the manner in which change takes place, and the ways organisational change might be interpreted.

In discussing how fiction operates TIERNEY (1993, 313) notes how it allows the author to 'rearrange facts, events and identities in order to draw the reader into the story in a way that enables deeper understandings of individuals, organizations, or the events themselves'. For me, the story 'works' and serves its purpose, but it works from a literary perspective. As TIERNEY argues.

Such perspectives reframe our analysis away from scientific standard of validity or trustworthiness, and toward more literary definitions of good literature. The reader does not judge the text according to standardized scientific criteria, or with the assumption that the text is meant to explain all such situations. Rather, the reader judges the text in a self-referential manner and might call upon the following questions in judgment: (a) Are the characters believable? (b) Are there lessons to be learned from the text for my own life? (c) Is the situation plausible? (d) Where does the author fit in the formation of the text? (e) What other interpretations exist? and (f) Has the text enabled me to reflect on my own life and work? (313)

Like the authors of poetic representations, ethnographic drama, narratives of the self and impressionist tales, TIERNEY does not advocate the use of his chosen genre at all times. He acknowledges that there are times when a more traditional case study is appropriate. That is, any story has multiple interpretations and representational styles. However, he does argue that, at times we need to create texts that enable the reader to reflect on his or her own life and see if the text resembles any sense of reality. By engaging the reader in the text the potential for a dialogue about the nature of reality is opened up beyond mere theoretical disagreements, so that we are forced to consider our own situations, our own lives.

12 The Problem of Criteria

The different tales as described suggest that researchers in general, and interpretive researchers in particular, need to look elsewhere for criteria to judge the product if their work if they choose to engage in experimental forms of writing. A starting point might be the world of literary criticism rather than the world of post-empiricist science. This suggestion becomes more compelling when we consider the views of BRUNER (1986) who proposes that there are two modes of cognitive functioning or two modes of thought, the paradigmatic or logico-scientific and the narrative modes,each of which provide distinctive ways of ordering experience and constructing reality. Although these two modes can be complementary they are irreducible to one another. Indeed, BRUNER warns that to reduce one mode to the other or to ignore one at the expense of the other will inevitably fail to capture the rich diversity of thought contained in each. Quite simply, each is a different way of knowing that has its own operating principles and its own criteria of well-formedness. As a consequence, each differ radically in their procedures of verification. How they convince and what they convince us of is also different - well formed arguments convince us of their truth whereas stories convince us of their lifelikeness. One verifies by eventual appeal to procedures for establishing formal and empirical truth whereas the other does not establish truth but verisimilitude.

A similar point is made by EISNER (1991) who argues that what is personal, literary, and even poetic can be a valid source of knowledge, even though this is consistently denied by those who hold a restricted 'scientific' view of what constitutes knowledge and truth. EISNER acknowledges that works of poetry and literature are not true in the literal sense, but suggests that they can be true in the metaphorical sense. To restrict truth to literal truth alone, is to restrict knowledge to those forms of discourse that can be literally true which for EISNER is problematic.

Scientific knowledge is seldom true in the literal sense......Especially in the social sciences where metaphor, analogical reasoning, and hypothetical constructs abound, literal truths are scarce. When we use literature, for example, to enlarge understanding, literal truth becomes and irrelevant criterion for appraising its utility. A piece of fiction can be true and still be fiction. Fiction, in the metaphorical sense is 'true to life'; it helps us to perceive, experience, and understand what we have previously neglected (108).

The issue of difference between alternative ways of knowing about, being in the world, and constructing truth has also been emphasised by SMITH (1989) who has consistently and convincingly argued the case that interpretive research is, at a deep philosophical level, different from postempiricist and critical forms of inquiry. More recently, SMITH (1993) has focused his attention specifically on the nature of criteria and how they operate to shape how judgments about 'good' or 'bad' research are made within different paradigms of thought (also see SPARKES 1992b, 1992c, 1994c). While this is not the place to rehearse this debate, one of the central issues for interpretive researchers raised by SMITH needs to be noted which relates to the nature of judgment in interpretive inquiry.

Judgments about the quality of research are not made with the application of abstract standards or rules; these judgments are practical accomplishments, undertaken within the context of dialogue and persuasion, that we work out as we go along. This is a process that has as its core issues of ethics and morals, not epistemological issues. Thus, interpretivists do not think of criteria as standards that make our judgments, as they are normally thought of, they see criteria as characterizing traits or values that influence our judgments. Moreover, these particular traits that are put forth as characteristic of good research are constantly subject to interpretation and reinterpretation as times and conditions change (SMITH, 1993, 139).

In view of the shifting terrain upon which judgments are continually made SMITH (1993) goes on to argue the need for interpretive researchers, when they address the problem of criteria, to begin by actually redefining the concept of criteria. How this redefinition takes takes place presents a major challenge to interpretive inquiry and other alternative research forms in the coming years. However, given the kinds of tales that are beginning to emerge in the literature, it is a task that cannot and should not be avoided.

13 Closing Thoughts

It is becoming increasingly difficult researchers PE and sport, and interpretive researchers in particular, to ignore the issues of representation that postmodernism signals for the ways in which we write ourselves, and Others, into and out of our texts. There are many ways to tell our tales and at this juncture there would seem to be an opportunity for us as a community to critique and re-vision writing in ways that increase our freedom to present texts in a variety of forms to different audiences. However, as RICHARDSON (1994, 523) comments, 'The greater freedom to experiment with textual form, however does not guarantee a better product. The opportunities for writing worthy texts - books and articles that are "good reads" - are multiple, exiting, and demanding. But the work is harder. The guarantees are fewer. There's a lot more for us to think about'.

Essentially, those who wish to write in different ways are left with a range of possibilities and problems (see SPARKES 1995). For example, given the nature of the review process that legitimises what actually gets published in scholarly journals, the referees within this process act as gatekeepers with great power. To some referees the notion of poetic experimentation might seem blasphemous and be rejected out of hand. Clearly, if impressionist tales, poetry or ethnographic fictions are to be accepted as legitimate forms of representation, then journal editors and referees will need to be persuaded to consider alternative formats for publication, and utilise different criteria of judgment. As LYONS (1992, 268) comments, 'qualitative sociology is not a dominant concern either for the profession as a whole or for those who control access to publication.

To add a post-modern description to the work will probably reduce access even further! Once textual criticism of dominant forms of representation is undertaken some raw nerves will be touched'.

For the moment it seems likely that the style of no-style will continue as the dominant form of representation for positivistic researchers and realist tales will be the main ones produced by interpretive researchers. This is not surprising since, after all, these tales have served us well in the past for particular purposes and will continue to contribute to our understanding in the future. They are certainly not to be dismissed lightly. However, their rhetorical features and the intellectual 'work' these perform are now evident and amenable to reflexive analysis. Of course, this is not to suggest that researchers of any paradigmatic persuasion within PE and sport should rush out and produce experimental texts in the spirit of textual radicalism. ATKINSON (1990, 180) argues, 'There is no need for sociologists all to flock towards 'alternative' literary modes. The point of the argument is not to suggest that suddenly, from now on, sociological ethnography should be represented through pastiche or literary forms. The discipline will not be aided by the unprincipled adoption of any particular textual practices, 'literary' or otherwise. On the other hand, we must always be aware that there are many available styles'. Furthermore, adopting other styles of representation is not an easy task and requires the development of a range of literary skills and sensitivities that may be sadly lacking within the PE and sport research community. In view of this, undoubtably, some experiments in narrative will fail. However, as TIERNEY (1993, 314) points out, 'others will succeed and, in doing so, they will enable us to see the world in dramatically different ways'.

One thing is for certain, the ways that we write and the manner in which we pass judgment has now become problematic and we cannot ignore this central aspect of our work. Our texts can no longer be taken to be innocent or neutral. In view of this ATKINSON (1991) suggests, we need to develop a reflexive self-awareness of the rhetorical and stylistic conventions we use, not with a view to substituting textual analysis for fieldwork, but rather to bring them within our explicit and methodological understanding. He emphasises that such reflexiveness is not easy since it would require an acquaintance with recent and contemporary literary theory along with parallel work on the poetics of economics, history, law, and so on. It is also recognised that it is far easier to copy a taken-for-granted model than it is to understand other genres, to manipulate their conventions, and to experiment with them. Therefore, as ROSALDO (1993, 62) argues in relation to the need for anthropologists to engage in experimental writing, 'Rather than discarding distanced normalizing accounts, the discipline should recover them, but with a difference. They must be cut down to size and relocated, not replaced. No longer enshrined as ethnographic realism, the sole vehicle for speaking the literal truth about other cultures, the classic norms should become one mode of representation among others...an increased disciplinary tolerance for diverse legitimate rhetorical forms will allow for any particular text to be read against other possible versions' (62). This would allow forms of writing that have been marginalized or banned altogether to gain legitimacy which could enable the discipline to approximate people's lives from a number of angles of vision, and incorporate an increasing variety of different voices. Such a tactic would better enable us to advance the PE and sport research project of apprehending the range of human possibilities in their fullest complexities.

Certainly, if we as a research community are to create the spaces for the new visions and voices then the telling of different tales has a part to play. Certainly there are risks, but I think they are worth taking. Indeed, as RICHARDSON (1994) notes, 'This is a time of transition, a propitious moment. Where this experimentation will eventually take us, I do not know. But, I do know, that we cannot go back to where we were' (524). I think RICHARDSON is right, there can be no going back for any researcher, whatever their paradigmatic persuasion, to the cozy self-deluding days when texts were seen as neutral and innocent representations of the realities of Others. The days of innocence are gone. All of us, as positioned authors are clearly implicated in the construction of any text and this needs to be acknowledged as we begin to reflect more deeply about how, and why, standard tales are told, as a prelude to seriously considering how alternative tales about PE and sport might be constructed in the future.

References

ATKINSON, P.: The ethnographic imagination: Textual constructions of reality. London: Routledge 1990.

ATKINSON, P.: Supervising the text. International Journal of Qualitative Studies in Education, 1991, 4, 161-174.

ATKINSON, P.: Understanding ethnographic texts. London: Sage 1992.

BAIN, L.: Research in sport pedagogy: Past, present and future. In: T. WILLIAMS; L. ALMOND; A. SPARKES (eds.): Sport and physical activity: Moving towards excellence. London: E & FN Spon 1990a, 3-22.

BAIN, L.: Visions and voices. Quest, 1990b, 42, 2-12.

BRUNER, J.: Actual minds, possible worlds. London: Harvard University Press 1986.

COLE, C.: The politics of cultural representation: Visions of fields/fields of visions. International Review for the Sociology of Sport, 1991, 26: 36-49.

DENZIN, N.: Representing lived experiences in ethnographic texts. In: N. DENZIN (ed.): Studies in symbolic interactionism, Vol. 12, London: JAI Press Inc. 1991.

DENZIN, N.: The art and politics of interpretation. In: N. DENZIN; Y. LINCOLN (eds.): Handbook of qualitative research. London: Sage 1994, 500-515.

EISNER, E.: The primacy of experience and the politics of method. Educational Researcher, 1988, 17, 15-20.

ELLIS, C.; BOCHNER, A.: Telling and performing personal stories: The constraints of choice in abortion. In: C. ELLIS; M. FLAHERTY (eds.): Investigating Subjectivity: Research on Lived Experience. London: Sage, 1992, 79-101.

FAHLBERG, L.; FAHLBERG, L.: A human science for the study of movement: An integration of multiple ways of knowing. Research Quarterly for Exercise and Sport, 1994, 62, 100-109.

FOLEY, D.: Making the familiar strange: Writing critical sports narratives. Sociology of Sport Journal, 1992, 9, 36-47.

FUSSELL, S.: Muscle: Confessions of an unlikely bodybuilder. London: Scribners 1991.

GEERTZ, C.: Works and lives: The anthropologist as author. Polity Press, Cambridge 1988.

HOOKS, B.: Narratives of struggle. In: P. MARIANI (ed.): Critical fictions: The politics of imaginative writing, Seattle, WA: Bay Press 1991, 53-61.

KOSONEN, U.: The running girl: Fragments of my body history. In: L. LAINE (ed.): On the fringes of sport, Sankt Augustin: Academia Verlag 1993, 16-25.

LYONS, K.: Telling stories from the field? A discussion of an ethnographic approach to researching the teaching of physical education. In: A. SPARKES (ed.): Research in physical education and sport: Exploring alternative visions. Lewes: Falmer Press 1992, 248-270.

MARCUS, G.; FISCHER, M. (eds.): Anthropology as cultural critique: An experimental movement in the human sciences. Chicago: University of Chicago Press 1986.

MCLENNAN, G.: The Enlightenment project revisited. In: S. HALL; D. HELL; T. MCGREW (eds.): Modernity and its futures. Cambridge: Polity Press 1992, 327-377.

MULKAY, M.: Sociology of science: A sociological pilgrimage. Milton Keynes: Open University Press 1991.

POOL, R.: Postmodern ethnography? Critique of Anthropology, 1991, 11, 309-331.

RICHARDSON, L.: Value constituting practices, rhetoric, and metaphor in sociology: A reflexive analysis. Current Perspectives in Social Theory, 1991, 11, 1-15.

RICHARDSON, L.: The poetic representation of lives: Writing postmodernist sociology. Studies in Symbolic Interaction, 1992, 13, 19-27.

RICHARDSON, L.: Writing: A method of inquiry. In: N. DENZIN; Y. LINCOLN (eds.): Handbook of qualitative research. London: Sage 1994, 516-529.

ROSALDO, R.: Culture and truth: The remaking of social analysis. London: Routledge 1993.

SCHEMPP, P.; CHOI, E.: Research methodologies in sport pedagogy. Sport Science Review, 1994, 3, 41-55.

SILVENNOINEN, M.: To childhood heroes. International Review for the Sociology of Sport, 1994, 29, 25-29.

SMITH, J.: The nature of social and educational inquiry: Empiricism versus interpretation. Norwood, NJ: Ablex Publishing Company 1989.

SMITH, J.: After the demise of empiricism: The problem of judging social and educational inquiry. Norwood, NJ: Ablex Publishing Corporation 1993.

SPARKES, A.: Paradigmatic confusions and the evasion of critical issues in naturalistic research. Journal of Teaching in Physical Education, 1989, 8, 131-151.

SPARKES, A.: Toward understanding, dialogue and polyvocality in the research community: Extending the boundaries of the paradigms debate. Journal of Teaching in Physical Education, 1991, 10, 103-133.

SPARKES, A.: Writing and the textual construction of realities: Some challenges for alternative paradigms research in physical education. In: A. SPARKES (ed.): Research in physical education and sport: Exploring alternative visions. Lewes: Falmer Press, 1992a, 271-297.

SPARKES, A.: The paradigms debate: An extended review and a celebration of difference. In: A. SPARKES (ed.): Research in physical education and sport: Exploring alternative visions. Lewes: Falmer Press, 1992b, 9-60.

SPARKES, A.: Validity and the research process: An exploration of meanings. Physical Education Review, 1992c, 15, 29-45.

SPARKES, A.: Self, silence and invisibility as a beginning teacher: A life history of lesbian experience. British Journal of Sociology of Education. 194a, 15, 93-118.

SPARKES, A.: Life histories and the issue of voice: Reflections on an emerging relationship. International Journal of Qualitative Studies in Education. 194b,7, 165-183.

SPARKES, A.: Research paradigms in physical education: Some brief comments on differences that make a difference. British Journal of Physical Education Research Supplement, 1994c, 14, 11-16.

SPARKES, A.: Writing people: The dual crises of representation and legitimation in qualitative inquiry. Quest, 1995, 47, 158-195.

STRATHERN, M.: Out of context: the persuasive fictions of anthropology. Current Anthropology, 1987, 28, 251-281.

TIERNEY, W.: The cedar closet. International Journal of Qualitative Studies in Education, 1993, 6, 303-314.

TIIHONEN, A.: Asthma - the construction of the masculine body. International Review for the Sociology of Sport, 1994, 29, 51-62.

TINNING, R.: Teacher education pedagogy: Dominant discourses and the process of problem-setting. Journal of Teaching in Physical Education, 1991, 11, 1-20.

VAN MAANEN: Tales of the field: On writing ethnography. Chicago: University of Chicago Press 1988.

WOOLGAR, S.: Science: The very idea. London: Tavistock Publications 1988.

YOUNG, K.: Perspectives on embodiment: The uses of narrativety in ethnographic writing. Journal of Narrative and Life History, 1991, 1, 213-24.

Michael Waring, Len Almond, Charles Buckley

Grounded Theory in Physical Education: Parental Influences on Participation in Physical Activity

Introduction

Studies have emerged documenting the level and kind of activity in which children are involved (CALE, 1994; SIMONS-MORTON et al., 1990; SALLIS et al., 1988; BARANOWSKI et al., 1987; Australian Health and Fitness Survey, 1985). However, few of these studies have focused on the reasons for participation. Any lack of understanding inhibits efforts to promote physical activity in this population, therefore to reduce this ignorance physically active and inactive children were interviewed to establish their reasons for participation or non-participation and the processes involved. The investigation, using grounded theory methodology, revealed numerous influential variables in differing contexts. This paper focuses on physical education, which is only one context, with specific attention to parental influences.

Grounded Theory

Grounded theory is a qualitative research approach that systematically analyses data to develop a substantive theory. It stems from the symbolic interactionist perspective as a 'new' Chicago School method introduced in the 1960's (DENZIN, 1992). There is movement backwards and forwards between inductive and deductive thinking within the theory, with ..."a constant interplay between proposing and checking. This back and forth movement is what makes our theory grounded!" (STRAUSS and CORBIN, 1990, 111).

GLASER and STRAUSS (1967) distinguish their theory from that of others by highlighting the evolutionary nature of their account through the identification of a set of 'interpreted' procedural steps, rather than the verification of a preconceived theory. Their claim is that data shapes the research process and its product in an innovative way. This allows data that is grounded (embedded in and faithful to the substantive area) to be identified, discarded, clarified and elaborated upon through simultaneous data collection and analysis. It differs from those theoretical frameworks which are developed in isolation to the particular setting, which may inhibit its innovative essence. From the accumulation of data, the researcher develops or 'discovers' the grounded theory (MARTIN and TURNER, 1986). One starts with an area of investigation and begins to evolve an appropriate theory from the relevant data specific to the situation under investigation.

The Focus

The sample compiled very active and very inactive boys and girls and their parents. A total of twenty seven children from year 7 (10-11 years) and year 8 (13-14 years) were selected by means of a 24 hour self-report questionnaire specifically designed for children (CALE, 1994). Each child was interviewed for approximately 45 minutes using a semi-structured interview format. All the interviews were recorded onto tape with the interviewees permission. The parents who agreed to be interviewed were asked the same questions as their child while following the same interview format. Each child was interviewed on two further occasions. The interviews ranged from thirty five minutes to one hour forty five minutes. Transcriptions of interviews were analysed following a grounded theory approach. The management of the data in this analysis was assisted by the use of a NUDIST (Non-numerical, Unstructured, Data, Indexing, Searching and Theorising) computer software package, in addition to a card indexing system. The N.U.D.I.S.T. software is a system for managing, organising and supporting research in qualitative data analysis projects.

Gatekeepers

A framework of opportunity exists that consumes all the choices a child has to make regarding their participation in physical activities. This framework is partially or completely constructed by the 'gatekeepers'. These gatekeepers consist of the child's parent(s), peers and school. Gatekeepers are those people who have the ability directly or indirectly to facilitate or inhibit physical activity. The framework for opportunity instigated and/or constructed by one or more of the gatekeepers is complicated. In terms of providing choices of physical activity for the child, none of the gatekeepers exist in isolation. Even though physical education exists within a school context, the evolving relationship with other gatekeepers and their influence on this context and the child's subsequent reasons for participation, remain important. A complicated juxtapositioning of interrelationships provides the 'cocktail' of experiences for each child's participation in various physical activities. By doing so it serves to structure the way in which they interpret and value their involvement in physical activity.

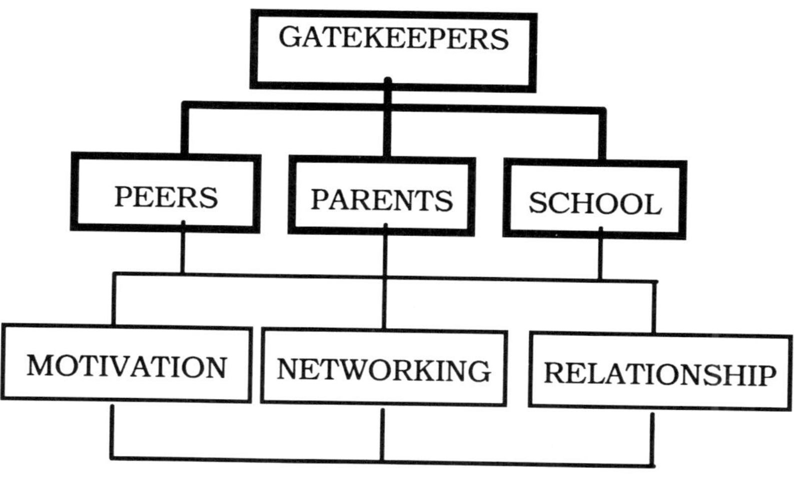

Figure 1. Networking (Guardian, Facilitator and Enforcer)

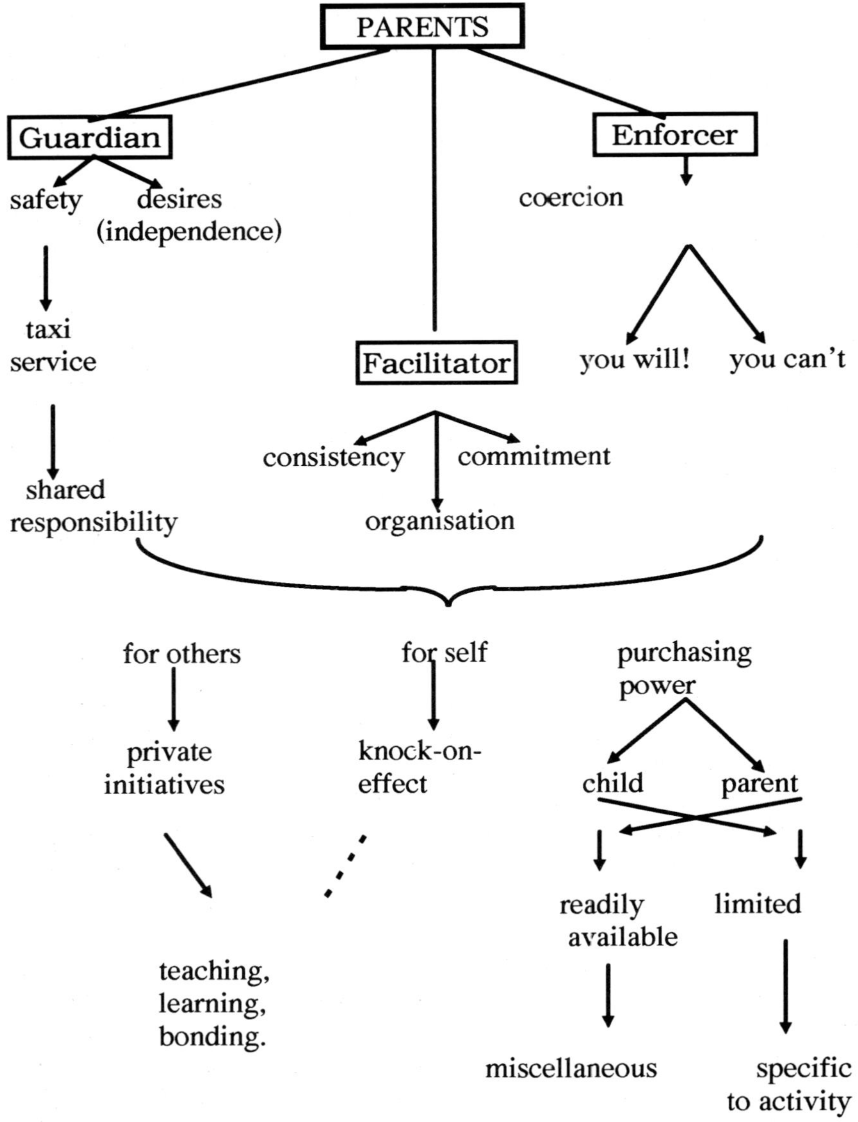

Figure 2. The Parent as "Guardian", "Facilitator" and "Enforcer".

Figure one identifies the gatekeepers (parents, schools and peers), each of which adopt the role of 'guardian', 'facilitator' and 'enforcer'. However, the manifestations of these roles is different for each one and is dependent on their interrelationship with the other gatekeepers. The relationship between the school and parents is a fundamental one. Together they facilitate the majority of physical activity in which children are involved. The influence of peers is, to a greater extent, influenced by such a relationship. A 'taster' of various physical activities can be initiated by any of the 'gatekeepers', but it is more commonly the role of the school. In this case, the parent as the 'guardian' (safety and caring for the well-being of their child), 'facilitator' (developing opportunities and access) and 'enforcer' (maintaining behaviour/activity within parentally perceived limits) assesses many variables to determine whether continued participation is realistic on a consistent basis (see figure two).
An overwhelming consideration for all 'gatekeepers' is the safety of the child before, during and after any activity. If this cannot be secured, especially for girls, the activity is not a viable one in the eyes of the parent(s).

> Father: Increasingly where possible under her own steam (*she makes her own way to activities*), but one has to be acutely conscious of the safety problem. Which is one reason why we actually said yes to the pony (to buy) because it's an environment in which she can have freedom and be safe.
> Mother: Well that was the appeal of the ice skating, as long as she promised not to go out of the rink I knew I didn't have to stay and watch her, she was safe in the ice rink.

Provision may be made by networking with other parents to offer the necessary supervision and/or transport on a shared basis. Distributing the "burden" of organisation, enables other commitments a parent and family members have to be maintained. The physical activity can then become a commitment on a regular basis if so desired. The notion of shared burden relates at another level too. If all the responsibilities for organising and executing activities rest with a single parent in the family, then even with some distribution of the burden amongst a network of parents, the choices for the child will remain limited because of the constant organisational pressure and preparation for their child's involvement in physical activity. Therefore, parental organisation of many variables is a key component that helps determine the amount of physical activity a child has access to on any consistent basis. The greater the organisational skills of the parent(s), the greater the likelihood of consistent physical activity in a child's lifestyle. Parents have to be organised and co-ordinated, as does the child.

> Mother: With most of the friends she would want to see, it can't be spontaneous because we then have to arrange them coming on the bus with her making sure that one of us is available to take them home. She asked someone over for Friday between school and going off to riding, well she had to check with me because of running her friend home. Of course she does spend a lot of time at the stables so squeezing anything else in is a bit difficult.

The economic and temporal constraints parents have to operate within and maintain are also important and influential variables. The degree of enjoyment and success a child has in physical education can be the incentive for the parent(s), child and school to seek additional opportunities for the child to participate in a particular physical activity outside of the physical education context. This exists along a continuum, at one end of which is the child who is an especially good performer in an activity, seeking not only increased frequency, but an increase in the standard of competition in a formally organised physical activity.

> Mother: She did it at school and became quite good. She's played all round for various local teams and now she plays for a bigger club. Other teams now want her to play for them instead next season, so I think she's going to join them.

Access to opportunities outside of the physical education context can create further opportunities for involvement in the activity which perpetuates the initial desire to experience a higher standard of performance and competition. At the other end of the continuum is the child who is dissatisfied with physical education. The child and their parent(s) may acknowledge the importance of physical activity. This is not necessarily because of the health benefits, but as a "management process", if they are doing this activity then they cannot be getting into trouble. Consequently they seek alternative activities to those experienced in physical education eg. horse riding.

> Mother: If she was joining in outside of school activities they would be not directly related to physical education, they'd be things like drama and that sort of activity, cookery, these are the sorts of things that she would get involved in rather than something physical.

Regardless of the position along the continuum previously discussed, the degree of organisation and commitment on behalf of the parent, as well as the child, is tremendous and cannot be underestimated when considering long term participation in their chosen activity.

Motivation and Relationships

The intervention of the parent in their child's physical education is influenced by their interpretation of the value of physical education, which is based on their own experiences at school, as well as any liaison with the school physical education department. A parent's view of physical education may be positively (or negatively) reconstructed as a result of contact with the school, as a consequence it may receive increased (decreased) recognition in their child's education.

> Mother: She's got a natural eye for the ball whatever it is, whatever size it is, she can do anything with it, she just does

> it, it's natural. Her teacher says it's just that natural thing, some kids have got it and she's lucky that she's got it.
> Father: The middle daughter's got it in a different way in that with the horses, she's got a good eye for judging distances, it's the same sort of thing but in a different way.

Alternatively, the experiences of the parent(s) in physical education at school may have been negative enough for them to readily succumb to any request by their child to refrain from physical education. Yet again the importance of a network of co-operation and dialogue between the school and parents is emphasised if participation is to be enhanced.

For both active and inactive children, it is acceptable to 'do' physical education if it offers them the right 'rewards' ie. that which emphasises and promotes what they feel is important to them and their friends. For example, "performance" within the physical education context is seen as a valuable attribute. Performance means that they are able to participate in the activity and perform the necessary manoeuvres competently (when compared with the average of the group) maintaining 'credibility' and 'acceptability' within the class.

> Father: She likes not to lack skill as opposed to being skilful. There's a subtle difference, because being skilful involves effort, lacking skill involves getting along. The social content would be critical really.

The cohesion of a particular peer group within the physical education context may act to dissolve this situation. Rather than the "group performance" standard being the baseline which is the "credible/acceptable" performance criteria, the standard of the peer group is taken as being "credible/acceptable". This becomes significant only to the peer group in question, be they elite or less able performers, physically active or inactive. Where there is a mixture of abilities within peer groups, the 'credible and acceptable' performance criteria is set in accordance with success for the less able performers. The judgement made here is created by the more able performer and based on the fact that their links and commitments outside of the physical education context (i.e. school, county, regional, club teams) allows them to be more accommodating to the ability of others in a short period of time such as a physical education lesson. If alternative opportunities to excel do not exist for the more able performer, there can be a conflict situation with resentment and confrontation which inhibits participation for all concerned in physical education.

Physical education can also reward children by giving them an opportunity to develop 'companionship' with peers. A shared experience which can be discussed and evaluated together is important to them. The experience, be it positive or negative, remains a common one, a focus for them to discuss and accept or reject together, building "companionship". Although this can occur in all curriculum areas the physical component of PE maintains a uniqueness in the school curriculum for children, which enhances the intensity of the 'bonding' process.

A 'fun' aspect to physical education is essential. Fun refers to a situation where performance and a commitment to experimentation in activities is encased in a non-threatening environment, that is overseen by a non-judgmental teacher. Such a situation allows the child to 'have a go' at the activity without being too concerned about the outcome. Consistency on behalf of the teacher is essential if participation is to be achieved and maintained. Most "fun" is gleaned from situations where the child can really experiment and practice, "having a go" at the activity without feeling that there will be a major autopsy of their performance (especially by the teacher). Mistakes occur, but it is the apparently casual nature of the feedback given by the teacher which is an important factor. The child wants to maintain a degree of anonymity within the class situation which allows them freedom to experiment, but also to 'learn' from the teacher.

> Mother: Yes that was always the thing at the rink. She was quite happy to be one of the crowd skating along as long as she wasn't one of the worst and she certainly wasn't going to stop talking long enough to be one of the best.

That advice given by teachers in a casual "try this..." approach, while the activity is in progress is seen as most positive by children. Prolonged involvement in an activity without it being broken up into small stilted components is preferable to enhance the trial and error process in experimentation and ultimately "learning". Given such a relaxed situation within the physical education context, there is a greater tendency for the participants (pupils and teacher) to "laugh and joke", as well as to be critical of their performance. The "laugh and a joke" does not equate to flippant uncontrolled behaviour, but is organised and controlled. However, the nature of the interactions between children and teacher is on a more relaxed and friendly plain. This relaxed openness and frankness resembles activities outside of the class context (at home or at break times), where children freely experiment with a variety of roles. It is of benefit to the child and physical education if this commonalty of experiences can be fused, so that they support each other. The greater the intrinsic desire, the greater the likelihood that participation in all forms of physical activity will become a component of their lifestyle now and in the future. While the physical education environment should remain non-threatening and "fun" in the eyes of the child, this does not exclude competition and the joy of winning. Competition is recognised as being desirable as long as it is developed with the same ethos and within the general remit of the non-threatening environment nurtured in the lessons. Winning against opponents multiplies the "fun" factor enormously, but is has to be the winning that is emphasised not the losing.

Conclusion

Approximately half of the physically active children in the study could not be considered very competent or elite performers with regards their physical performance in physical education. However, of those activities that they were involved in (which contributed to their high level of physical activity) they were more than averagely competent at them. There are serious implications for physical education here because all too often it is perceived by children and parents as being the 'games lesson'. Therefore, if a proportion of the highly active children are not involved in games of any kind outside of normal curricula time, this restricts the role of PE in promoting physical activity for them. Alternatively physical education has tremendous scope to turn children onto physical activity through the nature of its approach and influence on the other gatekeepers through a network of relations which it is not fully exploiting at this time.

References

AUSTRALIAN COUNCIL FOR HEALTH, Physical Education and Recreation Inc.: Australian Health and Fitness Survey. Edwardstown, KB Printing Services Pty. Limited 1987.

BARANOWSKI, T.; HOOKS, P.; TSONG, Y. et al.: Aerobic physical activity among third to sixth grade children. Journal of Developmental and Behavioural Paediatrics 1987, 8: 203-206.

CALE, L.: Monitoring Physical Activity in Children. Unpublished Ph.D. Thesis, Department of Physical Education, Sports Science and Recreation Management, Loughborough University, Loughborough, England, 1994.

DENZIN, N.K.: Symbolic Interactionism and Cultural Studies: The Politics of Interpretation. USA, Blackwell Publishing, 1992.

GLASER, B.G.; STRAUSS, A.L.: The Discovery of Grounded Theory. New York, USA, Aldine Publishing Company, 1967.

MARTIN, P.Y.; TURNER, B.A.: Grounded Theory and Organisational Research. The Journal of Applied Behavioural Science, 1986, 22 (2), 141-157.

SALLIS, J.F.; PATTERSON, T.L.; MCKENZIE; T.L.; NADER, P.R.: Family variables and physical activity in pre-school children. Journal of Developmental and Behavioural Paediatrics, 1988, 9, 57-61.

SIMONS-MORTON et al.: Children's frequency of participation in moderate to vigorous physical activities. Research Quarterly in Exercise and Sport, 1990, 61: 307-314.

STRAUSS, A.L.; CORBIN, J.: Basics of Qualitative Research Grounded Theory Procedures and Techniques. USA, Sage Publications, 1990.

TURNER, B.A.: The Use of Grounded Theory for the Qualitative Analysis of Organisational Behaviour. Journal of Management Studies, 1983, 20 (3), 333-348.

Fiona Dowling Næss

Conceptualising a Career in Teaching: A Life History Analysis of Norwegian Physical Educators

> "When you reach the top of the scale ... and I did that a good few years ago - there you are! I think that's rather frustrating or stupid, because whatever I do it won't be valued any higher. And as a subject teacher I'm on a scale 15 - and that's not very high - and I've already been there for years ... When you reach the top, you think, gosh, I'm not going to earn any more than *this*, and I've got another 30 years to go!"
> (Jorunn Andersen, 1993)

This is one teacher's remark concerning the career structure in the Norwegian school system: Jorunn is a subject teacher, that is to say she belongs on the lowest rung of the nationally imposed structure. Whilst it is essential to understand how this socially-constructed organisational pattern impinges upon the life and career of Jorunn, I believe that her comment reveals the limitations of a functionalist approach to the study of careers, with its emphasis on understanding the distribution of resources within organisations and the career paths of individuals through the ranks, because such studies reveal little about Jorunn the individual and Jorunn the teacher. As EVETTS (1992) states there is a danger that the reification of career structures can lead to them acquiring a 'phantom objectivity' which seems so all-embracing and rational that it can lead to the concealment of the fundamental nature of career, that is to say the relation between people. Statistically Jorunn may well represent a low-ranking, unambitious teacher without any upward mobility, and although, as the comment indicates, she is somewhat frustrated and despondent about her salary, after many hours of indepth interviewing I have discovered far from considering herself a career 'failure', Jorunn perceives herself to be a successful physical educator with a rich and rewarding career.

Indeed, given the intensely personal nature of teaching, it is surprising that there has been so little focus on the teacher as individual in our educational research (WOODS, 1987; GOODSON, 1991). If we are interested in deepening our understanding of pedagogical practice in order to enhance future educational experience, is it perhaps pertinent to respond to GOODSON's challenge to obtain a greater insight into the teacher as individual, rather than concentrating on the analysis of teachers' practice which he perceives to be a "vulnerable entry point" for executing change. A focus on teachers' careers is particularly relevant in Norway today because of the repercussions of a major reform period: a reform in which teachers are seen to be marginalised, and consequently, a reform which is having a profound effect upon the way teachers experience their jobs. What does it mean to have a teaching career, and in particular, a teaching career within physical education (PE) in Norway? More specifically, how can we study the lived experience of PE teachers? Within the confines of this paper, I propose to address two issues: first of all, the methodological problem of whose lives and careers do we study, and secondly, I wish to illustrate the potential power of life history work in contributing to our understanding of physical educators.

A recent study which has made a substantial contribution to our understanding of teachers' careers and lives is that of HUBERMAN (1989). Recognising the restrictions of a traditional, functionalist approach, he has built on life cycle research to provide a schematic model (see figure 1) which endeavours to take account of process.

Years of teaching	Themes/Phases	
1-3	Career entry: "Survival" and "Discovery"	
4-6	Stabilization	
7-18	Experimentation/ "Activism"	Reassessment/ "Self-doubts"
19-30	Serenity/ Relational distance	Conservatism
31-40	Disengagement: "Serene" or "Bitter"	

Figure 1: Huberman's schematic model of the teacher career cycle

He says the model should be seen as a heuristic device to help us to come to understand the complexity of teachers' careers, which acknowledges the idiosyncratic nature of career development and strives to portray the possibility for both continuity as well as discontinuity between the different phases in life. According to HUBERMAN, teachers' careers can be diagramatically represented by a single stream at career entry, through the stabilization phase, which is followed by multiple streams at mid-career, converging again into a single path at the end; depending on the previous trajectory this final phase can be either serene or acrimonious.

The model is useful in providing a framework for gaining an insight into the way in which individuals affect, and are affected by, their social environment, yet HUBERMAN (1989) himself warns of its limitations: "Modal trends such as these are suspect. Put together, they would probably describe no single individual in the sample, and only pieces of subgroups." GOODSON (1994) also fears that there is a danger that such models provide teachers with a script and can contribute to a self-fulfilling prophecy. With regard to our understanding of PE teachers, the model immediately poses problems in terms of the various phases outlined by HUBERMAN because several studies already indicate that a large number of PE specialists disengage from the subject area as early as in the mid-career phase rather than towards the end of the life cycle (SIKES, 1988; TEMPLIN, 1988; EVANS & WILLIAMS, 1989; TEMPLIN et al., 1991). How, then, can we better understand the life and world of the PE teacher?

I propose that the resurgence of the life history approach (PLUMMER, 1990) offers in fact a means by which the individual PE teacher's experiences can be revealed within a social and historical context, or in other words, offers the chance to study both the subjective and objective aspects of career. As BURGESS (1929) writes,

> "In the life history is revealed, as in no other way, the inner life of the person, his moral struggles, his successes and failures in securing control of his destiny in a world too often at variance with his hopes and ideals."

In studying the life of an individual PE teacher, we are able to see not only how various social, psychological, economic and religious factors influence the teacher's life choices, but we also are afforded the opportunity to reveal the social structures in which such choices are made. In other words, the life history has the potential to illuminate the dialectical process between the agency of individuals and the constraints of social structure (PLUMMER, 1983), as well as describing how new aspects of the self are brought into being (BECKER, 1970). In turn, we can learn more about the way these personal experiences shape pedagogical practice in PE.

Scholars in Britain and North America, who already have embarked upon the extensive process of collecting life history data from PE teachers via the use of semi-structured interviews, have begun to unveil deep insights into the lives and career of physical educators (SPARKES, 1994; TEMPLIN et al., 1994; SPARKES et al., 1990). Whilst each life history is unique, offering a means of explaining why an individual acts in a certain way rather than another, by studying a number of life histories common themes also emerge: we have gained, for example, a deeper insight into the multidimensional nature of marginality as experienced on both sides of the Atlantic with regard to subject knowledge, gender, age and sexual orientation. On reading the accounts of others' lives, I have been able to analyse and make better sense of my own experiences as a marginalised PE teacher in Britain and Norway, and thus as a part of the renaissance in life history work I have initiated a study of Norwegian physical educators.

The question many people pose is, whose lives and careers do you choose to study? At this point it is perhaps useful to offer a picture of the formalised and nationally operated career structure. Since 1961 teachers in Norway have been employed and receive a salary according to their educational qualifications and years of service, irrespective of the type of school in which they work, ie at the primary, middle or upper school level. There are four categories of teachers: subject teachers, teachers with a Bachelors Degree (4 years of study), teachers with a Master's Degree (6 or 7 years of study) and teachers who become administrative personnel. A PE teacher may belong to any of these categories with an education in PE and sports science or a combination of PE and other school subjects; in other words, a PE teacher may have a minimum of six months' or a maximum of six years' education in PE. There exist few tiers within the school structure, and in terms of 'upward mobility', a PE teacher must either gain further educational qualifications or move out of the teaching arena into administration in order to gain financial advancement and power; although it has to be said that in terms of the latter the financial gains are minimal and office working hours are longer. In some institutions it is possible to apply for the role of head of the PE section, but this depends on the size of the school and it is not always rewarded financially. Moreover, the latter is an internal appointment, often made on a rotational basis between the members of staff within a department, such that any increment in salary is not on a permanent basis. Alternatively another means of enhancing status is to become what is known as an 'øvingslærer' - a teacher who supervises student teachers on teaching practice - although strictly speaking in structural terms this type of 'promotion' is an external agreement between the individual teacher and an institute of higher education.

Thus a starting point for the selection of PE teachers whose life stories I want to gather might well be found in each of the various categories of teachers, although given the number of permutations in the Norwegian context and indeed, the difficulty of defining who constitutes a PE teacher compared to other countries such as in Britain and America where there is a minimum of three years of education, I have instead chosen strategic sampling. Governed by the traditions of interpretive and interpretive critical inquiry, I have selected 'interesting cases' based on prior research on the lives and careers of teachers (BALL & GOODSON, 1985; SIKES et al., 1985; ACKER, 1989; SPARKES et al., 1990; SPARKES & TEMPLIN, 1992) and my sociological imagination (MILLS, 1959). An alternative framework to that of the nationally operated career structure is provided by life-cycle research (LEVINSON et al., 1978), whereby as a starting point, I am interested in interviewing female and male PE teachers at different stages in their life cycle. In addition, I intend to focus on cases of marginality given its multifaceted roles within the context of PE, and as a result of preliminary research findings and in keeping with qualitative research, I am allowing data analysis to further inform my selection of cases, such that I now plan to interview, for example, teachers who have experienced the impact of severe injury. I am also open to the possibility for snowball sampling because as SPARKES et al. (1990) state it is an important strategy in terms of providing rich contrasts both within and between categories.

Within the confines of this short paper the task of doing justice to the life and experiences of a PE teacher is impossible; indeed, it should be noted that any life history is bound to the context in which it is recounted and interpreted. Moreover it is difficult to offer 'thick description' from the teachers' accounts of their lives, although what follows endeavours to stay true to the individual's narrative. I intend to show glimpses of the subjective realities of one Norwegian PE teacher, which have been contextualised and preliminarily analysed by me, in order to illustrate the potential of the approach to enhancing our understanding of what it means to be a PE teacher in Norway and of understanding why teachers teach the way they do by focusing on the issue of the 'substantial self'. The 'substantial self' refers to the most highly prized aspects of our self concept and the attitudes and values which are salient to them (NIAS, 1989), and a growing body of research argues that PE teachers, in socially constructing a career, seek to confirm their substantial sense of self which if seen to be negated or threatened, can lead to various forms of career disengagement (SIKES, 1988; EVANS &WILLIAMS, 1989; SPARKES, 1987, 1988, 1994a, 1994b; TEMPLIN et al., 1994).

I would like to present Jorunn Andersen, whom you fleetingly met in the opening section. We first met in her capacity as supervisor for PE student teachers and during the course of 16 hours of interviews she has given me the privilege of getting to know her better both professionally and personally; a process which continues today. Jorunn is of working class origens, she is 51 years of age and has 28 years of PE teaching experience, carried out at two schools - a 5 year period at an upper school early in her career and 23 years at a middle school. Her PE colleague during the past 23 years has been her husband. They have two sons who currently are studying to become PE teachers and coaches. Jorunn identifies herself as a gymnast, having taken part in troupe displays for many years and having been a coach for as long as she can remember! She 'trained' as a PE teacher and coach, with a special emphasis on dance, taking a two year course at a private college in Denmark, because the low grades she attained in her final school examinations barred her from studies in Norway. She later took some additional courses to qualify herself to teach in Norwegian schools. The overwhelming impression one gets of Jorunn today is that she loves her work, both as a PE teacher and a coach: as she says, "... it's enjoyable, it's what I can do and what I like doing best. I think it's been ... it *is* my life".

During our long conversations Jorunn has revealed various sides of herself, some of which she feels more positive about than others, all of which have been developed through her work in PE. The physical self is important because activity makes Jorunn feel good and it has provided an arena in which she can demonstrate mastery and control, compared to other forums in which she feels less secure. She nurtures this side of herself by regular training and she has also taken to the use of sunbeds to enhance her physical appearance. It has always been very important for Jorunn to play a physically active role in her PE lessons. With regard to her preference for different physical activities, Jorunn prioritises non-competitive sports, and indeed, non-competitiveness is another aspect of her substantial self: it is reflected in the way she teaches and her lack of participation in competitive situations at school or in the context of a vertical career. Jorunn sees herself as a caring individual and strives in particular to show warmth and understanding to her pupils in PE lessons and especially in the informal atmosphere of changing rooms. She also prides herself with professionalism, reinforced by the feedback she gets from pupils in terms of whether or not they have enjoyed and succeeded in the tasks she sets them, as well as by the reinforcement she values from being part of a PE student supervisory programme.

Jorunn is at odds to stress that her strengths lie within the practical, as opposed to the theoretical domain: she's at the grassroots where she belongs, and PE is served well by practically-oriented teachers such as herself. The image of the practitioner is manifested in her comments about the greater value of practical refresher courses, her revelations about her 'training' as opposed to her education, and by the constant comparison between PE on the one hand and theoretical subjects, involving a lot of planning on the other. I get the impression that Jorunn is not altogether at peace with her non-theoretical image and in a way it hints at a further underlying self which has been cultivated through her work in PE, namely her doubting self. Jorunn has doubts about her capacity to address groups including her colleagues, she has doubts concerning her ability to pursue further education, and in a sense she has doubts about her own opinions: throughout our conversations about her PE career she uses the plural form 'we', referring to her work as a joint effort between herself and her colleague-husband. It seems that at no stage she has benefitted from a word of encouragement from school administrators or colleagues concerning her personal and professional development; on the contrary, encouraging and positive comments have tended to rest at the practical or organisational level connected with the smooth-running of sports' days or after-school activities, serving to reinforce the practical image.

While the latter example of Jorunn's story provides us with an insight into the social structure in which she constructs her career and of its potentially constraining nature, she is however, generally speaking, unaware of this aspect and is satisfied with her life and work as a PE teacher: "I've found my niche in life .. I couldn't think of anything else.. I'd rather be doing." In her eyes, the one aspect of her life which can impose a threat is in fact her aging body: in the beginning of her 50s she notices how tiredness creeps over her body by the time the last bell rings, she notices a steady decline in her flexibility and strength which hampers her ability to demonstrate skills in lessons, and a hormone inbalance has led to periods of depression over the past year. She is trying to see the changes as inevitable and a natural part of aging, but the adjustments are considerable in terms of her physical and professional self. Her greatest worry is that the pupils might begin to perceive her as being too old to teach PE and she says if that were to happen she would have to give up. At the moment she has 11 years prior to retirement age, a retirement for which she and her husband already have great travel plans, but which so far does not represent disengagement and can be contemplated from afar. It will be interesting to see whether Jorunn continues to stave off feelings of negation of the self and adapts to the new demands placed upon her teaching by her aging body, because according to SIKES (1988) many aging physical educators find it difficult to 'age gracefully'.

I hope that this all too brief representation of certain aspects of Jorunn, the individual and the teacher, illustrates the value in studying a life. Other aspects of the tales she tells about herself reveal an array of central issues, illuminating her subjective world and the socially-constructed world in which she lives and works: namely, issues relating to gender, of socialisation into PE, technical rationality in PE, PE teachers as coaches and in other 'moonlighting' jobs, the marginalisation of the subject and its teachers, the politics of PE, lesson content and teaching strategies in PE lessons, and inservice training needs. Jorunn declares that she has found it an enlightening experience to recount her life to me and to reflect over the way her work in PE has developed. The capacity of life histories in pre-service and in-service education is promising (QUICKE, 1988; BUTT, 1989; SIKES & TROYNA, 1991; KNOWLES, 1992; SPARKES, 1993) and I believe that Jorunn's teacher-generated knowledge can help others, too, in critical reflection, either by directly relating to familiar situations or by providing contrasting stories of reality which cause them to challenge the taken-for-granted world of PE. By pursuing this project and gathering the life stories of other Norwegian physical educators, I hope to be able to provide some pieces in the highly patterned mosaic depicting teachers' lives and careers.

References

ACKER, S.: Rethinking Teachers' Careers. In: S. ACKER (ed.): Teachers, Gender and Career. Lewes, UK: Falmer Press 1989.

BALL, S.; GOODSON, I.: Understanding Teachers: Concepts and Contexts. In: S. BALL; I. GOODSON (eds.): Teachers' Lives and Careers. Lewes: Falmer Press 1985.

BECKER, H.: The Relevance of Life Histories. In: N. DENZIN (ed.): Sociological Methods: A Sourcebook. London: Butterworth 1970.

BURGESS, E.W.: Personality and the Social Group. Chicago: University of Chicago Press 1929.

BUTT, R.L.: An Integrative Function for Teachers' Biographies. In: G. MILBURN et al. (eds): Reinterpreting Curriculum and Research: Images and Arguments. Lewes, UK: Falmer Press 1987.

EVANS, J.; WILLIAMS, T.: Moving Up and Getting out: The Classed and Gendered Career Opportunities of Physical Education Teachers. In: T. TEMPLIN; P. SCHEMPP (eds.): Socialization into Physical Education: Learning to Teach. Indianapolis, Ind: Benchmark Press 1989.

EVETTS, J.: Dimensions of career: avoiding reification in the analysis of change. Sociology, 1992, Vol 26, No 1, 1-21.

GOODSON, I.: Comment at a seminar on life histories, Norwegian University of Sport and Physical Education, March 1994.

GOODSON, I.: Sponsoring the Teacher's Voice: teachers' lives and teacher development. Cambridge Journal of Education, 1991, Vol 21, No 1.

HUBERMAN, M.: The Professional Life Cycle of Teachers. Teachers College Record, 1989, Vol 91, No 1, 31-57.

KNOWLES, G.: Models for understanding pre-service and beginning teachers' biographies: illustrations from case studies. In: I. GOODSON (ed.): Studying Teachers' Lives. London: Routledge 1992.

LEVINSON, D. et al.: The Seasons of a Man's Life. New York: Alfred Knopf 1987.

MILLS, C.W.: The Sociological Imagination. New York: Oxford University Press 1959.

NIAS, J.: Primary Teachers Talking: A Study of Teaching as Work. London: Routledge 1989.

PLUMMER, K.: Herbert Blumer and the life history tradition. Symbolic Interaction, 1990, 13 (2), 125-144.

PLUMMER, K.: Documents of Life: An Introduction to the Problems and Literature of a Humanistic Method. London: George Allen & Unwin Ltd. 1983.

QUICKE, J.: Using Structured Life Histories to Teach Sociology and Social Psychology of Education: An Evaluation. In: P. WOODS; A. POLLARD (eds.): Sociology and Teaching: A New Challenge for the Sociology of Education. London: Croom Helm 1988.

SIKES, P.: Growing Old Gracefully? Age, Identity and Physical Education. In: J. EVANS (ed.): Teachers, Teaching and Control in Physical Education. Lewes, UK: Falmer Press 1988.

SIKES, P.; TROYNA, B.: True Stories: A case study in the use of life history in initial teacher training. Educational Review, 1991, Vol 43, No 1, 3-16.

SIKES, P.; MEASOR, L.; WOODS, P.: Teachers' Careers: Crises and Continuities. Lewes, UK: Falmer Press 1985.

SPARKES, A.: Life Histories and the Issue of Voice: reflections on an emerging relationship. International Journal of Qualitative Studies in Education, 1994a, Vol 7, No 2, 165-183.

SPARKES, A.: Self, Silence and Invisibility as a Beginning Teacher: a life history of lesbian experience. British Journal of Sociology of Education, 1994b, Vol 15, No 1, 93-118.

SPARKES, A.: Challenging Technical Rationality in Physical Education Teacher Education: the Potential of a Life History Approach. Physical Education Review, 1993, Vol 16, No 2, 107-121.

SPARKES, A.: The Micropolitics of Innovation in the Physical Education Curriculum. In: J. EVANS (ed.): Teachers, Teaching and Control in Physical Education. Lewes, UK: Falmer Press 1988.

SPARKES, A.: Strategic Rhetoric: a constraint in changing the practice of teachers. British Journal of Sociology of Education, 1987, Vol 8, 37-54.

SPARKES, A.; TEMPLIN, T.: Life Histories and Physical Education: Exploring the Meanings of Marginality. In: A. SPARKES (ed.): Research in Physical Education and Sport: Exploring Alternative Visions. Lewes, UK: Falmer Press 1992.

SPARKES, A.; TEMPLIN, T.; SCHEMPP, P.: Exploring Dimensions of Marginality: Reflecting on the Life Histories of Physical Education Teachers. Journal of Teaching in Physical Education, 1993, Vol 12, 386-398.

TEMPLIN, T.: Settling Down: An Examination of Two Women Physical Education Teachers. In: J. EVANS (ed.): Teachers, Teaching and Control in Physical Education. Lewes, UK: Falmer Press 1988.

TEMPLIN, T.; SPARKES, A.; SCHEMPP, P.: The Professional Life Cycle of a Retired Physical Education Teacher: A Tale of Bitter

Disengagement. Physical Education Review, 1991, Vol 14, No 2, 143-155.

TEMPLIN, T.; SPARKES, A.; GRANT, B.; SCHEMPP, P.: Matching the Self: The Paradoxical Case and Life History of a Late Career Teacher/Coach. Journal of Teaching in Physical Education, 1994, Vol 13, 274-294.

WOODS, P.: Life Histories and Teacher Knowledge. In: J. SMITH (ed.): Educating Teachers: Changing the Nature of Pedagogical Knowledge. 1987.

Rosetta McLeod

Analysing Performance in Physical Education - an Interactive Multimedia Approach

In Scotland, teachers and senior pupils engaged in the new Higher Grade Physical Education course, are making regular use of interactive multimedia. Since 1988, the Scottish Office Education Department (SOED) has promoted and supported a policy of introducing school- and college-based multimedia resources to meet a variety of staff development needs. The term "multimedia" here refers to play-back technology capable of delivering sizeable amounts of sound, still images, graphics and full-screen full-motion video controlled by a computer program. A significant development associated with the development of interactive multimedia packages in Scotland, has been the decision by the SOED to encourage education authorities to invest in technology for staff development by making funding available through specific grant arrangements. This has meant that the majority of our secondary schools now have access to rather expensive interactive video (IV) hardware provided for them by their education authority.

By 1994, experience with multimedia in Scotland had shown that this combination of video and computer technology offered a powerful tool to address the needs of teachers and schools in terms of staff development, and there was a growing interest in ways in which the technology could address the needs of the curriculum. Over recent years, there have been many new developments in Scottish Education, and in the 1993-94 school session, a new Physical Education course at Higher Grade level (for pupils around 16-18 years old) was on offer for the first time.

The experiential approach to the teaching of Physical Education, where pupils engage in, analyse and investigate physical activity in the practical context, is now well-established in Scottish schools. This is a challenging context and, in recent years, teachers have made use of videotape to help capture the transitory nature of physical activities and to vary their approaches to teaching and learning. The Higher Grade course, however, presents new challenges for teachers and pupils in terms of the width, depth and detail of analysis required both during class teaching and in student self-study work. It was felt that an interactive videodisc package which could help teachers and pupils become familiar with the requirements of this course, would be an extremely useful resource.

Because of the immensely visual nature of physical education, it is important that performances are seen clearly, perhaps from different camera angles, and that the viewer can make decisions on how to view the performances on the screen - at normal or fast speeds, in slow-motion or even frame-by-frame forward or back. Interactive video is the ideal technology for this type of detailed control and analysis of moving film. Consequently, an IV package, comprising a videodisc, computer software and paper-based support materials, was funded by the SOED and Grampian Region Education Department, in co-operation with the Scottish Interactive Technology Centre and Moray House Institute of Education. This package allows an in-depth analysis of the nature of Performance, a key feature of the Higher Grade course; provides an IV staff development resource with special emphasis on the development and assessment of Performance; and provides tutorials and tasks which give pupils a greater understanding of aspects of Performance. The content design, filming and editing of the videodisc was undertaken entirely in Grampian Region with a number of the authority's teachers, pupils and support staff being actively involved in the project. Software development was undertaken by the Scottish Interactive Technology Centre in Edinburgh.

One of the most exciting features of the Higher Grade Physical Education videodisc package is its flexibility of use. The two main sections, the Teacher Section and the Student Section, are targeted at the syllabus for Higher Grade, while the Database and the Tutorial Maker/Presenter facility allow for use by a variety of audiences in schools, colleges and even in the area of sports coaching. The videodisc contains footage of ten activities which were considered to be most popular in Scottish schools - athletics, badminton, basketball, dance, football, gymnastics, hockey, ski-ing, swimming and volleyball. The shooting of over 700 clips was planned carefully so that their analysis could be used to develop performance and to illustrate levels of attainments, thus helping teachers across the country to reach agreement and consistency in their assessment of pupil performance.

This concept of performance is at the heart of the course. According to the Scottish Examination Board's document "Arrangements in Physical Education 1993", "at Higher Grade, the course will engage pupils in an increasingly sophisticated and rigorous study of the ways in which physical activities are performed. performance will be the prime focus, a practical experiential base upon which skills and techniques, knowledge and understanding, analysis and evaluation are developed in an integrated way...Pupils will develop further the ability to assess and appraise performance. They will review their own practical endeavours and those of others in a series of contexts, requiring them to observe, describe and evaluate both process and product. Ways of analysing performance will evolve from this."

The Student Section of the package is designed to allow a two-prong entry route to the various Tutorials and Tasks. Selecting an activity will display a list of the various options which are available, and these are colour coded to show the Area of Analysis of Performance to which each relates. If, however, a student was working on an activity not represented in the package - golf, perhaps, or rugby - access to certain sections might still be appropriate by entry under a relevant Area of Analysis - Structures and Strategies, Appreciation of Action, Skills and Techniques, or Preparation of the Body.

Most frequently, students will enter the package by selecting an activity. If, for example, Swimming is selected, four different options will be offered: Learning and Developing Skills, and Concepts of Skill Development (both part of the Skills and Techniques Area of Analysis of Performance) and Governing Principles of Force and resistance and Governing Principles of Flotation and Propulsion (both part of Appreciation of Action). Clicking the mouse over Learning and Developing Skills will take the student to a sub-menu offering the Tutorial or two related Tasks. Logically, students begin by working through the Tutorial then apply the knowledge they have acquired by attempting a Task.

The materials within this Student Section are designed to support a variety of learning strategies: group use with or without a tutor, and individual learning. Students must read on-screen information, follow instructions, analyse moving film and listen to audio information. In this swimming Tutorial, for example, students must watch a swimmer, Laura, taking part in a race and, by using the on-screen control bar to play the full-screen video at various speeds (normal, slow-motion, or frame-by-frame) must reach an understanding of the weaknesses displayed by the swimmer and think of ways in which she might improve her performance. Students can also access an audio track to hear Laura's own assessment of her performance. It is, however, the on-screen control bar which is the key to the analytical process. Students are able to replay a clip of video instantaneously and control the speed of use in order to reach the depth of analysis and understanding required.

The next step is to select a Task and in this Swimming example, there is a choice between Analysing Stroke Technique and Analysing Starts and Turns. In each of these, the student will compare Laura's performance with that of Aislinn, a more accomplished performer, and will be able to record, through the keyboard, his/her opinions.

This input text can be saved to a floppy disc or printed out. In order to support the independent learner, a Reveal facility has been included. This gives an outline response to the Task in the event that the student requires some support. Many teachers have, in fact, described the IV resource as being rather like having an additional teacher in their department, able to provide relevant work for the pupils and to support their learning.

This then, is a brief example of how users will approach the various Tutorials and Tasks within the Student Section. Some of the Tasks require students to input their responses using the keyboard, while others refer them to record-keeping sheets provided in the paper-based support materials. In total, thirty-nine Tutorials and eighty-two tasks are included in this section across the ten activities, providing a highly flexible resource which can be used for supported self-study purposes by individuals or small groups with or without a tutor. The materials provide a reinforcement or extension of ideas and concepts introduced by the teacher during direct teaching.

The other main section of the package, the Teacher Section, focuses on Developing and Assessing Performance and offers a highly effective resource for staff development. The Developing Performance Tutorial and the two related Tasks aim to highlight for teachers the Key Aspects and Qualities of Performance which they should be helping students to develop during the course.

When a new, examinable course is offered to students for the first time, teachers are naturally concerned to ensure that their assessments of student performance are in accordance with national guidelines. Accordingly, the Assessing Performance Tutorial provides visual illustrations of Performance Bands, the criteria which teachers must apply when assessing the competence of their students' performance, and shows how assessment must take place under the three fundamental concepts of Control and Fluency, Effectiveness and Contexts. In this Tutorial, it is possible for teachers to call up video clips showing examples of Performance 1,2, and 3 in each of the fundamental concepts and across a number of activities. The clips available in this tutorial are not presented as definitive examples, but rather are offered as a stimulus to encourage professional debate about the mark bands.

After working through the Tutorial, teachers may then select a Task in order to try an assessment for themselves. From a menu they can select an activity, view a fairly comprehensive piece of video showing student performance, then reach their own decision on the Performance Band and the mark within the band. As in the Student Section, opinions can be recorded through the keyboard, and a Reveal option will then give a considered opinion with the Performance band and the final mark. This exercise provides a very effective staff development tool which focuses debate on particular performers and engages teachers in discussion on levels of performance. It has the advantage of allowing teachers to examine the assessment criteria eg. Performance Band 1 is described in this way: "The candidate consistently shows a high level of control and fluency in selecting, combining and performing skills effectively within a range of increasingly demanding contexts." Through use of the videodisc materials, teachers can have a visual representation of what this actually means. Students, too, have open access to the Teacher Section so that they can see the quality of performances they themselves should be aiming to achieve.

Apart from the Teacher Section and the Student Section, a number of flexible options are built in to the package. A database, accessible from any part of the package, offers a quick access route to video clips from all of the activities. The Athletics section of the Database, for example, allows users to find, within a few seconds, visual examples of the various skills involved in sprinting, high hurdling, high jump, long jump, shot putt and javelin. The Dance database is structured around Laban's Analysis and offers access to visual representations of skills in Action, Space, Effort and Relationship. For many pupils, the Database is the first port of call, with teachers encouraging them to compare a videotape of their own performance against the examples of good performance available here.

A great deal of the power of multimedia lies in the ability to tailor the content to match the varied needs of different target audiences. With this in mind, the Higher Grade Physical Education package includes a feature called Tutorial Maker/Presenter allowing users, both teachers and students, to compile their own multimedia presentations incorporating text, still or moving images and audio. This user-friendly software encourages teachers, for example, to select relevant clips of video or still frames and, by typing in their own text linked to the various visuals, they can create additional learning materials for pupils of varying ages and ranges of ability. Similarly, students can use this feature to compile their own audio-visual essays. It may soon even be possible for Higher Grade students to complete their 1200 word compulsory investigation using the Tutorial Maker/Presenter facility and submit a floppy disc to the Scottish Examination Board for assessment.

The Tutorial Maker software is extremely easy to use. To create a tutorial, users type in their text via the keyboard, identify the start and end frames of video which might illustrate points in the text, choose the appropriate audio channel from the two available and, finally, make a link between the text and the video by creating "hot text" ie. a word or phrase which appears in red as a signal to the reader that, by clicking on the red text, video clips can be accessed. For each piece of "hot text", up to five linked video clips can be selected, and these can be identified by referring to the Index in the User Guide, where frame numbers are provided. Speed of access to video clips is a powerful feature of IV, and, when frame numbers are typed in, the relevant piece of video will be displayed on the screen in just a few seconds. Within Tutorial Maker the complete presentation can be previewed and edited, with the selected video clips being shown in a small window on the screen. When the final presentation is played back in Tutorial Presenter, however, the video is displayed full-screen and the control bar is automatically present at the bottom of the screen. To provide ideas for using this facility, some Extended Tasks can be accessed in both the Student and the Teacher Sections. Students, for instance, might be required to answer an Extended Task on the topic of balance eg. "Dance, gymnastics and ski-ing are characterised by the demands placed on the performer's powers of balance. Bearing in mind that to sustain balance there are elements of strength and endurance to be applied by the performer, how would you advise these performers to develop strength and endurance for their specific event in order to improve balance? View the clips: dance 573-880; ski-ing 13150-13300; gymnastics 6726-7008 and 6054-6238."

At present, teachers around Scotland are beginning to create their own individual tutorials and tasks, and the exchange on floppy disc of these completed materials will provide an effective means of extending the use of the package.

The Higher Grade Physical Education package, therefore, highlights for teachers and their pupils the links between performance and its analysis, the integral nature of which is an essential feature of the curriculum design of this new course. For staff, the issues of developing and assessing performance are also addressed, with teachers being offered opportunities to develop their expertise within each area. In catering for the curricular and staff developments needs of the Higher Grade course, the videodisc package has tremendous potential, with the in-built facility for repackaging the visual images clearly demonstrating the power of IV technology. A click of the mouse on the control bar allows the sort of detailed analysis of images not previously possible, so that on-screen performances can be scrutinised in minute detail. A swimmer's racing turn, the arm action of a badminton player, a gymnast's forward walkover - these are some examples of the sorts of skills which particularly lend themselves to detailed analysis using slow motion or frame-by-frame controls.

It is not an exaggeration to say that this videodisc package is one of the most successful ever produced in Scotland. A review in the Times Educational Supplement described it as "one of the best designed and most flexible videodiscs I have seen. It combines many worthwhile design features with careful curriculum planning, and it fills a genuine gap in physical education. All 36 minutes of high quality video are used to the full, with options to view by still-frame, slow motion, forwards and backwards. It is hard to see how physical education teachers could fail to benefit from this disc."

More information about the Higher Grade Physical Education package is available from the Scottish Interactive Technology Centre, Moray House Institute of Education, Holyrood Road, Edinburgh EH8 8AQ.

Weimo Zhu

Computer-Intensive Statistics and the Assessment of Motor Behavior

Introduction

Computer-intensive statistics are a set of statistical techniques, including bootstrapping, randomization tests and Monte Carlo tests, in which extensive computations are heavily dependent upon modern high-speed digital computers, and the statistics generated are free from assumptions related to most classical statistics, such as the normal distribution. The name "computer-intensive statistics" came from DIACONIS and EFRON's influential introductory paper (DIACONIS & EFRON, 1983), and was sometimes referred to as "resampling statistics" (EFRON, 1982). Computer-intensive statistics are products of the modern computer age. In contrast with computing power available when classical statistics were developed, modern computing power is much faster and cheaper. Today's statisticians can afford more computations on a single problem than the world's yearly total expenditure for statistical computations in the 1920s! Computer-intensive statistics take advantage of the high-speed computing power of the modern digital computers. The payoff for such intensive computation is freedom from two major limiting factors that have dominated classical statistical theory since its beginning: the assumption that the data conform to a bell-shaped curve, and the need to focus on statistical measures whose theoretical properties can be analyzed mathematically (DIACONIS & EFRON, 1983).

Bootstrapping is used mainly for statistical inference. The Monte Carlo and the randomization tests have been used mostly in the area of significance testing. Occasionally, the jackknife statistic also is included in computer-intensive statistics (see ROBERTSON, 1991). The jackknife statistic is actually neither new nor computer-intensive. It was originally developed as a method to reduce the bias of an estimator. The main reason for including the jackknife statistic is that bootstrapping, one of the major computer-intensive statistics, was developed based upon the idea of the jackknife (EFRON, 1979). Statistics in both techniques are developed based upon sub-samples from a sample that is originally drawn from the population. However, the jackknife sampling is conducted in a more systematic way: Each observation is omitted, in turn, to generate sub-samples, while, in contrast, the bootstrap sampling is conducted randomly with replacement. Due to limited space, we will focus the following introduction on bootstrapping. Interested readers may refer to NOREEN (1989) for more details of the randomization and the Monte Carlo tests, and to MILLER (1974) for a more extensive review of the jackknife statistic.

Bootstrapping

Bootstrapping, invented by EFRON (1979), is a computer-intensive non-parametric statistical inference technique. Like other commonly used parametric inference statistics, bootstrapping also is based upon a sampling distribution, more specifically a bootstrap sampling distribution. The bootstrap sampling distribution, however, is developed based upon neither many repeated samples from a population nor any analytic formulas. To develop a bootstrap sampling distribution, we first draw a sample randomly from a population. Instead of drawing succeeding samples repeatedly from the population or computing parameters of the sampling distribution based upon existing analytic formulas, we redraw many sub-samples, which we call bootstrap samples, randomly *with replacement* from the sample. Thus, "bootstrapping" here actually means redrawing samples randomly from the original sample with replacement. Sample statistics, such as mean and median, are then computed for each bootstrap sample. Distributions of the bootstrap sample statistics are the bootstrapping sampling distributions of the statistics.

Statistics or estimates derived from the bootstrap sampling distributions are the bootstrap statistics. For example, the standard deviation of the bootstrap sampling distribution of the means is the bootstrap estimated standard error of the mean. In short, both parametric statistics and bootstrap statistics estimate parameters of a sampling distribution from a sample. Parameter statistics estimate the parameters based upon available analytic formulas, which are restricted, however, by related distribution assumptions, while bootstrap statistics estimate the parameters based upon the bootstrap samples, which are free from these assumptions.

The idea behind bootstrapping is quite simple. Although it is impossible to get many samples from a population ($\mathcal{F}$), it is possible to get repeated samples from a population of size *n* whose distribution approximates the population. Given a sample that is drawn randomly from the population, the cumulative distribution of the sample [$F_n(x)$], known also as the "empirical distribution function," is the optimal estimator of the population. Let X=(x1, x2, ..., xn) denote a random sample of size *n* from a population. If $\mathcal{F}$ denotes the cumulative distribution function of the population, then $F(x)=P(X \leq x)$, where $P(X \leq x)$ denotes the probability of yielding a value less than or equal to x. This allows the cumulative distribution of the sample of size *n* denoted by $F_n(x_{(i)})$ to become the maximum likelihood estimate of the population distribution function, F(x):

$$F_n\,(x_{(i)}) = \frac{i}{n} = \frac{\text{number of } x_1, x_2, \ldots, x_n \leq x_i}{n}, \qquad (1)$$

where *i* is, in fact, the cumulative frequency and *n* is the sample size.

Let us use a small sample of data to illustrate how the $F_n(x_{(i)})$ is developed and implemented. There were 20 observations in this sample (Table 1). The maximum value was 52, and the minimum value was 15, with a mean of 35.25 and a standard deviation of 11.05. After arranging the data into an order of increasing magnitude yields $x_{(1)} \leq x_{(2)}, \ldots, \leq x_{(n)}$, the cumulative distribution of the sample,

$F_{20}(x_{(i)})$, was computed (Table 1). For example, the cumulative frequency of x(2), i.e., value 18, was 2, and the corresponding $F_{20}(x_{(2)})$ was 0.10 (2/20), which meant that for this population, the probability of yielding a value less than or equal to 18 was 0.10.

Table 1: A sample of data and its cumulative distribution function

---

Raw data (n=20)

23 28 18 39 32 30 15 30 41 46 40 30 50 44 37 23 45 30 52 52

Ordered observations x(1) ... x(n)	15	18	23	28	30	32	37	39	40	41	44	45	46	50	52
Frequency	1	1	2	1	4	1	1	1	1	1	1	1	1	1	2
Cumulative Frequency	1	2	4	5	9	10	11	12	13	14	15	16	17	18	20
$F_{20}(x_{(i)})$	0.05	0.10	0.25	0.25	0.45	0.50	0.55	0.60	0.65	0.70	0.75	0.80	0.85	0.90	1.00

One of the nice features of the cumulative distribution function is that its value has a range from 0 to 1, and each χ value has its own corresponding cumulative proportion. For example, because the $F_{20}(x_{(1)})$ was 0.05 and the $F_{20}(x_{(2)})$ was 0.10, the cumulative proportion of the value 18, $CP_{(18)}$, was in the range: $0.05 < CP(18) \leq 0.10$ (see Table 1). Based upon the cumulative distribution function of the sample and its corresponding cumulative proportions, we can begin our bootstrap sampling process. First we generate a uniform random number between 0 and 1 using a random number generator (it is very important to have a good random number generator here). Then we determine the corresponding value of χ according to the cumulative distribution function. Say, for example, our first uniform random number generated was 0.4827, which, according the cumulative distribution function (Table 1), fell into the CP range of the value 32 ($0.45 < CP_{(32)} \leq 0.50$). The value of 32, therefore, was selected, and became the first observation in the first bootstrap example. We repeated this process twenty times (each bootstrap sample was the same size as the original sample), and the first bootstrap sample with 20 observations was generated.

Generally, 50 to 200 bootstrap samples are adequate to generate bootstrap statistics (EFRON & TIBSHIRANI, 1986). To build bootstrap confidence intervals, however, at least 1,000 bootstrap samples should be employed (EFRON, 1988). The computing algorithm of the bootstrapping, as we have already seen, is very straightforward: (a) generate a bootstrap sample randomly with replacement from the original sample, (b) compute bootstrap sample statistics and save them, (c) repeat (a) and (b) for at least 50 times, and (d) compute bootstrap estimates. The amount of computing required by most bootstrap applications, although considerable, is well within the capabilities of today's personal computers. Computing language codes for the commonly used statistics have been included in several introductory texts (see MOONEY & DUVAL, 1993 and NOREEN, 1989), and most statistical software packages, such as SAS and SPSS-X, have the capacity to conduct bootstrapping with some programming. Also, several computer programs specializing in bootstrapping (see BOOMSMA, 1991 and LUNNEBORG, 1987) have been developed.

In summary, bootstrapping is a statistical approach to making inferences about population parameters, but it differs fundamentally from traditional parametric statistics in that it employs large numbers of repetitive computations to estimate the shape of a statistic's sampling distribution, rather than depends upon distribution assumptions and analytic formulas. Thus, the major advantage of bootstrapping over traditional parametric statistics is that it may sometimes be better to draw conclusions about the parameters of a population strictly from the sample at hand (e.g., a sample with small n), than to make perhaps unrealistic assumptions about the population. Bootstrapping has great application potential in assessment and data analyses in our field because many of our data distributions are skewed (e.g., pull-up data in fitness testing), and many of our researchers use small samples in their studies. For more information about bootstrapping, refer to the introductory texts by EFRON and TIBSHIRANI (1993) and a more technical reference by EFRON (1982).

An Example

To demonstrate the advantages of computer-intensive statistics over traditional parametric statistics in some statistical situations, we will use an example to show how to make a bootstrap statistical inference. Say, for example, a group of researchers wanted to determine if there is a difference in the upper body strength between boys and girls. They decided to use chin-ups as the strength measure, and the median as the statistic to measure central tendency because they knew already that the chin-ups data were not distributed normally. After randomly collecting a sample from both the boy and the girl populations, the researchers computed the medians for both boy and girl samples, and found a difference between the medians. They soon realized, however, that there was no way for them to determine the accuracy of their statistical inference because there was no theoretical reason to believe that the difference between the two sample medians was distributed normally, nor was there any analytic formula for them to compute standard error and confidence interval for the statistic. Let us see how bootstrapping can help them determine the accuracy of the difference between two sample medians.

Step 1: Draw a Random Sample

To make a bootstrap statistical inference of the parameters of a population (the median difference in this case), first we need to draw a sample from the population. Because we are interested in the difference between the medians in girl and boy chin-ups performances, we draw a girl sample (*n*=20), as well as a boy sample (*n*=20) from an existing data base (*N*=8,800). These samples and their statistics are illustrated in Table 2.

Table 2: Chin-ups raw data, bootstrap samples, and median difference

Raw data											Median
Boys (n=20):	14,	3,	16,	1,	8,	2,	4,	2,	6,	1,	5
	1,	18,	0,	5,	24,	14,	3,	5,	10,	12	
Girls (n=20):	0,	0,	1,	0,	0,	0,	5,	2,	2,	3,	0
	0,	1,	0,	0,	0,	0,	0,	0,	0,	0	

Unsorted	Bootstrap Sample Median		
Bootstrap Sample	Boys	Girls	Difference
1	3.0	0.0	3.0
2	4.0	0.0	4.0
3	5.0	0.0	5.0
4	5.5	0.0	5.5
5	4.0	0.0	4.0
...		...	
4996	6.0	0.0	6.0
4997	5.5	0.0	5.5
4998	3.5	0.0	3.5
4999	4.0	0.0	4.0
5000	5.0	0.0	5.0

Step 2: Redraw Bootstrap Samples

Next, we need to redraw many bootstrap samples from the sample so that a bootstrap sampling distribution can be developed. To make a bootstrap statistical inference, as indicated earlier, at least 1,000 bootstrap samples should be redrawn. To ensure that our inference will not be affected by inadequate bootstrap samples, we decide to redraw 5,000 bootstrap samples. More specifically, first we developed the cumulative distribution functions of the samples using the original boy and girl samples, respectively. We then generated a uniform random number from which a corresponding observation was selected from both boy and girl original samples. This was repeated 20 times so that two n=20 bootstrap samples, one for boys and another for girls, were generated. A total 5,000 such bootstrap samples were generated for both boys and girls, respectively. These procedures were completed by BOJA (BOOMSMA, 1991), a bootstrapping computer program.

Step 3: Compute and Sort Sample Statistics

To develop a bootstrap sampling distribution, first compute bootstrap sample statistics. The sample statistic we computed was the difference between the medians of the boy and the girl bootstrap samples. For example, the median of first boy bootstrap sample was 3.00, and the median of first girl bootstrap sample was 0.00. The difference between the two medians was 3.00. Similar computations were repeated for all 5,000 bootstrap samples. For clarification, the first five and the last five boy and girl bootstrap sample medians and their differences are illustrated in Table 2. We then sorted all the median differences, which consisted of the bootstrap sampling distribution of the median difference, and plotted them in Figure 1. As we expected, the distribution was not distributed normally.

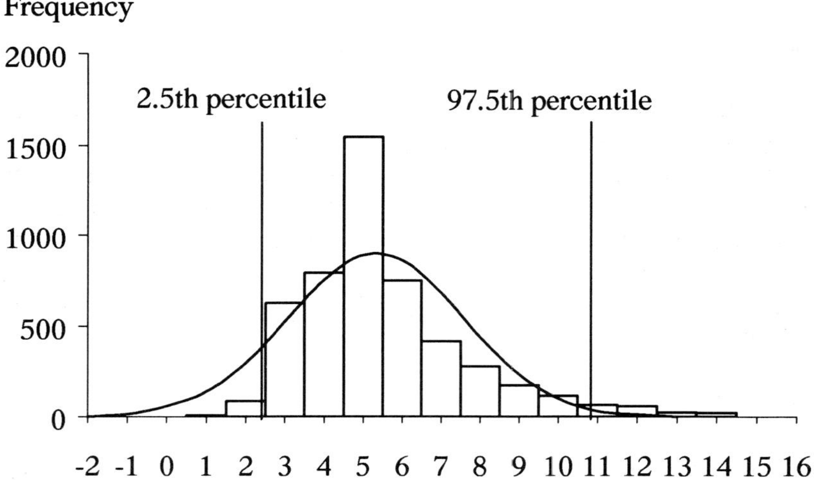

Figure 1 Sample Median Difference in Chin-Ups Performance

Step 4: Develop a Confidence Interval

To develop a statistical confidence interval, first determine an a-level. Usually, we set the a-level at 0.05. Accordingly, the corresponding percentiles for locating lower and upper endpoints of the confidence interval should be the 2.5th (0.05/2) percentile and the 97.5th (1-0.05/2) percentile, respectively. To determine the lower endpoint of the confidence interval, we simply counted up from the smallest sorted statistic (the median difference) to the 125th smallest value, which was 2.50. This was our lower endpoint of the confidence interval. Similarly, we counted down from the highest value to the 125th highest value, which was 11.00. This was the upper endpoint of the confidence interval. Thus, our statistical inference of the population median difference (q) could then be determined:

$$P(2.50 \leq q \leq 11.00)=0.95 \text{ (see Figure 1).}$$

Step 5: Make Statistical Inference Decision

Based upon the bootstrap confidence interval developed, we could make our statistical decision. First, we concluded, with 95 % confidence, that the interval between 2.50 and 11.00 covered the true median difference between boy and girl chin-ups performances. Because zero was not included in the confidence interval, we further concluded, with 95 % confidence, that the boys' chin-ups performance was statistically significantly higher than the girls' performance.

Conclusion

The development of new computer-intensive statistics has provided us not only a non-parametric approach to analyzing data to which parametric statistics are not appropriate, but also a new way to explore those statistics that traditionally cannot be applied due to violation of statistical assumptions or lack of analytic formulas. The major advantage of computer-intensive statistics over traditional statistics is that sometimes it may be better to draw conclusions about the parameters of a population strictly from the sample at hand, rather than by making perhaps unrealistic assumptions about the population. Finally, computer-intensive statistics should not be considered inexorable to the parametric statistics, but rather as an alternative, when the parametric statistics are not appropriate or not available.

References

BOOMSMA, A.: BOJA: A program for bootstrap and jackknife analysis [Computer program]. Groningen, The Netherlands: iec ProGAMMA, 1991.

DIACONIS, P.; EFRON, B.: Computer-intensive methods in statistics Scientific American, 1983, 248 (5):116-130.

EFRON, B.: Bootstrap methods: Another look at the jackknife. The Annals of Statistics, 1979, 7:1-26.

EFRON, B.: The jackknife, the bootstrap and other resampling plans. Philadelphia, PA: Society for Industrial and Applied Mathematics. 1982.

EFRON, B.: Bootstrap confidence intervals: Good or bad? Psychological Bulletin, 1988, 104: 293-296.

EFRON, B.; TIBSHIRANI, R.: Bootstrap methods for standard errors, confidence intervals, and other measures of statistical accuracy. Statistical Science, 1986, 1:54-77.

EFRON, B.; TIBSHIRANI, R.: An introduction to the bootstrap. New York: Chapman & Hall 1993.

LUNNEBORG, C.E.: Bootstrap applications for the behavioral sciences Educational and Psychological Measurement, 1987, 47: 627-629.

MOONEY C.Z.; DUVAL, R.D.: Bootstrapping: A nonparametric approach to statistical inference. Newbury Park, CA: Sage Publications 1993.

MILLER, R.G.: The jackknife: A review. Biometrika, 1974, 61: 1-15.

NOREEN, E.W.: Computer-intensive methods for testing hypotheses. New York: John Wiley 1989.

ROBERTSON, C.: Computational intensive statistics. In: P. LOVIE, A.D. LOVIE (eds.): New developments in statistics for psychology and social science New York: The British Psychological Society Routledge, 1991: 49-80.

Élaine Tanguay, Georges Lemieux, Nicole Dufresne, Jacques Chouinard

The Written Description as a Method for Measuring Skill Analysis Ability

1. Theorical Framework

Skill analysis has largely been proclaimed as one of the most important teaching skills for the process of motor skill learning (ARMSTRONG, 1984; HOFFMAN, 1977; PINHEIRO, 1989). It is also the teaching skill that comprises the largest percentage of the teacher's time during a physical education class (BARRETT, 1979).

Skill analysis has been studied in relationship with different variables: the relationship between a teacher's competency in analyzing motor skill performances and variables such as the observer's professional experience, the observer's performance ability, and the observer's knowledge of the skill (REIKEN, 1982). The strategies used in measuring the observer's competency, comprise some features that make them somewhat questionable from a naturalistic point of view. First, most of these studies use experimental procedures in which the subjects analyze the filmed performance of one student or athlete. In the gym, teachers usely don't observe the filmed performances of their students. They observe live performances of many students of different ability levels, moving in different directions, at different speeds. Second, and more important for the topic at hand, is the response system these studies use to measure the competency of the observer: questionnaires on which the subject indicates whether the observed performance is identical or not to the model performance (ARMSTRONG & HOFFMAN, 1979); drawings from which the subject choose the one best representing the observed performance (IMWOLD & HOFFMAN,

1983); verbal identification and visual discrimination of the critical features of the skill observed (WILKINSON, 1986); identification of the performance errors from a prepared list (ARMSTRONG, 1977); identification of corrective statements needed to improve the performance (NIELSEN & BEAUCHAMP, 1991). According to HOFFMAN (1976), the response system used to evaluate the observer's competency must be clear and concise, while measuring the observer's perceptual and diagnostic proficiencies. However, some authors find the response systems used in studies in skill analysis somewhat restrictive to the observer. According to REIKEN (1982), the task presented to the observer sometimes modifies his natural process of analyzing a motor skill performance. In her opinion, the task presented to the observer should indeed measure his perceptual and diagnostic abilities, but it should also re-create his natural way of analyzing a performance. Such a task would be one requiring the observers to indicate which features occur, rather than which do not.

Considering these findings, it appeared worthwhile to design a response system where the observers would, in writing, describe the performances they observed, identify their critical features and specify the errors they detected in these performances. This response system would permit the researchers to measure the observers' knowledge about the motor skills analyzed and their perceptual and diagnostic abilities. It was designed as part of a study on the effect of a training program in skill analysis.

2. Purpose of the Study

The purpose of this study is to determine the validity and the reliability of a response system used to measure the observers' ability to analyze live motor performances.

3. Methods and Procedures

3.1 Subjects

Twenty-three freshmen, majoring in physical education, volunteered for the study. When asked about additional education (inservice, etc.), none mentioned any particular training in skill analysis.

3.2 Training Program in Skill Analysis

The training program consisted of a two-week unit of three-hours sessions which took place two times per week. The purpose of the training program was to provide a method with which the students can organize movement knowledge around a common framework of ideas and principles, in order to analyze different motor performances. As HOFFMAN would put it "provide a generic framework for categorizing and considering various physical skills“ (1977, 44). No special attention was bestowed on the learning of the written description.

3.3 Testing Procedure

The subjects analyzed live performances of five motor skills, chosen to represent a variety of movements. For each observation, the subject's position was set at about 3-4 meters from the performer, with a 90° angle. The observers were asked to observe the performance once, and then were allotted four minutes to execute the following tasks in writing: describe, as precisely as possible and chronologically, the performance observed, identify it's critical features (check), and specify the performance errors detected in the performance. Each performance was videotaped for futur validation.

3.4 Data Analysis Procedures

3.4.1 Description of the Performance

The method developed to analyze the content of the written description was induced from conversations with expert teachers in different sport activities. Five categories were identified for the analysis: number of movement components and critical features mentioned in the description, chronology of the description, phases of the movement mentioned and the accuracy of the description. Each category was allotted a number of points and the maximum score attainable was 100 points. The best description was the one receiving the highest score.

3.4.2 Identification of the Critical Features

This task was designed to verify with certainty if the subjects knew the critical features of the motor skill observed. After having described the performance, the observers identified with a check the statements which, in their opinion, were related to the critical features of the motor skill. The analysis of the content consisted in counting the number of critical features identified and compare them to a list drawn by experts.

3.4.3 Identification of the Performance Errors

This task was designed to evaluate the subjects' ability in identifying errors observed in the performance. They were asked to specify the errors observed. The analysis consisted in counting the number of errors identified and verify their accuracy by using the videotape.

3.5 Assessing the Validity of the Analysis

The main question in this study concerned the extend to which the response system permitted the observers to describe what they actually saw. In order to determine this, the following procedures were undertaken. The researchers randomly chose the response sheets of twelve subjects, which they filled out after having observe a student perform a pirouette. Two coders were trained to analyze the response sheets. The accuracy of the written description was established by comparing the response sheets with the videotaped performance. Coders independently read each statement, compared it with the recorded performance, and determined if the statement was accurate or not.

The accuracy of the identification of the critical features was done by comparing the critical features identified by the observer with a list drawn, after agreement was reached, by two experts in the sport activity. Again, both coders carried out this task independently. This method is similar to the used by other investigators such as WILKINSON (1986).

The accuracy of the identification of the performance errors was established by comparing the response sheets with the videotaped performance. Two experts in the sport activity together read each statement, compared it with the recorded performance, and jointly determined its accuracy.

3.6 Assessing the Reliability of the Analysis

Between reliability was assessed by comparing the analysis of the two coders. The following formula for intercoder agreement was used:

$$I.C.A. = \frac{\text{Agreements}}{\text{Agreements} + \text{Disagreements}} \times 100$$

Within reliability was established through a test\re-test technique. The procedure used to analyze the response sheets was repeated a week later.

4. Results

4.1 Validity of the Analysis

The results indicate a level of validity fluctuating between 90 % and 95 %, as measured by the level of accuracy of the description. This finding suggests that the written description is useful in measuring the observers' perceptual ability. However, a number of subjects indicated errors in their description. For example "... (during the pirouette), the head of the performer did not turn last." This behavior has already been mentioned by REIKEN (1982) in her study with gymnastic coaches. Her results indicate that coaches tend to describe the presence of features rather then their absence, those features being correctly or incorrectly executed. In this study, the categories used to analyze the written description focused on the presence of features, but did not permit us to distinguish between the correctly and the incorrectly executed components, as seen by the observers. Thus, this omission may somewhat affect the validity of the analysis of the description, because it does not permit the researchers to identify precisely in what way the observers see the components of the performance.

4.2 Reliability of the Analysis Procedure

The levels of within reliability and between reliability of the written description, the identification of the critical features and the identification of the performance errors were found to fluctuate from 90 % to 100 %, depending on the performance analyzed.

5. Conclusion

Our results indicate that the written response sheet is a valid response system to measure the perceptual and diagnostic abilities of participants, engaged in a training program in skill analysis.

However, to improve the use of this response system, it might be worthwhile beforehand, to measure the writing ability of the participants. A participant with limited writing capacity may not be evaluated to his full potential.

Also, it might be preferable to limit the number of movement components, because some participants use the chunking technique to store information while observing a performance. Thus, they tend to write only key words that refer to a number of movement components. For example, one participant wrote this about the starting position of the performer: "... the performer's body is in fifth position." Another participant described with detail the same position, because he did not know the position's name. When counting the number of movement components, the latter participant has more components than the former. However, this does not mean that the latter participant is a better observer than the former. In conclusion, as the results indicate, this response system is valid and reliable. It can be use with large groups or with individuals.

References

ARMSTRONG, C.W.: Research on movement analysis: Implications for the development of pedagogical competence. In: M. PIÉRON; G. GRAHAM (eds.): Sport Pedagogy. Human Kinetics, Champaign, 1984, 27-32.

ARMSTRONG, C.W.; HOFFMAN, S.J.: Effects of teaching experience, knowledge of performer competence, and knowledge of performance outcome on performance error identification. Research Quarterly, 1979, 50 (3), 318-327.

BARRETT, K.R.: Observation for teaching and coaching. Journal of Physical Education and Recreation Jan., 1979, 23-25.

HOFFMAN, S.J.: Competency-based training in skill analysis: Designing assessment systems. In: R.S. STADULIS (Ed.): Selected papers from the 1976 research symposia of the AAHPER National Convention. Human Kinetics, Champaign, 1976, 3-12.

HOFFMAN, S.J. :Toward a pedagogical kinesiology. Quest, 28 (10), 1977, 38-48.

IMWOLD, C.H.; HOFFMAN, S.J.: Visual recognition of a gymnastics skill by experienced and inexperienced instructors. Research Quarterly for Exercise and Sport, 1983, 54 (2), 149-155.

NIELSEN, A.B.; BEAUCHAMP, L.: The effect of training in conceptual kinesiology on feedback provision patterns. Journal of teaching in physical education, 1991, 11, 126-138.

PINHEIRO, V.E.D.: Motor skill diagnosis: Diagnostic processes expert and novice coaches. PHD dissertation, Pittsburgh: University of Pittsburgh, 1989.

REIKEN, G.: Description of women's gymnastic coaches' observations of movement. PHD dissertation, NewYork: Columbia University, 1982.

WILKINSON, S.: Effect of a visual discrimination training program on the acquisition and maintenance of physical education students' volleyball skill analytic ability. PHD dissertation, Columbus: Ohio State University, 1986.

Virgina G. Overdorf, Lisa Plescia, Kathy S. Gill

Coaches' Perceptions and Actual Knowledge about Issues Related to Nutrition and Weight Control

A common, but rarely talked about problem in American competitive sports, is that of eating disorders. The rise in prevalence of eating disorders in American society has been well documented over the last decade (HALMI, FALK, & SCHWARTZ, 1981; LEVENKRON, 1982; MITCHELL & ECKERT, 1987). More recently the rising prevalence of eating disorders among the athletic population has been acknowledged as problematic. In fact, a 1988 study (BURCKES-MILLER & BLACK) suggested that male athletes are up to 15 times and female athletes forty times more likely to have an eating disorder than the general American public. This higher prevalence may be related to the pressures associated with modern sports competition, and the desire to gain any possible competitive edge.

The prevalence has not subsided, yet few American educational institutions have instituted programs to educate athletes about proper diets and appropriate weight control methods. Many concerned health experts feel far more could be done to prevent the severe complications of eating disorders.

In order for athletes to understand important principles of weight control and nutrition, they must be educated. Studies (LOOSLI, BENSON, GILLIEN, & BOURDET, 1986; WERBLOW, FOX, & HENNEMAN, 1978) have underscored that female athletes have poor nutrition knowledge, but several others (PARR, PORTER, & HODGSON, 1984; WELCH, ZAGER, ENDRES, & POON, 1987; WERBLOW, FOX, & HENNEMAN, 1978) have indicated a positive relationship between nutrition knowledge and diet behavior. Such knowledge should be forthcoming from athletic coaches or administrators, or their designated representatives. However, a recent study by OVERDORF and GILL (1994) indicated that 78 % of female high school athletes never had a coach speak to the team about proper weight loss and nutrition, and it was even more rare for representatives from the athletic administration to address the topic.

While there are undoubtedly many reasons why this problem is being overlooked, one reason might be that coaches are not knowledgeable about nutrition and proper weight control methods, nor about eating disorders themselves. There may be an educational issue with coaches that must be addressed prior to expecting transmittal of information on these critical topics to athletes. This study was designed to examine that issue by looking at what coaches claim to know about nutrition and eating disorders, and what they actually know.

Method

Subjects

Participants in this study included 42 coaches of female sports in four New Jersey high schools, 53.7 % male and 46.3 % female, with an education level of BA = 54.3 %; MA = 20 %; and MA+ = 26 %. The length of time coaching was as follows: 1-5 years = 46 %; 6-10 years = 20 %; and over 10 years = 34 %. Coaches volunteered to participate in this study, along with their athletes. Each coach was informed that his/her participation was not mandatory and that participation could be terminated at any time. The coaches represented a cross-section of sports including field hockey, basketball, tennis, softball, track and field, gymnastics, volleyball, swimming and soccer. Fifty-four percent of them had been coaching six or more years.

Procedure

A signed consent form was obtained from each participant. All subjects completed two inventories, a survey and a quiz. Both questionnaires were completed anonymously and complete confidentiality was assured. The survey was completed first, handed in, and then the quiz was obtained and completed. All questionnaires were immediately placed in an envelope by the site coordinator. The envelopes were then sealed and returned to the investigator. The survey and quiz took between 15-20 minutes to complete.

Measures

Coaches' Nutrition and Weight Survey (CNWS). This inventory was developed by two of the investigators. It requested demographic information followed by items about weight control and nutrition. The format provided multiple choice, with multiple responses permitted on some items, and forced-choice questions. Test-taking time averaged between 9-11 minutes for this inventory.

Coaches' Nutrition and Weight Quiz (CNWQ). This quiz was developed by two of the investigators, and it was designed to evaluate actual knowledge, as well as application of that knowledge regarding nutrition and weight loss information contained in the survey. Twenty multiple choice and forced-choice questions were included, with time to complete this quiz averaging between 7-9 minutes.

Results

Nutrition

On the CNWS, 91 % of the coaches rated their nutrition knowledge as average or better, while only 40 % had taken any formal classes in nutrition. Yet with such a high self-rating of nutrition knowledge, only 14 % of the coaches knew what percentage of simple carbohydrates should constitute athletes' diets, while less than half (40 %) were able to identify sources of complex carbohydrates. Eleven percent of the coaches thought athletes should have a high protein diet, while most of them (80 %) still believed that muscle is gained by eating proteins. Furthermore, only 8 % were able to identify sources of low fat. In spite of the limited knowledge identified, more than half of the coaches frequently discussed sports nutrition with their team.

Weight Control

In regard to issues of weight control, 40 % of the coaches believed that athletes would improve their performance if they lost weight. In communicating this belief to the team, 34 % claimed to have shared it several times or more, and 36 % had spoken to individual athletes about losing weight on many occasions (Table 1).

Table 1. Coaches' Communication about Weight Loss

	TO ATHLETE	TO TEAM
NEVER	57	48.7
ONCE	8	29.0
SEVERAL TIMES	31	28.0
CONSTANTLY	2	0

Of the 76 % of the coaches who said they tracked their athletes' weight, the predominant method for monitoring weight loss was visual inspection (37 %) rather than actual measurement (Figure 1).

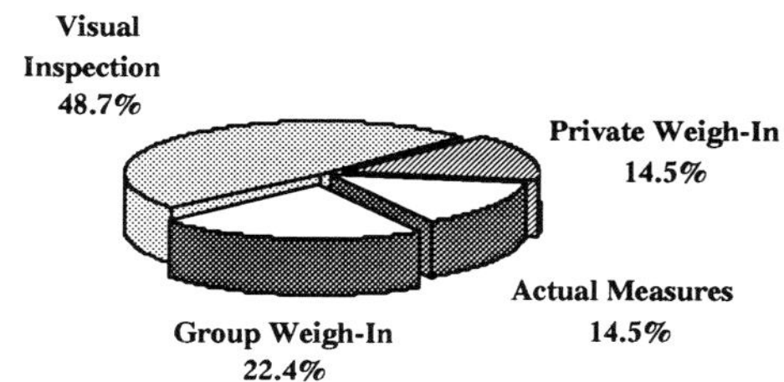

Figure 1. Methods used by coaches to monitor weight.

Group weigh-ins was the second method of choice reported by coaches. In a related study (OVERDORF & GILL, 1994), the athletes of these coaches surprisingly presented discrepant perceptions. Only 3.1 % of the athletes reported that their coaches used group weigh-ins, 1.7 % said they used private weigh-ins, 0.7 % said their coaches measured body fat, while 4.7 % allowed that their coaches might monitor their weight through visual inspection. In fact, most of them (89 %) did not think their coaches monitored their weight at all.

Responses to several questions about eating disorders resulted in some interesting responses. Seventy-seven percent of the coaches thought that weight loss had to exceed 15 % in order to reflect an anorectic condition. Moreover, 82 % of the coaches thought that body image distortions occurred equally among male and female adolescents, suggesting a lack of awareness of the greater risk for eating disorders among female athletes. Finally, 68 % of the coaches thought they had an athlete with an eating disorder, and 60 % of them said they would like more information on eating disorders.

Discussion

This study supports the findings of WOLF, WIRTH, and LOHMAN (1979) and PARR, PORTER, and HODGSON (1984) that coaches are not well-prepared in nutrition knowledge, with the caveat that coaches' self-ratings tend to be higher than their actual knowledge. While 91 % of the coaches rated their nutrition knowledge as average to very good, similar to PARR et al.'s data (1984), almost two-thirds (60 %) of them had never had a formal nutrition course. Moreover, this study indicated that coaches are particularly poorly prepared in nutrition knowledge application, the very activity that is most critical in their interaction with athletes on this important topic.

The coaches also appeared to have limited knowledge about weight control. A majority of them did not talk about weight control, and when they did, it tended to be to the team. Such communication runs the risk that an athlete with a lower self concept may think that the coach is telling her to lose weight, and may do so to please the coach, even though weight loss is contraindicated.

For the 76 % who do monitor their athletes' weight, they tend to do so by visual inspection (37 %) rather than actual measurement. This form of monitoring enables an athlete with a weight loss problem to effectively hide in her baggy or big clothing and to escape detection. Of the 28 % who tracked their athletes' weight through weigh-ins, 17 % of them utilized group weigh-ins. The subliminal message sent to an athlete when weighed in front of her/his peers is that you had better lose weight or everyone will know. Coaches utilizing this method of weight tracking are manipulating their athletes in undesirable ways.

Poor nutritional information, coupled with admonishment to lose weight to improve performance without explanations about how to do so, could be just the combination that results in compulsive eating behavior and the use of pathogenic weight control methods. In a vulnerable athlete, these patterns could develop into serious eating disorders. If there is no early intervention, these eating disorders can progress to the point of being resistant to treatment. Coaches, the first line of defense, must know the warning signs or initial changes in order to be able to intervene before the problem becomes too large. Therefore, it is critical to emphasize prevention in order to reduce the prevalence of these disorders in American society. Prevention lies in the proper education of those to whom athletes turn for knowledge regarding nutrition and weight control, their coaches.

Acknowledgement. This study was supported by a grant to the primary investigator from Ronald McDonalds Children's Charities.

References

BURCKES-MILLER, M.E.; BLACK, D.R.: Male and female college athletes: Prevalence of anorexia nervosa and bulimia nervosa. In: Athletic Training, 1988, 23, 137-140.

HALMI, K.A.; FALK, K.R.; SCHWARTZ, E.: Binge eating and vomiting: A survey of a college population. In: Psychiatric Medicine, 1981, 11, 697-706.

LEVENKRON, S.L.: Treating and overcoming anorexia nervosa. Charles Scribners Sons, New York 1982.

LOOSLI, A.R.; BENSON, J.; GILLIEN, D.M.; BOURDET, K.: Nutrition habits and knowledge in competitive adolescent female gymnasts. In: The Physician and Sportsmedicine, 1986, 14(8), 118-130.

MITCHELL, J.E.; ECKERT, E.D.: Scope and significance of eating disorders. In: Journal of Consulting and Clinical Psychology, 1987, 55, 628-634.

OVERDORF, V.G.; GILL, K.S.: Body image, weight and eating concerns, and use of weight control methods among high school female athletes. In: Women in Sport and Physical Activity Journal, 1994, 3(2), 69-79.

PARR, R.B.; PORTER, M.A.; HODGSON, S.C.: Nutrition knowledge and practice of coaches, trainers, and athletes. In: Physician and Sportsmedicine, 1984, 12(3), 127-138.

WELCH, P.K.; ZAGER, K.A., ENDRES, J.; POON, S.W.: Nutrition education, body composition, and dietary intake of female college athletes. In: The Physician and Sportsmedicine, 1987, 15(1), 63-74.

WERBLOW, J.A.; FOX, H.M.; HENNEMAN, A.: Nutritional knowledge, attitudes, and food patterns of women athletes. In: Journal of the American Dietetic Association, 1978, 73, 242-244.

WOLF, E.M.; WIRTH, K.C.; LOHMAN, T.G.: Nutritional practices of coaches in the big ten. In: Physician and Sportsmedicine, 1979, 7(2), 112-124.

Jacalyn Lund

Authentic Assessment: Have We Finally Found User Friendly Evaluation?

Think for a moment about how much our world has changed in the past 20 years. Fiber optics and lasers enable us to communicate with people around the world as if they were next door. Computers used to be housed in buildings instead of being located on desk tops and carried around in briefcases. Documents can be faxed all over the world, and even to the local schools if children forget homework assignments. Who knows, maybe some day faxes for gym clothes will even be invented!

To prepare students for this innovation and change, schools are having to change as well. The skills and knowledge valued in tomorrow's society will be very different from those valued when many of us were in schools. Computer literacy is becoming as important as the three R's. The ability to apply knowledge is becoming more valued than memorizing facts. Students have opportunities to work together in groups or teams to solve problems instead of always working independently. An integrated approach to learning is becoming more popular in which thematic curriculums attempt to show how subjects, such as math, reading, and physical education, can be taught around a topic rather than only teaching them as independent entities.

This change in curriculum, coupled with calls for accountability and school reform, has led educators to look for new and better ways to assess student knowledge. Alternative assessments have become increasingly more popular in the era of school reform as dissatisfaction over multiple choice and/or standardized tests increases. Part of the dissatisfaction occurs because standard forms of assessment look at indicators of learning rather than at the "real thing." Too often students can calculate math problems using formulas, but don't know if they are to use the area or perimeter formula when figuring out how much carpet to get for the living room. Students can score well on vocabulary and spelling tests, but can't write a decent letter of application for a job.

In physical education, we have lots of opportunity to directly assess skill because much of our subject is performance related. The soccer community would never dream of deciding the winner of the World Cup on the basis of which team was the best at juggling the soccer ball. Football fans will never let the Super Bowl become a punt, pass, and kick contest. Pitting Duke against Arkansas for the National Collegiate Basketball Championship on a multiple choice basketball rules test just won't work.

Unfortunately, physical education teachers fail to utilize the advantages of our profession when trying to determine if students have reached the movement and educational goals of physical education. Indirect indicators are used rather than direct observations of performance. Multiple choice tests are substituted for being able to use rules while playing a game. Skill tests, done in closed settings, are used to determine game skill. These assessments do have their place, however they should not be the final goal for teachers. Alternative assessments allow teachers to observe student ability to play tennis, dance, or swim as a part of assessment, thus taking physical education to a higher level of achievement.

As a secondary school teacher, I changed my grading/evaluation system every year. The conventional assessments I used were adequate, but I was looking for something that did a better job of assessing my goals. I wish I would have known about alternative assessment then, as that would have helped me put the pieces together and better align my goals and assessment.

Authentic assessment, alternative assessment, and performance assessment are all terms describing tests that attempt to measure acquisition of knowledge from a holistic standpoint in an effort to improve assessment and learning. The purpose of this paper will be to provide a brief introduction to various forms of alternative assessments. Definitions and examples will be offered, as the components of alternative assessments are explained. The paper will conclude by pointing out some of the advantages and problems associated with alternative assessment.

Alternative Assessment

Definitions for alternative assessment range from being anything other than a conventional and/or multiple choice test to CUNNINGHAM's (in press) which follows:

> a group of techniques that: (a) focus on the evaluation of products or performances that are considered important in their own right not just as indicators of some other valued outcome; (b) are intended to determine how well a student can use knowledge, rather than how much knowledge a student possesses; and (c) emphasize "higher level," more complex learning.

The above is a more comprehensive and accurate representation of alternative assessment. It will be used to represent alternative assessment in this paper.

Alternative assessments give students a chance to integrate and apply knowledge and skills as the teacher determines whether or not the instructional or learning goals have been met. Students are required to actively accomplish complex and significant tasks while using prior knowledge, recent learning, and relevant skills to solve realistic or authentic problems (LINN, BAKER, & DUNBAR, 1991). Responses are generated rather than chosen, as they would be on more conventional testing formats (HERMAN, ASCHBACHER, & WINTERS,

1992). Figure 1 may be a useful way to look at how traditional and alternative assessments differ.

* Emphasize higher level/complex learning
* Products are considered meaningful in their own right
* Measure application of knowledge
* Activity accomplish complex and significant tasks
* Direct observation of performance * Tasks have a realistic thread
* Students generate/create a response.

Figure 1 Characteristics of Alternative Assessments

The term alternative assessment is often used interchangeably with performance assessment. I prefer the term alternative assessment because it implies that we are doing something differently than we did in the past. This is not to say that the assessment that we have done in the past is inappropriate, I am merely recognizing that alternative assessments do something differently and have additional requirements to satisfy.

The term performance assessment can be confusing, especially for those teaching physical education. Physical educators have assessed performance for many years, however, they have not necessarily used alternative performance assessments. A distinction needs to be made between performance assessments and assessments of performance. A physical education skill test or fitness test would be an assessment of performance. Most skill and fitness tests do not meet the requirement of being complex and significant tasks. Being able to perform a tennis forehand against a wall 20 times is quite different than using a tennis forehand against an opponent in a game situation. The latter requires a student to move into position to play the ball and place the ball away from the opponent so as to score a point. The tennis game fulfills the requirement of being complex and a task that is considered important in its own right. The student has to be able to choose when the forehand is an appropriate shot. A conventional skill test may be a more appropriate way to assess the forehand in isolation. The alternative assessment would determine if, in fact, the student had sufficient skill to use the forehand in a meaningful context.

Grant Wiggins, a noted authority on authentic assessment, describes a soccer player he coached who could do 2 on 1, 3 on 2, and 4 on 3 drills, but was incapable of seeing and reacting to those situations as they occurred during game play (WIGGINS, 1993). Although the drills can be a way to learn and practice skills, the student needs to be able to use these skills in an applied setting before one could say that the player really understands the concept. Drills are not the appropriate level to assess student understanding, although they are an important part of the teaching process. Assessment during drills can provide valuable feedback. However, when the teacher assesses skills in an applied context, students are able to understand how the parts relate to the whole.

Alternative assessments give teachers a mechanism for looking at skills in a realistic setting. Students progress from being able to set and bump the volleyball accurately in a drill or skill test, to playing a game and using strategy to defeat opponents. *Plies* and *grande battements* become part of an art form as they are choreographed into dances. Talents can be demonstrated in a meaningful form and as students "stretch" and grow while being assessed.

Examples of Alternative Assessments

Although alternative assessment can assume several forms, the most common ones used in physical education include essays, oral discourses, exhibitions and event tasks, and portfolios. They will be described next.

Written Essays

Written essays are not limited to traditional papers as the name might indicate. Since this is an alternative assessment, the student must generate a product while demonstrating understanding. A health teacher in Kentucky had students look at cancer statistics for their area. Students did a lot of research at area libraries and hospital for this project. They looked at incidence of cancer for their county and compared it to that for the rest of the state. They decided local citizens needed to be more about cancer, which resulted in additional research about causes, detection, and prevention. The final "written essay" was an informational brochure which they distributed at a local mall as part of a cancer awareness campaign.

Oral Discourse in Physical Education

Oral discourses may not be practical for a physical education class of 60, but they do have their place. A teacher may allow a student to coach an activity or sport and then engage that student in a discussion of game strategy, offenses and defenses so that the student's level of understanding and application can be determined.

A teacher educator might talk with a student after a case study has been read or a teaching video watched. During the discussion the teacher educator could determine the extent to which the student understood the effective teaching practices noted during the observation or reading. In both these examples, teachers need to prepare criteria prior to the conversation so that the teacher can determine whether or not the student has met the goals for the assignment.

Exhibitions and Event Tasks

Exhibitions are comprehensive demonstrations of a student's skills or performance (FEUER & FULTON, 1993). Students are required to produce some type of live performance that demonstrates their skill. This could be done individually or in groups for an outside audience or for the class. An example of this might be choreographing a rope jumping routine, for which criteria had been established, and then presenting it to the class.

Event tasks are a form of exhibitions that can be completed in a single class period. The term is one used in the state of Kentucky. Event tasks pose questions to students or present hypothetical situations or problems which the student or a group of students must resolve. The completeness of the response is then assessed by the teacher using a predetermined criteria or scoring rubric. An example of an event task might be creating a game for a group of classmates that involves manipulative skills combined with locomotor and non-locomotor movement. Students are given several pieces of equipment with which to create a new game. A scenario can be added to give this task a touch of reality. For example, you might tell students that they are creating the game because they are in charge of the recreation for an annual family picnic.

Portfolios

Portfolios are collections of a student's work assembled over time (FEUER & FULTON, 1993). Students select the pieces that are to be included in the collection which they feel will demonstrate that they have met the goals or criteria for the project. The portfolio does not incorporate every paper generated by a student in that class, but rather only the best papers or the student's personal favorites. Thus, as students create their portfolios, they also must evaluate their work as they decide which pieces to include. Cover letters are added which guide the reader through the portfolio, explaining why certain items were included over others and how the items in cluded demonstrate that the student has met the criteria for learning. This student evaluation of the portfolio is a necessary component. Students are given the opportunity to redo pieces which are substandard or remove others when something better is completed. Faculty in higher education should be quite familiar with portfolios as most, if not all, colleges and universities require portfolios to document promotion and tenure advancements.

A physical education teacher might have students prepare a fitness portfolio. This may include initial fitness testing results, a prescription for improving current levels of fitness, a log documenting workouts, a journal describing the training program, a concluding fitness assessment, and an overall review of the success of the program, possible changes, and future commitment to physical activity. A portfolio designed to demonstrate fitness knowledge expertise would contain different documentation than one demonstrating personal fitness.

Our student teachers are asked to assemble portfolios. These are used to document a variety of teaching behaviors that the student has acquired while completing our program and during student teaching. These portfolios become a resource for the preservice teacher as the job search begins.

Authentic Assessment

Authentic assessments allow teachers to view learning holistically in a realistic setting. Several components are integrated as a student demonstrates multi-dimensional activities. Authentic assessments are alternative assessments that are terminal assessments. That is, they are direct measures of the skills that students should be able to do in the context of the game or activity. The tasks are real. Playing a team, individual, or low organized game, performing dance or gymnastics routines, or participating in outdoor education excursions would all be examples of authentic assessment tasks. The game does not have to be a part of a league nor does the dance performance have to be for an outside audience in order for the assessment to be authentic. A teacher education program could consider how a student teaches a class while being observed and/or video taped as a form of an authentic assessment.

The reform movement in Kentucky has chosen to use alternative assessment to determine whether or not students have met the state learning goals. Several criteria have been developed to look at the quality of the assessments used for teaching and testing. They are:

1. *Essential* vs. tangential - The "big idea" should be represented. The task done by students is important. Students don't just gather tools, they actually do the work.
2. *Authentic* vs. contrived - The processes appropriate to the discipline are used and students value the task. The assessment has a component of realism.
3. *Rich* vs. superficial - The assessment should lead to other problems and raise other questions. It should be pregnant with possibilities.
4. *Engaging* vs. uninteresting - Students should find the assessment thought provoking. They should want to persist in completing the assessment and perhaps go beyond the original requirements.
5. *Active* vs. passive - The student is the worker as meaningful products are created. There is a deepening of understanding on the topic as students interact with other students.
6. *Feasible* vs. infeasible - The assessment should be safe. Students should not be limited by time, materials, or equipment.

* ***Essential*** vs. Tangential
* ***Authentic*** vs. Contrived
* ***Rich*** vs. Superficial
* ***Engaging*** vs. Interesting
* ***Active*** vs. Passive
* ***Feasible*** vs. Infeasible

Figure 2 Kentucky's Criteria for Judging Assessments

Choosing the Right Assessment

The type of alternative assessment chosen would depend on the learning goals or the unit. If a teacher was doing a unit on endurance running, he/she could teach about training components (frequency, intensity and time), target heart rates, and pacing. If the teacher wanted to assess the training process, a log of the distances and times that were completed as part of this assignment could be required along with a discussion about the implications of these for training toward the ultimate endurance goal. This would be an example of a written essay. In it the teacher would be looking for evidence that demonstrated such things as an understanding of sound conditioning practices, integration of knowledge about training, pacing, and perhaps an evaluation by the student of the process. If the teacher had been interested in assessing an affective domain goal, indications of voluntarily running outside of class might have been listed in the original criteria.

An exhibition task could require a student to determine his/her distance running pace and then maintain that pace for a certain mileage. One criteria might be to observe whether or not the student began at a pace that would allow him/her to finish the entire distance. This distance would be such that the student could demonstrate endurance-type running, but would not be as far as an endurance race might entail.

The student might actually enter a race after having completed the training or do a bonified distance/endurance race in conjunction with others in the class. The assessment criteria might be based on whether or not the student completed the race and if he/she met the target time or if projected split times were reached. A final product that included student reactions and reflections might be added to the documentation on splits and target times.

This same unit could beassessed with a portfolio which might include such things as research on training components, a training log to document distances, a student diary that talked about how he/she felt after each training episode, a chart on resting heart rate to see if this decreased, and/or a summary paper that discussed what was learned and how this was applied. The components included in this portfolio might be suggested by the teacher as ways to demonstrate expertise, but the final choice of what to include, is left to the student.

Proponents contend that students find alternative assessments more meaningful than tasks such as running laps. Many assessment choices are possible. The type of assessment chosen by the teacher is determined by the teacher's instructional goals.

Creating Alternative Assessments

There are 4 basic steps to creating alternative assessments. This next section will provide a brief introduction to each of those.

1. *Set an instructional goal.* The teacher must decide what he/she wants students to be able to do as the result of instruction. There may be several goals a teacher wishes to accomplish during the instructional unit but they might not all be assessed. If the goal is important to the teacher, the best way to ensure learning is to hold students accountable through assessment.

2. *Prioritize the goals.* Instruction may include several goals but the assessment should focus on a limited number of them. Trying to assess too many things can get confusing. The number of goals selected to must correspond with the time available to accomplish them. The more goals a teacher chooses to assess, the longer the unit of instruction will be. A teacher needs to allow adequate time to teach the material students are expected to master.

3. *Select the type of assessment task to best measure your goals.* For example, if the goal is to teach students the game of badminton, the assessment might revolve around a badminton tournament with other students or an outside club. Other instructional goals might be satisfied by having students give a demonstration of their skills at a shopping center or nursing home. Preservice teachers might be required to set up a badminton clinic for a local high school. The task possibilities are virtually endless as long as they will measure the teacher's instructional goal(s).

4. *Determine the rubric or standard by which the task will be judged.* To say that students will play a badminton game is not specific enough. A standard or criteria must be set so that the level of expertise that

students will be expected to achieve is determined in advance and the students know how they will be assessed.

Setting the rubrics in advance is helpful from two standpoints. First, they will help determine the method and content of instruction needed to achieve the goals. Secondly, students know the scoring rubric in advance. They understand the criteria by which they will be assessed, and as instruction progresses, they will be aware of how close they are to achieving the goal. This will provide feedback throughout the learning process, without students having to depend on the teacher as the sole source of information/feedback.

The same task can be used to measure different types of learning. For example, a badminton game could look at skill, strategy, knowledge of rules, or good sports behavior. When using the same task to assess multiple goals, an analytic scoring rubric can be used to look at each component separately, or a holistic rubric can be created that will look at the entire piece or performance. Holistic scoring is usually simpler and faster than analytic because you have only one set of criteria (rather than two or three) with which to judge the performance (HERMAN et al., 1992). Another strategy for assessing multidimensional tasks is to score a piece holistically, noting the analytic dimensions that are strong or weak.

The scoring rubrics in physical education should pay attention to both process and product. Getting a serve over the net isn't important, from an educational standpoint, if the technique isn't correct. Also, since complexity is a component of alternative assessment, shot placement and strategy must be present. Rubrics should address instructional goals to ensure that these will be met. The more time allotted to instruction, the more complex the goals and rubrics can be. The key is matching the rubrics with the goals.

Specifying the criteria and defining the rubrics are important so that all alternative assessments are graded by the same standard. Rubrics help assure inter-rater reliability (DORAN, BOORMAN, CHAN &

HEJAILY, 1993). Scorers can drift away from the original criteria if they are not stated clearly enough. This is similar to the observer drift that can occur during observational research studies.

Because our profession requires overt student responses, creating alternative assessments in physical education is in many respects easier than for other subject areas. Being able to play a game, create a dance, or go on a camping trip requires students to synthesize knowledge and apply it at a holistic and higher cognitive level. The difficulty with physical education assessments often lies in the absence of a permanent product to which a teacher can refer for assessment. Video taping a student performance may be one way to eliminate that problem.

Advantages of Alternative Assessment

This section will be discuss the strengths and positive aspects of alternative assessment.

1. Alternative assessments allow the teacher to make direct observations of student work. With written tests on rules, an assumption is made that people who do well on them know the rules and people who do poorly, do not. Skill tests indirectly measure playing expertise as the components of the game are taken away from the context of the game. With alternative assessment one can see the student in action within a game setting. Authentic assessment is a direct observation of what this person knows and can actually do in a meaningful context.

A volleyball official might be able to pass a volleyball rules test, but may not be able to apply these rules while officiating a game. Conversely, a person might not be able to pass a written test because of a number of problems, but can be a great volleyball official. Test anxiety, inability to understand the written interpretation of the rules, reading something into the question that makes a different answer more desirable, being a slow reader, or taking the test out of a person's native language could all lead to poor multiple choice scores. These are just a few examples of why watching a person officiate a game might be a better indicator of actual ability than a written test.

2. With alternative assessment, students have to understand the material in order to complete the assessment task. Knowing the facts isn't enough. Demonstrating knowledge on a rules test does not guarantee that a person can apply them in a game. Knowing the terminology of effective teaching does not mean that a person is a quality teacher. Alternative assessments call upon students to apply the skills and knowledge they have learned (STIGGINS & BRIDGEFORD, 1985).

3. Alternative assessments tend to have good instructional alignment. The goals, tasks, and assessments are all congruent when alternative assessments are used because they tend to be interwoven. Instructional alignment is a sound educational practice that leads to higher levels of achievement (COHEN, 1987).

4. Students usually have longer periods of time to do the assessments. In many respects, this is an instant society. An answer from a student is expected immediately. The person who can shoot back an answer is more highly regarded than one who thinks before speaking. Research indicates that if a teacher waits before expecting an answer, the student will have time to formulate a higher order response. This past semester a student teacher did an outstanding job in the classroom but was paranoid about passing the National Teachers Exam (NTE) certification test. The problem was not lack of knowledge. She panics when doing multiple choice tests that have time limits. Alternative assessments can help alleviate this problem for students.

5. Authentic assessments tend to be more interesting and more realistic. Writing lessons plans for an actual teaching practicum is much more challenging than writing them to turn in to a teacher for a

grade. Knowing that one will be relying on the knots tied for a belaying class makes knot tying a little more meaningful. Learning to dance is a lot more fun when the student will be able to use these skills at an upcoming school function. I have observed that students seem to enjoy the challenges presented with alternative assessments often causing them to spend more time on the task than the teacher may originally have envisioned.

6. Alternative assessments can provide quality feedback to students. Since students are told of the assessment before instruction begins, they know the final goal and criteria. Having this information can provide feedback to students as they proceed through the unit, which is a definite benefit to students (SPADY, 1988). Assessment can actually occur throughout the learning in a formative fashion instead of being tacked on at the end. Formative evaluation is much more important to the instructional decisions that a teacher must make on a day-to-day basis (LINN, 1990).

7. In some instances, the assessment and the task are one and the same, which saves instructional time. Some physical education teachers claim that they do not assess students because it takes too much time away from instruction. Using alternative assessments can be an effective solution to this problem because assessment and teaching are interwoven. Alternative assessments also allow teachers to assess multiple aspects of a task rather than single dimensional ones. For example, an alternative assessment may require a student to play a game of tennis. Assessment for knowledge of rules, stroke topography or skill analysis, knowledge of strategy, and acceptable sport behavior and etiquette can occur during this game.

8. Alternative assessments can be context specific. Valid and reliable skill or multiple choice tests may not take into consideration the amount of time you have available to teach, the number of students in your class, the initial starting skill level of students, strength and age of the student, and so forth. When setting standards for alternative assessments, context can be taken into consideration, thus

setting up students for possible success in less than ideal teaching situations.

9. Assessment by observation is formalized with alternative assessments. Many teachers already use observation very effectively as their primary means of informal assessment (WILSON, 1970). By setting criteria, the process becomes more structured. Instead of giving arbitrary letter grades, students can see where they stand with regard to the criteria that have been established.

10. Current educational trends lead us to over-test students and then do little with the results. A prime example of this is the teacher who administers fitness tests and then puts the data on the shelf instead of using it to guide instruction and motivate students. Alternative assessments tend to be purposeful and useful throughout instruction. By setting standards in advance, students know what they are expected to achieve. Deficiencies can be corrected during instruction. Both the students and teachers have feedback about performance. Yes, the teacher is teaching toward the test, but when the test is a worthwhile goal, what is wrong with this approach?

Concerns Connected with Alternative Assessment

Although alternative assessments have many positive attributes, there are some issues and concerns that must be addressed.

1. One of the biggest criticisms of alternative assessments concerns validity and reliability. Validity and reliability are possible with alternative assessments, but they narrow the range of possible answers and responses) and require others to score results.

If alternative assessments are not used for high stakes accountability and testing (i.e. tests that decide whether a student will graduate, get a scholarship, or if a school will receive funding), accurate determination of validity and reliability is not as critical. Few if any teachers currently spend time making sure that their tests are valid and/or reliable (STIGGINS, CONKLIN & BRIDGEFORD, 1986). Therefore, with many classroom assessments, validity and reliability are not being sacrificed when alternative assessments are used, the test format is simply being changed. For high stakes accountability, reliability, validity, and/or some equivalent are necessary. Perhaps new standards to address these issues will have to be created for alternative assessments (MOSS, 1992). Many experts are grappling with this issue.

Reliability may be one important component, but not the only possibility for judging the worth of a test. "If reliability is put on the table for discussion, if it becomes an option rather than a requirement, then the possibilities for designing assessment and accountability systems that reflect a full range of valued educational goals becomes greatly expanded" (MOSS, 1994, 10). Reliability is just one factor to be considered in judging the quality of assessment.

2. The teacher has to realize that there are many correct ways to answer the questions asked or the problems generated through alternative assessments. A teacher has to be open to accepting these responses. This is not always easy to do.

3. Alternative assessments are costly in terms of the time that they require to administer and score. Tests, however, often determine what students deem to be important and what they prepare and study (WIGGINS, 1989b). If performance was improved as the result of using alternative assessment, this might help offset the concern over time and monetary expense of assessment. Assessing the wrong component is expensive as well. Since alternative assessments tend to be direct measures of assessment, this latter issue is less likely to happen. For state level assessment, sampling techniques, where not every student is tested, can be 'used to keep costs down (POPHAM, 1993).

The purpose of the assessment must be examined and then the decision made of how much expense to incur. The ultimate purpose of assessment should be to improve teaching and learning. This must be the primary focus when deciding how to assess.

4. Peripheral factors must be considered when determining the type of assessment to be used. The assessment must be written so that teachers are assessing what they actually want students to know. Giving first grade students an assignment that involves reading and writing skills would not be appropriate because several of them may have limited expertise. Our students in Kentucky were recently asked to do a writing sample on a given topic. If they didn't know much about Greek architecture, they were not able to showcase their writing talents. A class of 60 students with one ball would not allow a perspective teacher much opportunity to demonstrate teaching expertise.

5. The terminology with alternative assessment has not been clearly defined (WORTHEN, 1993). Whenever an idea becomes as popular as this one has, it is bound to suffer growing pains. There are discrepancies in the literature about terminology. Although some sources (HERMAN et al., 1991) say that the terms alternative assessment, performance assessment, and authentic assessment can be used interchangeably, others make definite distinctions between the them. Performance and portfolio assessment are seen as two entities (CUNNINGHAM, in press). Authentic and performance assessments are differentiated in one place (MEYER, 1992) yet in another source, authenticity is seen to be a vital component of all performance assessment. (WIGGINS, 1989a).

Since most of the literature comes from academic areas, physical education is forced to interpolate and extrapolate information and definitions from this knowledge base. I'm sure this point will be debated at this conference and many other places before consensus about definitions is reached.

Conclusion

As a teacher, I struggled for many years to find a grading and evaluation system that worked for me. I have now come to realize that part of the problem was that I wasn't making full use of assessment. I was using conventional techniques that allowed me to assess the pieces. Alternative assessments allow meaningful assessments for students. Instead of focusing on independent skills, I could have had students use their skills in game settings and evaluate them at that level. After all, that was my ultimate goal. I just didn't realize that that type of assessment was legitimate. By weaving assessment throughout instruction, it becomes an integral part of learning. Students understand what they are expected to accomplish and thus are better able to achieve teacher expectations.

I want to clarify that I am not advocating the elimination of multiple choice tests or skill tests from instruction. The teacher must determine instructional goals and then decide what will be the best way to evaluate whether or not a student has achieved them. In my program, these tests were an intermediate step, but they were not the final goal that I wanted to accomplish. Hence the need for alternative assessment.

We must have discussions about alternative assessments relative to physical education so that our definitions become more clear and understandable. Until this is done, practitioners and teacher educators alike will be caught in this confusion and the confusion will neither be healthy or helpful.

Students tend to enjoy these assessments because they typically are more challenging than traditional tests. They allow students to combine knowledge in a meaningful way. When students are more motivated, their final product tends to be of a higher quality. Moreover, alternative assessments are actually fun to create and challenging to administer.

For these reasons, I am personally excited about alternative assessments. Authentic assessments are the ultimate form of these, as students become involved in real world accomplishments. Teachers can directly assess behaviors they want their students to achieve with authentic assessments, making them user-friendly. More significantly, students become more active participants in the teaching/learning process as instruction and assessment are interwoven.

Alternative assessments do not have to be intimidating. They can be administered in conjunction with the learning tasks and not drain time away from instruction. Students know what is expected of them from the beginning and can work toward that end. I challenge our test and measurement colleagues to start including this approach to assessment in their classes. It's time for educators to start thinking differently about education and alternative assessment could be a wonderful start.

References

COHEN, S.: Instructional alignment: searching for a magic bullet, Educational Researcher 1987, 16 (8), 16-20.

CUNNINGHAM, G.: Assessment in the Classroom: Constructing and Interpreting Tests. New York: Macmillan Publishing Company (In press).

DORAN, R.; BOORMAN, J.; CHAN, F.; HEJAILY, N.: Authentic assessment: an instrument for consistency, The Science Teacher 1993, 60 (6), 37-40.

FEUER, M.; FULTON, K.: The many faces of performance assessment, Phi Delta Kappan 1993, 74 (6), 478.

HERMAN, J.; ASCHBACHER, P.; WINTERS, L.: A Practical Guide to Alternative Assessment. Alexandria, VA: Association for Supervision and Curriculum Development 1992.

LINN, R.: Essentials of student assessment: from accountability to instructional aid, Teachers College Record 1990, 91 (3), 422-436.

LINN, R.; BAKER, E.; DUNBAR, S.: Complex performance-based assessment: expectations and validation criteria, Educational Researcher 1991, 20 (8), 15-21.

MEYER, C.: What's the difference between authentic and performance assessment?, Educational Leadership 1992, 49 (8), 39-40.

MOSS, P.: Shifting conceptions of validity in educational measurement: implications for performance assessment, Review of Educational Research 1992, 62 (3), 229-258.

MOSS, P.: Can there be validity without reliability? Educational Researcher 1994, 23 (2), 5-12.

POPHAM, W.: Circumventing the high costs of authentic assessment, Phi Delta Kappan 1993, 74 (6), 470-473.

SPADY, W.: Organizing for results: the basis of authentic restructuring and reform, Educational Leadership 1988, 46 (2), 4-8.

STIGGINS, R.; BRIDGEFORD, N.: The ecology of classroom assessment, Journal of Education Measurement 1985, 22 (4), 271-286.

STIGGINS, R.; CONKLIN, N.; BRIDGEFORD, N.: Classroom assessment: a key to effective education, Educational Measurement? Issues and Practice 1986, 5 (2), 5-17.

WIGGINS, G.: A true test: toward more authentic and equitable assessment, Phi Delta Kappan 1989a, 69 (9), 703-713.

WIGGINS, G.: Teaching to the (authentic) test, Educational Leadership 1989b, 46 (7), 41-47.

WIGGINS, G.: Assessment: authenticity, context, and validity, Phi Delta Kappan 1993, 75 (3), 200-214.

WILSON, R.: Determination of evaluative devices for adequate assessment levels of competence in certain physical education activities. Office of Education (DHEW) Washington, D.C. Bureau of Research 1970. (ERIC Document Reproduction Service No 047-338).

WORTHEN, B.: Critical issues that will determine the future of alternative assessment, Phi Delta Kappan 1993, 74 (6), 444-454.

4. Changes in Society - Chances for Adapted P.E.

Claudine Sherrill

Individual Differences, Adaptation, and Creativity Theory: Applications and Perspectives

Adapted physical activity is accepted as an academic discipline, subdiscipline, or area of specialization in many universities and countries (DEPAUW & SHERRILL, 1994; DUNN & MCCUBBIN, 1991; SHERRILL, 1988). In others, adapted physical activity (like the people it serves) is neglected, ignored, or devalued. Beliefs, attitudes, and practices vary tremendously, but adapted physical activity is increasingly accepted as an independent sport science worthy of the same attention as other theoretically-based fields of study.

The purpose of this paper is to invite pedagogy scholars to consider the meanings of adapted physical activity both within the university teacher preparation context and the home-school-community service delivery or empowerment context. What theories and practices do adapted and regular physical education share? What is our potential for growing and maturing together? Why do we need each other?

Many Meanings: A Historical Overview

Adapted physical activity has many meanings, partly because it has been associated with different populations over the ages. Historically, we trace our origins to the curative and therapeutic uses of exercise in ancient China, Greece, and Rome. In this respect, we are similar to sports medicine (HOLLMANN, 1992). Many of the first university-based adapted physical education specialists in the United States were physicians, physical therapists, armed services medical personnel, or individuals who had seriously considered a career in medicine. Their main interest was individuals with physical disabilities and/or health impairments, and they relied on a rich body of knowledge extending from the Swedish medical gymnastics movement of the 1800s through the remedial and corrective physical education era (LEONARD, 1923; MCKENZIE, 1909; RATHBONE, 1934), to the initial evolution of adapted physical education philosophy in the 1950s.

In the 1960s and 1970s, in the United States, the population served by adapted physical education shifted drastically when children born with developmental disabilities began receiving services in public schools rather than in state institutions. The new placement trend resulted in a total revision of the adapted physical education knowledge base, a close reliance on special education, and eventual departure from the medical model. Some leaders advocated merging adapted physical education and special education into a new field of study called special physical education (FAIT, 1966), but the majority viewed adapted physical education as a more accurate term for the interdisciplinary or crossdisciplinary body of knowledge they were helping to create.

The year 1973 marked the beginning of an international movement with the founding of the International Federation of Adapted Physical Activity (IFAPA) in Quebec, Canada. Subsequent biennial conferences in Belgium, USA, Great Britain, Canada, Australia, and Japan have recently attracted 600 to 800 professionals who share scholarly work. Human Kinetics publishers encouraged shifting of school-based terminology (adapted physical education) to the broader, lifespan vision (adapted physical activity) by publishing conference proceedings by this title in the early 1980s (EASON, SMITH, & CARSON, 1983) and initiating a journal called *Adapted Physical Activity Quarterly*, in 1984.

Adapted physical activity has become an umbrella term used worldwide to devote philosophy, beliefs, attitudes, and practices pertaining to home-school-community delivery systems that empower individuals of all ages and capabilities to engage in healthy, meaningful, satisfying physical activity (DOLL-TEPPER, DAHMS, DOLL, VON SELZAM, 1990; SHERRILL, 1993). As such, adapted physical activity is an equal-status partner to regular physical activity or sport pedagogy.

Underlying adapted physical activity philosophy is the reality that professionals in most settings lack the resources (time, energy, money, expertise) to meet all needs of all people. Even when attitude, training, and motivation are optimal, situations arise that require consultant or other kinds of assistance. Facilities of the future will employ teams of professionals who have varied interests and competencies that are specifically matched to a broad spectrum of individual differences. We will not expect a regular physical educator or recreator to function alone in one setting and an adapted physical activity specialist to function alone in another setting. Both will function in numerous roles in many and varied settings that provide lots of choices and challenges. Our philosophy and practices will be inclusive, built on cooperation and collaboration among team members. Before this can happen, however, we must change attitudes of most everyone involved.

Changes and Challenges Pertaining to Attitude

Adapted physical activity must be conceptualized first and foremost as attitude change (MORISBAK, 1990; SHERRILL, 1993). An extensive body of literature documents perceived lack of competence and other variables as barriers to integration and inclusion of individuals different from oneself (DOWNS & WILLIAMS, 1994; HEIKINARO-JOHANSSON & SHERRILL, 1994; SCHMIDT-GOTZ, DOLL-TEPPER, & LIENERT, 1994; RIZZO & VISPOEL, 1992).

New research studies must attempt to answer questions about how and why. Regular and adapted physical activity professionals must collaborate in the design and conduct of such research. Illustrative of this new thrust is the research by KOWALSKI (1994) and colleagues at Adelphi University in New York, who have shown the efficacy of infusion strategies in changing attitudes.

Social and Political Construction of Knowledge

Adapted physical activity, like other areas of knowledge, is socially and politically constructed. Its theory and practices are specific to history and culture and the ways our respective societies value or devalue individual differences. Always adapted physical activity has sought to serve individuals that comprise social minorities on the margin of mainstream inclusion and acceptance. Always adapted physical activity has been shadowed by discrimination, prejudice, and stereotyping.

Increasingly, adapted physical activity acts as a catalyst and conscience in promoting integration and access. Adapted physical activity is becoming a political movement in the same sense as feminism, which now advocates for acceptance of all forms of diversity.

In the USA, this commitment grew out of the civil rights movement of the 1960s. For the first generation of university teacher-trainers in adapted physical education, shaping the new curriculum was associated with the service orientation of President John F. Kennedy, "Ask not what your country can do for you; ask what you can do for your country!" Those of us who loved physical education and sport wanted it for all people. We were particularly saddened by research reporting exclusion of children with mental retardation from school physical education instruction (BRACE, 1968; FAIT, 1966).

Professional preparation specialization training that led to Master's and Doctoral degrees began in 1967, with enactment of legislation in the USA that made federal grant money available to colleges and universities which were willing to create graduate level academic specialization in adapted physical education and therapeutic recreation. The mission was to convince large numbers of young prospective teachers to overcome their fears and prejudices and develop careers that combined physical education, special education, and the social psychology of individual differences. This was not easy, and it is still not easy. Various strategies have been used. One has been federally funded graduate assistantships and scholarships to finance the graduate education of adapted specialists. Also some full time university positions in adapted physical education have been funded by federal monies. In a sense, the behavior modification principle of pairing something good (money) with something unknown and anxiety-provoking (individual differences or children no one wanted) has been operative...

Advocacy Theory and Practice

I share this case study of USA professional preparation to emphasize that government intervention and/or money from big business and industry are often needed to fight prejudice and discrimination. Recognition of this fact has led adapted physical activity leaders to develop a body of knowledge called advocacy theory and practice (SHERRILL, 1993). **Advocacy** is action aimed at promoting, maintaining, or defending a cause, like the rights of individuals with disabilities. Courses of study on advocacy include units on attitude change, assertiveness training, support networking, legislation, and litigation. We cannot leave the development of this knowledge to chance. Regular physical education needs advocacy also, and adapted physical activity professionals have skills that should be used to promote and maintain high quality physical education instruction for all children.

The cultural/economic foundations of fighting prejudice and creating equal opportunity vary widely, of course, from state to state and from country to country. The challenges eventually will broaden teacher training from its focus on classroom and school activity to an emphasis on home-school-community relationships. Issues of acceptance, inclusion, self-esteem, motivation, and locus of control extend beyond school boundaries and challenge adapted physical activity to shape a new image.

Contemporary Definitions of Adapted Physical Activity

The definition of adapted physical activity has clearly changed from programming for students who cannot safely or successfully participate in regular physical education to programming that encompasses the total lifespan and the total ecosystem (i. e., individuals with special needs, their families, teachers, classmates, and significant others). We no longer automatically remove the student from the regular classroom. Instead, we consider how the environment can be altered, how attitudes can be changed, how support services can be provided, and how multiple placements can be used (BLOCK, 1994; DAVIS & BURTON, 1991; DEPAUW & GOC KARP, 1994; HEIKINARO-JOHANSSON, SHERRILL, HUUHKA, & FRENCH, 1995; KOWALSKI, 1994).

Let us consider two new definitions of adapted physical activity: long and short versions of essentially the same ideas. The long version is:
Adapted physical activity is crossdisciplinary theory and practice related to **lifespan** activity of individuals whose function, structure, or appearance requires expertise in (a) assessing and adapting **ecosystems** and (b) facilitating societal changes necessary for

- equal access
- integration/inclusion
- lifespan wellness
- movement success
- empowerment/self-actualization

A short version of this might be: *Adapted physical activity is crossdisciplinary philosophy, attitudes, knowledge, and skills central to psychomotor service delivery and empowerment for individuals of all ages whose differences from the norm require expertise in adaptation.* Note how these definitions avoid such negative terms as disability and handicap. They stress instead uniqueness, diversity, and individual differences because we work with **whole** people. Disability is only one part of an individual just as gender is a part and race/ethnic group and religion are parts.

Individual Differences and Adaptation Theory

Adapted physical activity then academically is comparable to women's studies or ethnic group studies. It is, however, plagued by the historic, pervasive discrimination that able-bodied and able-minded persons feel toward individuals they perceive as different. Erving GOFFMAN (1963) has emphasized that disability is an **undesired difference** that no one would choose. In this way disability is different from other categories like gender, race, and religion that comprise part of our identity.

GOFFMAN (1963) posited **stigma** theory to help explain attitudes and practices toward undesired differences. Stigma is a Greek word for **branding**, which comes from the ancient Greece practice of branding individuals, slaves, or prisoners believed to be bad or not quite human because of crimes, or political beliefs, or other differences.

Social psychologists like KATZ (1981) have produced research that indicates that the able-population, the majority, is not prejudiced per se by disability but rather the **difference** that disability connotes. From childhood on, our society socializes people to embrace similarity, to become as others are, to make friends with and choose as spouses people who are similar to self. Whole cultures fight, kill, and seek to eliminate humans perceived as different and thus, in some way, threatening.

How much we teach that could be called similarity theory! In the early years of adapted physical education, leaders stressed that people with disability were more similar than different to us. Therefore, we could feel more and more comfortable as we explored our similarities. This then led to positing that the pedagogy could be similar, we should just try harder. This approach, to some extent, works but it devalues the part of the individual that is different. It is like saying gender or race or socioeconomic status do not matter. Research shows that all of the variables that make us different or unique do matter in adapting or creating pedagogy that works (HEIKINARO-JOHANSSON et al., 1995; SCHMIDT-GOTZ et al., 1994).

Individual differences theory is a body of knowledge posited by SHERRILL (1993) that recognizes continuous assessment of the individual and his/her ecosystem as the central focus of service delivery and empowerment. This theory rejects the use of characteristics, categories, and labels in studying individuals with disabilities and providing services for them. Instead, the emphasis is on the dynamical systems at play in both **inter** and **intra** individual and ecosystem differences. Instead of the word **characteristic,** we use assessment terminology like indicators, descriptors, variables, and observations. We base individualized education programs on what we assess, not characteristics associated with specific disabilities.

Note adaptation in our new definitions. **Adaptation** is the continuous, dynamic, and bidirectional process by which individuals and the environment reciprocally change one another. Adaptation theory, first posited by Ernst KIPHARD (1983) of Germany, stresses assessment of both the individual and the environment and strategically modifying each. Out of adaptation theory come practices like ecological task analysis (DAVIS & BURTON, 1991) and various attitude change interventions.

Creativity Theory

Creativity is the problem-solving, reflective process by which adaptation is planned and executed. Creativity has been factor analyzed by GUILFORD (1952), TORRANCE (1962), and others into specific behaviors that must be assessed and taught separately. **Fluency**, is asking, "How many ways?" -- exploring every possible question and solution. **Flexibility** is shifting easily from one ecological dimension to another (time, space, size, color): Using all the perceptions and emotions to explore ecological relationships and interactions. **Originality** is stretching the mind for the different or unique solutions that no one else has described. **Elaboration** is playing with details, thereby organizing and evaluating the effects of different variables, individually and in unique combinations.

Whereas these creativity components are in the cognitive domain, SHERRILL (1993) emphasizes that creative behaviors in the affective domain are essential also to the adaptation process, particularly to pedagogical strategies pertaining to integration and inclusion. Specifically, professional preparation programs should aim to teach the creative behaviors of acceptance, imagination, curiosity, caring, and courage.

Creativity enables professionals to find and envision uses of new resources. Among the most valuable of the resources that adapted physical activity specialists support are individuals with disabilities, who often possess new insights because of their different life experiences and therefore are excellent at adaptation. In the future, individuals with disabilities increasingly will be employed as teachers and administrators.

Individuals with disabilities are the world's largest social minority (SHAPIRO, 1993). This minority encompasses approximately one of every six people. This vast resource already has been instrumental in changing attitudes of many persons, like myself, away from the old medical model that traditionally has guided much of professional preparation and service delivery toward a new social minority model (see Figure 1 in appendix). This model was given to me by Duncan Wyeth, a leader in cerebral palsy sports, who has stimulated much of my creative thinking about adapted physical activity over the past 10 years. Note that Figure 1 summarizes much of the content of this paper.

New Concepts of Disability

Individuals with disabilities increasingly are providing leadership on new and different ways to view disability. Likewise, they are shaping our professional vocabulary. In adapted physical activity, we refer to **individuals with disabilities** and **disability sport** because this is the preferred terminology of the disability community (SHAPIRO, 1993).

Research by Nancy WEINBERG (1988) at the University of Illinois and others is indicating that disability is not necessarily always perceived as bad or tragic or negative. As early as 1973, research began to appear that showed no significant differences between the ratings of people with and without disabilities on life satisfaction, frustration, and happiness. The only significant difference was on ratings of difficulty of life. This difficulty did not increase their feelings of frustration with life or lower their feelings of satisfaction or happiness.

Other research has centered on the wish question: If you were given one wish, would you wish that you are no longer disabled? Findings generally are only about 50 % saying yes.

So there are tremendous individual differences among people with disability. It appears that even the word **disability** must be redefined. **Disability** today refers to individual differences in appearance, structure, or function that are perceived as undesirable by self and/or others. This leaves open the idea that the difference may be undesirable only to others. For people with disabilities, the difference may simply be a neutral fact of life. More and more, we will come to realize that disability is socially constructed through reciprocal interactions between self and others.

Disability, and hence adapted physical activity knowledge, is specific to culture and history and moderated by time of onset, nature of difference, socioeconomic status, gender, ethnicity, lifestyle choices, and the multitude of roles, expectations, aspirations, and perceptions that each individual incorporates into self and conveys to others.

Celebration of Individual Differences

In the decades to come, adapted and regular physical activity professionals will increasingly view themselves as equal-status partners in meeting the challenges created by social and political changes. Society increasingly will celebrate individual differences and value all human life. Together, we will explore individual differences, adaptation, and creativity theory as one of many conceptual frameworks designed to implement more fully the sport for all philosophy.

References

BLOCK, M.: A teacher's guide to including students with disabilities in regular physical education. Baltimore, MD: Paul H. Brooks, 1994.

BRACE, D.: Physical education and recreation for mentally retarded pupils in public schools. Research Quarterly, 39, 1968: 779-782.

DAVIS, W.E.; BURTON, A.W.: Ecological task analysis: Translating movement theory into practice. Adapted Physical Activity Quarterly, 8 (2), 1991: 154-177.

DEPAUW, K.P.; DOLL-TEPPER, G.M.: European perspectives on adapted physical activity. Adapted Physical Activity Quarterly,6, 1989: 95-99.

DEPAUW, K.P.; GOC KARP, G.: Integrating knowledge of disability throughout the physical education curriculum: An infusion approach. Adapted Physical Activity Quarterly, 11(1), 1994: 3-13.

DEPAUW, K.P.; SHERRILL, C.: Adapted physical activity: Present and Future. Physical Education Review, 17(1), 1994: 6-13.

DOLL-TEPPER, G.; DAHMS, C.; DOLL, B.; VON SELZAM, H. (Eds.): Adapted physical activity; An interdisciplinary approach. Berlin: Springer-Verlag, 1990.

DOWNS, P.; WILLIAMS, T.: Student attitudes toward integration of people with disabilities in activity settings: A European comparison. Adapted Physical Activity Quarterly, 11(1), 1994: 32-43.

DUNN, J.M.; MCCUBBIN, J.A.: Preparation of leadership personnel in adapted physical education. Adapted Physical Activity Quarterly, 8(2), 1991: 128-135.

EASON, R.L.; SMITH, T.L.; CARON, F. (Eds.): Adapted physical activity: From theory to application. Champaign, IL: Human Kinetics. 1983.

FAIT, H.: Special physical education (2nd ed.). Philadelphia: W.B. Saunders, 1966.

GOFFMAN, E.: Stigma: Notes on management of a spoiled identity. Englewood Cliffs, NJ: Prentice-Hall, 1963.

GUILFORD, J.: A factor analytic study of creative thinking. Report from the psychological laboratory, No. 8, University of Southern California, Los Angeles, 1952.

HEIKINARO-JOHANSSON, P.; SHERRILL, C.: Integrating children with special needs in physical education: A school district assessment model from Finland. Adapted Physical Activity Quarterly, 11(1), 1994: 44-56.

HEIKINARO-JOHANSSON, P.; SHERRILL, C.; HUUHKA, H.; FRENCH, R.: Adapted physical education consultant service model to facilitate integration. Adapted Physical Activity Quarterly, 12 (1), 1995: 12-33.

HOLLMANN, W.: Sports medicine: Fundamental aspects. In: H. HAAG, O. GRUPE, & A. KIRSCH (Eds.): Sports science in Germany (pp. 105-118). Berlin: Springer-Verlag, 1992.

KATZ, I.: Stigma: A social psychological analysis. Hillsdale, NJ: Lawrence Erlbaum, 1981.

KIPHARD, E.: Adapted physical education in Germany. In: R. EASON, T. SMITH; F. CARON (Eds.): Adapted physical activity: From theory to application. Champaign, IL: Human Kinetics, 1983: 25-32.

KOWALSKI, E.M: A comparative analysis of preservice students' attitudes towards teaching individuals with disabilities. In: AIESEP (Ed.): Volume of Abstracts, Presentation at AIESEP World Congress, Berlin, 1994: 204.

LEONARD, F.E.: A guide to the history of physical education. Philadelphia: Lea & Febiger, 1923.

MCKENZIE, R.T.: Exercise in education and medicine. Philadelphia: W.B. Saunders, 1909.

MORISBAK, I.: Adapted physical education: The role of the teacher and pedagogical practices. In: G. DOLL-TEPPER, C. DAHMS, B. DOLL, & H. v. SELZAM (Eds.): Adapted physical activity: An interdisciplinary approach. Berlin: Springer-Verlag, 1990: 235-243.

Rathbone, J.: Corrective physical education. Philadelphia: W.B. Saunders, 1934.

RIZZO, R.L.; VISPOEL, W.P.: Physical educators' attributes and attitudes toward teaching students with handicaps. Adapted Physical Activity Quarterly, 8,1991: 4-11.

SCHMIDT-GOTZ, E.; DOLL-TEPPER, G.; LIENERT, C.: Attitudes of university students and teachers towards integrating students with disabilities in regular physical education classes. Physical Education Review, 17 (1), 1994: 45-57.

SHAPIRO, J.P.: No pity: People with disabilities forging a new civil rights movement. New York: Times Books/Random House, 1993.

SHERRILL, C. (Ed.): Leadership training in adapted physical education. Champaign, IL: Human Kinetics, 1988.

SHERRILL, C.: Adapted physical activity, recreation and sport: Crossdisciplinary and lifespan. Dubuque, IA: Wm. C. Brown, 1993.

TORRANCE, E.P.: Guiding creative talent. Englewood Cliffs, NJ: Prentice-Hall, 1962.

WEINBERG, N.: Another perspective: Attitudes of people with disabilities. In: H.E. YUKER (Ed.): Attitudes toward persons with disabilities. New York: Springer, 1988: 141-153.

Medical Model	Social Minority Model
· Disability is equated with being defective, inferior, or less than.	· Disability is equated with being different; different is *not* less than, it is simply being different.
· A wide spectrum of biological/psychological anomalies and deficits exists.	· There is only one shared experience: social stigma.
· Teminology tends to be very negative.	· Terminology tends to be positive or neutral with person-first emphasized.
· Discussion is about defects, problems, or characteristics.	· Discussion is about individual assessment data, personal strengths and weaknesses.
· Goal is to give advice/ prescription to patient.	· Goal is to empower individual to assume active role in self-actualization.
· Graphics are passive.	· Graphics are active.

Figure 1. Old and new models that guide adapted physical activity philosophy and practices. From C. Sherrill (1993). Adapted physical activity, recreation, and sport: crossdisciplinary and lifespan, p. 48.

Chris Visscher, J. Paul Dresen, Marcel L.M.P. Haane

Education of Physically Handicapped Youths for Careers as Sports Instructor

1 Introduction

In the Netherlands the education of youths who want to be sports- or recreation instructor takes place at a Central Institute of Education of Sports Instructors (CIOS). After a 3-year education the graduates can work in organised sports, in care or they can start their own business. Young physically handicapped people too asked whether they could be admitted to an education in sports (VAN LUMMEL and HAANE, 1986).

Information is available of physically handicapped students who follow the regular education system (VISSCHER, 1983). Training of physically handicapped students at a school in which motor abilities and physical loads play an important part is unique, anyway in the Netherlands.

In 1988 the CIOS in Arnhem (the Netherlands) started an education programme for physically handicapped youths. The central question of this 4-year project was: "Is it possible to train physically handicapped youths for careers as recreation and sports instructor?“ It must be added that "education" in this context is defined as "enabling the student to meet the course requirements of a CIOS programme by making some adjustments to the existing, standard programme".

The teaching model for physically handicapped students should in fact be realized within the existing teaching model and yet should yield the results desired. The fact is that handicapped graduates from CIOS will be allowed to and will have to lead able students. So the handicapped students should follow as many lessons as possible together with the regular students (BOSSCHER, 1979, W.V.C., 1981).

First we will describe the admission procedure, then we will outline the adjustments in the teaching model and third we will look at the success of the project in terms of how many students were able to finish the programme and how many dropped out. Thereafter we will make some special remarks about the integration of handicapped and regular students. Finally we will give a short answer to the central question and make some general remarks.

2 Admission Procedure

For candidates for this project the following starting points were applied:

1 Candidates will be trained for a certificate of the same value as regular students.
2 Candidates should be able to follow the existing training programme.
3 Adapted exercises for the handicapped are a hundred percent equivalent to the usual execution.

This means that in order to be able to follow the existing training, limits had to be set to the degree of handicaps of the candidates. Admission of handicapped students also means that there should be willingness to adjust the training programme without endangering obtaining the final requirements.

The admission procedure consisted of the following parts:
1. Checking the legally required certificate or admission document.
2. A medical test.
3. A test for motor ability.
4. The AGAS, which is a general scale to measure one's attitude to his or her own handicap.

There were 38 persons who were really interested in this project. Not all of them were acceptable. After this very serious selection fifteen candidates were accepted. The students had a wide range of disabilities. There were students with an amputated leg or an amputated arm, a serious hearing problem, hemiplegia, or persons who were confined to a wheelchair. Extra provisions were made for them, such as sports-wheelchairs and an interpreter for deaf students. Without these special provisions these students would not be able to follow the programme.

3 Adjustments of the Programme and the Teaching Path

Very important is that the degree requirements were not changed. Adjustments were made as to how the requirements were met. The original structure and teaching paths were based on four handicap categories.

Table 1 Handicap categories

Cat.	Description	number of students
I	Less or not motorially handicapped (Students can follow almost the whole training programme)	4
II	"Walkers" (Motorial or organic handicap that has little influence on movements "Amputated" (students with a prosthesis)	5
III	Wheelchair-users	3
IV		3

Generally, students of the same handicap category required the same adjustments.

In relation with the handicap categories the following adjustments were made:

* A general courseload reduction to about 90 % of the regular programme and scratching an optional subject. These course reductions did not oppose the requirements, established by the Government.
* Subjects with low participation were replaced by subjects that matched the physical abilities of the persons involved. To this end subjects like table tennis and archery were added to the curriculum.
* Adapted exercises were equivalent to the usual execution. For example wheelchair basketball was equivalent to regular basketball.
* Extending the course duration and the possibilities of extra lessons and examinations.
* More student guidance, especially on personal, medical and academic matters.

Research has been done into which part of the curriculum should be followed by the handicapped, apart from the able students and which part, depending on the category of handicap, together with the regular students.

In the second and third grade of a CIOS education, students choose subjects in which to specialize. Because not all students from one category of handicap chose the same subject, individual teaching paths were necessary. The need to switch to individual teaching paths is also prompted by the fact that many students from the project had a delay during their first year of study. They were behind compared to the other students in their own category and a more individual programme was necessary. So all the changes and adjustments could not prevent academic related problems and lack in progress.

4 Results and Discussion

The project was evaluated by means of questionnaires, interviews and observations. Of the 15 students:

* was one student able to finish in three years;

* got five students their degree after an extension of three months to one school year;
* did one student not finish his study because of a car accident;
* dropped eight students out of the programme prematurely;

The actual handicap did not play a crucial part in successfull completion. The graduates are spread evenly over the range of handicaps and handicap categories.

The results must be seen in conjunction with the experimental character of the project. A number of students were admitted although there were doubts about their physical, cognitive and social competence in relation to the demands of the CIOS programme.

How the results of the handicapped students are related to those of the regular students is shown in table 2.

Table 2 Comparising of handicapped and able students

CIOS certificate in	Handicapped (N=15)	Regular (N=158)
* 3 years	6.6 %	26.6 %
* Passed with delay	33.3 %	49.4 %
* Stopped study	60.0 %	24.0 %

Apart from physical demands, large cognitive and especially psycho-social demands were placed on the students. A physical handicap in a sports and body-oriented programme can result in a very heavy pressure to want to prove oneself, which led to overtraining in some students (BUFFONE, 1984).

Having a physical handicap in a sports and body-oriented schooling has clear characteristics that are tied to the handicap in relation to this education. The fact that every drop-out indicated that at the start of their study they did not feel handicapped, but started feeling handicapped during their study is an extremely striking example (BIELEFELD, 1986, BENSON and JONES, 1992). Not being able to do something motorial has very different dimensions within this education than it has in other regular education systems. The ruling body culture makes the status of physical performance in this education very high. An extra is that the physical performance is immediately perceptable to everybody and asserts its influence (VISSCHER and TER WISSCHA, 1993). This is contrary to achievements on the cognitive subjects, where the achievements will mostly be known at a later stage and will also often be more obscure. This valuation of performance is typical for a sports education but can increase the pressure on a handicapped student considerably (FOX, 1992).

Answers to other research questions regarding the acceptation of handicapped students by fellow students, showed that there was a large degree of acceptance. Of the able students 80,8 % were positive or very positive about the handicapped fellow students. There were 99 able students involved in this research by means of a questionnaire. For the regular students there was also an extra teaching effect, expressed as a greater feeling of appreciation for the education one is getting. The greater the degree of acceptance, the greater the experienced appreciatory value (significant $p < 0.01$).

5 Conclusion

1. When we return to the central question, whether it is possible to train physically handicapped youths for careers as recreation or sports instructor we can say: "It is possible, however, students should satisfy certain conditions but the training programme should realize the adjustments needed and offer much extra support.“
2. The proposed model for disabled students should be structured to allow a student an extension of the course duration.

3. It is important that during admission procedures not only physical and cognitive skills are examined but also the student's acceptance and manner of dealing with his own handicap.
4. A satifactory emotional stability and social competence are important qualities for following a CIOS programme.
5. The education of handicapped students must be optimally integrated into the present programme. A good affiliation with the current structure prevents the unnecessary stigmatizing of handicapped students.

References

BENSON, E.; JONES, G.: "Psychological implications of physical activity in individuals with physical disabilities". In: T. WILLIAMS, L. ALMOND; S. SPARKES (eds.): Sports and physical activity - Moving towards excellence. London: E & SPON, 1992, 221-228.

BIELEFELD, J.: Körpererfahrung, Grundlage menschlichen Bewegungsverhaltens. Göttingen: Hubert & Co, 1986.

BOSSCHER, R.J.: About the social value of integration of practising sports by the physically handicapped. Amsterdam: Vrije Universiteit, 1979.

BUFFONE, G.W.: "Exercise as a therapeutic adjunct". In: J.M. SILVA; R.S. WEINBERG (eds.): Psychological foundations of sport. Champaign: Human Kinetics Publ., 1984, 445-451.

FOX, K.R.: "The complexities of self-esteem promotion in physical education and sport". In: T. WILLIAMS; L. ALMOND; A. SPARKES (eds.): Sports and physical activity - Moving towards excellence. London: E & FN SPON, 1992, 383-389.

LUMMEL, R.C. VAN; HAANE, M.L.M.P: Gehandicapten op het CIOS? De Vriescheborg Haarlem 1986.
(Handicapped student at the CIOS)

Ministery of Welfare, Health and Culture (Culture, Recreation and Social Work). Practising sports by handicapped people. Den Haag: Her Majesty's Stationary, Policy Paper 1981.

VISSCHER, C.: Integratie van gehandicapte kinderen in het reguliere onderwijs. Groningen: RuG, Scriptie 1983.
(Integration of handicapped children in the regular schoolsystem)

VISSCHER, C.; TER WISSCHA, J.T.: Sporten, waarom zou ik? Een onderzoek naar de effecten van een sportvormingsprogramma voor lichamelijk gehandicapten en chronisch zieken. Groningen: Universitair Centrum Sportresearch, 1993.
(Participate in sports, why should I?)

Pauli Rintala, Niina Raappana, Sanna Vallittu, Douglas Collier

Changes in Perceived Competence of Children with Developmental Language Disorders after Psychomotor Training

Perceived competence is viewed as an important variable in academic achievement and in the acquisition of coping behaviors that enable a child to thrive in school and social environments including physical education. In addition to perceived competence other terms like self-concept are also found in the literature (e.g., CHAPMAN, 1988; HOPPER, 1988; KARPER and MARTINEK, 1983; MARTINEK and KARPER, 1982; ROGERS and SAKLOFSKE, 1985). Perceived competence can be seen more situation specific than self-concept, and it has gained acceptance as an element of self-concept development (ULRICH and COLLIER, 1990). Hence, perceived competence is viewed as the self-evaluation of domain-specific skills.

We know very little about the development of perceived competence in special populations, especially children with developmental language disorders. The term 'specific developmental language disorder', also called dysphasia (BISHOP and ROOSENBLOOM, 1987) is used when a child's language development is slow, restricted and/or deficient. The condition manifests itself in receptive and/or expressive language having no attendant neurological or psychiatric disturbances (ZANGWILL, 1978).

Perceived competence is seen as an important mediator of participation in physical activity (GRUBER, 1986; HARTER, 1978, 1981; SONSTROEM, 1984). The amount of success or failure that a child achieves in a particular domain will influence perceptions of competence thus influencing further participation. Programs based on motology or "Motopädagogik" (motor education) (e.g. KIPHARD, 1990), have been used for a long time in Germany and found out to be helpful for children's physical development (e.g. DOLL-TEPPER, 1987). Recently similar program successfully improved the physical performance of children with developmental language disorders (RINTALA and PALSIO, 1994). However, the effects of those programs on perceived competence have not been empirically tested. Therefore, the purpose of this study was to examine the changes of perceived competence after the eight-week motology based psychomotor program as well as the congruence between a student and a teacher rating of the students' perceived competence.

Methods

Subjects and Design

Subjects participating in this study were 30 elementary school children between the ages of 7 and 11 years. All were diagnosed with specific developmental language disorder based on their medical files. The students were in self-contained classrooms located adjacent to the other elementary school classrooms in the same school building.

In this field study, the non-randomized control-group pretest-posttest design was used. The experimental group consisted of three classes: First graders, (n=7); Second/third graders, (n=8); and Third/fourth graders, (n=7), altogether 22 students. One class (2-3 graders, n=8) served as a control group. From practical reasons all the groups were intact classes.

Instrumentation and Testing Procedures

A modified, illustrated-verbal version of the HARTER's (1982) Perceived Competence Scale for Children (SARLIN, 1990) was used to measure perceived competence. The modified version had been found feasible when testing elementary age students among Finnish population (SARLIN, 1990), and it was chosen for this study for comparative reasons. The test consisted of 23 items: six for physical competence, six for social competence, four for cognitive competence, and seven for self-esteem. Each item included a text and a figure with three choices to choose from (Fig. 1).

Figure 1. An example of perceived physical competence evaluation sheet. After SARLIN (1990.)

One classroom teacher, familiar with the test, administered the test before and after the psychomotor program for all students. Each group was assessed separately as a class; the teacher read each item loud and every student marked his/her choice of option.

Psychomotor Program

The experimental group participated in the program for eight weeks. The program was carried out three times a week, for 30 minutes. Before each session there was a warm-up game containing ball, tag, and musical games. After the session the review discussion about students' experiences during the session was held. Additionally, a fine motor skill program was carried out twice a week for 45 min. It's goal was to develop students' manual dexterity. In both programs, positive and realistic feedback was emphasized in teaching. Also the content of the program was individually planned, based on age and skill level, for each of three experimental groups and the sessions advanced from easier to more difficult. The control group participated in normal school work including physical education twice a week between the tests.

The main goal of the psychomotor program, based on the philosophy of motology (e.g. KIPHARD, 1990), was to improve fundamental motor skills and perceived competence of students. The psychomotor program which aims at personality education through movement, i.e., through basic motor and perceptual experiences, consisted of 11 stations where ball handling, climbing, rolling, jumping, balancing etc. skills were practiced. The equipment included different kinds of balls, a ladder, mats, hoola-hoops, jump ropes, benches, targets, bars and a mini-trampoline.

Data analysis

Perceived competence was divided into physical and general perceived competence. As in the SARLIN (1990) study, physical competence constituted its own factor in the factor analysis. Perceived physical competence was composed of six items and perceived general competence consisted of the rest of the 17 items (social, cognitive and self-esteem). The means of both physical and general competence raw score sums were calculated. The significance of differences between pre- and posttests and between the student and teacher ratings of perceived competence was determined using Wilcoxon test for small samples sizes.

Results

The perceived competence instrument had eight items which were opposite to eight other items and could be used to calculate the consistency of the answers. From 16 correlation coefficients, which varied from .27 to .78, 14 were significant.

The psychomotor program was implemented between the Winter '93 and Spring '93. Perceived competence did not change significantly in any of the groups.

How realistically the students perceived their competence was investigated by comparing the students' and teachers' ratings (SILON and HARTER, 1985) and was called congruence of the perceived competence. It was assumed that the bigger the difference between the ratings, the more unrealistic the student's perceived competence was.

First graders in the experimental group perceived their physical and general competence, before and after training, significantly higher than their teachers did (p=.018 - .028) (Fig. 2).

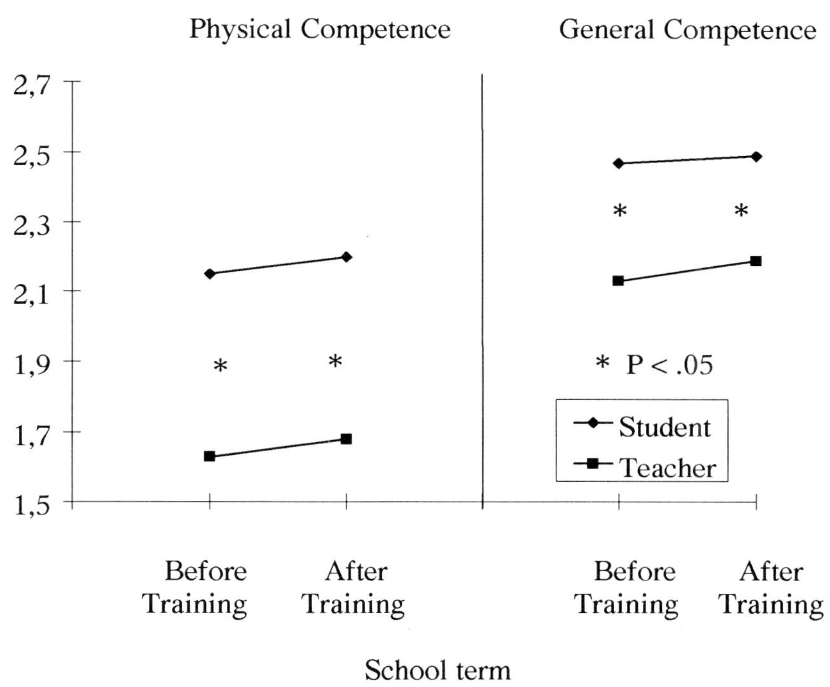

Figure 2. Congruence of Perceived Competence
First grade

With respect to Second/third and Third/fourth graders in the experimental group, the students' perceived competence was not significantly different from teachers' (before: p=.465 to p=.675; after p=.447 to p=.893) and was considered realistic both before and after training.

The control group perceived itself similarly to the same age (Second/third graders) experimental group, but differently from the teacher's view of their perceived physical competence. The posttest score was significantly different from the teachers' view (p=.028) (Fig. 3).

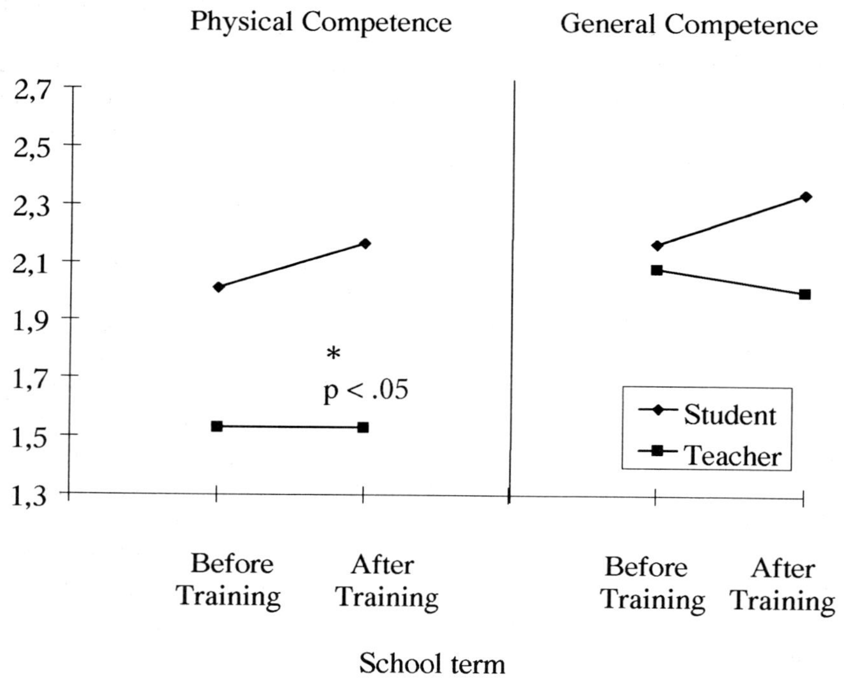

Figure 3. Congruence of Perceived Competence
Control Group

Discussion

There has been little research conducted on the effect of physical activity programs on psychosocial development in special populations (GIBBONS and BUSHAKRA (1989). The current study investigated the effect of an 8-week program on students with developmental language disorder. No significant changes were found in perceived competence upon the conclusion of the program. Although JOHNSON et al. (1968) and SMITH and EASON (1988) observed improvement in self-concept after eight-week physical activity programs, SONSTROEM (1984) suggested that physical activity programs should last at least 15-20 weeks in order to improve self-concept. As the psychomotor program in this study continued for eight weeks, this may have not been long and/or effective enough to improve perceived competence. Other factors affecting perceived competence (e.g., school, home, friends and recreational activities) may not have been adequately controlled.

If we accept the premise that the teachers' ratings of student competence were accurate, first graders (7 years of age) with developmental language disorders saw their perceived competence as unrealistically high both before and after the psychomotor program. These findings support GALLAHUE's (1989) position that children assess their competence unrealistically before the age of eight. The other experimental groups (second/third and third/fourth graders) had physical and general perceived competence that were the same as their teachers', indicating that they perceived their competence realistically. The control group participated in normal school work including physical education twice a week between the tests. Its perceived competence changed from realistic to unrealistic from pre- to posttest.

Although some research indicate that children with disabilities exhibit lower perceived competence than children without disabilities, results are not all uniform (CRAFT and HOGAN, 1985; HARTER, 1988; JONES, 1985). When we compared the level of perceived competence between the students in this study and the students without disabilities examined by SARLIN (1990), it was found that students with developmental language disorders had lower level of perceived physical competence, but the level of perceived general competence did not differ from students without disabilities. It has been hypothesized (CAUSGROVE DUNN & WATKINSON, 1994: SILON & HARTER, 1985) that perceived competence is affected by peers and, as well, depends on the comparison group. Thus, the students in this study who were in the special classrooms might have compared themselves academically to peers in the same school.

The assessment of underlying structure of perceived competence of children with language disorders is problematic. Due to their communication deficit, filling out the questionnaire form is difficult. Therefore, special attention must be given to a student who requires help in the testing situation.

In conclusion, the eight-week psychomotor program is too short to allow changes in perceived competence, but in future studies the special attention should also be on the content of such programs.

References

BISHOP, D.; ROOSENBLOOM, L.: Childhood language disorders: classification and overview. In: W. YULE; M. RUTTER (eds.): Language development and disorders. Mac Keith Press, London, 1987, 16-41.

CAUSGROVE DUNN, J.L.; WATKINSON, E.J.: A study of the relationship between physical awkwardness and children's perceptions of physical competence. Adapt Phys Activity Q, 1994, 11, 275-283.

CHAPMAN, J.W.: Learning disabled children's self-concepts. Review of Educational Research, 1988, 58, 347-371.

CRAFT D.H.; HOGAN, P.I.: The development of self-concept and self-efficacy: Considerations for mainstreaming. Adapt Phys Activity Q, 1985, 2, 320-327.

DOLL-TEPPER, G.M.: Effects of physical education on children with learning disabilities. In: M.E. BERRIDGE; G.R. WARD (eds.):

International perspectives on adapted physical activity. Human Kinetics, Champaign, 1987, 19-24.

GALLAHUE, D.L.: Understanding motor development in children, John Wiley & Sons, New York 1989, 2nd ed.

GIBBONS, S.L.; BUSHAKRA, F.B.: Effects of Special Olympics participation on the perceived competence and social acceptance of mentally retarded children. Adapt Phys Activity Q, 1989, 6, 40-51.

GRUBER, J.J.: Physical activity and self-esteem development in children: Meta-analysis. In: A. STULL; H. ECKERT (eds.): Effects of physical activity on children. American Academy of Physical Education Papers 19. Human Kinetics, Champaign, 1986, 30-48.

HARTER, S.: Effectance motivation reconsidered - Toward a developmental model. Human Development, 1978, 21, 34-64.

HARTER, S.: A model of intrinsic mastery motivation in children: Individual differences and developmental change. In: W.A. COLLINS (ed.): Minnesota symposium on child psychology. Erlbaum, Hillsdale, NJ, 1981, Vol. 14, 215-255.

HARTER, S.: The perceived competence scale for children. Child Development, 1982, 53, 87-97.

HARTER, S.: Causes, correlates and functional role of global self-worth: A life-span perspective. In: J. KOLLIGIAN; R. STERNBERG (eds.): Perception of competence and incompetence across the life-span. Yale University Press, New Haven, CT, 1988, 67-97.

HOPPER, C.: Self-concept and motor performance of hearing impaired boys and girls. Adapt Phys Activity Q, 1988, 5, 293-304.

JOHNSON, W.R.; FRETZ, B.R.; JOHNSON, A.: Changes in self-concepts during a physical development program. Res Quarterly, 1968, 39, 560-565.

JONES, C.J.: Analyses of the self-concepts of handicapped students. Remedial and Special Education, 1985, 6 (5), 32-36.

KARPER, W.B.; MARTINEK, T.J.: Motor performance and self-concept of handicapped and non-handicapped children in integrated physical education classes. Am Cor Ther J ,1983, 37, 91-95.

KIPHARD, E.: Motopädagogik [Motopedagogy], Modernes Lernen, Dortmund 1990, 4th ed.

MARTINEK, T.J.; KARPER, W.B.: Entry level motor performance and self-concept of handicapped and non-handicapped children in mainstreamed physical education classes. A preliminary study. Percept Motor Skills, 1982, 55, 1002.

RINTALA, P.; PALSIO, N.: Effects of physical education programs on children with learning disabilities. In: K. YABE; K. KUSANO; H. NAKATA (eds.): Adapted physical activity: Health and fitness. Springer, Tokyo 1994, 37-40.

ROGERS, H.; SAKLOFSKE, D.H.: Self-concepts, locus of control and performance expectations of learning disabled children. J Learn Dis, 1985, 18, 273-277.

SARLIN, E.-L.; TELAMA, R.; BOVELLAN, A.-K.; ROMPPAINEN, A.-M.: Effects of daily physical education on motor fitness, ball handling, gymnastic skills and perceived physical competence among elementary school children. In: R. TELAMA; L. LAAKSO; M. PIERON; I. RUOPPILA; V. VIHKO (eds.): Physical education and life-long physical activity. Reports of Physical Culture and Health, Jyäskylä, 1990, 73, 501-507.

SILON, E.L.; HARTER, S.: Assessment of perceived competence, motivational orientation, and anxiety in segregated and mainstreamed educable mentally retarded children. J Educ Psych, 1985, 77, 217-230.

SMITH, T.L.; EASON, R.L.: Effects of success-oriented reading and motor program on self-concept of children referred for learning disability. Percept Motor Skills, 1988, 67, 94.

SONSTROEM, T.J.: Exercise and self-esteem. In: R.L. TERJUNG (ed.): Exercise and sport science reviews. Collamore Press, Lexington, 1984, 12, 123-150.

ULRICH, D.A.; COLLIER, D.H.: Perceived physical competence in children with mental retardation: Modification of a pictorial scale. Adapt Phys Activity Q, 1990, 7, 338-354.

ZANGWILL, O.L.: The concept of developmental dysphasia. In: M.A. WYKE (ed.): Developmental dysphasia. Academic Press, London 1978, 1-11.

Nicolette H.M.J. van Veldhoven, Vincent Gulmans, Adri Vermeer, Paul Helders

Physical Competence in Children with Cystic Fibrosis: A Pilot Study

Introduction

Cystic Fibrosis (CF) is a common fatal genetic disease and a frequent cause of chronic pulmonary disease in children and adolescents. During the past two decades these patients have experienced a steady improvement in life expectancy and in their overall quality of life (HEYERMAN, 1991; VAN DEN BRANDE, 1990). Exercise tolerance in patients with CF is gradually reduced as the disease progresses and has been found to correlate with the severity of airway obstruction and clinical status (VAN DEN BRANDE, 1990; BAR-OR, 1986). Maximum work capacity is practically normal in mildly and moderately affected patients (STRANGHELLE, 1988).

Improving the physical condition of children with CF can be important for two reasons. First, recent data suggest that physical conditioning can improve bronchial clearance and increase the endurance of the respiratory muscles (BAR-OR, 1986). Second, there is a motivational effect. Improvements in condition will be experienced as self-rewarding for the child as physical potential increases. Usually, when the child can do more, it creates feelings of success and pleasure. The more a child knows about what controls personal success and failure, the higher the perceptions of physical competence, i. e. perceived physical competence (HARTER, 1978). Success leads to expectations about future success and thus the child will continue with physical training (CONNOLLY, 1974).

Therefore, it will be important to know how children assess their physical strain. This assessment is called perceived exertion. The individual's perception of exertion during physical work is interesting when studying man at work or during leisure time activities, and in epidemiological evaluation of daily exercise intentions (BORG, 1982). In BORG's opinion, perceived exertion is the single best indicator of the degree of physical strain.
There is no information available on the relation between exercise (in)tolerance and perceived exertion and perceived physical competence.

The aim of this study was to investigate the relation between physical condition, perceived exertion and perceived physical competence.

Methods
Subjects

Thirteen 7 to 12-year-old children with CF (mean 11.2 yr; six boys and seven girls) were selected to participate in the study. All the children were patients treated at the Utrecht University Children's Hospital. Only the children who were free of fever, did not cough more than usual and were not short of breath when resting, could participate in the investigation.

Procedure

After a visit to the physiotherapist of the CF outpatient unit, the child was tested for 45 minutes. Three tests were administered.

Physical Condition Test. This test consists of an exercise test (c1-c5) and several pulmonary function tests (c6-c10) and measurement of height and weight (c11).
The exercise test was performed on an electronically-braked cycle ergometer (Bosch ERG 501). The initial load of 35 Watt for five minutes was increased by 10 Watt every minute. The pedalling frequency was 45-55 rpm. Exercise was stopped when the subjects

could no longer continue despite encouragement, or when arterial oxygen saturation (SaO2) had decreased to less than 80 % of the baseline level. SaO2 and heart(pulse) rate (HR) were recorded continuously with an oximeter (Nellcor N-200 E Pulse oximeter).

The test was performed once, in the presence of a physiotherapist and a researcher. The subjects were encouraged to exercise every minute to the best of their ability. The maximum physical exertion was defined as the maximum work rate maintained during one minute (Wmax).
During the exercise test the following variables were measured: c1 Arterial oxygen saturation at 5 minutes (SaO25); c2 Arterial oxygen saturation at maximum physical exertion (SaOmax); c3 Heart(pulse) rate at 5 minutes (HR5); c4 Heart(pulse) rate at maximum physical exertion (HRmax); c5 Maximum Wattage (Wmax).
Before exercise the following pulmonary function tests were measured (Jaeger, Masterlab): c6 Forced vital capacity (FVC); c7 Forced expiratory volume in one second (FEV1); c8 Maximal expiratory flow at 50 % of the expiratory volume (MEF50); c9 Forced expiratory volume 1 / forced vital capacity (FEV1/FVC %); c10 Residual volume / total lung capacity (RV/TLC %).
Also height and weight were measured: c11 Body Mass Index: Weight/Height ^{2} (BMI).

The physical condition test scores were expressed by c1 - c11. Two items of the physical condition test, HR5 and RV/TLC %, correlated negatively with the other items. Both showed that a lower score indicated a better condition, contrary to the other scores. Therefore both items were recoded.
Two values were extended, namely HRmax (c4) and BMI (c11). They showed less variation.
The analysis of homogeneity for the physical condition tests reveals that Cronbach's alpha is .94.

Borg Scale. The Borg Scale scores were administered during the exercise test (Modified Borg Scale, BORG 1982). Before this administration, the subjects were thoroughly instructed. The subjects were asked about the subjective rating of perceived exertion at the beginning and at the end of every minute of cycling: 'To what degree are you out of breath now?' 'How tired are your muscles now?' according to a standard rating scale with scores which ranged from 0 - 10 (from nothing at all, weak, moderate to very, very strong). The category scale was noted on a board in front of the cycle ergometer. The different verbal expressions of dyspnea and exhaustion were noted according to their ratio properties.

Borg scale scores were administered every minute. Correlations between the different scores on different times were very high (.92). Therefore, three measurements in time (5, 8 minutes and maximum) give a good overall impression of the whole test. The Cronbach's Alpha of the Borg scale is .94.

Perceived Competence Scale. The translated version of the perceived competence scale (HARTER, 1985) was used (ROSSUM, 1987). This Dutch version of the test contains five separate subscales, namely selfworth (8 questions), physical appearance (7 questions), scholastic competence (7 questions), social competence (8 questions) and physical competence (12 questions). This questionnaire was administered to the subjects individually after the exercise test. This research has only used the scores on the subscale physical competence. Each item was scored from 1 to 4, with a score of 1 indicating low perceived physical competence and a score of 4 reflecting high perceived physical competence. To measure the perceived physical competence, scores on this subscale were added up.

Cronbach's Alpha of the perceived physical competence scale, after removing item 24 because the correlation was under .20, is used for the remaining 11 items .84.

A remark has to be made about the fact that this study concerns a sample of thirteen children: reliability values might be based on coincidence. However, all the tests used here have already been tested for reliability for 'normal' children. The results give an indication of the use of these instruments for research with children with CF.

Data Analysis

The scores on the Borg Scale range from '0', the maximum score, to '10' the minimum. For a comparison of the tests, all scores were transformed to Z-scores.
Statistical procedures, according to Spearman's or Kendall's methods of rank correlation (rs), were performed to establish correlations between the instruments. A two-tailed test was used. Significance was accepted at the 0.05 level.

Results

Correlation between Physical Condition and Perceived Exertion

In Figure I, it is demonstrated that there is a significant linear correlation (Kendall Spearman r_S=.75, p=.002) between the Physical Condition Test and the Borg Scale. Children who performed less well on the cycle ergometer, felt more quickly exhausted and short of breath. Children who achieved better results showed less feelings of exhaustion and shortness of breath.

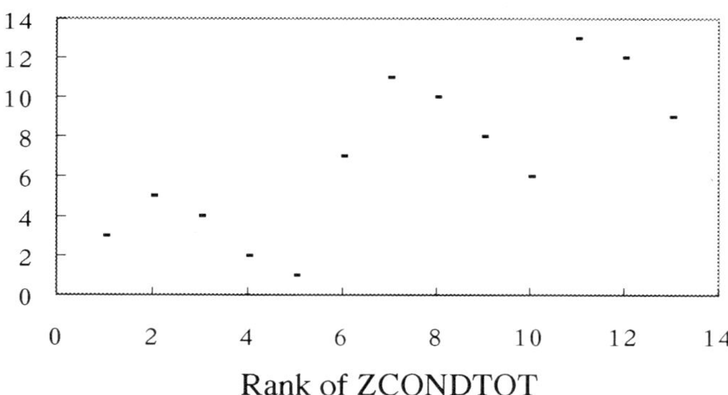

Figure I. Correlation between Physical Condition Scores and Borg Scale Scores.

'Rank of zborgtot' is the total score of the Borg scale. First the total score is standardized and then classified. `Rank of zcondtot' is the total score of the condition-scale. First the total score is standardized and then classified.

Correlation between Physical Condition and Perceived Physical Competence

Figure II shows the correlation between the Physical Condition Test and the Perceived Physical Competence Scale. There is a (moderate) significant linear correlation (Kendall Spearman r_S=.68, p=.006).
One points deviates from the mean regression line (bottom right). This indicates that one child underestimated his potential.

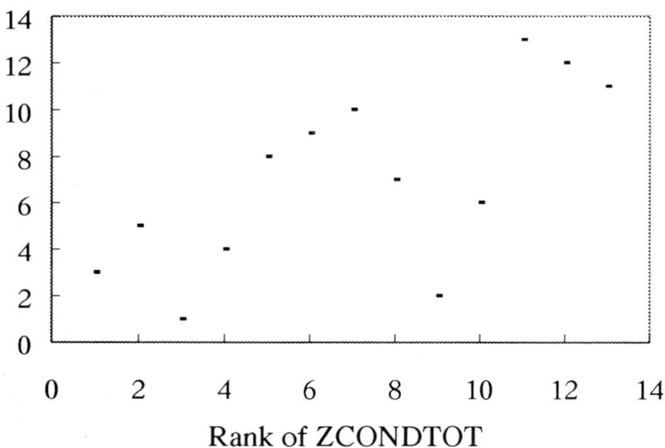

Figure II. Correlation between Physical Condition Scores and Perceived Physical Competence Scores.

`Rank of zcomptot' is the total score of the competence-scale. First the total score is standardized and then classified. `Rank of zcondtot'' is the total score of the condition scale. This score is first standardized and then classified.

Discussion

The purpose of this study was to investigate perceived exertion and perceived physical competence, and the assessment of this in children with CF at the age of 7 to 12 years. During the research period thirteen children were available for participation. Because of the small sample, conclusions must be drawn with caution.
The research question concerned the relationships between tests. A significant correlation was found between the Physical Condition Test scores and the Borg Scale scores (Figure I): these results imply that children with a relatively better condition show feelings of

breathlessness and exhaustion to a lesser extent. This is consistent with GOLDBERG (1990) and SILVERMAN et al. (1988). They posit that in the use of the Borg Scale by patients with lung diseases, the perceived shortness of breath during exercise is reproducible and correlates with the physiological measurements indicating the intensity of the effort.

Also a significant correlation was found between the Physical Condition Test scores and the Perceived Physical Competence Scale scores (Figure II). From this result it can be deduced that children with a low level of physical performance perceive their physical competences accordingly. One child underestimated its potential. The majority of the children who perform well are aware of this and judge their abilities efficiently. This is in line with the competence theory (VAN ROSSUM, 1992) which supposes that perceived competence has a linear correlation with performance. It is not in accordance with the results of BAARDMAN (1992) which showed that children with fewer physical abilities, had an unrealistic view of their own abilities. The conclusion of VEERMAN (1992), that children with emotional and behavioural problems show no deviant perceived competence scores compared with normal schoolchildren, corresponds to the results of this study.

The similarity between figure I and figure II is striking. The general idea children have about themselves physically also applies in the specific situation of the cycle test.

The results of this study indicate that in children with CF the capacity of physical strain corresponds linearly to perceived physical competence. Children with a poor condition show a lower level of perceived competence and vice versa. Moreover, perceived exertion during an exercise test corresponds to physical performance.

According to HARTER's theory, children with less exercise potential will avoid exercise because they do not wish to be confronted with problems of their difficulties. In this case, if it is possible to improve the child's condition he/she can regain his/her faith in his/her own exercise potential. And with that, perceived competence will also increase.

Further research in the effectiveness of physical exercise programmes in children with CF is necessary.

Acknowledgement
We gratefully acknowledge the support of Dr. B. Baarda.

References

BAARDMAN, I.: Enige kanttekeningen bij het competentie concept (Some comments on the concept of competence). Bewegen en Hulpverlening, 1992, 9, 187- 198.

BAR-OR, O.: Die Praxis der Sportmedizin in der Kinderheilkunde. New York, Heidelberg, Berlin: Springer-Verlag 1986.

BORG, G.: Psychophysical bases of perceived exertion. Medicine and Science in Sports and Exercise, 1982, 14, 377-381.

BRANDE, J.V.L. VAN DEN: Kindergeneeskunde (Child Medicine). Utrecht: Bunge 1990.

CONNOLLY, K.J.; BRUNER, J. (eds.): The growth of competence. London: Academic Press 1974.

GOLDBERG, B.M.D.: Children, Sports, and Chronic Disease. The Physician and Sportsmedicine, 1990, 18 (10), 45-56.

HARTER, S.: Effectance motivation reconstructed: Toward a developmental model. Human Development, 1978, 21, 34-64.

HARTER, S.: Manual for the self-perception profile for children. Denver: University of Denver 1985.

HEYERMAN, H.G.M.: Studies in the Clinical Management of Cystic Fibrosis. Leiden: thesis 1991.

ROSSUM, J.H.A. VAN: Motorische competentie en gedrag: het ei van Columbus of een lege dop? (Physical Competence and behaviour: Just the thing or a shell?) Bewegen en Hulpverlening, 1992, 9, 266-273.

ROSSUM, J.H.A. VAN; VERMEER, A.; BONN, S. VAN DEN; DEELSTRA, H.; KOLK, W. VAN DER: Het competentiebegrip en motorisch gedrag. Een toepassing in de motorische remedial teaching. (The Concept of Competence and Motor Behaviour. An implementation in Motor Remedial Teaching). Tijdschrift voor Orthopedagogiek, 1987, 26, 515-524.

SILVERMAN, M.; BARRY, J.; HELLERSTEIN, H.; JANOS, J.; KELSEN, S.: Variability of the Perceived Sense of Effort in Breathing during Exercise in Patients with Chronic Obstructive Pulmonary Disease. American Review of Respiratory Disease, 1988, 137, 206-209.

STRANGHELLE, J.K.: Physical Exercise for Patients with Cystic Fibrosis: A Review. International Journal of Sports Medicine, 1988, 9, 6-18.

VEERMAN, J.W.: Competentiebeleving bij kinderen met emotionele en gedragsproblemen (Perceived Competence in Children with Emotional and Behaviour Problems). Bewegen en Hulpverlening, 1992, 9, 143-255.

5. Sport in the Life Span

Charles Buckley, Len Almond, Michael J. Waring

Socio-Cultural Factors Affecting British Children's Involvement in Sport and Physical Activity Implications for Educational and Leisure Policies

Interest in children's involvement in physical activity has grown in recent years from perceived links between inactive lifestyles and health related problems in adulthood, together with a concern about opportunities for the development of health through physical education programmes. The need to develop a deeper understanding of primary-school-aged children's participation in sport and exercise is vital as it is often thought that attitudes and habits are determined in early-childhood.

Existing evidence indicates that there are gender differences among children's activity patterns. Surprisingly little research has been concerned with why individuals do not become involved in various forms of physical activity or the reasons why boys are more active than girls.

Whilst the importance of socio-cultural factors affecting children are recognised social research has, for some time, focused almost entirely on formal sport socialization studied from a deterministic and unidirectional perspective. Attention needs to be given to how or why significant others become influential and to the factors that may lead to a lack of involvement in certain forms of activity.

Children's Activity Patterns

Research into activity levels of children in Britain is sparse when compared to the United States, Canada and Australia; furthermore such research has in general focused on adults and adolescents, only recently have researchers begun to explore activity patterns of younger children (e.g. ARMSTRONG and BRAY, 1991, SLEAP and WARBURTON, 1990; 1992). Existing evidence suggests that activity levels of British children are low, indeed ARMSTRONG and MCMANUS (1994), in summarizing research evidence state "The current level and pattern of children and adolescents' physical activity is a cause for serious concern. Girls appear to be less active than boys and girls' level of physical activity decreases as they move through secondary school." (p. 26). Following publication of the Allied Dunbar National Fitness Survey (1992) and Health of the Nation, together with a political climate which has become more supportive of the cause for health promotion, increased attention has been developed in the issue of childhood inactivity. However, in light of all the evidence which suggests the need to promote active lifestyles little is known about the determinants or correlates of physical activity among children (SALLIS et al., 1992).

Existing Research

Factors affecting decisions regarding levels of involvement in physical activity are complex and may vary across time and location. Thus, existing research should be viewed as having limited potential for generalizing to wider populations, and assumptions regarding similarities across cultures should be critically assessed. It is recognised that factors such as age, gender, socio-economic status, ethnic background and location will have an effect on participation in activity, however, these areas have been relatively unexplored, especially in Britain. Examples of existing studies from abroad include:

- Socio-economic status as a key determinant of health related behaviour (GOTTILEB and CHEN, 1985; SUNNEGARDH et al., 1985).
- Race and ethnicity as factors effecting levels and type of involvement (GOTTILEB and CHEN, loc.cit.; TAYLOR, BARANOWSKI and SALLIS. In press).
- Influence of parents/peers (GREENDORFER et al., 1981; KLESGES et al., 1984; KUNESH et al., 1992).

- The importance of environment as potentiating and/or limiting behaviour (KLESGES et al., 1990; MORRIS, 1988; SALLIS et al., 1990; WAXMAN and STUNKARD, 1980).

Research in the psychological domain which provides invaluable information in developing understandings of the decision-making processes involved with young children and activity far outweighs socio-cultural studies. If researchers are to fully appreciate children's perspectives on sport and physical activity they must address the relevance of the social environment and of socialization influences affecting children's psychological processes (BRUSTAD, 1992).

Socialization Research into Sport and Physical Activity

Early socialization research has been criticised for its deterministic nature - based on the assumptions that people are passive learners and internalise normative influences in the environment. Such models ignore the content and dynamics of the social relationships through which socialization occurs (COAKLEY, 1993). These criticisms have led to social scientists adopting alternative models based on socialization as interaction approaches - such a shift in focus is supported at a theoretical level (ALANEN, 1990; GIDDENS, 1979; WENTWORTH, 1980) and through research (ANDERSON et al., 1986; BATES, 1975), which suggest that socialization is an interactive and bidirectional process. This view of socialization as an interactive process of construction draws attention to social relations and social action rather than individual responses to the social environment. Such an approach can be used to effectively understand the effects and relationships between the dynamics, context and role the individual child plays in determining levels of physical activity. Despite their potential, interactive studies have received limited attention in the sociology of sport.

Socialization research has also concentrated primarily on formal sport (KUNESH et al., loc. cit.), such a narrow focus limits the potential for considering other physical activity choices such as exercise or physically active play which may produce health benefits. In addition, existing research is limited in developing understandings of why or how significant others become influential (HASBROOK, 1989; HASBROOK and HORN, 1985).

There are few interactionist studies on which to draw to demonstrate their potential for understanding children's participation in physical activity, in particular when considering British children.

COAKLEY and WHITE (1992) used an interactionist model in a study of participation decisions made by a sample of British adolescents using in-depth interviews. Results suggested that young people were not passive learners in the socialization process - they negotiated participation decisions in the light of how they saw participation fitting in with the rest of their lives. Examples of other studies using an interactionist model (e.g. COAKLEY, 1992; KUNESH et al., loc. cit.; STEVENSON, 1990) also tend to focus on adolescent age groups. Considering the general acceptance that attitudes and beliefs are established in early childhood it is more than surprising that so few studies attempt to provide insights into socialization of young children into physical activity.

Existing research provides few insights about specific differences between levels of participation in physical activity, the correlational effects between independent variables, or the social contexts in which they occur (COAKLEY, 1993). Future research in the area needs to focus on understanding the complex and dynamic processes involved rather than generating specific empirical facts of a descriptive nature. GREENDORFER (1993) suggests that "sport socialization research needs to take on a totally different direction from that pursued in the past. Immediate changes might include experimenting with different theoretical perspectives; approaches that take into account theories other than social learning may be fruitful ... alternative research designs could be applied; empiricist traditions and survey research could be replaced with naturalistic and ethnographic methods" (p. 12).

Female Socialization into Physical Activity and Sport

Gender differences in levels of physical activity of British children have been reported, studies show boys to be more active than girls (e.g. The Sports Council for Wales 1987; DICKENSON, 1987; WILLIAMS, 1988; The Northern Ireland Fitness Survey 1989; ARMSTRONG et al., 1990a, 1990b, 1990c, 1991) and/or that activity levels decrease with age (e.g. DICKENSON, loc. cit.; The Sports Council of Wales loc. cit.; The Northern Ireland Fitness Survey, loc. cit.). More recent studies by THIRLAWAY and BENTON (1993) support these findings - they suggest that boys are more active primarily because they play more team games, perhaps they suggest, as there is a greater range of team games available for boys to play, such as football, rugby and cricket and that these receive wide media attention providing boys with numerous sporting role models.

A number of existing studies indicate that gender stereotyping occurs very early in a child's life (see GREENDORFER, loc. cit.) with parents providing different play opportunities and having different expectations for their children. There have been numerous investigations and discussions surrounding the issue of the school and its influence in stereotyping children into specific gender roles (e.g. SCRATON, 1986; TALBOT, 1993). Such research findings provide insights into apparent differences of levels of activity especially in secondary schools where it appears that differences in levels of participation are exaggerated (THIRLAWAY and BENTON, loc. cit.). A number of recommendations for changes in educational and leisure policy have been made in light of these findings. Such recommendations include giving "issues of equality greater legitimacy and visibility within ITE courses as well as more generally within the institutions in which these are based" (FLINTOFF, 1993, 197), challenging stereotypes of masculinity and femininity through an awareness of language (WRIGHT, 1991), the use of role models in demonstrations and direct observation intervention by teachers when pupils overtly stereotype (SCRATON, 1992); assessing the relevance of co-educational settings for physical education lessons in secondary schools (EVANS et al., 1985); dispelling existing beliefs amongst some coaches about sex differences in motor performance especially of pre-adolescent children. The power of the school, only recently conceptualized as a site of ideological struggle (SPARKES, 1989) is recognised as a powerful mechanism for transmitting values and beliefs to pupils. Research has revealed that patterns of behaviour in physical education emphasize orderliness and achievement, conformity, inequality and a movement standard that is masculine, athletic, and competitive (BAIN, 1985).

The potential use of socialist feminist theory has been discussed in the literature (e.g. BRAY, 1988; SCRATON, 1992). However, as yet, it has not been exploited in the context of young children and activity patterns. This seems surprising in contemporary British society currently characterised by large scale innovations such as the National Curriculum and its inherent political ideologies. With its emphasis on the importance of historical analysis and capitalist patriarchy, socialist feminism as a framework has obvious relevance for analysing gender inequalities based on ideologies of masculinity and femininity in primary schools. Similarly, with an emphasis on class divisions it could provide insights into sexual divisions in leisure opportunities such as access to sports classes, influences of out of school opportunities and experiences for physical activity (SCRATON, 1992). Exploring the potential of Hargreaves' ideas on sport in which women become involved in: "A co-operative new venture with men for qualitative new models in which differences in the sexes are unimportant" (1993, 183) deserves consideration in terms of potential relevance for young children and the games they play and, more importantly, have organized for them. A search for new game forms which draw on the positive attributes of children's natural play which do not highlight gender differences between girls and boys may be a way forward to increased participation.

Conclusion and Recommendations for Future Research

So far, researchers have made limited progress in understanding the complexities of socio-cultural factors affecting young children's participation in physical activity. The use of a socialist feminist framework to determine the effects of gender on levels of participation through an interactionist approach, using appropriate qualitative methodologies, might illuminate a number of relevant factors affecting girls levels of participation in physical activity. It must be recognised however, that many interrelated factors mediate such a process and, the contribution of other frameworks and perspectives should be incorporated in developing further insights into the complexities of socio-cultural influences. Possibilities for such future research might include combining 'interactive' socialization theory with:

- Bourdieu's notion of capital, the body and social class. Investigations in this area might provide insights into the effectof social class on levels of activity in educational sports and leisure settings.
- Gramsci's notion of hegemony - in investigating the extent to which "physical education helps create and maintain the actual hegemonic ideology and unjust social conditions" (FERNANDEZ-BALBOA, 1993, 231) and the extent to which such ideologies inhibit or promote physical activity in schools. Such a framework provides obvious opportunities for examining issues in the context of commercial developments designed to afford opportunities for youngsters to take part in organised activities.
- Theories of children's play - There are many divergent areas of interest within this category. Such an analysis might use Huizinga's ideas on the nature of play in investigating levels of activity at play periods and/or lunch times. This might also provide opportunities for investigating gender differences in children's activity patterns across cultures. CARVALHO and SMITH (1990) studied children's perceptions of the gender appropriateness of five common playground activities in both England and Italy and found gender stereotyping to lessen with age. ARCHER (1989) suggests that there

is some evidence for an increase in girls' actual participation in football in England. The relationship between actual participation of boys and girls in physical activities and their perception of gender differentiation regarding these activities remains an interesting issue for future research.

Insights and developments in psychological aspects of children's motivations have contributed towards an understanding of children's activity patterns yet there is a dearth of studies, particularly in Britain relating to socio-cultural factors affecting participation. The need to be aware of such issues in a rapidly changing modernist society (some would argue post-modernist e. g. BEST and KELLNER, 1991) is vital if educators, parents, youth leaders and other concerned policy makers are to make informed decisions regarding provision and encouragement for children in sport and physical activity.

References

ALANEN, L.: Rethinking socialization, the family and children. In: P.A. ADLER; P. ADLER (Eds.): Sociological Studies of Child Development, JAI Press, Greenwich 1990, 13-28.

ANDERSON, K.E.; LYTTON, H.; ROMNEY, D.M.: Mothers' interactions with normal and conduct-disordered boys: who effects whom? Developmental Psychology, 1986, 22, 604-609.

ARCHER, J.: Childhood gender roles: structure and development. The Psychologist, 1989, 9, 367-370.

ARMSTRONG, N.; BALDING, J.; GENTLE, P.; WILLIAMS, J.; KIRBY, B.: Peak oxygen uptake and physical activity in 11 to 16 year olds. Paediatric Exercise Science, 1990a, 2, 349-358.

ARMSTRONG, N.; BALDING, J.; GENTLE, P.; KIRKBY, B.: Patterns of physical activity among 11 to 16 year old British children. British Medical Journal, 1990b, 301, 203-205.

ARMSTRONG, N.; BALDING, J.; GENTLE, P.; KIRKBY, B.: Estimation of coronary risk factors in British schoolchildren: a preliminary report. British Journal of Sports Medicine, 1990c, 24(i), 61-66.

ARMSTRONG, N.; BRAY, S.: Physical activity patterns defined by continuous heart rate monitoring. Archives of Disease in Childhood, 1991, 66, 245-247.

ARMSTRONG, N.; WILLIAMS, J.; BALDING, J.; GENTLE, P.; KIRBY, B.: Cardiopulmonary fitness, physical activity patterns and selected coronary risk factor variables in 11-16 year olds. Paediatric Exercise Science, 1991, 3, 219-228.

ARMSTRONG, N.; MCMANUS, A.: Children's fitness and physical activity, a challenge for physical education. The British Journal of Physical Education, 1994, Spring, 20-26.

BAIN, L.L.: The hidden curriculum re-examined. Quest 1985, 37, 145-153.

BATES, J.E.: Effects of a child's imitation versus non-imitation of adults' verbal and non-verbal positivity. Journal of Personality and Social Psychology, 1975, 31, 840-851.

BEST, S.; KELLNER, D.: Postmodern theory, critical interrogation, Macmillan, 1991, London.

BRAY, C.: Sport and social change: socialist feminist theory. Journal of Physical Education Recreation and Dance, 1988, 59, 50-53.

BRUSTAD, R.J.: Integrating socialization influences into the study of children's motivation in sport. Journal of Sport and Exercise Psychology, 1992,14, 59-77.

CARVALHO, A.M.A.; SMITH, P.K.: Playground activities for boys and girls: developmental and cultural trends in children's perceptions of gender differences. Play and Culture, 1990, 3, 343-347.

COAKLEY, J.J.: Burnout among adolescent athletes: a personal failure or social problem? Sociology of Sport Journal, 1992, 9, 271-285.

COAKLEY, J.J.: Sport and socialization. Exercise and Sports Science Reviews, 1993, 21, 169-200.

COAKLEY, J.J.; WHITE, A.: Making decisions: gender and sport participation among British adolescents. Sociology of Sport Journal, 1992, 9, 20-35.

DICKENSON, B.: Survey of the activity patterns of young people and their attitudes and perceptions of physical activity and physical education in a local education authority M Phil, Loughborough University.

EVANS, J. et al.: Some thoughts on the political and pedagogic implications of mixed sex groupings in the physical education programme. Paper presented to the Sociology of Physical Education Conference, 1985, Manchester University.

FERNANDEZ-BALBOA, J.M.: Sociocultural characteristics of the hidden curriculum in physical education. Quest, 1993, 45, 230-254.

FLINTOFF, A.: Gender, physical education and initial teacher education. In: J. EVANS (Ed.): Physical education sport and schooling, Falmer Press 1993, London, 184-204.

GIDDENS, A.: Central problems in social theory, University of California Press, Berkley 1979, 96-130.

GOTTILEB, N.H.; CHEN, M.: Sociocultural correlates of childhood sporting activities and their implications for heart health. Social Science Medicine, 1985, 21, 533-539.

GREENDORFER, S.L.: Gender role stereotypes and early childhood socialization. In: G.L. COHEN (Ed.): Women in sport: issues and controversies, Sage, California 1993, 3-14.

GREENDORFER, S.L.; EWESON, M.E.: Gender differences in childrens socialization into sport. Research Quarterly for Exercise and Sport 52, 1891, 301-310.

HARGREAVES, J.: Gender on the sports agenda. In: A.G. INGHAM; J.O. LOY (Eds.): Sport in social development: traditions, transitions and transformations, Human Kinetics, Leeds 1993 167-185.

HASBROOK, C.A.: Reconceptualizing socialization. Paper presented at annual meeting of the North American Society for the Sociology of Sport, Washington D C, 1989.

HASBROOK, C.A.; HORN, T.S.: Childhood socialization into sport: some theoretical and methodological considerations. Paper presented at the annual meeting of the North American Society for the Sociology of Sport, Boston 1985.

KLESGES, R.C.; COATES, T.J.; MOLDENHAUER; KLESGES, B.; HOLZER J.; GUSTAWSON, J.; BARNES, J.: The FATS: an observational system for assessing physical activity in children and associated parent behaviour. Behavioral Assess, 1984, 6, 333-345.

KLESGES, R.C.; ECK, L.H.; HANSON, C.L.; HADDOCK, C.; KLESGES, L.M.: Effects of obesity, social interactions and physical environment on physical activity in pre-schoolers. Health Psychology, 1984, 9, 435-449.

KUNESH, M.A.; HASBROOK, C.A.; LEWTHWAITE, R.: Physical activity socialization: peer interactions and affective responses among a sample of sixth grade girls, Sociology of Sport, 1992, 9, 385-396.

MORRIS, E.K.: Contextualism: the world view of behaviour analysis. Journal of Experimental Child Psychology, 1988, 46, 289-323. Northern Ireland Fitness Survey, A report by the division of physical and health education, Queens', University of Belfast, 1989.

SALLIS, J.F.; HOVELL, M.F.; HOFSTETTER, C.R.; ELDER, J.P.; CASPERSON, C.J.; HACKLEY, M.: Distance between homes and exercise facilities related to the frequency of exercise in San Diego residents. Public Health Reports, 1992, 105, 179-185.

SALLIS, J.F.; SIMONS-MORTON, B.G.; STONE, E.J.; CORBIN, C.B., EPSTEIN, L.H., FANCETTE, N., IANNOTI, R.J., KILLEN, J.D., KLESGES, R.C., PETRAY, C.K., ROWLAND, T.W.; TAYLOR, W.C.: Determinants of physical activity and interventions in youth. Medicine and Sports Science, 1992, 24:6, 248-257.

SCRATON, S.: Images of femininity and the teaching of girls physical education. In: J. EVANS (Ed.): Physical education sport and schooling, Falmer Press, London 1986, 139-153.

SCRATON, S.: Shaping up to womanhood, gender and girls' physical education, Open University Press, Buckingham 1992.

SLEAP, M.; WARBURTON, P.: Physical activity patterns of primary school children, Health Education Authority, 1990.

SLEAP, M.; WARBURTON, P.: Physical activity levels of 5-11 year old children in England as determined by continuous observation Research Quarterly for Exercise and Sport 63, 1992, 3, 238-245.

SPARKES, A.: Culture and ideology in physical education. In: T.J. TEMPLIN; P.G. SCHEMPP (Eds.): Socialization into physical education: learning to teach, 315-338, Benchmark Press, Indianapolis 1989.

Sports Council for Wales , Exercise for health - health related fitness in Wales, Heartbeat Report, 1987, No 23.

STEVENSON, C. L.: The athletic career: some contingencies of sport socialization. Journal of Sport Behaviour, 1990, 13, 103-113.

SUNNEGARDH, J.; BRATTEBY, L.E.; STOLIN, S.: Physical activity and sports involvement in 8 and 13 year old children in Sweden. Acta Paediatrica Scandinavia, 1985, 74, 904-912.

TALBOT, M.: A gendered physical education: equality and sexism. In: J. EVANS (Ed.): Physical education sport and schooling, Falmer Press, London 1990, 74-89.

THIRLAWAY, K.; BENTON, D.: Physical activity in primary and secondary school children in West Glamorgan. Health Education Journal 1993, 52, 1, 37-41.

WAXMAN, M.; STUNKARD, A.: Caloric intake and expenditure of obese boys. Journal of Paediatrics, 1980, 96, 187-193.

WENTWORTH, W.M.: Context and understanding: an inquiry into socialization theory, Elsevier, New York, 1980.

WILLIAMS, A.: Physical activity patterns among adolescents - some curriculum implications. Physical Education Review, 1980, 11 (1), 28-39.

WRIGHT, J.E.: The contribution of teacher talk to the production and reproduction of gendered subjectivity in physical education PhD thesis, 1991, University of Wollongog, Australia.

Hans Peter Brandl-Bredenbeck, C. Roger Rees

Physical Self-Concept in German and American Adolescents

1 Introduction

Both in Germany and in the United States sport is perceived as a stabilizing influence in the lives of adolescents. By encouraging a positive physical self-concept sport is supposed to help adolescents cope with the physical and emotional problems of maturation. However, empirical evidence concerning this assumption is rare and often contradictory (see MIRACLE/REES, 1994) for a review of the American research).

If one looks at these hypotheses from the point of view of the current German and American societies, interesting aspects of research concerning the physical self-concept of adolescents in the USA and in Germany appear. This presentation examines how the physical self-concept of adolescents is affected by differences in the cultural setting and by sports involvement.

2 Theoretical assumptions

French sociologist, Pierre BOURDIEU (1982), has elaborated a socio-cultural theory of great sophistication. He suggests that the symbolic value which is accorded to a particular position in social space is defined by the amount (and structure) of social, cultural and economic capital possessed by the individual (BOURDIEU, 1983). BOURDIEU refers to the idea of different capitals in order to show that social reproduction does not occur accidentally. The way the forms of capitals are acquired ensures a certain continuity as far as social structures are concerned.

Economic capital refers to money, goods and other values. In order to define our role in society and to attempt our goals we do not only rely on our economic capital. *Social capital* is defined by the structure and function of our social network. In terms of BOURDIEU our friends and relationships represent a form of capital. This social capital is partly built on corporeal characteristics. Specifically among adolescents the constitution of a group and the social status within a group of peers is often linked to physical appearance, physical performance and/or body styling. *Cultural capital* is the amount of culturally inherited and individually acquired "cultivation". This cultural capital appears in embodied and institutionalized forms. High school diploma, university degrees and professional skills belong to the latter form of cultural capital. Embodied cultural capital is represented by the way people walk, talk, dress and eat. Embodied cultural capital, however, is not represented by the things people posess. It can be seen and evaluated by the way people are.

"You never get a second chance to make a first impression". This quote from an advertisement for clothing reflects the function of the embodied social and cultural capital, which according to BOURDIEU are important components of what he calls "habitus" (cf. 1982: 175). Acquiring social and cultural capital, however, is often limited by the amount of economic capital a person has. The "habitus", however, is the transformation of cultural and social living conditions into an embodied, unconscious device, which rules people's behavior and taste. The way people walk, talk and dress, or what kind of sports they do and how they treat their bodies, reveals the deepest disposition of their habitus (BOURDIEU, 1982: 307).

Bearing in mind this function of the different forms of embodied capital the body has to be seen as a powerful social ressource; it is at the center of BOURDIEUs general theory of social reproduction. In this paper we do not want to argue whether the physical capital is a subsection of cultural and social capital (BOURDIEU, 1983) or whether it has to be seen as a separate form of capital like SHILLING suggests (1993a: 58). The more important issue is how these forms of embodied capital are linked to the physical self-concept of adolescents and whether the physical self-concept is influenced by differences in the cultural setting and by sports involvement.

It is not difficult to understand the idea that the human body may be used as a form of capital. For example, a lot of people all around the world have jobs which require no special mental skills. It is sufficient to use one's own body and thus earn some money. An extreme example would be male and female prostitutes who use their bodies in order to earn a living (cf. SHILLING, 1993a: 57). In this case the conversion of the physical capital into another form of capital, e. g. money, is evident. The evidence might be less clear but still can be seen in the case of male bodybuilders who are sometimes hired to work as bouncers or in the case of professional sportsmen and women where the conversion of physical capital into other forms of capital is more sophisticated. Nobody would seriously doubt, however, that top athletes are able to convert their embodied capital into socially useful forms of capital. For example, male athletes could get jobs because of their popularity gained through sport and via the help of the old boys network. Thus, embodied social capital can be very useful in the working world. The conversion of embodied cultural capital, can be of the same importance as embodied social capital and as instutionalized cultural capital (e. g. high school diploma, university degrees, job training) when applying for a job. "Indeed, the importance of managing the body, dress, manner and speech in obtaining elite jobs is reinforced by those studies which suggest that qualifications serve only as an initial screening device, rather than actually determining employment selection decisions" (SHILLING, 1993a: 68).

For teenagers the body gains special importance as a bearer of status symbols. Indeed, the body is used as the central means to acquire recognition from peers or adults as well as to achieve a minimum of social recognition and success, since adolescents can only present their bodies. "Using one`s body as a source of power is an indicator of not having more reliable, less endangered and above all more powerful resources of trade like: money, property, connections, professional titles, etc." (ZINNECKER, 1989: 310). In the field of sports this way of using the body can be seen very clearly.

Youth and the presentation of one`s body in a youthful, active, and athletic way is not only legitimate, as we can see in the daily life. A lot of people are wearing track suits and sport shoes, even when they are not on their way to do sports. Being young and athletic is also a means of distinguishing oneself from other individuals, that means to yield profit through distinction. Thus, the process of differentiation, which BOURDIEU (1982) calls distinction can be used as a means of gaining higher social status.

The youthful, attractive body becomes a desirable object for all members of society and therefore is strongly sought after. One of the common paradigms of postmodern societies is that the body is a medium and point of reference for meaning-giving subjectivity. That means that in postmodern society where contradictions and complexity go beyond the individual's control the body becomes a means and realm for exerting power and control. The centralization and rediscovering of the body is evident in almost all areas of society. The emphasis layed on the body, fitness, and the youthful-athletic look are all facets of this phenomenon.

In the U.S.A. as well as in Germany the ideal of "physical appearance" and "body styling" is closely connected to the picture of a youthful, athletic and dynamic body. Physical fitness is evaluated so positevely that it is even supposed to be a means through which individuals can contribute to improve society (GLASSNER, 1989). Running, for example, has become a symbolic and practical physical antidote to the malaise of modernity. Thus, physical activity is supposed to be able to enhance morality.

It is important, however, to mention that the significance of the young-looking body is not only a form of capital for the younger generation. In the context of our age-defying society the younglooking body is emphasized and thus assigned a high symbolic value. Youthfulness is a desirable characteristic for everyone. This is even more true taking into account that youth as a life time period has significantly been extended in postmodern society. In a recent survey on youth in Germany, for example, the range of age was from 14 to 30 years (cf. 'Der Spiegel' 19.9.1994). Furthermore, power in society is no longer exclusively attributed to the older generation. The shift of power towards younger people is not only due to their ability in handling modern technology but is also significantly influenced by their physical capital.

3 Hypotheses

In Germany, the country of great philosophers, the body and the physical performance has always played a minor role compared to the intellectual performance. In this tradition it is still more important to acquire and to own institutionalized forms of social and cultural capital. In the society diploma, degrees and certificates have still a higher reputation than the embodied forms of social and cultural capital.

In the USA, however, the embodied forms of social and cultural capital refer to other historical roots. It is evident that building the new nation demanded more physical than intellectual power. In the New World there was less need to acquire diploma or other institutional forms of capital. The only thing that counted was the economic performance.

In further developing and changing the tradition of the muscular christianity idea the young American nation emphasized succes through one's own physical performance. In this historical process economic superiority often was equalized with moral superiority. Not only in a general social context, but also in a sports context "moral power was transmuted into physical power." (MROZEK, 1983: 169). Showing physical power by winning in sports led to the idea that winning shows moral superiority and that sport builds character. This idea was reinforced by the incorporation of sports in the educational system. Especially in the USA, where the varsity system underlines the competitive aspect of sport, participation and succes in sport is supposed to pay off later. Athletes know how to cope with difficult situations and thus are well prepared for the working world. It is even assumed that their popularity gained through sport and the social background of the old boys network could help them to get a better job than non-athletes (see MIRACLE/REES, 1994: especially Chapter 6).

We contend that competitive sport plays a more important role in American schools than in schools of any other country. In Germany, for example, competitive sport takes place in clubs. The emphasis of sport in school is more on physical education, that means on teaching physical abilities in order to make the children have fun and to enable the children to participate in lifetime sport activities.

Hypothesis 1: *These differences in historical, societal and cultural settings strongly affect the physical self-concept in German and American adolescents. Taking into account the seemingly higher emphasis on body related aspects in America we expect the American adolescents to evaluate their body concept more positive than their German counterparts*

Adolescents are influenced by this renaissance of the body in postmodern society in a special way. During puberty and adolescence the body plays a very important role. During this phase of change teenagers are exposed to a series of developmental tasks (HAVIGHURST, 1972), which according to social-psychologists, are closely related to the change or construction of a positive body-concept (OERTER/MONTADA, 1987). The body-concept becomes a decisive dimension of adolescents` self-concept.

The importance of the body is not only to be seen on an intra-individual level, but also on an inter-individual level. That means that adolescents gain status in their peer group via their social application of the body. Studies about the hierarchy in peer groups showed that athletes are more popular than non-athletes and that they even belong to those groups with the highest status (MIRACLE/REES, 1994; REES, 1995). Participation in sports - this is one theoretical assumption - gives teenagers the opportunity to experience their body, its performance and a personal sense of accomplishment. In this area succes can be attributed directly to one's own body-related performance. In this athletic performance, teenagers have the opportunity to enhance the value of their bodies, or in Bourdiean terms, to build more body capital. In the social field of sports adolescents learn to use their bodies as a source of power and capital.

Hypothesis 2: *We assume that teenagers, in whose lives sport plays an important role, evaluate their bodies more positively than those for whom sport only plays a minor role*

4 Method

The results presented here are based on the data of a quantitative survey. A questionnaire was answered by 7th, 9th and 12th grade students in the USA (New York and Memphis/Tennessee) and Germany (Berlin [west and east], Northrhine-Westphalia [former West-Germany] and Brandenburg [former East-Germany]). This presentation will be based on the data from New York (n=989) and Berlin (n=1086).

Body-concept in German and American adolescents is measured by a quantitative instrument which has been validated and applied succesfully in the context of German sport and youth research (cf. MRAZEK/HARTMANN, 1989; BRETTSCHNEIDER/BRÄUTIGAM, 1990). This instrument has been adapted to the American context. The translations of the items have been discussed in a bilateral workshop in order to assure that the application of the research instrument is possible in the USA. Furthermore we tried to take into account the methodological problem of equivalences, meaning that translation and retranslation of the items is not considered to be sufficient, but you also to contextualize the contents into the respective countries.

5 Results

In a first approach a factor analysis (with varimax rotation) for the item-scale representing the physical self-concept was calculated. The factor structure of the body concept for the adolescents in Berlin and in New York revealed to be identical. The same factors are extracted and the factor loadings for the items belonging to the same factors are similarily high. These results, however, do not allow the conclusion that the body concept in both cultural settings is similar or even identical. The only conclusion we can draw at this point is that the research instrument is a sound basis for further analysis in both countries.

In order to test our first hypothesis that American (New York) adolescents are supposed to evaluate there physical self-concept higher than their German (Berlin) counterparts two items have been selected. The items used in this analysis are: 1) "I like my body"; 2) "In comparison to others I am good-looking". The selection of these two items is based on the initial assumption that a positive evaluation of one's physical self-concept serves as a stabilizing element in the lives of adolescents. Furthermore the theoretical approach, which suggests that social and cultural capital is being built via the body, supports analysing those items that express the distintive character of one's own body within its social and cultural context.

The differences in the self-evaluation as far as the selected items are concerned are striking. Figure 1 shows the answers to the item "I like my body". On the one hand ***54 %*** of the answers of the Berlin adolescents are in the middle ranges "more true than false" and "more false than true". Those groups that scored positive answers ***(25.4 %)***, that means "mostly true" (14.0 %) and "true" (11.4 %) and negative answers "mostly false" (8.5 %) and "false" (12.1 %) have nearly the same quantity **(20.6 %)** (mean Berlin=3.60). On the other hand only **28.4 %** of the New York adolescents range in the "undecided area". **16.1 %** score negatively on this item [with the groups being 9.2 % scoring "false" and 6.9 % scoring "mostly false"] whereas **55.5 %** say that it is mostly true (21.4 %) or even true (34.1 %) that they like their body (mean NY=4.38).

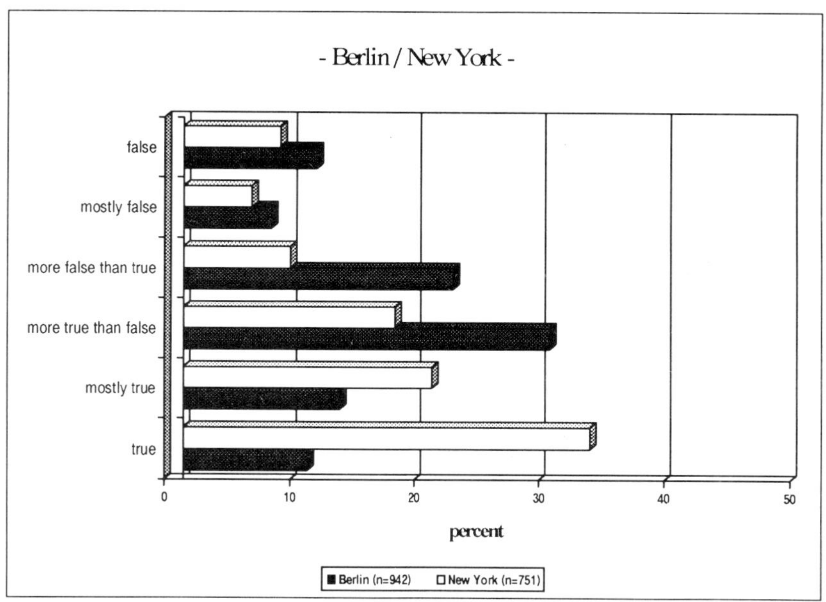

Figure 1: "I like my body"; Berlin/New York

Figure 2 shows the answers to the item "In comparison to others I am good-looking". The tendency of New York adolescents scoring higher than the compared Berlin age group is replicated. **51.6 %** of the New York adolescents tend to say that it is "mostly true" (22.4 %) or even "true" (29.2 %) that they are good-looking compared to others (mean NY=4.30). Only **26.7 %** of the Berlin adolescents have such a positive view as far as their physical appearance is concerned. It is remarkable, however, that only **14.7 %** in New York [7.7 % "false" and 7.0 % "mostly false] and **15.3 %** in Berlin [8.1 % "false" and 7.2 % "mostly false"] think really negatively about their physical appearance in comparison to others (mean Berlin=3.71).

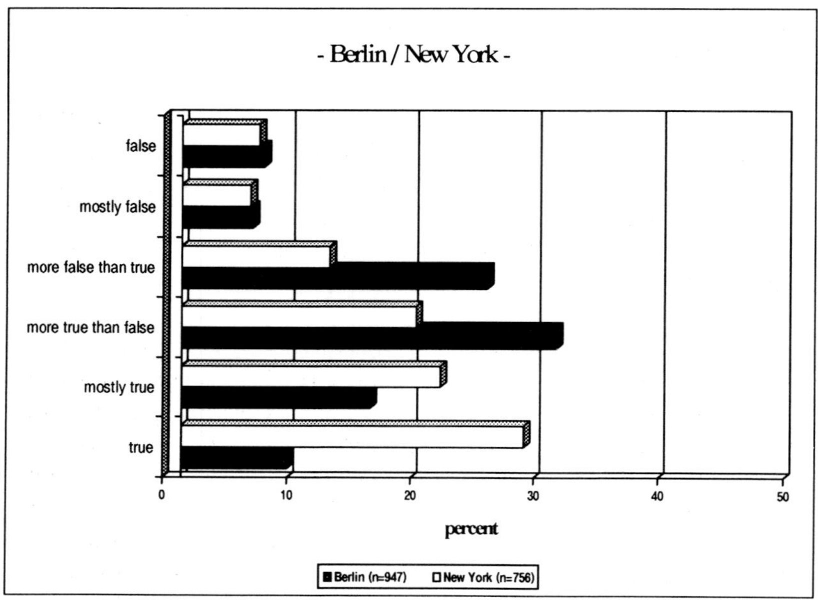

Figure 2: "In comparison to others I am good-looking"; Berlin / New York

As far as the physical self-concept scale is concerned, there is a general tendency of the New York adolescents to score more positevely. What makes the New York adolescents so self-confident about their body? Are they more aware than their German counterparts of their bodies being a form of social and cultural capital? Isn't this result a contradiction to the findings that American teenagers, generally speaking, are less fit than their German counterparts and that the percentage of body fat of American teenagers has continously increased in the last years (a tendency not yet to be found in Germany)?

As we have seen, the scores on the physical self-concept are not independent of societal and cultural settings. As we hypothesized American adolescents evaluate their physical self-concept more positively than their German counterparts. The extent to which differences can be seen, however, is surprising.

Although the enormous differences as far as the evaluation of the physical self-concept is concerned need further interpretation, the first hypothesis is confirmed. In the final discussion of this paper we will present some additional aspects for an interpretation that might help to explain these differences between New York and Berlin adolescents.

The second hypothesis was that teenagers in whose lives sport plays an important role, evaluate their bodies more positively than those for whom sport only plays a minor role. In order to test this hypothesis it is necessary to build subgroups according to the self-assessed importance of sport in the daily life. For this we used a measure developed by CURRY in his research on self-identity (CURRY, 1993; CURRY/WEANER, 1987). The adolescents were asked to rate the importance of sport on a scale ranging from 0 to 100. The subgroups that we developed are the following: *sport is of no importance* (0 to 19), *sport is slightly important* (20 to 39), *sport is moderately important* (40 to 59), *sport is more important* (60 to 79), *sport is very important* (80 to 99) and *sport is the most important thing* (100).

Generally speaking, sport in the lives of New York adolescents is a little more important than it is in the lives of the Berlin adolescents. (mean New York = 72.87 and mean Berlin = 69.32; level of significance = .002)

On the left-hand side of the following figure (3) one can see the six subgroups according to their self-assessed importance of sport.

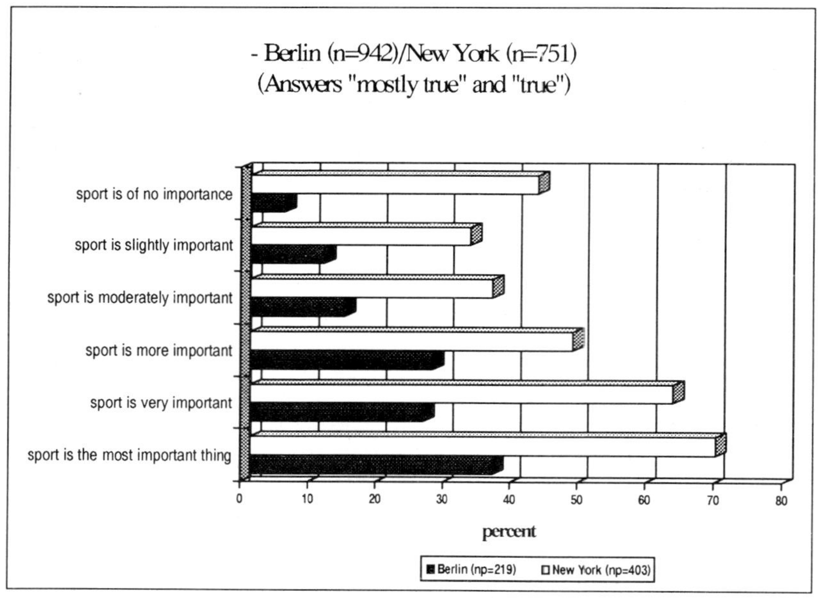

Figure 3: "I like my body"; Relationship between the importance of sport and body concept in Berlin and New York

Taking into account that we want to show the relationship between the importance of sport and a positive evaluation of the physical self-concept the graphics describe the positve answers ("mostly true" and "true") on the selected items. This graphic is to be read like this: As far as the Berlin adolescents are concerned, only 6.5 % among those who said sport being of no importance in their life rated the positive answers on this item. The higher the self-assessed importance of sport, the more the Berlin adolescents tend to say that they like their body, with the percentage being 37.4 % for the positive answers among those who said sport is the most important thing. The graphic shows very impressively that the New York adolescents scored differently. Independent of their affiliation to a subgroup the New York adolescents score very positively on this item. Even the group that says that sport is of no importance in their lives scored more positively on this item (44.1 %) than those Berliners that said that sport is the most important thing. Nevertheless, the positive evaluation of one's own body within the New York sample increases with the growth of the importance of sport, with the agreement on the answers "mostly true" and "true" being 70.3 % among those who said that sport is the most important thing.

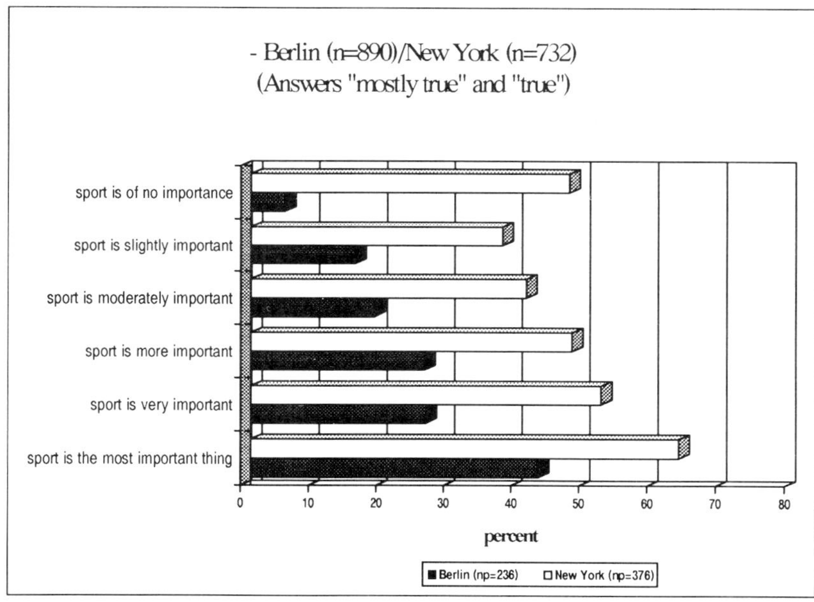

Figure 4: "In comparison to others I am good-looking"; Relationship between the importance of sport and body concept in Berlin and New York

The answers to this item generally replicate the already mentionned tendency. In Berlin the importance of sport is significantly related to the way adolescents score on the item "In comparison to others I am good-looking". The higher the importance of sport the more positive the assessement. In the social comparison the New York adolescents evaluate their personal outlook very positively. The importance of sport seems to have no effect on the evaluation. Indeed, even that group of New York adolescents that said sports is not important at all scored higher (48.6 %) on this item than the Berlin adolescents for whom sport is the most important thing.

The second hypotheses reveals to be partly true. In Germany the self-assessed importance of sport shows significant influence on the evaluation of the physical self-concept. The American adolescents, however, seem to evaluate their physical self-concept independently from the individually assessed importance of sport. The presented results indicate a confounding effect. The importance of body-related aspects in New York seems to be determined on a more general level and/or by other variables than the importance of sport. It may be that American and German adolescents use different criteria in interpreting the importance of sport. Specifically, American adolescents' rating of sport does not appear to be attached to their own perceived physical ability to the extent that it is in Germany. Such an interpretation indicates a higher status of the body in American compared to German adolescent culture. In America the body is important for everyone, whether they are athletic or not.

6 Discussion

As we hypothesized the New York adolescents, generally speaking, evaluate their physical self-concept more positively than their Berlin counterparts. As far as this result is concerned the extent to which differences can be observed is striking. These differences and the fact that the evaluation of the physical self-concept of New York adolescents holds independent of the importance of sport suggests the interpretation that corporeal characteristics play a more important role in New York compared to Berlin.

In terms of the socio-cultural approach New York adolescents are building more body capital than their Berlin counterparts. Perhaps American adolescents are more aware of the fact that their body is able to produce embodied social and cultural capital and thus they are working on it. This could be due to the general emphasis on corporeal aspects in American society. The social reinforcement of bodily aspects underlines the younglooking and fit person. By doing so, the adolescents, owner of all these required qualities, are able to gain social status in the peer group as well as in the "adult society" via their body.

Sociologically the US-society in comparison to German society is based on more and stronger dichotomies (e. g. rich-poor, success-failure, victory-defeat). Consequently there is a much smaller middle class in the USA than in Germany. On the one hand, in the United States everyone, regardless to his social background, can be succesful. The myth "from a dish washer to a millionaire" is still alive. But on the other hand, adolescents can anticipate that economic success is very difficult to achieve. In both societies, however, young people want to be independent, yet a great number of them remain economically dependent till they have acquired institutionalized forms of cultural capital (university degrees and vocational training). The access for all adolescents to these forms of cultural capital is more limited in the USA (private education) than it is in Germany (public education). In order to improve their position in the social space in the present and to avoid the failure in the long run adolescents are looking for a means which can be of help. The body capital is such a means, which seems to be more of use in the USA than in Germany.

The degree to which the above described phenomenon differs in both societies, however, needs further interpretation. A few examples might help to show, that it is more than a subjective assumption, that the physical capital plays a more important role in the USA than in Germany. In the USA the norm to look good and feel great is ubiquitous. Almost all new forms of movement and fitness (e. g. aerobics, walking, rollerblading, etc.), whose goal was to create or uphold a fit and fat-free young, dynamic body, were developed and became very popular in the USA. In Germany these new trends always appeared with delay. They have not become as popular and they have not reached the status of a social norm like in the USA. In the USA a lot of companies made fitness programs available to their employees because out of shape employees cost the company money and give it a bad image (GLASSNER, 1989). Although large German companies sometimes offer fitness facilities the message is not the same. Moreover, people in the USA who don't smoke, "eat right" and do exercise get lower insurance rates (GLASSNER, 1989). In Germany insurance rates are not yet affected by the state of health or the degree of physical activity of an individual. The health insurance companies, however, want to raise the insurance rates for those people participating in sports, because injuries in sports costs them big money.

Exercise today is not simply a way to get a workout (POWERS, 1992: 286). Especially in the USA it is an entry into a realm of fantasy peopled by cult figures like Jane Fonda and Cher, anorexic Barbie dolls and detailed-styled Jackie Joyner-Kersees, muscle packed California dream men and Shaquil O'Neal "Shaqattacks". In a world where these cult figures still serve as role models and where the economic success can easily be related to the physical performance, the already existing importance of corporeal characteristics is even more emphasised.

Taking into account these examples the emphasis on a youthful and fit body seems to be an integral and important part in the North American culture whereas in Germany people regard their body capital important, yet the social status is lower.

7 References

BOURDIEU, P.: Die feinen Unterschiede. Kritik der gesellschaftlichen Urteilskraft. Frankfurt/Main: Suhrkamp Verlag 1982.

BOURDIEU, P.: Ökonomisches Kapital, kulturelles Kapital, soziales Kapital. In: R. KRECKEL: Soziale Ungleichheiten. Band 2. Göttingen 1983, 183-198.

BRETTSCHNEIDER, W.-D./BRÄUTIGAM, M.: Sport in der Alltagswelt von Jugendlichen. Forschungsbericht. Düsseldorf 1990.

CURRY, T.: The Effects of Receiving a College Letter on the Sport Identity. In: Sociology of Sport Journal 1993, 10, 73-87.

CURRY, T./WEANER, J.: Sport Identity Salience, Commitment, and the Involvement of Self in Role: Measurement Issues. In: Sociology of Sport Journal 1987, 4, 280-288.

Der SPIEGEL: Wochenmagazin vom 19.9.1994.

GLASSNER, B.: Fitness and the Postmodern Self. In: Journal of Health and Social Behavior, 1989, 30, 180-191.

HAVIGHURST, R.J.: Developmental Tasks and Education. New York 1972

MIRACLE, A./REES, R.: Lessons of the Locker Room. The Myth of School Sports. Amherst. New York 1994.

MRAZEK, J./HARTMANN, I.: Selbstkonzept und Körperkonzept. In: W.-D. BRETTSCHNEIDER/J. BAUR/M. BRÄUTIGAM: Sport im Alltag von Jugendlichen. Schorndorf: Karl Hofmann Verlag 1989, 218-230.

MROZEK, D.: Sport and American Mentality, 1880-1910. Knoxville, TH: University of Tennessee Press, 1983.

OERTER, R./MONTADA, L.: Entwicklungspsychologie. München. Weinheim 1987.

POWERS, R.G.: Sports and American Culture. In: L.S. LUEDTKE: Making America. The Society and Culture of the United States. North Carolina 1992, 272-288.

REES, R.: What Price Victory? Myths, Rituals, Athletics and the Dilemma of Schooling. In: A. SADOVNIK (Ed.): Knowledge and Pedagogy: The Sociology of Basil Bernstein. Norwood, NJ. Ablex 1995, 371-383.

SHILLING, C.: The Body, Class and Social Inequalities. In: J. EVANS (Ed.): Equality, Education and Physical Education. London. Washington D.C. 1993a, 55-73.

SHILLING, C.: The Body and Social Theory. London. Newbury Park, CA, 1993b.

ZINNECKER, J.: Jugend, Körper und Sport im Zivilisationsprozeß. In: W.-D. BRETTSCHNEIDER/J. BAUR/M. BRÄUTIGAM: Sport im Alltag von Jugendlichen. Schorndorf: Karl Hofmann Verlag 1989, 296-310.

Paul De Knop, Lars Magnus Engström, Berit Skirstad, Maureen R. Weiss, Marc Theeboom

Sport and Youth: Problems and Features of Youth Sport

Introduction

This paper[1] reports on the international project "Children, Youth and Sport", which was conceived as a collaborative venture between some members of the Committee "Sport and Leisure" of the International Council of Sport, Science and Physical Education (ICSSPE). Subsequently, at a meeting of this committee which was held in Malaga in July 1992, other youth sport researchers were invited to contribute to the project. Some 20 representatives from around the world expressed their interest, and at a further meeting in May 1993 in Stockholm, a plan was agreed for a book on multinational trends in youth sport. The main objective of the project was: (a) to contribute to the general knowledge about how youth sport in contemporary societies is organized, (b) to explain how and why youth sport patterns change and develop, (c) to provide information concerning interesting campaigns, and (d) to look into the future of child and youth sport.

Methodology

At the outset, it was decided that the project would be loosely structured to enable different countries to participate according to their resources and interests. A secondary but important aim was to foster international collaborative work on youth sport, while seeking

---

1 This paper is adapted from *Worldwide Trends in Child and Youth Sport*, by P. De Knop, L.M. Engstrom, B. Skirstad, M.R. Weiss (Eds.), In Press, Champaign, IL: Human Kinetics. Copyright, 1996 by Human Kinetics Publishers, Inc. Adapted with permission.

to gain a better understanding of the peculiar features of each society through cross-national comparison.

In many respects the methodology adopted in cross-national comparative research is no different from that used for within-nation comparison or for other areas of sociological research. It can be descriptive, evaluative and/or analytical. The descriptive or survey approach, which will usually result in a state of the art review, is generally the first stage in any large-scale international comparative project and it is also the method adopted in this project.

The project was aimed at analyzing recent trends in child and youth sports within different countries on a number of aspects (i.e., organizational networks, sport participation and promotional campaigns). Child and youth sports were defined as all sport activities outside the physical education curriculum for youngsters between 6 and 18 years of age. This means that schoolsport as an extra-curricular activity was also included. It was decided to provide the possibility for each contributor to define sport activity in their own specific way.

Data was collected from five continents including the following 20 countries: Australia, Belgium, Brazil, Canada, China, Denmark, England, Finland, Germany, Israel, Japan, the Netherlands, New Zealand, Norway, Poland, Portugal, Scotland, Spain, Sweden, and the USA.

It was not the intention to concentrate on the comparison of basic, quantitative data on youth sport participation in these countries, but rather on detecting broad worldwide trends in child and youth sport. Therefore, answers to the following questions were sought:

- are there any worldwide trends and developments in child and youth sport?
- what are the trends in sport participation in developing countries in comparison with those in, for example, western industrialized countries?

- what are the main problems youth sports are faced with ?
- what are the main trends in the youth sport campaigns and in youth sport policy?

The project has resulted in the making of the book "Worldwide Trends in Child and Youth Sport" to be published by Human Kinetics and edited by De Knop, Engström, Skirstad, and Weiss. Next, is a brief overview of the project's most important conclusions, trends and recommendations.

Conclusions

One of the project's most important findings is that sport can be regarded as the most popular leisure time activity among children and youth. In most countries which were involved in the project, at least half of all children in their early teens are active in various sports. It is interesting to note the similarity that exists between the countries concerning the organization and content of children's sport. Most of the youth sport activities take place in a sport club or in extra-curriculum training in school.

More boys than girls are active. This is especially true in traditional and team sports, where competition is a fundamental part. This finding is not surprising as most of these sports are based on male values, with emphasis on competition and performance. While most boys can strengthen their masculine identity through success in competitive sport, it is unclear to what extent sport success influences girls' identity. Sometimes success in sport may even mean a risk for the female identity. However, sports segregate the sexes like few other phenomena. It is very seldom that boys and girls take part in sports together.

Some of the most common sports played by youth are soccer among boys and swimming among both sexes. Jogging, cycling, and walking are the most popular activities outside a sport club. There are hardly any popular sports that are played in a specific country solely.

Sport has thereby become an international phenomenon with performance and rules that are known by almost all individuals regardless of nationality and language.

In those countries where studies about the social recruitment to sport have been conducted, findings show that middle class children are overrepresented. The membership of a sport club is often related to gender, social class, and family situation. The most common motives for taking part in youth sports are characterized by intrinsic values like enjoyment and social reasons. These motives are more common than investment values like success in competition and better performance.

Only a few countries refer to a specific system for finding and training young talents. However, this does not mean that there is a lack of interest in other countries regarding this matter. On the contrary, the ambition to find talents is often very high, but the ways to develop a future top athlete might be different. In most cases, talented children remain in their original clubs until their teens, while at the same time take part in various national and international tournaments.

Trends in the Development of Child and Youth Sport

Going through all the data, a number of trends and problems regarding child and youth sport can be noticed. For example, the number of opportunities for participating in sport for youngsters has increased substantially in the last 10 years. Also, more and more children have become interested in organized sport. This increase has been remarkable, particularly among girls. Especially in countries such as Sweden, Norway, Finland, and Germany, girls' sport habits have come to resemble the boys'. However, recently, the interest for organized sports seems to have come to a breakpoint in many countries and is now decreasing, which many sport organizations regard as a problem.

Another trend is the institutionalization of sport. The traditional sports, such as team sports, are not played spontaneously to the same extent as before. In some countries, spontaneous sport practice has almost disappeared. Children´s knowledge about and performance in sport have become more and more differentiated and the extent and intensity of physical activity have become more varied. Today, one can identify two extreme groups of children: on the one hand, highly trained children and on the other hand, physically inactive children. As a result, the physical capacity and sport skill vary considerably between children and these variations tend to increase - making these two groups even more distinct.

Adult sports has indeed influenced children's sports to a large extent. Norms and values of adults are dominating. In many sports, children are looked upon as if they were small adults. As a result, children's sport has become more serious, less playful and too much organized. Children are not allowed to play to the same extent as before. Organizers of different sports are competing for the children's interest, which leads to a decrease of the age when children start to be members of sport clubs and also to a lack of cooperation between the clubs.

As a result, children are introduced to sports at an earlier age than before. In many of the countries included in this project, 50 % of the children start at the age of 7 or 8 or even younger. Sport participation, on the one hand, is a dynamic process whereby young people's involvement is characterized by moving in and out of a wide range of activities with a considerable amount of experimentation. However on the other hand, there is a trend towards specialization in sport, where all the concentration and physical effort must be paid to one, or at the most, two sports. The interest in many of the traditional sports like gymnastics and athletics seems to decrease, while the interest in new sports like judo and girls' soccer increases.

The number of dropouts is increasing with increasing age. This is especially distinct among girls. This is reported from all countries where researchers have studied this phenomenon. During adolescence, there is an increasing decline in number of participants.

Contemporary western competitive sports are characterized by a high degree of seriousness, a focus on results, and a highly structured system of competition. A similar development can be noticed within children´s sport. The increasing economical and social meaning of success (compared with getting other prizes) in top sports leads to a harder acting within (and without) the limits of the rules, and an increasing temptation to use illegitimate drugs (e. g., doping) to achieve a desirable victory. This development among top-level athletes is for many people even a threat against children and youth sport.

It is reported from several countries that there are problems to get qualified leaders. In this context, the need for adequate education as well as the occurrence of financial problems are mentioned. There is a heavy dependency on volunteers which creates a high turnover and an uncertainty of quality of leadership and coaching.

Recommendations

Children's sports can serve many purposes. Sport can be a meaningful occupation for many children and give them a life-long interest in physical activity as an important part of a healthy way of life and as a source of joy and relaxation. Sport can also make a platform for future elite sportsmen and women and is a way for self-realization and success for young people with a talent for sports. For many children, sport is also an important environment for upbringing and it fills an important function in society's culture reproduction, where significant values in our culture are being recreated and carried over to the next generation.

It is, however, very doubtful if children's sports, with the development that has been drawn up above, can fulfil to a full degree any of these purposes. Our definite opinion is that the course must be changed and, with this in mind, we would like to conclude with a number of recommendations.

Sports among children must be made more accessible. It should be located close to residential areas. The possibilities to try different sports must increase considerably, thus creating better conditions for a varied physical activity and also diminishing the importance of parents' interests and life conditions.

Play and learning must come first, that is, the intrinsic value of sports must have priority. To stress the investment value one-sidedly is a misdirected ambition from adults and, as a matter of fact, a strange and forced-upon element in children's world of sports.

Training must be rich in variations and individualized. A firmly controlled and formalized training can counteract its purpose. The activities of sport clubs should aim at trying to develop talent in the best way possible instead of trying to find talents. A selection of individuals, as well as a pronounced specialization, should not be made before reaching the teens. The great variations in the maturing process among individuals make all prognoses that are made before the teens very uncertain.

A child's relation to sports, to his or her own body and the experience of his or her own physical ability is the result of a learning process. To learn a sport is, however, not only a question of learning motor skills. It is also a question of learning norms and a set of values, of how to behave oneself, and of a style of life. Children are socialized into sports and thereby also into the value system of sports. Youth sport is one of our most important environments for upbringing. Sports must therefore also be valued as such and given rightful importance in children's lives and development. Perhaps sport is the most important normsetter, second only to family and school. On the strength of its range and importance, sport must mediate and recreate essential values for the continued existance of our culture. In other words, it fills the function of reproducing culture. Therefore, it is of utmost importance that sport should follow a sound ethical code. In this context, the leader's personality, style of life and acting is an important factor.

Maybe one of the greatest challenges facing youth sport today and in the near future is to set up a cooperative and coordinate approach by schools and clubs with the purpose to offer sports as an educational environment for all children which enables them to develop at their own speed according to their own interests.

Terry McMorris, Peter Bunyan, Tim Holder

Relationship Between Selected Psychological Variables Before and After an Outdoor Pursuits Expedition

1. Introduction

To some people participation in outdoor pursuits, such as walking, scrambling, climbing, abseiling and caving, is a pleasurable experience, which provides them with much enjoyment. To others such activities are to be avoided. Nevertheless, many college physical education programmes include compulsory outdoor education courses. The purpose of this study was to examine the interrelationship between sensation seeking, perceived competence (PC), state anxiety and perceptions of enjoyment (PE) before and after a compulsory outdoor pursuits expedition, which was part of an outdoor education course.

It has been claimed that enjoyment is experienced when motivational needs are met (WANKEL and SEFTON, 1989). In outdoor pursuits this need may be the desire for challenge and adventure or simply experiencing the sensations of nature. Both of these drives are part of what ZUCKERMAN (1979, 1983) described as sensation seeking. According to ZUCKERMAN (1971, 1979), individuals possess an "optimal level of sensation." Some people require a great deal of stimulation for arousal to occur, these would be high sensation seekers. Other people need only a minimal level of stimulation, these are low sensation seekers. High sensation seekers tend to seek out exciting activities, while low sensation seekers avoid activities which, to them, are too stimulating (ZUCKERMAN, 1979, 1983).

Following a long period of research into sensation seeking, ZUCKERMAN (1971) subdivided sensation seeking into four categories: thrill and adventure seeking (TAS), environmental seeking (ES), boredom susceptibility (BS) and disinhibition (Dis). High levels of TAS are indicative of individuals who seek challenging and dangerous activities. ES persons are less concerned with danger and challenge but more with "experience for its own sake " and the "feel" of nature. BS people are easily bored by repetition of experience and predictability and have a preference for a variety of experiences. Dis is a sign of people who lack social inhibitions and enjoy partaking in such activities as heavy social drinking, "wild parties" and gambling (ZUCKERMAN, 1971). ZUCKERMAN (1971) found moderate but significant correlations between the sub-categories and claimed that they were not independent factors, but, he added, that there were some clear differences.

One would expect the TAS component of sensation seeking to be strongly correlated to voluntary participation in outdoor pursuits. Indeed enjoyment of participating in such activities was claimed by ZUCKERMAN (1971) to be an indicator of TAS. It is not surprising then to find that TAS has been shown to be significantly correlated to voluntary participation in risky sports (STRAUB, 1982; ROWLAND, FRANKEN and HARRISON, 1986). STRAUB (1982), however, found that ES and BS were better predictors of voluntary participation than TAS. This supports ZUCKERMAN'S (1971) claim that these sub-categories are not independent factors. This assertion has been further supported by the fact that the total scores on the sensation seeking scale (SSS) have generally shown a significant relationship between high levels of sensation seeking and voluntary participation in risky activities (HEYMAN and ROSE, 1980; STRAUB, 1982; ROWLAND et al., 1986).

The relationship between sensation seeking and voluntary participation in risky activities and/or enjoyment of such participation may be explained by the interaction between sensation seeking and state anxiety. ZUCKERMAN (1983) stated that low sensation seekers demonstrate higher levels of state anxiety and more rapid increases in state anxiety than high sensation seekers when risky activities are to be undertaken. While this relationship may well affect the amount of PE, the situation could be further complicated by the person's PC in the activities to be encountered. BANDURA (1977) claimed that one of the major causes of state anxiety occurred when individuals perceived the task that was to be undertaken as being beyond their capabilities. While those who perceived themselves as being capable of carrying out the task, demonstrated little state anxiety and would "anticipate satisfaction."

The literature, both empirical research and theoretical, has focused on the relationships between sensation seeking and voluntary participation; sensation seeking and state anxiety; PC and PE. No research has attempted to examine a possible inter-relationship between all of these factors. Both theory and research findings suggest that it would be reasonable to hypothesise that there will be an inter-relationship between sensation seeking, PC, state anxiety and PE in a group of individuals engaging in a compulsory outdoor pursuits expedition. Furthermore, the possibility of one or more of the variables acting as predictors of state anxiety, PC and PE requires examining as it could provide very useful information to instructors about how to interact with students during an expedition.

2. Method

Forty-one first year B.Ed. (Hons.) physical education majors completed part of ZUCKERMAN's (1979) SSS, before and after undertaking a compulsory outdoor pursuits expedition. The Dis sub-scale was omitted because there is no evidence that this scale has any relevance to the other variables being measured (STRAUB, 1982). Furthermore, as the experimental design meant that the scale could not be completed anonymously and the Dis scale contains many questions which relate to activities which student teachers may not wish their tutors to know about, it was decided that its inclusion could affect the honesty of the answers.

The subjects also completed PC and PE questionnaires, before and after the expedition. Content validity was claimed for the questionnaires and reliability was established by a test re-test method. Thirty-one first year B.Ed. (Hons.) physical education majors, who were not part of the experiment, but who were about to take part in a similar expedition, completed the questionnaires on two separate occasions, which were one week apart. Reliability coefficients were determined by the Spearman Rank Correlation method.

The expedition lasted five days and took place on Dartmoor (England). It included walking, scrambling, climbing, caving and abseiling. The students slept in tents except for one night spent in the open. Selected students were interviewed by the third author, who was unknown to them, following the end of the expedition. The interviews were semi-structured and the students were selected on the basis of their scores on the SSS. They represented high, average and low sensation seekers. Twenty subjects were, also, administered a modified version of the Competitive State Anxiety Inventory-2 (CSAI-2) (MARTENS, BURTON, VEALEY, BUMP and SMITH, 1983), thirty minutes prior to their first experience of caving. The only modification to the CSAI-2 was that statements referring directly to competition against an opponent were modified to refer to successfully completing the task.

3. Results

Spearman Rank Order Correlations for the test re-test scores on the PC and PE questionnaires both demonstrated high correlations, $r=0.95$ ($p<.001$) for PC and $r=0.87$ ($p<.001$) for PE. It was, therefore, accepted that these questionnaires were reliable. The inter-correlations matrix for SSS, TAS, ES, BS, PC and PE for both pre- and post-expedition are shown in table one.

Table 1. Inter-correlations matrix for SSS, TAS, ES, BS, PC and PE. Pre-expedition results below the diagonal and post-expedition above.

	SSS	TAS	ES	BS	PC	PE
SSS		.73**	.62**	.63**	.37**	.52**
TAS	.69**		.27*	.21	.48**	.60**
ES	.68**	.30*		.08	.06	.14
BS	.65**	.20	.16		.10	.23
PC	.46**	.61**	.31*	.12		.70**
PE	.49**	.50**	.37	.15		

** p<.01, * p<.05.

Stepwise multiple regression analyses, with PC as the dependent variable and TAS, ES and BS as the predictor variables, showed that for both pre- and post-expedition, TAS was the only variable in the equation, R^2 =.47 (p<.01) pre-expedition and R^2=.26 (p<.01) post. With PE as the dependent variable and TAS, ES, BS and PC as the predictor variables, PC was the only variable in the equation pre-expedition, R^2=.44 (p<.01). Post-expedition both PC, (R^2=.52, p<.01), and TAS were accepted in the equation, multiple R^2=.59 (p<.01).

SSS correlated significantly with cognitive anxiety (r=-.68, p<.01), somatic anxiety (r=-.81, p<.01) and self confidence (r=.70, p<.01) prior to the first experience of caving. Perception of caving competence (PCAV), which was determined from the relevant questions in the PC questionnaire, also, correlated significantly with cognitive anxiety (r=-.70, p<.01), somatic anxiety (r=-.57, p<.01) and self confidence (r=.59, p<.01). Stepwise multiple regression analyses were also carried out to determine the best predictors of cognitive anxiety, somatic anxiety and self confidence. The predictor variables were TAS, ES, BS and PCAV. PCAV was the only variable in the equation for cognitive anxiety (R^2=.59, p<.01), while ES (R^2=.55, p<.01) and TAS, multiple R^2=.74 (p<.01), were accepted in the equation for somatic anxiety. TAS (R^2=.49, p<.01) and ES, multiple R^2=.72 (p<.01) were the variables in the equation for self confidence.

Comparison of the SSS, PC and PE pre- and post-expedition results, using the Wilcoxon Signed Rank Test, showed that there was no significant difference for SSS, although BS did demonstrate a significant decrease (p<.01). Neither TAS nor ES were significantly altered. Both PC and PE showed significant (p<.01, in both cases) increases.

4. Discussion

The results of the experiment provide partial support for the hypothesis that there would be an interaction between sensation seeking, state anxiety, PC and PE before and after a compulsory outdoor pursuits expedition. The pre- and post-expedition correlations between SSS, TAS, and ES are in agreement with STRAUB (1982) and ROWLAND et al. (1986) and support ZUCKERMAN's (1971) contention that TAS and ES are "not independent, but nevertheless separate identities." The fact that BS did not correlate significantly with TAS and ES, however, failed to support ZUCKERMAN's (1971) claim for that sub-scale and supports BALL, FARNILL and WANGEMAN's (1984) assertion that BS measures a dimension of sensation seeking that is essentially different to TAS and ES.

That PC should correlate significantly with SSS, TAS and ES pre-expedition was expected but, surprisingly, post-expedition PC correlated significantly only with SSS and TAS. Furthermore, the strength of these correlations had fallen. This may be accounted for by the experience of the expedition itself. Prior to the expedition the subjects had little knowledge of the nature of many of the tasks to be undertaken, therefore PC may have been determined to a large extent by their desire, or lack of it, for sensation seeking, rather than a judgement of the skill required for successful completion of the tasks. The results of the stepwise multiple regression analyses pre- and post-expedition with PC as the dependent variable and the sub-scales of SSS as the predictor variables supports this possibility. Pre-expedition TAS accounted for 47 % of the variance in PC but post expedition this had fallen to only 26 %. The post hoc interviews further supported this contention, as the low sensation seekers stated that PC rose post-expedition because they had successfully completed the tasks but they still did not wish to repeat the experience.

That ES failed to significantly correlate with PC post-expedition may also be explained by information provided in the post hoc interviews. Most subjects did not find the environmental stimuli very demanding, probably because the weather during the five days was moderate, with subjects not being faced by extremes of cold, heat or damp. Several low sensation seekers, however, did find the height of the climbs and the sensations of caving somewhat intimidating. This suggests that ES may have only had a bearing in extreme situations.

The correlations of PC with PE both pre- and post-expedition support the claims of BANDURA (1977), NICHOLLS (1984) and ROBERTS (1984), that individuals are likely to enjoy activities in which PC is high and dislike undertaking activities in which PC is low. Stepwise multiple regression analyses with PE as the dependent variable and TAS, ES, BS and PC as the predictor variables showed that pre-expedition PC accounted for 44 % of the variance with the other factors failing to add significantly to the predictive value. Post-expedition PC accounted 52 % of the variance while PC and TAS, together, accounted for 59 %. This change in prediction level may be explained by the changes in the relationship between PC and TAS from pre- to post-expedition. As stated earlier, pre-expedition PC was highly related to TAS but post-expedition this diminished. The interviews suggested that post-expedition PE was not only related to PC but also the drive for thrill and adventure.

Significant correlations between PE, SSS, and TAS were expected based on previous research into sensation seeking and choice of activity (HEYMAN and ROSE, 1980; ROWLAND et al., 1986). However, the failure of ES to correlate significantly with PE post-expedition raises a question concerning the relationship between PE and sensation seeking and is in disagreement with STRAUB (1982).

ZUCKERMAN (1983) stated that TAS by its very nature should correlate significantly with enjoyment of adventurous activity. However, he explained that unless other sub-scales, particularly ES, also significantly correlated then the claim that the relationship between PE and SSS was due to an underlying genetic drive, would be questionable. The pre-expedition results suggest that such a drive was present, however, the post-expedition results fail to support such a claim. As stated earlier, the post hoc interviews showed that the experience may not have been extreme enough for ES to have been a significant variable in this particular expedition. The results may, also, have been affected by the nature of this specific group of subjects. They scored comparatively low on the ES scale compared to the TAS scale. Being physical education majors it would not be surprising to find that TAS accounted for an unusual proportion of the overall SSS scores compared to ES and BS. Similar results have been found with groups that have occupations in which conformity to the norms of society would be expected (ZUCKERMAN, 1983).

The significant correlations between CSAI-2 results and SSS scores support ZUCKERMAN's (1983) assertion that sensation seeking affects state anxiety. Similarly the significant correlations between PCAV and CSAI-2 results support the claims of NICHOLLS (1984) and ROBERTS (1984) that PC and state anxiety are related. Indeed, NICHOLLS (1984) stated that "test-anxiety scales" refer directly to perceived ability and that "the action ingredient of test anxiety scales is perceived competence."

Stepwise multiple regression analyses with TAS, ES, BS and PCAV as the predictor variables and each of the CSAI-2 sub-scales as dependent variables showed somewhat contradictory results. PCAV was the only variable in the equation for cognitive anxiety, however ES and TAS were the best predictor variables for somatic anxiety and self confidence. These results suggest that cognitive anxiety is linked to the intellectual perceptions of ability while somatic anxiety and self confidence are related to underlying drives and resultant emotions.

The failure of the SSS scores to be significantly changed by the experience of the expedition supports the notion that sensation seeking is a genetically based personality factor (FULKER, EYSENCK and ZUCKERMAN, 1980). This is further supported by the TAS and ES results but not the BS scores. It is difficult to explain why the BS results should have shown a significant decrease and this change may merely be a reflection of the relatively low reliability of this sub-scale (ZUCKERMAN, 1971).

The pre- to post-expedition results pertaining to PC scores provides empirical evidence for BANDURA's (1977) claim that successful completion of a threatening task can be used to increase PC. Post hoc interviews, however, suggested that this is only possible with low sensation seekers if goals are not set too high and tasks are graded so that they can opt for experiences that do not exceed their TAS levels or that are not perceived as too demanding. Low sensation seeking subjects stated that they needed a great deal of assurance from the instructors during tasks that they perceived as technically demanding and tasks which were not technically demanding but in which state anxiety was likely to be high due to environmental factors, e.g. caving. A number of subjects stated that they would have opted out of undertaking such tasks, had they not had faith in the ability of the instructors.

Increases in PE from pre- to post-expedition undoubtedly resulted to some extent from increases in PC thus supporting BANDURA (1977). The interviews, however, showed that other factors affected PE, particularly group cohesion, this was especially so for low sensation seekers, many of whom looked upon undertaking the activities as an onerous burden but worth the effort in order to enjoy the affiliation with other members of the group.

To summarise, the results of this experiment demonstrated an interrelationship between sensation seeking, PC and PE, however, the relationship appears to have been mostly due to the individuals', scores on the TAS sub-scale of the SSS. PE appears to be related more to PC than to sensation seeking although the desire for TAS may be a predictor of PE. PCAV was the best predictor of cognitive anxiety but somatic anxiety and self confidence were best predicted by TAS and ES, suggesting that inner drives may affect these factors more than intellectualisation about ability. Furthermore, it was shown that an increase in PC does not necessarily lead to a desire to repeat the experience.

5. References

BALL, J.; FARNILL, D.; WANGEMAN, J.F.: Sex and age differences in sensation seeking: some national comparisons. British Journal of Psychology, 1984 75, 257-265.

BANDURA, A.: Self-efficacy: towards a unifying theory of behavioural change. Psychological Review, 1977, 84, 191-215.

FULKER, D.W.; EYSENCK, S.B.G.; ZUCKERMAN, H.: A genetic and environmental analysis of sensation seeking. Journal of Research in Personality, 1990, 14, 261-281.

HEYMAN, S.R.; ROSE, K.G.: Psychological variables affecting scuba performance. In: C.H. NADEAU; W.R. HELLIWELL; K.M. NEWELL; G.C. ROBERTS (Eds.): Psychology of Motor Behavior and Sport-1979, Human Kinetics, Champaign, ILL, 1980, 180-188.

MARTENS, R.; BURTON, D.; VEALEY, R.S.; BUMP, L.; SMITH, D.E.: Development and validation of the Competitive State Anxiety

Inventory-2. In: R. MARTENS; R.S. VEALEY; D. BURTON (Eds.): Competitive Anxiety in Sport, Human Kinetics, Champaign, ILL, 1983, 117-190.

NICHOLLS, J.G.: Achievement motivation: conceptions of ability, subjects experience, task choice and performance. In: Psychological Review, 1984, 3, 328-346.

ROBERTS, G.C.: Towards a new theory of motivation in sport: the role of perceived ability. In: J.M. SILVA; R.S. WEINBERG (Eds.): Psychological Foundations of Sport, Human Kinetics, Champaign, ILL, 1984, 214-288.

ROWLAND, G.L.; FRANKEN, R.E.; HARRISON, K.: Sensation seeking and participation in sporting activities. In: Journal of Sports Psychology, 1986, 8, 212-220.

STRAUB, W.F.: Sensation seeking amongst high and low risk male athletes. In: Journal of Sports Psychology, 1982, 4, 246-253.

WANKEL, L.; SEFTON, T.M.: A season long investigation of fun in youth sports. In: Journal of Sport and Exercise Psychology, 1989, 11, 355-366.

ZUCKERMAN, M.: Dimensions in sensation seeking. In: Journal of Consulting and Clinical Psychology, 1971, 36, 45-52.

ZUCKERMAN, M.: Sensation Seeking: Beyond The Optimal Level of Arousal, Erlbaum, Hillside, NJ 1979.

ZUCKERMAN, M.: Sensation seeking in sports. Personality and Individual Differences, 1983, 4, 285-292.

6. Competitive Sport

Winfried Joch

Imitation, Continuity or a New Conception of the Talent-Promotion in Germany

The talent issue became the focus of attention in sport many years ago. Each person involved knows that the prospect of competitive sport and the international development of performance in sports is governed considerably by the way talent questions are treated e. g. which programme gains acceptance for the promotion of talents in order to grant them an optimal chance of development. The quest of talent-promotion and the way it is treated is very much connected to the chance of survival of competitive sport. Failures are almost irreversible.

Naturally, the fascination of these talent-issues was soon recognized and accordingly, sport-science took a critical look at many different areas of talent:
"There is an immense attraction in the quest for talent (what is this?), in the optimal search strategy (does anything like this exist?), and in the standardized plan of promotion (is that really desirable?); and accordingly the scientific observation of talent-projects seems to suggest itself more than anything else" (HAGEDORN/JOCH/ STARISCHKA, 1989, 7).

1. About the General Difficult Situation in Germany

In 1968 the first boarding schools were founded in "West"-Germany, aimed to carry out a systematic talent-promotion. And up to the end of the 80's, there was a whole host of those separate activities, which were linked with the BAL (German Association of Peak Performance), the sport federations, the regional sport association, some ministries of education and art, and several local institutions. But the outcome and the success was rather low. Therefore, the BAL representatives summarized: *"The entire German sport-system still shows (...) big structural deficits and a lack of content, in reference to the search for talents"* (FRIEDRICH/HOLZ, 1989/5, 6). Accordingly a completely new conception of the talent-promotion was announced.

When in 1990 with the German reunification the successful GDR sport-system was dissolved, the suggestion was made to integrate these positive experiences into the "West"-German-system. Especially in the field of junior training, the GDR success was indisputable and over many years the secret model of "West"-German sport managers. But the structure of both German systems proved on the one hand to be established too deeply and on the other hand to be too different from each other, so that an integration was only carried out in arduous tiny steps, neglecting essential elements of the GDR-system accordingly. These endeavours of integration were overshadowed by the continuous doping discussion, which discredited the GDR system insistently and was used as a preferable object of criticism.

In addition most of the GDR coaches, the main guarantors of success, could be kept only occasionally in the preferably honorary system of the "West"-German sport.

In the question of talent-promotion, the German sport is confronted with the alternative either to accept the recipe of success or - if this was possible - only those parts which formerly safeguarded the success but which were not politically indoctrinated. But the recently united German sport may maintain the "West"-models. Or a new one could be worked out, which would be an entirely new conception based on empirical knowledge and scientific recognitions which were gained over the last 30 years.

2. The Canon of Concurring Realizations

The comparatively long and continuous research, more or less coordinated with coaches and practical basic conditions in the different kinds of sport and their associations, has lead to a series of realizations and agreements which are hardly questioned concerning their relevance for talent-promotion. Five of the most important issues are discussed below:

2.1 The Relevance of Training

Talent development is a dynamic process which becomes prominent in training. Talented persons are recognized in training and are usually neither traced through single diagnostic methods - tests or sightings - nor exclusively recruited through the regional competitive system. Training is constitutive for talent-promotion.

In a different wording: *"Sportive talent and training are inseparably connected with each other and are mutually dependent. Sportive talent develops only in a determined and effective training"* (THIESS 1989/5, 11).

2.2 Versatility as a Foundation

Versatility is one of the general accepted and undisputable condition of junior training and talent-promotion. Accordingly it is hardly questioned "that in the training for beginners concerning children and juniors there should be an emphasize on versatility in the sport specific process, methodically as well as with regard to content" (THIESS, 1991, 5-9). But this versatility is not valid without exceptions; rather is the emphasis on the intentional side of the process, therefore aimed at the achievement of a high sportive performance by the talented person at the end of the longterm and systematic training. This "intentional versatility" (JOCH, 1992, 67-70) comprises as a foundation of talent-promotion the methodical abundance of variation and a selection out of the nearly unlimited supply of possible movements as well as their careful study. It is not essential to learn everything - as a kind of multi-talent - but rather to acquire those things which are important and indispensable for the intented aim.

2.3 Training as a Long Term Process

The process of training concerning the talent-promotion is characterized by a gradual adaptation which is additionally reinforced by continuity and performance. The duration of this process is the condition for process in the required progression - the progression of strain, the performance capability and development - which should be stable, sufficiently prepared and in no way a real test to the organism.

- Training within the framework of talent-promotion is considered to be a process of learning: Experiences should be gathered and digested which refers to biological-adaptive processes as well as to psychological and social processes. The childlike need for a change of situations, for new impressions and mobility/agility has to be gradually introduced in the learning process, which should always be directed at the intended object - the achievement of a high sporting standard. If this should happen in a responsible way, it has to be a gradual and an individual way of learning.
- The feature of gradual processes has a special meaning for the intensification of training demands and the physical-motor endurance parameter. Without the gradual intensification of training-demands and their timely and systematic preparation, it is very likely that the entire organism gets overworked which sooner or later effects negatively the performance development.

- Especially during the initial stages of talent-promotion and the first phases in which promotion measures are taken, there can arouse a danger caused by the accelerated demands: talented children are very often in a high starting position concerning their motor acitivity in comparison to other children of the same age. In addition they usually improve these abilities much faster which results in their being very soon on a very high level, a level which had not been prepared and stabilized systematically and continuously. Trainer sometimes feel tempted to accelerate their training even more being with that no longer careful and thorough. This will inevitably result in neglecting the principle of gradual processes. The training programmes are consequently treated in double-quick time and sometimes important phases are missed out.

2.4 Exceptional Performance

Those children who should be supported in their sportive talent do need to be interested and to have a certain inclination to exert a special performance. In the research of general talent, these aspects receive major consideration and therefore they also receive adequate attention in recognizing sportive talents:

1. *"The child shows very clearly an exceptional inclination in managing certain tasks.*
2. *The child manages the task with a certain kind of fondness and with no trouble at all. Doing so it shows an interest and willingness to perform with even better results.*
3. *Talent is developed in early years, being very much influenced by education and promotion of their surroundings"* (MICHEL/NOVAK, 1983, 43-44).

Consequently, it becomes most important "to make out those children who have decisive personal qualification at their disposal" and are capable of development to promote them and to enable them to sportive performances" - (THIESS, 1989, 11). This claim covers three main aspects: finding - promoting - qualifying.

2.5 Regularity and Development

With that the most important issue of the relation between regularity and development is mentioned. It should be taken into account that the development of sportive talents is determined by an area of conflict, constituted by the long-term and continuous preparation, based on a planned and systematic training on the one hand, and by spontaneity, coincidences and unpredictability on the other. The talent issue should not be considered as a mono-causal chain consisting of the mere regulations of in- and output. It is rather characterized to a high degree by the criteria of relative originality and non-linear dynamic processes. Therefore, the course of talent-development is not very often predictable.

3. Difficulties in Realization

The German sport-system has three basic areas of talent promotion at its disposal. But each of them has to work under the restrictions of institutionalized basic conditions.

3.1 The sport-club: they are responsible for the self-organized and independent sport and they arrange competitions. Thus they control - based only on the general agreements of the regional associations - the general promotion of achievements and with that become responsible for the talent-promotion. Even if some measures of promotion occure at first outside of their area of responsibility, sooner or later the agreement of these local sport clubs is needed.

But these sport clubs have considerable difficulties in coping with the tasks of talent promotion: depending on honorary support, forced to calculate with a high degree of fluctuation, provided only with very modest financial capacities, and in the great majority more or less orientated on an average (national) rather than on an international level of performance, they do not have the required resources to take on the "burden" of talent-promotion on their own.

3.2 Supporting units: In the late 60's, the German sport association developed a supplementary supporting unit which has resulted so far in the "Olympic-base-system". This system comprises full-time offices and scientific and social support which are synchronized with the club activities. They are mainly designed to support the club in those situations, where these are no longer able to maintain an optimal chance of promotion. This system obviously offers lots of different advantages but cannot deny several major disadvantages, such as in the lack of variety of interests and developing possibilities, the isolation of the children in sport "ghettos" away from their familiar environment.

3.3 Especially those people who tried to justify a talent-promotion in an educational context have recommended schools and with that school sport as the main place for talent-promotion. A real success however was hardly tracable. And recent experiences from the former GDR-system displays very effectively which way to go, if you really want to be successful: isolation of the best, specialisation of coaches and trainers, scientific approaches based on a long-term continuity. The "West"-German schools were in no way able to fulfill those criterias. Nevertheless, does the demand for school-sport as one component in talent-promotion remain justifiable. Accordingly, a central question arises out of these reflections: Each institution which has recently been involved with talent-promotion was able to provide a definite solution without any major disadvantages. To display and to assess these issues it is helpfull to draw up a list of standards, based on recent recognitions about talent-promotion. These should always form a foundation if you try to maintain a human competitive sport. This list is mainly orientated at the problems of development.

4. Development as a Model

Talent-promotion is a process of development; it follows general principles of development.

4.1 The Issue of Scope and Its Restrictions

According to OERTER development is a process "nearly without any limitations." For talent-promotion the amount of scope results on the one hand out of the mutual dependence of motor-activities, coordinative capabilities and motor skills (JOCH, 1988, 15-18), and on the other hand out of the connection of these qualities with other areas of personality, such as recognition, intelligence, motivation and the somatic-dimensions (GUILFORD, 1964). And as it is impossible to detect talented people with any degree of certainty, and the developing processes are by no means compatible to the conditions of adults, it becomes obvious that there is a definite need for special strategies, which should put great store to the individual changes and developments without interfering too much with them. Such a theory can be described as "growing without interference".

This theory has a long tradition in education. It is based on inert capacities and defines interventions generally as designed only to keep away negative influences. The process of self-development is considered to be most important. The talent will find its own way to develop - just like a plant which extracts the essential substances from its surrounding.

Educationalists can only support these inert processes of nature; and they will do that most effectively in avoiding any unnecessary interference. Consequently if talent-promotion takes this theory into consideration it should believe and trust in inert capacities and accordingly try to avoid any adaptive processes and influences from outside. If for example street football is considered as one pool for football players the idea behind that statement is definetely related to the theory of "growing without interference". Finally, talent will find its way, inspite of various different influences.

But there certainly exist a quite different point of view concerning these matters. A quite contrary view assumes that every scope of development has to be restricted radically in order to form people in the required way. The former GDR system has practiced this in political and in social matters. Therefore, sport (and with that talent-promotion) as well as nursing homes, schools and sport associations were used as one constituent of the monopolitical system. Only actual results were of importance and personal aims in life of athletes, coaches and teachers were not considered at all. In reference to the actual sporting reality this meant a reduction of scope and was noticeable in strict, standardised training plans, the procedure of selection and the way days, months and years were organized. Everything was planned towards only one target: success. Although there were maybe some exceptions to the rule, this idea was usually pursued with a high degree of perfection and control. Today talent-promotion has to find a "third" way in order to establish a more suitable conception out of these extremes.

4.2 Integration and Social Basic Conditions

Decisions concerning such a third way always depend on whether the promotion of talents are accepted as a main part of social basic conditions. The development of the (sporting) individual is very much connected to the personal social environment, into which extend the society is able or willing to support and appreciate these talents. So there definitely is a strong relation between talents and society; or to put it in a more provocative phrase: each society has adequate talents, but these are only perceptible, if the society wants to afford and support them.

Values which depend on the social environment manifest themselves in the moral concept of the people, who are part of this environment. If these moral concepts interfere with requirements of a sporting career, this will effect inevitably the general sporting standard. So if "ghettos" of a sporting mono-culture - where success is made possible through systematic training - are not in accordance with the general values of the society, this has an effect on the exploitation of the entire "pool" of talents. The following list represents a few demands which are a result of these reflections:

- sport schools under the premise of isolation are not adequate
- the appropriate amount of time for training should always stand in a reasonable relation to other activities
- teachers and coaches who are in charge of talented people, should consider their job as one aspect of organizing one's life, rather as the only possible way.

The basic condition, standards and values which are characteristic of a free society should be the foundation of talent-promotion in Germany.

4.3 Variable Conditions of Performance

The scepticism towards the achievement of young people as a criterion for talent diagnostic is very reasonable. This scepticism is mainly based on the principle that sporting performance is considered as a developing process in dependence on condition and perspective. That means there is by no means such a thing as a stable and universal condition of performance. (THIESS, 1989/5, 110). The aspect of improvement of performance and the development in general, should stand in the centre of interest in the discussion of talent issues, rather than the mere registration of temporary results.

Two main topics are relevant in this respect: The capacity of adaptation and progression:
- the capacity of adaptation refers mainly to the biological system and the way it reacts and adapts to exercise
- the capacity of progression deals with the problem of how far it is possible to optimize the capacity of performance of individual (motor) features in their relation to the complex sporting performance.

Therefore, talent-promotion is designed to look ahead. It is always important to build on the basis of present conditions in order to prepare the appropriate and individual prospects. During the preparation you should not do anything which might interfere with future targets.

5. Summary

Talent promotion is not tied to any specific institution. Its effectiveness depends to a high degree on the competence with which the talent-training is carried out: a competence which is based on the assumption that goals from the distant future take priority, rather than present achievements. Three aspects should be considered in the realization of such a training:

- measures obtain their specific qualities, their meaning and their practical effect only in connection with the particular aspect of promotion. Exclusively within the concrete measures it becomes possible to detect the talent. The most important measure is training.

- promotion in its entirety: talent-promotion does not exclusively refer to the development of sporting capacities, but should be extended to personal development as well. One necessary condition for that is certainly the actual sporting performance, together with areas like intelligence, motivation, perceptive facultaties, somatic dimensions, needs and attitudes.

- the (sporting) talent can function as an important consolidation of social norms and standards, in so far as socialisation and social standards are basic features of the talent-promoting process. The effectiveness of the promotion is very much influenced by its degree of compatibility concerning values and norms of the prevailing form of society. But on the other hand it is very much characteristic for a society how resources are treated and what is done to support and develop these.

References

FRIEDRICH, E.; HOLZ, P.: Ein Konzept zur Talentförderung im bundesdeutschen Leistungssport. Leistungssport, 1989, 5, 5-10.

GUILFORD, J.P.: Persönlichkeit. Beltz, Weinheim 1964.

HAGEDORN, G.; JOCH, W.; STARISCHKA, S.: Sportwissenschaft und Sportpraxis. In: Kultusminister NRW (ed.): Talentsuche und Talentförderung. Ritterbach, Frechen, 1989, 7.

ISRAEL, S.: Die bewegungsbedingte körperliche Adaption als biotisches Prinzip. Theorie und Praxis der Körperkultur 2, 1988, 86-94.

JOCH, W.: Das sportliche Talent. Meyer & Meyer, Aachen 1992.

MARTIN, D.: Zur sportlichen Leistungsfähigkeit von Kindern. Sportwissenschaft, 1982, 3, 255-274.

MICHEL, G.; NOVAK, F.: Stichwort "Begabung". In: Kleines psychologisches Wörterbuch, 8 ed. Herder, Freiburg 1983.

OERTER, R.: Moderne Entwicklungspsychologie. 12 ed. Ludwig Auer, Donauwörth 1973.

THIEß, G.: Die Auswahl sportlicher Talente in der DDR. Leistungssport, 1989, 5, 11-14.

THIEß, G.: Allgemeine Regeln für die effektive Gestaltung des Anfängertrainings von Kindern und Jugendlichen. Leistungssport, 1991, 5, 9-11.

Carlyn Zaniboni

Elite High School Students and P.E.: A Case Study

Our problem was to introduce and evaluate a Human Movement program established and implemented within a unique educational setting. The program, in its initial year, was implemented at Boston University Academy and served Year 9 -10 students.

MERCURIO, LAMBERT and OESTERLE, in an attempt to answer the question of educating our country's youth, stress that an "important aspect of school-college relations is providing college-level academic experiences for talented high school youth." (1983, 74). Boston University Academy attempts to do just that. Boston University Academy was founded in the Fall of 1993 and serves as a private high school for motivated students grades 9-12. The Academy is located on Boston University's campus and utilizes much of the University's facilities and resources.

The Academy was founded on many principles and is structured to nurture and inspire motivated students with a passion for learning. The classics-based curriculum employs an integrated approach and exposes the students to many facets of education while connecting various disciplines. Human Movement and the physical education program are integral and essential parts of this holistic curriculum and this factor was not just talk, as it so often turns out to be.

The structure of the Academy is unique in relation to other private high schools. In their fourth year, the status of the students makes them both seniors at the Academy, and freshmen at Boston University. Should they decide to attend another university, they will enter that university with advanced freshman standing. This approach seeks to eliminate the wasteful spring semester that many high school seniors experience after they've already been accepted to a University and before they finish their senior year. The Academy's program intends to facilitate motivated learners with directional ambition and utilize this potentially wasted semester. GREENBERG (1982) addresses this need for more high school-college collaboration, and the "apparent readiness of significant numbers of high school undergraduates to handle the rigors of college-level study," he also notes that "many areas of curricular redundancy in the last two years of high school and the first two years of college" move secondary schools towards collaborative programs (1982, 79).

Research reveals a number of collaborative efforts between high schools and colleges in the U.S.A. One program seeks to bridge high school students into further collegian academic endeavors. The Advanced Placement Program developed in the 1950s, renders examinations, which if passed, give students credit for college-level courses and also exempt them from some prerequisites. Kenyon College offers a "School-College Articulation Program that provides high school students courses at their high schools which can be transferred towards college credit at Kenyon." (WATKINS, 1983, 14.). Kenyon will also send a transcript of completed course-work if the student chooses to attend another school (WATKINS, 1983).

Many other universities offer summer courses and extended courses to help high school students achieve, yet perhaps the two programs which resemble that of Boston University Academy, have been implemented at Seattle University and the University of California at Berkeley. Seattle University in cooperation with Seattle Preparatory school created the Matteo Ricci College which enables students to earn a high school diploma and a college degree through a six year plan. They spend three high school years on the preparatory campus and three on the University's campus. At the University of California-Berkeley, nominated high school seniors are allowed to take two courses per semester at the university which will count towards a university degree at Berkeley or be transferred to another college/university (WATKINS, 1983). These programs, and that of Boston University Academy all seek and cater to the motivated student within the actual university setting. Therefore, planning and implementing a physical education curriculum within the university environment and for a special population of students became an unusual, yet welcomed, task.

The Human Movement program was designed to serve these unique students. The philosophy, structure, and implementation of this program compliments the integrated curriculum approach of the Academy and is supported by the founders and faculty. Faculty and administrative support enhances the program's success and illustrates a facilitating bridge between the traditional subjects and the physical education curriculum.

During the initial stages of development, Academy administrators conferred with University coaches and activity/skills course instructors. Failing to find what they wanted in a physical education program, they sought the professionals within the Human Movement Program at Boston University's School of Education. The Human Movement Chairman, Dr. John CHEFFERS, advised the founders on an innovative program and its structure. It was decided that a part-time director would be needed to teach and oversee the two day a week program. Mr. David STONE was hired and then an assistant, Carlyn ZANIBONI, was added. The two, both graduates of Boston University, entered the program with exuberance and unrelenting dedication. They believed whole-heartedly in the success of the program and worked long hours with little pay. Their efforts in conjunction with cooperation from many University representatives resulted in preliminary recognition, support and success.

This study addresses the following questions; Is physical education needed by elite highly intelligent individuals? How do you structure a human movement program within a classics-based curriculum? What methodology was employed to evaluate the program, and what were the results?

Method

The subjects included all 36 of the Academy students. They were 13-15 year olds participating in a physical education program which occurred twice a week on Wednesdays and Friday afternoons from approximately 1:30-3:15 p.m.

The methodology included both qualitative and some quantitative research. The two physical educators participated in every class and unit. CHEFFERS Adaptation of Flanders Interaction Analysis (CAFIAS) was used quantitatively, as an observational tool for several units and activities (CHEFFERS, MANCINI, and MARTINEK, 1980). Data regarding a stress lecture, a crew lesson, and a sailing unit was collected to observe the interactions between instructor and students as well as analyze and evaluate student participation and involvement. The involvement of students was measured with Individual Reaction Gestalt- Version III (IRGIII) (CHEFFERS and CROWLEY-SULLIVAN, 1990), an instrument that describes involvement, emotional inferences, and violence. It is used in group and individual activity.

Qualitative procedures for evaluation included student fitness and nutrition diaries or journals and interviews with Academy faculty and administrators. As part of the curriculum, students were required to maintain fitness and nutrition journals in which they provided tangible reflection and feedback to the two human movement educators.
The guidelines students used were as follows:

1. All handouts given to you in class are to go into the diary.
2. All materials and journal entries having to do with the same unit, are to be kept together in chronological order.
3. You must make an entry in the diary every Wednesday and Friday, commenting on the day's activity and experience.

Questions and requirements for the entries included:

(a) What new knowledge did you gain today? Cite at least two examples.
(b) What did you feel was the most interesting or fun part of today's activity? Try to be specific.
(c) Are there any areas of the present activity not being taught that you would like to learn?
(d) Please use the rest of the blank space to comment.

The educators collected and commented on the entries approximately every three to four weeks. Entries were assessed on a one to three scale. The two teachers acknowledged detailed feedback, constructive comments, and general organization as evaluative criteria.

A second qualitative method of informal interviewing was employed to attain reflection and initial evaluation by Academy faculty and administrators. Three people were interviewed. One was the Director of Admissions and Student activities, the other was the Headmaster of the Academy and a Vice-President of Boston University, while the third was a Physics teacher and newly-appointed Administrative Dean. All three were asked the same open-ended questions and given opportunity to reflect openly on various components of the program. Samples of the questions can be found in Figure 1.

Methodology

Questions Asked During Informal Interview

1) As (Academy position held), what do you think of the human movement/physical education program here at Boston University Academy (B.U.A.)?

2) A great deal of controversy surrounds the purpose of human movement and physical education in schools, do you see a purpose for it at B.U.A.?

3) What kind of changes do you see in the students before and after P.E.? Through your interactions, do you hear students reflecting on the human movement program?

4) What aspects of the B.U.A. human movement program do you find unique? Does this program contrast or run parallel to your own personal physical education experiences?

5) Agassiz Village is an integral part of the human movement program, can you see why?

6) What changes would you make in the human movement program?

7) Do you think the integration of human movement across other disciplines would enhance the quality of physical education at B.U.A.?

8) What would Boston University Academy be like without the human movement program?

Figure 1. Questions asked during interviews

Curriculum Design

Prior to developing the curriculum, Academy students answered a questionnaire regarding previous physical education experiences. They were asked which activities they enjoyed and which activities they would like to see as part of their Academy physical education curriculum. Results from the questionnaire and valuable input from Boston University professors led to the development of a comprehensive curriculum.

The curriculum centers around five organizing centers, the Agassiz Village-Residential field experience, the fitness and nutrition journals, and the two day a week, extended period/class structure. The five organizing centers were developed by Dr. John CHEFFERS and the two physical educators (see Figure 2.).

Figure 2. Human Movement Curriculum Organizing Centers

A variety of curriculum units resulted from and formulated around the students' interests and the five organizing centers. For example, the Heart, Lung, Health, and Nutrition center was addressed through a weight training unit and other cardiovascular fitness activities. The following activities resulted from each center:

1. **Heart, Lung, Health and Nutrition (HLH)** - Weight Training, Power Walking, Stress Management Lecture, Nutritional Intake Records and Evaluation, and Cardiovascular activities.

2. **New and Traditional Games** - Soccer, Ultimate Frisbee, Basketball, New Games, Softball, Water Polo, and Volleyball.
3. **Integration of Movement with Academic Subjects** - Physics and Sailing, Nutrition and Physiology, and the Agassiz Village Residential Field experience.
4. **Life Long Sports and Extra School Activities** - Sailing, Crew, Ice-Skating, Swimming, Self-defense/Tae Kwon Do and Skiing.
5. **Intramural and Extra mural Sports** - Flag football, Basketball, Volleyball, and Interscholastic Scrimmages.

A description of the curriculum would not be complete without an explanation of the Agassiz Village Residential Field Experience and its curriculum developed by Dr. John CHEFFERS, and implemented by the Human Movement Department at Boston University's School of Education.

Dr. John CHEFFERS explains the Agassiz experience as actually a school, away from school, with a difference. The program has four major themes and is composed of approximately eight activities. The students travel to northern Maine, about 3 hours from Boston and stay at a camp called Agassiz. Agassiz has cabins, a dining hall, various recreation halls, tennis/basketball courts, and it situated overlooking an aesthetic and beautiful lake. The program has an academic emphasis and integrates academic skill with movement experiences. There is a focus on group activities including non-competitive teams/games with a demand for cooperative work and approaches. Agassiz Village also promotes an environmental emphasis with an appreciation of nature as well as it's relevance to the student's lives. Lastly, an adventure component guides activities which increase self-concept, self-confidence, and problem solving abilities. The actual activities include: orienteering, adventure, archery, drama, night adventure, creative dance, new games, and environmental sensitivity (CHEFFERS, 1994).

Results-Interviews and Diaries

Student Evaluation of the Program

The students liked it! There is a very positive outlook on human movement and physical education. The following excerpts were taken from student's journals to illustrate the programs initial success. The journals act as tangible tools to monitor progress for both the teacher and student. They are organized in reference to the five organizing centers.

Life Long Sports and Extra School Activities

Susan* reflects on her experiences in crew:

"Today was a lot of fun. We went out on the barge. I realized that the only way you're going to get the thing to move is if you all pull together. The other thing that I learned is that we had a hard time working together, because everyone was at a different level....I think that actually rowing was the most fun thing about today."

Jake* reflects on the skating unit:

"Today was a very interesting day, the reason I say this is because I actually skated backwards decently. I am far from Bobby Orr, but it certainly was an improvement that I actually moved this time....it was a lot of fun actually being a decent skater, as I discovered that one tends to enjoy things more when one is good at them. Now if I could just learn how to stop....."

The students were asked to individually reflect on the Agassiz Village experience on a separate piece of paper. They were asked to give general feedback, comments, and describe their feeling before, during, and after camp. They were also asked to include any

* * Fictitious Name

suggestions for improvement or changes in the curriculum at Agassiz Village. Here is what resulted:

"..The camp gave me a chance to learn more about my friends and fellow students. The food wasn't that great, but the rolls were good. I think we should go to the camp every year and help the new students."

"I must admit that when I first learned that we would be going to camp Agassiz I held the trip in contempt. I have never enjoyed camp, but I did have some fun at Agassiz and it was a worthwhile journey into the world of cooperation... My favorite activity was the night walk, it was just me and nature."
"I thought Agassiz Village was cool."

Intramural and Extra Mural Sports

Sarah reflects on intramural flag football:
"We played football after school, in the rain, Mr. Stone is right, its great!! Our team won, I really enjoyed today.

HLH-Heart, Lung, Health, and Nutrition

Christopher reflects on power walking:
"Today we did a power walk and I really enjoyed doing it. It was a good time to walk with my friends, and I was really surprised, too that I was able to do it. I wasn't even really tired in the end. In fact, I found it very refreshing... I never thought of walks like that as exercise never thought of it as something like a sport are there competitions in power walking?"

Reflection on the stress management lecture proved positive:
"Today was a little different, we had a stress lecture instead of regular gym. At first I was really upset, because I hate lectures. Dr. Yeager was great... He spoke about stress management and how we can deal with daily stress. He made us see and understand that if we didn't

know how to control and deal with our stress our **resistance** could break down making us sick... We did a couple of exercises which were fun and enlightening hope we have more stress management lectures."

New and Traditional Sports

Michael's entry on basketball reflects on this more traditional sport:
"Today I learned a number of things, and we did various drills such as dribbling, and passing which improved my skills. Also I learned how to play several games. Today's most enjoyable activity was playing the games. Though drills are helpful, games put them all together. Also my competitive nature makes me want to play games. This program is wonderful and does not need to be improved."

An entry on soccer from another Paul:
"Ah, the return of "warm-ups". Stretches are fine, but after a warm-up I'm ready to cool down! On the positive side, these warm-ups are much more worthwhile than simply running "the gym class loop" as I've done for the past five years... My team lost, but what's important is that I participated and I even made an "assist". I think this means that I kicked the ball to a teammate who then scored a goal. I don't believe I've done that before."

Integration of Movement with Academic Subjects

General journal reflections on the entire human movement curriculum and reflections concerning the integration of P.E. with other subject areas included:

"... It added a sense of purpose to the activity, I hope to enjoy physical education even more as we begin a new crew unit next week."

"..Compared to past years, gym was a lot of fun ... this year with an extended period, it is really helpful. It allows us to play a full game and learn the rules to it.... another great thing was that we tried a great variety of activities, I don't think I played one activity that I disliked."

Faculty Evaluation of the Program

The student journals were one form of qualitative data collected, the others included the informal interviews mentioned before. Answers to the questions included:

Question One:
"B.U.A. is a different kind of school. We encourage our students to explore. The human movement program gives then a chance to do physical activities that they would not normally have an opportunity to do."

"This is the first time someone has designed a physical education program that has lasting benefits for kids as they grow older and enter adult life."

Question Two:
"Yes, absolutely, it is easy in a strongly emphasized academic school to ignore this subject, yet students need to realize that exercising their brain is not the only important thing in life. Cooperative learning helps them in their academic endeavors as well."

"Extremely important that they learn at an early age that the body requires exercise and typically most of them had little interest in P.E., but now most of them have found it enjoyable and valuable."

Question Three:
"The kids love it!"

Question Four:
"Experiences, no, Philosophy, yes. I went to a private high school where we had to play three competitive sports a year and it generated a 'you are good, you are bad' attitude. I began to think 'I am not a sports person' .Yet this program gives them a chance to sample so many different sports in an environment that allows them to experiment without pressure."

"It is completely different from my own P.E. experiences, mine were standard traditional activities and this program incorporates more life long sports."

Question Five:
"Agassiz is a little 'Microcosm of Society' in which the darkest and brightest sides of students can be seen. Some kids desperately did not want to go and pleaded not to attend, yet I didn't talk to one single student who didn't enjoy it. I think one single notion was emphasized and that was to never let fear prevent you from trying something new whether you are good at it or not. You may find you like and enjoy it. I think it was good that I went because the students see the faculty members as humans. I liked the fostering and explorative attitude. There is nothing more liberating than conquering fear."

"I don't know all the details because I didn't go to the camp, but it brought them all together like even a year didn't do."

"30 % did not want to go. 100 % want to return."

Question Six:
"Aside from easier access to facilities I wouldn't change anything except for maybe the addition of some extra mural and competitive interscholastic sports."

Question Seven:
"Yes, I like the idea that you relate P.E. to Physics and other academics."

"I think the integration is very important because it runs parallel to the style of teaching we have here at B.U.A., the hands on activities that are related to other events and the relation of academics to world events."

"Some of the students were talking about Agassiz and telling me that 'there's good physics up there."

Question Eight:
"For some it is the best part of the whole week. The fun component. The students would be a lot more lethargic and the P.E. program may be the only exercise they get."

"The human movement program is as innovative as any of our other academic programs, with out it, it would be a culture shock."
"Without it, the B.U.A. would offer a less rich program. People might think it is just a group of brainy nerds instead of a school with a very interesting human movement program in which students are taught to exercise in every facet of their lives. Academic and Physical."

Results Systematic Observation

CAFIAS-(Teacher-Student Interactions and Interaction Patterns) SAILING

Interaction patterns showed that one third of the lesson was teacher-information giving (5-5) which led to extended teacher direction giving (6-6) and then predictable student responses (6-8). Sometimes, the questions asked generated responses with interpretation (4-8).

The teacher contribution was higher and the student contribution was lower than national norms (72 % and 27 % respectively). The content was teacher oriented at 55 %. The student initiation ratios (24 %) and the teacher's use of questions/acceptance was low (18 %). The teacher was the sole teaching agency and the data was collected during one whole session.

Crew

Three distinct interaction patterns resulted from crew:

1) (5-5) - One third of the lesson was given through extended teacher information giving.
2) (6-6-8-8) - The teacher gave long directions followed by extended student rote functioning.
3) (9-9) - This pattern showed some extended student activity.

The teacher and student contributions differed from national norms (58 % and 41 % respectively) in that there was more student contribution than normal. The teachers interest on content (42 %) was normal. All other rations were low. The class structure was whole with the teacher as the sole teaching agent.

Individual Reaction Gestalt III-(Student Involvement)

Stress Management Lecture

The Individual Reaction Gestalt III (IRG III) showed that student involvement in the lecture was high with a great deal of controlled emotions. The IRG III observer system also illustrated some group work.

Discussion

This study shows the importance and the necessity of a human movement program at Boston University Academy. BEAUCHAMP, DARST, and THOMPSON state that a "quality program must also show evidence of student learning or achievement" (BEAUCHAMP, DARST, and THOMPSON, 1990, 92) The entries from the student's journals and other feedback illustrates their progress and their learning.

Faculty interviews also revealed general excitement and approval of the program. Willingness on the part of the faculty to accept the human movement program, and unrelenting support added to the initial success of the program.

The systematic observation data revealed some differences between the crew and sailing activities. Sailing has a narrower constriction than crew, however, they both contained a great deal of teacher direction, talk, and student predictable behavior. The nature of the two sports renders these findings understandable.

There is ghetto mentality surrounding many high school physical education programs in this country and, perhaps, world wide. This program and its success is intent on defeating this mentality. The organizing centers in which the exciting activities (sailing, crew, Agassiz village, etc.) are developed upon, act as a solid backbone for a fledging program of great promise.

Obviously, the Hawthorne effect has presented itself in this study. The newness and the preparation of the program contributed to its domino success. This action research illustrates that physical education programs can be not only popular, but effective.

References

BEAUCHAMP, L.; DARST, P.; THOMPSON, L.: Academic learning time as an indication of quality high school physical education. Journal of Physical Education, Recreation, and Dance, 1990, 61, 92-95.

CHEFFERS, J.: Agassiz village. Paper Available from Author. 1994.

CHEFFERS, J.; CROWLEY-SULLIVAN, E.: The Instruments of Involvement (Individual Reaction Gestalts Versions I, II, III, IV). Boston University Publishing 1990.

CHEFFERS, J.; MANCINI, V.; MARTINEK, T.: Interaction Analysis: An Application to Nonverbal and Verbal Activity. Association for Productive Teaching, 1980.

GREEN, J.: State academies for the academically gifted. Phi Delta Kappa Educational Foundation. University of Illinois 1993, 1-41.

GREENBERG, A.: High school/college articulated programs: pooling resources across the abyss. NASSP Bulletin, 1982, 66, 79-86.

MERCURIO, J.; LAMBERT, L.; OESTERLE, R.: College credit earned in high school: comparing student performance in project advance and advance placement. College and University, 1983, 59, 74-86.

RICE, P.: Attitudes of high school students toward physical education activities, teachers, and personal health Physical Educator, 1988, 45, 94-99.

WATKINS, B.: How some colleges and high schools are already cooperating. Chronicle of Higher Education, 1983, 7, 14.

Xiaolin Yang, Risto Telama, Lauri Laakso

Parental Influences on the Competitive Sports and Physical Activity of Young Finns - a 9-Year Follow-Up Study

Introduction

Existing research suggests that families, specifically the parents, play a significant role in socializing their children into sports and physical activities. These studies have indicated that parents, particularly fathers, have a large influence on their children's participation (GREENDORFER & LEWKO, 1978; SAGE, 1980). The influence of the parents can be explained in terms of social learning. The parents' positive attitude and social support have been generally acknowledged to have a direct bearing on the development of a child's self-esteem, social skills, and cognitive abilities. It has been noted that the parents' support has a positive connection with the pleasure and interest of the child in sports (WOOLGER & POWER, 1993) and with the leisure-time physical activity of young people (ANDERSSEN & WOLD, 1992), while the parents' negative attitude correlates negatively with the child's enjoyment of sport (OMUNDSSEN & VAGLUM, 1991; SCANLAN & LETHWAITE, 1988). Parents also provide their children with role models.

High expectations are one effective way in which parents can influence their chiidren's participation in sports and physical activities. Moderate expectations in the area of sport, which are in accordance with a child's perceived competence, positively affect a child's motivation, but too-high expectations can cause anxiety and distress for the child. Over-expectation is in danger of becoming oppressive and is likely to cause the child to drop out from sport (BRUSTAD, 1988; GOULD et al., 1982; ORLICK, 1974; SCANLAN &

LEWTHWHITE, 1988; ROBERTS & TREASURE, 1992) and may even result in burnout (FEIGLEY, 1987; SMITH, 1986). Because parents who are active in sports can provide active role models and their attitudes towards sport are positive, it may be supposed that they also have higher expectations concerning their children's sports participation. Therefore we suggest that the level of parents', particularly fathers' physical activity explains their children's participation in sports. Furthermore, parental expectations vary with the socioeconomic status of families. Parents from different social classes can have quite different attitudes towards the physical activity, and participation in sports of their children (COAKLEY, 1987; LAAKSO & TELAMA, 1978; 1981).

Although many recent studies have touched upon the dropout problems in competitive sport among young athletes, there is a lack of longitudinal studies. Also, until recently, little research has been concerned with the importance of parental influences for the continuity and development of sporting and physical activity from childhood to young adulthood. The present study, therefore, attempts to find out how the effect of parental background (e.g., physical activity and socio-economic status) influences children's habitual physical activity, as well as participation in or dropping out of sport; and how the parental influence predicts children's involvement in later physical activity.

Material and Methods

The material to be presented was drawn from the data base of the Cardiovascular Risk in Young Finns program, which has been implemented in Finland since 1980. There were 316 boys and 319 girls, a total of 635, in the 9-year-old age groups; 321 boys and 327 girls, a total of 648, in the 12-year-old age groups; 286 boys and 312 girls, a total of 598, in the 15-year-old age groups. The same subjects were surveyed in a 9-year follow-up study. In 1989 they were 18, 21 and 24 years of age respectively (Table 1).

Table 1 Numbers of subjects' responses to questions of physical activity by cohort, age and gender in a 9-year follow-up study

	Boys				Girls			
Measurement year	1980	1983	1986	1989	1980	1983	1986	1989
Cohort (Age in 1980)	N	N	N	N	N	N	N	N
1971 (9)	316	296	247	228	319	279	249	266
1968 (12)	321	256	187	200	327	293	236	263
1965 (15)	286	210	157	191	312	248	189	245

Physical activity and sport were measured by means of a short questionnaire. Questions concerned frequency of leisure-time physical activity, intensity of physical activity, amount of sports club training, participation in sports competitions, and habitual way of spending leisure time. The physical activity index (PAI), ranging from five to fourteen, was a sum of these five variables. The coefficient of internal consistency (Cronbach's alpha) was calculated for all age groups as an indicator of the reliability of the sum index. The coefficient varied from .44 to .76. (TELAMA et al., 1994; YANG, 1993).

Parents' physical activity was measured by a simple question: how much do they engage in physical activities? (1 = a little to 3 = regularly). In cross-tabulations, cases of no father were treated as a category of their own; and in correlations, as missing data. Father's socioeconomic status was coded into five categories (1 = high, 2 = medium, 3 = low, 4 = farmer and 5 = no father).

Results

The frequency of participation of children and adolescents in sports in three age cohorts is showed in Figure 1. Approximately 80 % of the boys and 65 % of the girls at the age of 9 and 12 were involved in physical activity twice a week or more. The highest values for participation in sports club training once a week were found in both boys and girls at 12 years of age. Comparisons between the three cohorts show that the proportion of boys and girls who participated in sports club training at 12 years of age had increased by about 10% from 1980 to 1983. Children's sports and physical activity decreased most from the age 12 to 15, and then the trend of the curve for the participants was similarly downwards in each cohort. Boys were more active in sports than girls during childhood. The percentage of physical activity in boys decreased continuously as age increased, while in girls it seemed to be relatively stable after the age of 15. At the ages of 21 and 24 women are more active than men.

Figure 1 see appendix

The fathers' physical activity was significantly related to physical activity index (PAI) of 9-year-old boys and girls, and gave a significant prediction of PAI values three, six and nine years later (Table 2). The mothers' physical activity had a significant, but very low correlation with girls' PAI values. Fathers' physical activity in 1980, when children were 9-year-olds, predicted children's physical activity in 1983 and 1986 as well as fathers' physical activity in 1983 and 1986.

Table 2 Correlation of parents' physical activity (P.A.) with children's physical activity index (PAI) by age and gender in follow-up (pairwise)

	Father's P.A.			Mother's P.A.		
Years	1980	1983	1986	1980	1983	1986
Boys' PAI (9 yrs.)						
1980	.19*			.09		
1983	.19**	.12		.01	.06	
1986	.28**	.19**	.27**	.13*	.12	.14*
1989	.30**	.18*	.21**	.05	.02	.07

(12 yrs.)						
1980	.23**			.15*		
1983	.17*	.13		.08	.10	
1986	.15	.14		.01	-.02	
1989	.12	-.03		.03	-.01	

	Father's P.A.[1]			Mother's P.A.		
	1980	1983	1986	1980	1983	1986[2]
Girls' PAI						
(9 yrs.)						
1980	.20**			.14*		
1983	.15*	.11		.15*	.09	
1986	.20**	.14*	.16*	.14*	.10	.11
1989	.23**	.16*	.12	.11	.15*	.14*
(12 yrs.)						
1980	.14*			.11*		
1983	.11	.12		.16*	.20*	
1986	.04	.13		.08	.14*	
1989	.06	.07		.10	.07	

[1] When calculating correlations, "no father" has been treated as missing data.
[2] Parents' physical activity was not measured in 1989.
* p<0.5, ** p<,01.

In order to see the influence of single parents (no father in the family), the means of PAI values were calculated in four groups (Figure 2, see appendix). Children of high-activity fathers were more likely to take part in habitual physical activity than those of low-activity fathers. Boys and girls who had a single parent were generally similar to those of low- or moderate-activity fathers.

Except in one case (12-year-old boys, medium/low status), there were no relationships between the fathers' socioeconomic status and their children's physical activity index (Figure 3, see appendix).

The children were divided, according to the three years' follow-up, into four categories: *Actives*, who participated in sports club activities at least once a week in both measurements; *Beginners*, who started to participate in sport after the first measurement; *Dropouts*, who dropped out of sport after the first measurement; and *Outsiders*, who did not participate in sport at all in both measurements. Children of active fathers were significantly and clearly more persistent in sport and less likely to drop out of sport than those of passive fathers (Figure 4). Interestingly, the proportion of active boys and girls with a single parent was found to be higher than that of those with passive fathers; or even with moderate-activity fathers, in the case of boys. Figure 5 showed that the influence of the mothers' physical activity was similar to that of the fathers', but there was no statistically significant differences between the groups among boys.

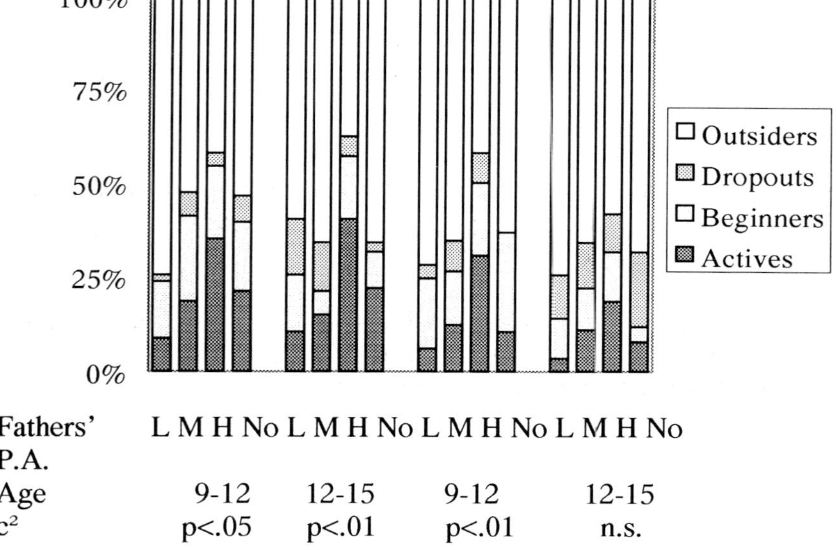

Figure 4 Percentages of children's participation in and dropping out of sport related to fathers' physical activity (P.A.) by age and gender in a 3-year follow-up study

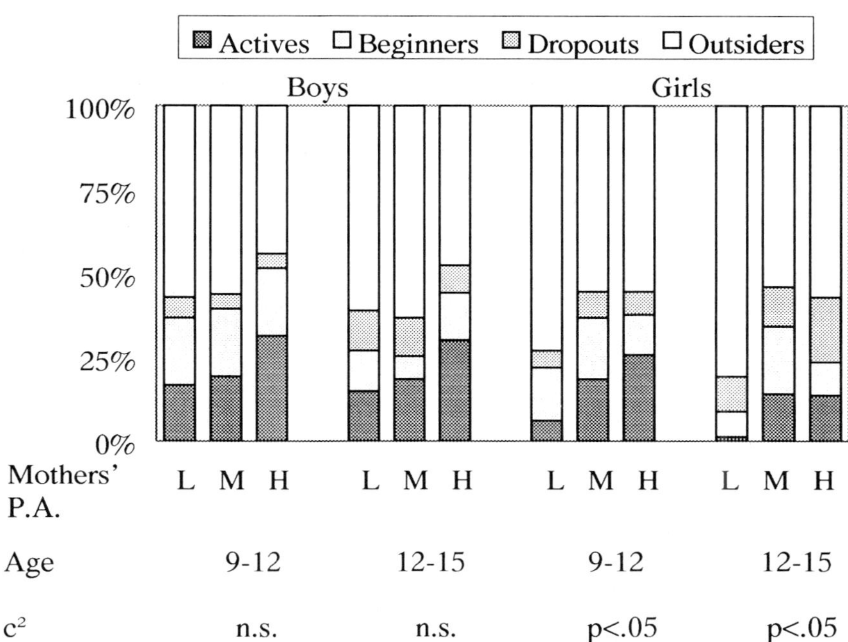

Figure 5 Percentages of children's participation in and dropping out of sport related to mothers' physical activity (P.A.) by age and gender in a 3-year follow-up study

Girls whose fathers belong to the highest status were much more likely to continue training than the girls in other groups, but no difference was found in the boys (Figure 6).

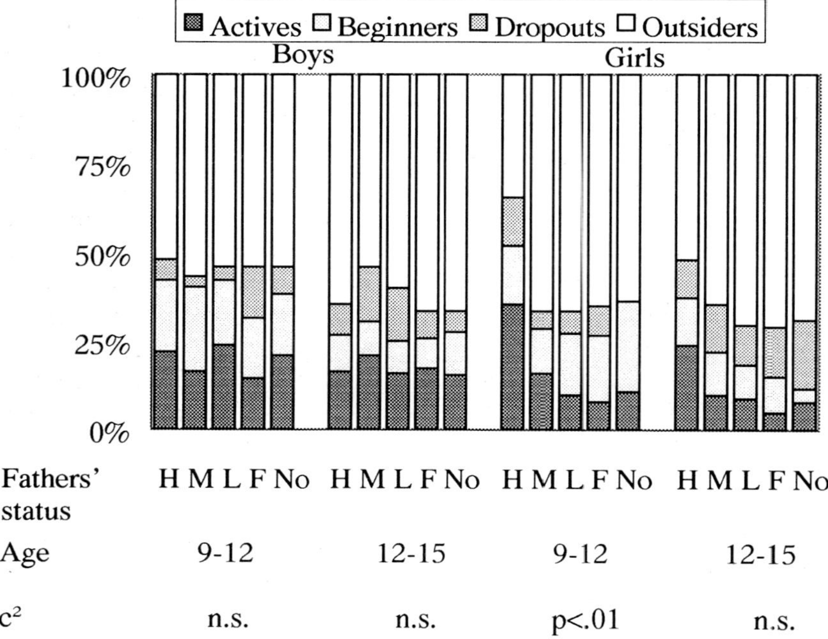

Figure 6 Percentages of children's participation in and dropping out of sport related to fathers' social status by age and gender in a 3-year follow-up study

Discussion

One explanation for the relationship between children's and parents' activity levels is role-modeling according to social learning theory (BANDURA, 1977), which proposes that human beings can learn from observing and modeling the behavior of significant others. Children's participation in, or dropping out of sports is strongly associated with parental attitudes and behavior in regard to sport and physical activity; the influence of the father being particularly important. The present results indicate that the extent of the parents' physical activity is particularly related to children's sports club activity in childhood.

The 9-year-old children of fathers who engage in regular physical activity tend to be more involved in sports activities than the children of passive fathers. Active fathers tend to be more encouraging about organized sports to their sons at the age of 12 than to their daughters of the same age. The mothers' physical activity only correlates with the sporting activity of girls; not with that of boys. During this period the number of those who have remained active in sport, and the number of new starters is large; and the rate of dropouts is small. It is possible that these parents' expectations of athletic achievements are higher for their sons than for their daughters. Children who decide to continue their involvement in sport, or else to change or withdraw from sport are affected both by parental expectations and behavior, and by the expectation of satisfaction for themselves (GREENDORFER, 1986; PATRIKSSON, 1988). It is also possible that children who want to participate in sports require a positive attitude and support from their parents (TELAMA et al., 1994).

One interesting finding is that the percentage of children with single parents who participate in sports club activity is higher than that of those with passive fathers, or even, among boys, with moderate-activity fathers. It seems that for children's participation in sport, no father is better than a passive father. This may indicate the bad influence of a passive role model; or it may be that the mother tries to compensate for the deficiency of the father. This result runs counter to the hypothesis presented by COAKLEY that "children with single parents have limited exposure to sports activities early in their lives (1987, 44)."

The process of sport socialization is a two-way process between children and their parents. On the one hand the parents' attitudes and behavior towards sports as a potential value influence their children's interest in sports; and on the other hand, the children who become athletes and achieve sporting success may change their parents' lifestyle (HASBROOK, 1986; MCPHERSON et al., 1989; SNYDER & PURDY, 1982; TELAMA & VANHAKKALA-RUOHO, 1981).

The results indicate that girls of fathers with high status are more likely to be involved in sports activities than those of fathers with low status, and of farmers. The finding that there is no significant difference between the fathers' socioeconomic status and boys' sports participation in a 3-year follow-up study is different from previous results (LAAKSO & TELAMA, 1981; MCPHERSON et al., 1989). This may be connected to what we know about the development of modern (or post-modern) society. The increased extent of individualization and privatization, and the relinquishing of traditional norms may mean that the young generation is less dependent on its social background. The interesting point, however, is that the physical activity of fathers has a strong relationship to boys' sports participation. This may mean that sports participation in general is less dependent on social background.

The parental influence is a predictor of children's involvement in later physical activity. The present results indicate that the fathers' physical activity predicts the 9-year-old boys' and girls' habitual physical activity nine years later as they get older. It seems that the fathers' physical activity is especially important when children are at the age of 9. The influence of fathers on children's physical activity is slightly stronger than that of mothers. The impact of mothers seems to be a greater influence on girls' physical activity. The present study agrees with the findings of GREENDORFER and LEWKO (1978) that fathers would appear to be more important socializing agents than mothers, especially in childhood and adolescence.

Acknowledgements: This study was supported by the Finnish Ministry of Education and LIKES Research Center, Jyväskylä, Finland.

References

ANDERSSEN, N.; WOLD, B.: Parental and peer influences on leisure-time physical activity in young adolescents. Research Quarterly for Exercise and Sport, 1992, 63 (4), 341-348.

BANDURA, A.: Social learning theory. Englewood Cliffs, NJ: Prentice-Hall 1977.

BRUSTAD, R.J.: Affective outcomes in competitive youth sport: The influence of interpersonal and socialization factors. Journal of Sport & Exercise Psychology, 1988, 10, 307-321.

COAKLEY, J.J.: Children and the sport socialization process. In: D. GOULD; M.R. WEISS (eds.): Advances in pediatric sport sciences, Vol. 2: behavioral issues. Champaign: Human Kinetics Publishers, 1987, 43-60.

FEIGLEY, D.A.: Coping with fear in high level gymnastics. In: J.H. SALMELA; B. PETIOT; T.B. HOSHIZAKI (eds.): Psychological nurturing and guidance of gymnastic talent, 1987, 13-27.

GOULD, D.; FELTZ, D.; HORN, T.; WEISS, M.: Reasons for attrition in competitive youth swimming. Journal of Sport Behavior, 1982, 5, 155-165.

GREENDORFER, S.L.: The dropout phenomenon: Sociological perspectives. Paper presented at the American Alliance for Health, Physical Education, Recreation and Dance Convention, (Cincinnati, OH), 1986, April 10-13.

GREENDORFER, S.L.; LEWKO, J.H.: Children's socialization into sport: A conceptual and empirical analysis. Paper presented at 9th World Congress of Sociology, Uppsala, Sweden 1978.

HASBROOK, C.A.: The sport participation - social class relationship: Some recent youth sport participation data. Sociology of Sport Journal, 1986, 3, 154-159.

LAAKSO, L.; TELAMA, R.: Sport activities of Finnish youth with special reference to young school leavers. In: Research Institute of Physical Culture and Health, Yearbook 1978, Jyväskylä, 1978, 27-36.

LAAKSO, L.; TELAMA, R.: Sport participation of Finnish youth as a function of age and schooling. Sportwissenschaft, 1981, 1, 28-45.

MCPHERSON, B.D.; CURTIS, J.E.; LOY, J.W.: The social significance of sport. An introduction to the sociology of sport. Human Kinetics Book. Champaign, III 1989.

OMUNDSSEN, Y.; VAGLUM, P.: The influence of low perceived soccer and social competence on later dropout from soccer: a prospective study of young boys. Scand J Med Sci Sports, 1991, 1, 180-188.

ORLICK, T.D.: The athletic dropout - a high price for inefficiency. Canadian Association for Health, Physical Education and Recreation Journal, 1974, 21-27.

PATRIKSSON, G.: Theoretical and empirical analysis of drop-out from youth sport in Sweden. Scandinavian Journal of Sports Sciences 1988, 10(1), 29-39.

ROBERTS, G.C.; TREASURE, D.: Children in Sport. Sport Science Review 1992, 1 (2), 46-64.

SAGE, G.C.: Parental influence and socialization into sport for male and female intercollegiate athletics. Journal of sport and social issues 1980, 4 (2), 1-13.

SCANLAN, T.K.; LEWTHWAITE, R.: From stress to enjoyment: Parental and coach influences on young participants. In: E.W. BROWN; C.F. BRANTA (eds.): Competitive sports for children and youth. Champaign Ill: Human Kinetics Books 1988, 41-48.

SMITH, R.E.: Toward a cognitive-affective model of athletic burn out. Journal of Sport Psychology, 1986, 8, 36-50.

SNYDER, E.E.; SPREITZER, E.A.: Family influence and involvement in sports. Research Quarterly, 1973, 44 (3), 249-255.

SNYDER, E.E.; PURDY, D.A.: Socialization into sport: Parent and child reverse and reciprocal effect. Research Quarterly for Exercise and Sport, 1982, 53 (3), 263-266.

TELAMA, R.; LAAKSO, L.; YANG, X.: Physical activity and sport participation of young Finns. Scand J Med Sci Sports, 1994, 4, 65-74.

TELAMA, R.; VANHAKKALA-RUOHO, M.: Children's participation in competitive sports and the family. In: L. BOLLAERT; P. DE KNOP (eds.): Family sport and leisure. ICSPE 1981.

TELAMA, R.; YANG, X.: Children's sport participation as a predictor of physical activity in young adulthood. Paper presented at the 36th ICHPER World Congress, Tokyo, Japan, August 18-22 1993.

WOOLGER, C.; POWER, T.G.: Parent and sport socialization: Views from the achievement literature. Journal of Sport Behavior, 1993, 16 (3), 171-189.

YANG, X.: Longitudinal analysis of Finnish children's and youths' participation in competitive sport and physical activity. Licentiate thesis. Jyväskylä: Department of Physical Education, University of Jyväskylä 1993.

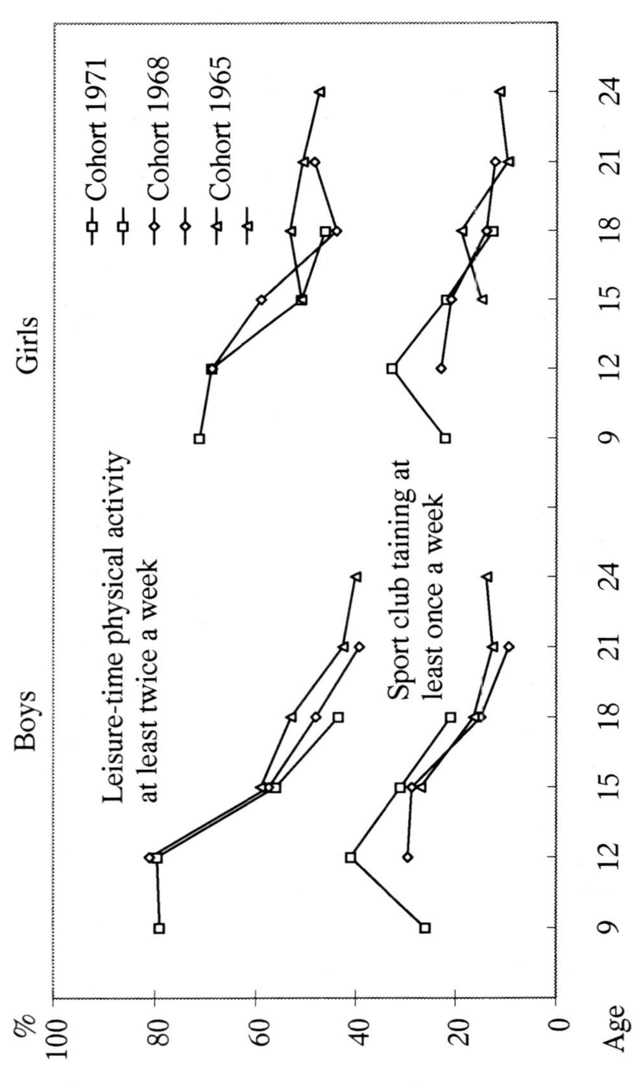

Figure 1. Percentages of children's participation in sport and physical activity by age, gender and cohorts in follow-up

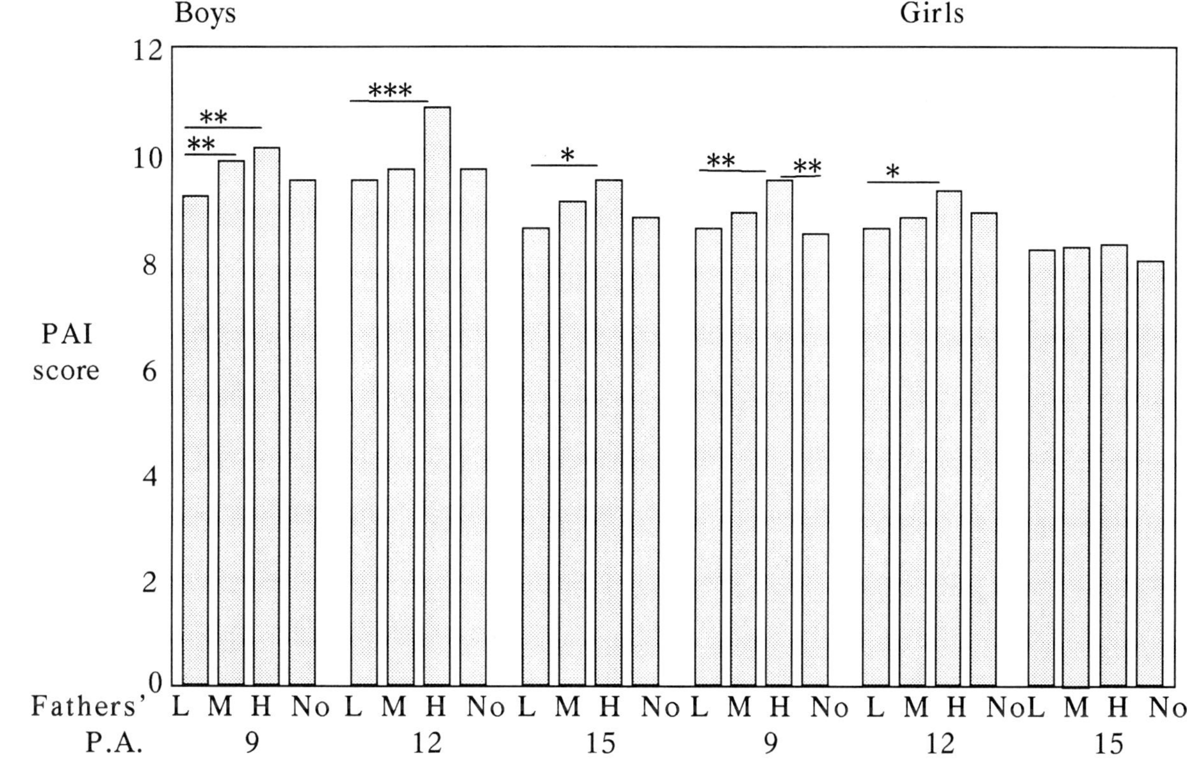

Figure 2. PAI scores of children related to fathers' physical activity (P.A.) by age and gender in 1980

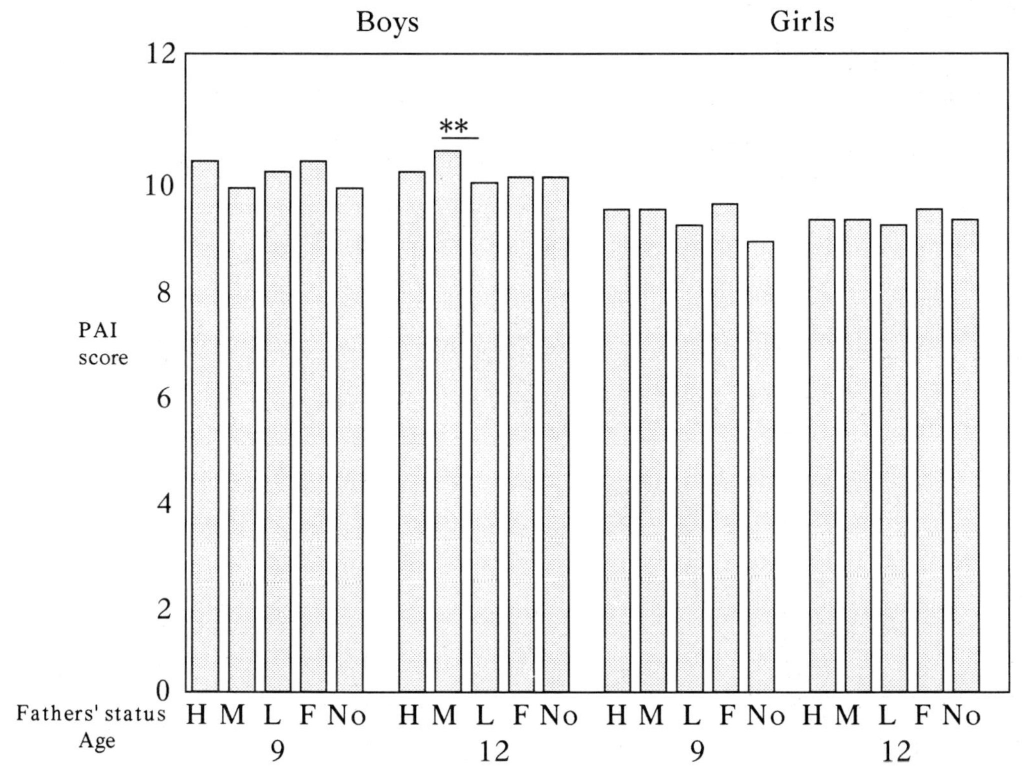

Figure 3. PAI scores of children related to fathers' social status by age and gender in 1980

AIESEP is a non-governmental professional organization of universities and institutions supporting physical education, sport sciences, in particular sport pedagogy. Besides institutional membership, individual faculty members who promote the field of sport pedagogy and science through research, publication, and other forms of professional communication and study are welcome. Through the AIESEP organization of member institutions and faculty, international cooperation in scholarly pursuits is extended. AIESEP's goal is to promote the integration of knowledge in sport sciences and to provide scholarly opportunities for their application in the broad field of sport pedagogy. The broad mission recognizes the close relationship between the scholarly scientific study of professional preparation and research in professional practice.

Board Members (1994-1998)

Prof. Dr. John Cheffers, Boston University (President)
Prof. Dr. Maurice Piéron, Université de Liège (Secretary General)
Prof. Dr. Marielle Tousignant, Université Laval (Vice-President)
Dr. Len Almond, Loughborough University (Vice-President)

Prof. Elida Alfaro, Instituto Nacional Educación Física Madrid
Dr. Zvi Artzi, Wingate Institute
Prof. Dr. Henrique Barreiros, Faculdade de Motricidade Humana, Lisboa
Prof. Dr. Gary Barrette, Adelphi University
Prof. Dr. Wolf-Dietrich Brettschneider, Freie Universität Berlin
Mrs. Ann De Lacy, Liverpool Institute of Higher Education
Prof. Dr. Karen DePauw, Washington State University
Dr. Gudrun Doll-Tepper, Freie Universität Berlin
Prof. Dr. Ron Feingold, Adelphi University
Prof. Dr. Manoel José Gomes Tubino, Universidade Gama Filho, Rio de Janeiro
Mr. Jean Francis Grehaigne, Université de Bourgogne
Dr. Ken Hawkins, University of Ballarat

Mr. Fred Hirst, Liverpool Institute of Higher Education
Prof. Mario A. Lopez, Instituto Nacional de E. Física, La Plata
Prof. Dr. Claude Paré, Université du Québec à Trois-Rivìeres
Prof. Dr. Risto Telama, University of Jyväskylä
Prof. Dr. Margrit Safrit, The American University, Washington DC
Prof. Dr. Bohumil Svoboda, Universita Karlova Praha